Sustainable Development for Hospitals and Clinics

Supaprawat Siripipatthanakul
Bangkok Thonburi University, Thailand

IGI Global
Scientific Publishing
Publishing Tomorrow's Research Today

Vice President of Editorial Melissa Wagner
Director of Acquisitions Mikaela Felty
Director of Book Development Jocelynn Hessler
Production Manager Mike Brehm
Cover Design Jose Rosado

Published in the United States of America by
IGI Global Scientific Publishing
701 East Chocolate Avenue
Hershey, PA, 17033, USA
Tel: 717-533-8845 | Fax: 717-533-7115
Website: https://www.igi-global.com E-mail: cust@igi-global.com

Library of Congress Cataloging-in-Publication Data

Names: Siripipatthanakul, Supaprawat, 1973- editor
http://id.loc.gov/rwo/agents/n2025004519
Title: Sustainable development for hospitals and clinics / edited by: Supaprawat Siripipatthanakul.
Description: Hershey PA : IGI Global Scientific Publishing, [2026] | Includes bibliographical references. | Summary: "Healthcare improves public health, but waste harms individuals and the environment. Sustainable healthcare services are needed in a fast-changing world. This book discusses methods to safeguard the environment in healthcare and address sustainability research. Chapters discuss sustainability, healthcare, and digital change, emphasizing how resource efficiency and accountability can lessen environmental impact"-- Provided by publisher.

Identifiers: LCCN 2024055212 (print) | LCCN 2024055213 (ebook) | ISBN 9798369398005 hardcover | ISBN 9798369398012 paperback | ISBN 9798369398029 ebook
Subjects: LCSH: Medical informatics--Case studies | Health services administration--Data processing--Case studies | Sustainable development--Case studies
http://id.loc.gov/authorities/subjects/sh2008112409 | LCGFT: Case studies. https://id.loc.gov/authorities/genreForms/gf2017026140
Classification: LCC R858 .S868 2025 (print) | LCC R858 (ebook) | DDC 610.285--dc23/eng/20250320
LC record available at https://lccn.loc.gov/2024055212
LC ebook record available at https://lccn.loc.gov/2024055213
British Cataloguing in Publication Data
A Cataloguing in Publication record for this book is available from the British Library.

Table of Contents

Detailed Table of Contents

ChatGPT simulates human interactions with AI. The qualitative study examines ChatGPT use and ethics in Thai healthcare. This research combines secondary data from Scopus, Web of Science (WOS), and Google Scholar to construct an interview tool to illuminate ChatGPT implementation in healthcare. Twelve (12) Thai users were purposively sampled for qualitative interviews in this study. Five professionals employ Word Cloud, Grammarly, and Turnitin for plagiarism and AI writing checks to analyze content. ChatGPT makes it easier for strategic planners, healthcare practitioners, and researchers to get vital information. ChatGPT can provide knowledge with responses, support for suggestions, and valuable ideas from previous reviews; generate topic article ideas; and individually disseminate public information about epidemics, public health, and health-related questions.

This chapter demonstrates how digital technology and AI enhance individual dental care and learning. Digital dentistry tools are expanding opportunities for dental staff, practitioners, students, and patients. Due to the pandemic and the prevalence of contagious diseases, distance learning has become more efficient, accessible, and effective. This chapter presents a systematic study of Scopus, Web of Science (WOS), and Google Scholar papers mainly from 2021 to 2025, employing purposive

This chapter describes how Malaysian healthcare providers in Penang promote ESG-aligned sustainability through digital solutions. Digitalization improves operational efficiency, environmental performance, and patient-centered care, according to stakeholder theory, institutional theory, and the resource-based view. Digital tools like EMRs, AI-assisted diagnostics, blockchain-based records, and telemedicine platforms can improve healthcare delivery and system resilience, according to a PRISMA analysis of policy initiatives, institutional practices, and ESG principles. The findings show that Penang's healthcare providers encourage lowering of ecological footprints and administrative redundancies. The study identified technological inequalities, data governance challenges, and regulatory control difficulties, despite achieving promising results. ESG performance, ethical digital stewardship, and cross-border health regulations need improvement. Policymakers, administrators, and global health strategists use the insights to promote sustainable digital health.

Numerous studies show that mobile apps improve clinic services. They inform patients of diagnoses, treatment plans, and pricing, service, and facility options. The systematic review detects plagiarism using Word Cloud and Grammarly. The English versions of Google Scholar, Web of Science (WOS), and Scopus databases use AI writing similarity checks to examine scientific article material from 2021 to 2025. Mobile apps boost management, communication, and marketing, but they also increase patient outcomes and organizational performance in dental clinics. This technique could minimize healthcare utilization and clinic management costs using mobile apps for translation, management, and digital marketing. Medical professionals and patients have various commercial mobile app options. However, mobile app resource costs and low user adoption make cost-benefit analysis problematic.

Foreword

A key crossroads has been reached in the healthcare industry, characterized by environmental, social, and economic concerns that have never been seen before. Not only do hospitals and clinics serve as sites for healing, but they also make substantial contributions to energy consumption, waste generation, and the utilization of scarce resources. The notion of sustainable development provides a revolutionary vision for healthcare. This vision incorporates environmental responsibility, social equality, and economic viability into the day-to-day operations of clinical facilities as well as the planning of long-term strategic initiatives.

Within the context of restructuring hospitals and clinics for the future, this foreword provides an introduction to the crucial role that sustainability plays. Sustainable healthcare facilities are setting new benchmarks for excellence in various areas, including the adoption of green building designs and renewable energy systems, the implementation of digital technologies, and the development of patient care models that are inclusive. They adhere to the principles of environmental stewardship, prioritize the health and safety of both patients and healthcare personnel, and ensure that economic viability is maintained to provide universal access to medical care.

As the demand on healthcare systems to adapt to climate change, global pandemics, and demographic shifts continues to increase, sustainable development is no longer an option; rather, it is an absolute necessity. Through the promotion of innovation, the encouragement of collaboration, and the dedication to ethical principles, hospitals and clinics have the potential to become effective agents of transformation that are sustainable.

This book explains the various approaches, challenges, and opportunities associated with constructing a sustainable healthcare organizations. There are high hopes that it will motivate health policymakers, healthcare leaders, practitioners, and academics to take courageous actions toward a healthier and more sustainable world.

Penpim Phuangsuwan
College of Management, University of Phayao, Thailand

Preface

Sustainable development in hospitals and clinics has evolved from an aspirational objective to an essential strategy in response to escalating environmental issues, growing healthcare needs, and the need for equitable access to quality care. This study examines the methods by which healthcare facilities might achieve sustainability through the incorporation of eco-friendly practices, the promotion of social fairness, and the enhancement of economic efficiency. Sustainable healthcare systems safeguard planetary health while enhancing long-term patient welfare and institutional resilience through energy-efficient infrastructure, waste reduction, inclusive health services, and technological innovation. This prelude urges readers to consider the pressing need for transformation in healthcare delivery, as hospitals and clinics confront the challenges of climate change, resource depletion, and an aging population, while offering a framework for integrating sustainability into their operations.

The book comprises eight chapters that aim to empower academic leaders and strategic planners to facilitate sustainable development in hospitals and clinics, encouraging researchers to adopt collaboration, creativity, communication, and critical thinking among researchers, organizations, and industries.

CHAPTER OVERVIEW

Chapter 1: A Case Study of Sustainable Development in Hospitals in Thailand Using ChatGPT

Dr. Supaprawat Siripipatthanakul, Bangkok Thonburi University, Thailand

Mr. Somboon Chaiprakarn, Sarasas Suvarnabhumi Institute of Technology, Thailand

Dr. Sorasun Rungsiyanont, Department of Oral Surgery and Oral Medicine, Faculty of Dentistry, Srinakharinwirot University

Dr. Penpim Phuangsuwan, University of Phayao, Thailand

This chapter is about how ChatGPT simulates human interactions with AI. The qualitative study examines the use of ChatGPT and its ethics in Thai healthcare. This research combines secondary data from Scopus, Web of Science (WOS), and Google Scholar to develop an interview tool that sheds light on the implementation of ChatGPT in healthcare. Twelve (12) Thai users were purposively sampled for qualitative interviews in this study. Five professionals employ Word Cloud, Grammarly, and Turnitin for plagiarism and AI writing checks to analyze content. ChatGPT makes it easier for strategic planners, healthcare practitioners, and researchers to get vital information. ChatGPT can provide knowledge through responses, support suggestions, and valuable ideas from previous reviews; generate topic article ideas; and disseminate public information about epidemics, public health, and health-related questions individually.

Chapter 2: Sustainable Dentistry Using Artificial Intelligence (AI) for Digital Education and Business among University Dental Hospitals

Dr. Supaprawat Siripipatthanakul, Bangkok Thonburi University, Thailand

Dr. Sorasun Rungsiyanont, Oral Surgery and Oral Medicine, Srinakharinwirot University

Dr. Sutithep Siripipattanakul, Kasetsart University

This chapter demonstrates how digital technology and AI enhance individual dental care and learning. Digital dentistry tools are expanding opportunities for dental staff, practitioners, students, and patients. Due to the pandemic and the prevalence of contagious diseases, distance learning has become more efficient, accessible, and effective. This chapter presents a systematic study of Scopus, Web of Science (WOS), and Google Scholar papers mainly from 2021 to 2025, employing purposive sampling, PRISMA criteria, and content analysis. Digital education, chat forums, and digital publications can engage instructors, students, and patients, boosting academic accomplishment, continuing education, and patient and community dental healthcare understanding based on knowledge and attitudes. Moreover, dental marketing with digital business provides fast, personalized services.

Chapter 3: Sustainable Clinic Management Based on Practices and Human Resource Management (HRM)

Dr. Pongsakorn Limna, International College, Pathumthani University

Dr. Sutithep Siripipattanakul, Kasetsart University

This chapter examines how Human Resource Management (HRM) serves as a strategic driver of healthcare sustainability in a systematic analysis of sustainable clinic management. The study employed data collection and analysis based on peer-reviewed publications from 2020 to 2025, sourced from Scopus, Web of Science, and Google Scholar, utilizing the PRISMA framework. The findings indicate that green human resource management (GHRM) and digital transformation are converging to bring operational sustainability initiatives and HRM strategies closer together. Electronic medical records, telemedicine, and virtual HR processes are helping clinics reduce environmental impact and boost efficiency. HRM also increases employee engagement, diversity, well-being, and ecological responsibility. Sustainability and human capital development improve clinic resilience and long-term performance while supporting global sustainability goals. The best practices and strategic advice for clinic administrators and policymakers wanting to implement sustainability across all levels of healthcare management.

Chapter 4: Sustainable Private Hospitals Based on Prices, Services, and Facilities

Dr. Parichat Jaipong, Manipal GlobalNxt University

Dr. Chok Nyen Vui, School of Business, Manipal GlobalNxt University

This chapter explores how sustainable private hospitals balance profitability with environmental responsibility and social equality by integrating sustainable principles into their pricing, services, and facilities. This chapter employed the PRISMA METHOD for systematic review analysis. The findings entail delivering value-based treatment and transparent pricing, giving comprehensive services that prioritize preventive care and patient education, and constructing and managing facilities with a focus on energy efficiency, waste minimization, and a healthy environment. Sustainable private hospitals reduce environmental impact and operational expenses while simultaneously enhancing reputation and promoting long-term community welfare, thereby attracting patients and ensuring financial sustainability.

Chapter 5: Healthcare Digitization and Sustainability of Penang Healthcare Providers: A Case of Medical Tourism

Dr. Seng Loong (Stanley) Kok, Manipal GlobalNxt University

Dr. Patcharavadee Sriboonruang, Kasetsart University

This chapter describes how Malaysian healthcare providers in Penang promote ESG-aligned sustainability through the use of digital solutions. Digitalization improves operational efficiency, environmental performance, and patient-centered care, according to stakeholder theory, institutional theory, and the resource-based view. Digital tools like EMRs, AI-assisted diagnostics, blockchain-based records, and telemedicine platforms can improve healthcare delivery and system resilience, according to a PRISMA analysis of policy initiatives, institutional practices, and ESG principles. The findings show that Penang's healthcare providers encourage reducing ecological footprints and administrative redundancies. The study identified technological inequalities, data governance challenges, and regulatory control difficulties, despite achieving promising results. ESG performance, ethical digital stewardship, and cross-border health regulations need improvement. Policymakers, administrators, and global health strategists use the insights to promote sustainable digital health.

Chapter 6: Sustainable Development Based on Mobile Apps for Translation, Management, and Digital Marketing in Clinics

Dr. Sutithep Siripipattanakul, Kasetsart University
Dr. Parichat Jaipong, GlobalNxt University
Dr. Penpim Phuangsuwan, University of Phayao, Thailand

This chapter discusses how mobile apps enhance clinic services. They inform patients of diagnoses, treatment plans, pricing, service, and facility options. The systematic review detects plagiarism using Word Cloud and Grammarly. The English versions of Google Scholar, Web of Science (WOS), and Scopus databases use AI writing similarity checks to examine scientific article material from 2021 to 2025. Mobile apps enhance management, communication, and marketing, while also improving patient outcomes and organizational performance in dental clinics. This technique can minimize healthcare utilization and clinic management costs by utilizing mobile apps for translation, management, and digital marketing. Medical professionals and patients have various commercial mobile app options. However, mobile app resource costs and low user adoption make cost-benefit analysis problematic.

Chapter 7: Online Purchase Intentions among Healthy Drink Consumers: A Sustainable Healthcare Sector Model

Dr. Parichat Jaipong, Manipal GlobalNxt University

This chapter discusses healthy drink products that have gained popularity among consumers worldwide due to their environmental and health benefits. According to the trend of healthy drink consumption, the industry has flourished and expanded into various consumer product and service categories. To explore purchasing behavior related to healthy drink products, this study applied the theory of planned behavior (TPB), a method for predicting consumer behavior that has been widely used in various research areas in recent years, based on the studies using the PRISMA method. Based on the literature review, the TPB model (attitude, subjective norms, and perceived behaviour control) that incorporates E-WOM and perceived value was examined in this study to predict online purchase intentions among Thai consumers of healthy drinks. The study also shows TPB factors and perceived value significantly direct the effect on purchase intention in healthy drink products. The results can be applied to any related healthy products industry and used to develop a strategy for customer intention.

Chapter 8: Sustainable Development in Hospitals for Elderly Dysphagia In Geriatric Dentistry

Dr. Penpim Phuangsuwan, University of Phayao, Thailand
Dr. Sorasun Rungsiyanont, Srinakharinwirot University
Dr. Patcharavadee Sriboonruang, Kasetsart University
Dr. Sutithep Siripipattanakul, Kasetsart University

This chapter is about sustainable development. Treating dysphagia in older patients in geriatric dental facilities requires a comprehensive approach that encompasses environmental, social, and economic considerations. This chapter uses PRISMA for systematic review meta-analysis. Related keywords determined the 2021-2025 scholarly paper selection. We used thematic and content analyses. Adjusted diets reduce waste and make better use of resources, which benefits the environment. Socially, it requires equal access to specialized treatment, patient-centered methods that consider individual needs, and well-supported staff. Financially, cost-effective strategies, preventive dental treatment to prevent dysphagia, and long-term value are needed. Geriatric dentistry promotes oral health to prevent and alleviate dysphagia. This improves the quality of life for older patients and ensures resource-efficient healthcare.

Through thoughtful collaboration among researchers and professors on these diverse themes, "Sustainable Development for Hospitals and Clinics" offers academic leaders and strategic planners insights into enhancing sustainable development for hospitals and clinics.

Supaprawat Siripipatthanakul

Chapter 1
A Case Study of Sustainable Development in Hospitals in Thailand Using ChatGPT

Supaprawat Siripipatthanakul
https://orcid.org/0000-0001-6671-2682
Bangkok Thonburi University, Thailand

Somboon Chaiprakarn
https://orcid.org/0000-0001-5357-5201
Sarasas Suvarnabhumi Institute of Technology, Thailand

Sorasun Rungsiyanont
Srinakharinwirot University, Bangkok, Thailand

Penpim Phuangsuwan
https://orcid.org/0000-0003-2371-7998
University of Phayao, Thailand

ABSTRACT

ChatGPT simulates human interactions with AI. The qualitative study examines ChatGPT use and ethics in Thai healthcare. This research combines secondary data from Scopus, Web of Science (WOS), and Google Scholar to construct an interview tool to illuminate ChatGPT implementation in healthcare. Twelve (12) Thai users were purposively sampled for qualitative interviews in this study. Five professionals employ Word Cloud, Grammarly, and Turnitin for plagiarism and AI writing checks to analyze content. ChatGPT makes it easier for strategic planners, healthcare practitioners, and researchers to get vital information. ChatGPT can

DOI: 10.4018/979-8-3693-9800-5.ch001

provide knowledge with responses, support for suggestions, and valuable ideas from previous reviews; generate topic article ideas; and individually disseminate public information about epidemics, public health, and health-related questions.

1. INTRODUCTION

ChatGPT's capabilities have amazed everyone since its November 2022 launch. ChatGPT provides real-time, evidence-based suggestions for clinical decision assistance, such as pharmaceutical interactions, treatment choices, and clinical guidelines. Healthcare is increasingly using AI. AI-based chatbots can promote health, educate, and influence behavior. Health chatbot uptake must be predicted by examining motivation, but rare research studies have examined acceptance. AI-led health chatbot engagement has been proposed (Nadarzynski et al., 2019; Dhunnoo, 2023). The OpenAI GPT-3-enabled Natural Language Generation (NLG) model ChatGPT can improve e-commerce, education, entertainment, finance, health, news, and productivity through chat. Thus, ChatGPT has current and future uses in various industries on how this technology may customize consumer content. ChatGPT helps businesses enhance customer service efficiency and effectiveness (George & George, 2023). ChatGPT was used several times to evaluate medical query responses: ChatGPT exchanges on medical topics that this version answers rapidly but summarizes internet literature. Mistakes were found in medical query responses, as the firm noted on the ChatGPT web page. The data was also limited until September 2021. Recognizing its medical limitations and learning from past responses are positive traits (Vaishya et al., 2023). The third iteration of OpenAI's ubiquitous language model is ChatGPT-3. The 2020 publication is one of the most advanced large language models. It is learning to retrieve massive amounts of text data from the Internet to generate human-like text and execute NLP tasks like text completion, summarization, and translation. The conversational AI language model ChatGPT-3 was launched on November 30, 2022, and is widely used in health and medical sciences. It has been praised and criticized since its inception. In this article, the researchers examined ChatGPT-3's healthcare applications. First, we retrieved the chatbot's material on NLP, health service perks, and IOT types. Next, relevant literature is reviewed to confirm the contents. It can become DocGPT based on limited literature (Iftikhar, 2023). Teachers found that ChatGPT answered regular questions and let them focus on more essential duties (Limna et al., 2023).

Ethical problems are raised by ChatGPT, including the potential for privacy violations, the risk of obtaining inaccurate information, the possibility of algorithmic bias, and the potential for the connection between the physician and the patient to become more unstable. In order to guarantee that artificial intelligence is utilized in a manner that is both responsible and beneficial within the healthcare sector, it is necessary to address these problems acceptably. Ethical concerns about ChatGPT in education include worries about the chatbot's accuracy and the loss of instructor engagement. Privacy and data security were also significant concerns. The discussion about ChatGPT may help educators and policymakers decide whether to use ChatGPT. Ethical concerns include data privacy, AI biases, and the potential consequences of incorrect health-related information provided by ChatGPT (Rivas & Zhao, 2023; Limna et al., 2023; Wu et al., 2024; Hua & Jiang, 2024).

According to sustainable development goals (SDGs) and sustainability, all nations must contribute to such an ambitious aim. The theme has multiple dimensions and perspectives and involves stakeholders that can combine digitization with sustainability, support food security and sustainability in emerging economies, identify the link between technological progress and sustainable development, and optimize processes using available resources. Female gender and youth contribution to the SDGs must also be considered. Additionally, comprehending creative objects connects memories to present existence. Sustainable tourism practices can promote regional economies and turn cultural heritage management into a sustainable development tool. Several early-life activities can address health-related sustainability challenges, especially technology adoption in healthcare promotion and its success using technology and AI (Ali et al., 2023; Sribanasarn et al., 2025).

Therefore, ChatGPT is an AI-powered chatbot that mimics human speech. It can write articles, essays, job applications, comments, and poems to text prompts. ChatGPT's ethical issues in healthcare should be addressed. Thus, this qualitative study uses qualitative interviews to explain ChatGPT in healthcare. The study aims to explain ChatGPT's usage in the healthcare sector and focus on the ethical concerns and challenges that ChatGPT may face in healthcare settings.

1.1 Research Objective

This study explained the acceptability of ChatGPT in identifying potential barriers or facilitators to healthcare services and promotion. The research may benefit person-based health chatbots, such as ChatGPT, in this study for sustainable development goals (SDGs), and its sustainability in the healthcare sector.

1.2 Research Question

How is ChatGPT used in Thailand's healthcare sector to promote sustainable hospital development and daily life?

2. LITERATURE REVIEW

2.1 ChatGPT in the Healthcare Sector

Generative Pretrained Transformer (GPT) is an innovative AI that can write human-like language. OpenAI created the AI language model ChatGPT. GPT, built and trained on a large corpus of text data, responds to natural language questions that match user needs. This technique has several medical uses. One barrier to ChatGPT implementation in healthcare is the need for accurate and current data. GPT needs updated medical data to make reliable suggestions and treatments. GPT could achieve this using reliable data from regularly updated sources (Javaid et al., 2023). Healthcare researchers must be cautious in unrest. General readers, healthcare experts, and NLP scientists can learn about ChatGPT's medicinal applications. PubMed has been used to search for 'ChatGPT' yields published papers. An inclusion criterion and taxonomy are suggested to narrow search results and identify publications. The present iteration of ChatGPT performed moderately or "passing" in various tests and is unreliable for clinical deployment because it was not developed for clinical purposes. Specialized NLP models trained on (bio)medical datasets remain superior for essential clinical applications. (Aydın & Karaarslan, 2022). OpenAI's huge language model, ChatGPT, is a powerful medical tool. By analyzing medical papers, ChatGPT could be used in many medical applications. ChatGPT is medically used. ChatGPT simplifies complex tasks and improves patient care, clinical decision-making, and healthcare professional communication. ChatGPT has privacy, ethical, and medical bias issues. Despite these challenges, ChatGPT has shown great promise to change healthcare delivery and medicine. (Muftić et al., 2023).

ChatGPT can enable remote patient monitoring and tailored healthcare. Patient self-treatment and AI-driven infodemics are also risks. It advises healthcare practitioners and policymakers on ChatGPT ethics and safety. SWOT analysis guides ChatGPT and other language model development. Comment on ChatGPT's application in healthcare and its potential effects on patient care and public health (Zaman, 2023). ChatGPT is the first large language model (LLM) to reach a broad public audience. Rapid use and exploration by the general population have sparked concerns about its appropriate incorporation in numerous professions. We debated ChatGPT's use in education, research, and healthcare in a virtual and in-person panel. Former ChatGPT users were more likely to use it in more situations. ChatGPT in teaching was the most ambiguous of the three cases. The merits and downsides of using this technology in education, research, and healthcare were examined. ChatGPT's acceptability and ideal use in education, research, and healthcare were debated. LLMs like ChatGPT should be discussed in education, healthcare, and research. Adoption has dangers and unexpected challenges, so a planned and controlled approach would prevent harm (Hosseini et al., 2023). ChatGPT can help doctors and other healthcare workers improve services. It can create automated systems that give doctors tailored advice. It can be used to construct intelligent health systems that provide patients with personalized medical advice based on their medical history. Additionally, ChatGPT can be used to create systems that detect and treat health concerns. It can also create virtual agents who provide tailored health advice and support. Due to their direct patient engagement, chatbots will transform the healthcare business and eliminate privacy problems (Kalla & Smith, 2023).

ChatGPT improved scientific writing, research equity, and versatility in healthcare education, healthcare research (efficient dataset analysis, code generation, literature reviews, saving time to focus on experimental design, and drug discovery), and healthcare practice. ChatGPT raised ethical, copyright, transparency, legal, bias, plagiarism, lack of creativity, false content with hallucinatory risks, inadequate knowledge, improper citations, cybersecurity, and infodemic concerns. Healthcare education, research, and practice may change with ChatGPT's potential applications. Due to its limitations, this AI chatbot should be used cautiously. ChatGPT cannot write scientific articles until the ICMJE/COPE rules are changed. Emergency action is needed to involve all healthcare education, research, and practice stakeholders. It will assist in creating an ethical code for acceptable ChatGPT use in healthcare and academics (Sallam, 2023). ChatGPT, a chatbot powered by artificial intelligence, has quickly risen to prominence in numerous fields, including medical education and healthcare literature. This hybrid narrative review, conducted collaboratively by human authors and ChatGPT, seeks to summarize and synthesize the current understanding of ChatGPT in the medical literature during its first four months. Using a search strategy in the PubMed and EuropePMC databases, 65 and 110 publications were obtained, respectively. There is the influence of ChatGPT on medical education, scientific research, medical writing, ethical considerations, diagnostic decision-making, automation potential, and criticisms. The findings indicate a growing corpus of literature on ChatGPT's applications and implications in healthcare, emphasizing the need for additional research to evaluate its efficacy and ethical concerns (Temsah et al., 2023). Just months after its launch, ChatGPT has garnered attention in many industries, including healthcare. Recently, researchers claimed it passed the U.S. medical licensing exam. Few empirical studies have evaluated whether ChatGPT is valued and accepted by the public in healthcare. A model of factors affecting user acceptance of ChatGPT for healthcare was developed to understand the public's propensity to get AIGC apps like ChatGPT. This paradigm integrates the unified theory of acceptance and use of technology (UTAUT) and the Trust, Perceived Risk, and Perceived Illness Theory. It aimed to reveal ChatGPT adoption factors for healthcare services (Kong & Fu, 2023).

2.2 Acceptability of ChatGPT in Health Consultations

Trust may be necessary for ChatGPT adoption. Please note that ChatGPT was not designed for healthcare. Thus, overusing it for health advice may lead to erroneous information and health dangers. ChatGPT must improve its ability to distinguish between queries it can address and those it should refer to health care specialists. Although excessive confidence in AI-powered chatbots like ChatGPT is risky, shared accountability and collaboration between developers, subject matter experts, and human factors researchers can reduce these risks (Choudhury & Shamszare, 2023). ChatGPT is a powerful and popular AI language model. It is trained to understand and produce human language for automated customer service, chatbots, and content development. It has many benefits but could be misused to communicate harmful safety information. A diverse collaboration of specialists examined nine examples across safety domains to assess ChatGPT's safety guidance. Using mobile phones while driving, supervising children around water, crowd management, fall prevention in older people, air pollution when exercising, helping a distressed colleague, managing job demands to avoid burnout, and fitness app data protection. There are risks to using ChatGPT for safety advice. ChatGPT produced false or harmful claims and stressed individual accountability, which may have caused ecological fallacy. ChatGPT should be used cautiously for safety-related information, expert verification, ethical considerations, and safeguards to ensure users understand the limitations and receive appropriate guidance, especially in low- and middle-income countries. The investigation reminds us that, as AI technology advances, public safety must be considered (Oviedo-Trespalacios et al., 2023). The healthcare market has changed rapidly because of technical, economic, and societal changes since the epidemic. Telehealth consultations are more accessible due to broadband connectivity, higher insurance reimbursement rates, and provider and patient acceptance. These innovations create a powerful new healthcare industry rival not limited by regional limits. Traditional medical providers fear new competitors would threaten their data, so they don't share it. (Yaraghi, 2023).

Self-diagnosis and health intentions of ChatGPT users are explored. Healthcare routinely uses ChatGPT despite its unsuitability. Improve and adapt the technology instead of discouraging its use in healthcare. Developers, providers, and policymakers must collaborate to use AI chatbots properly in healthcare. By understanding user preferences and making decisions, AI chatbots like ChatGPT anticipate user demands and give accurate health information. It increases health literacy and access. AI chatbots in healthcare should be studied for their long-term effects on self-diagnosis and integration with other digital health initiatives to improve patient care and results. To create and utilize AI chatbots like ChatGPT to improve healthcare and consumer health (Shahsavar & Choudhury, 2023).

ChatGPT has the potential to enhance healthcare systems. Nevertheless, concerns regarding the reliability and source of information provided by AI chatbots were the primary obstacles. ChatGPT has been a significant asset to the field of digital health during its initial development. However, it is crucial to address its precision, reliability, and potential legal implications. It is not advisable to rely solely on current ChatGPT and other chatbots to diagnose or treat patients without human supervision, as they are unreliable. To thrive in the healthcare industry, AI chatbots must possess high trustworthiness. Subsequent investigations should compare ChatGPT's therapeutic outcomes concerning other artificial intelligence chatbots (Temsah et al., 2023).

ChatGPT is becoming increasingly popular and has numerous applications in clinical medicine. ChatGPT produces precise lists of differential diagnoses, aids in clinical decision-making, enhances clinical decision support, and offers valuable insights for cancer screening. ChatGPT has delivered accurate disease and medical information with its advanced question-answering capabilities. ChatGPT produces patient clinical letters, radiology reports, medical notes, and discharge summaries, enhancing the efficiency and precision of healthcare practitioners. Promising avenues for future research encompass the fields of real-time monitoring and predictive analytics, precision medicine and personalized therapy, the utilization of ChatGPT in telemedicine and remote healthcare, and the integration of current healthcare systems. ChatGPT enhances clinical decision-making and improves patient care by complementing the experience of healthcare practitioners. Nevertheless, ChatGPT possesses both positive and negative aspects. Researchers must evaluate the advantages and disadvantages of ChatGPT. Recent advancements in clinical ChatGPT research indicate possible risks and difficulties. Like ChatGPT, it will provide direction and assistance for AI research on health-related topics (Liu et al., 2023).

2.3 Ethical Concerns about ChatGPT in the Healthcare Sector

ChatGPT, as a disruptive technology, can potentially improve healthcare access. However, its application as a medical chatbot raises concerns. Since ChatGPT is not a licensed medical expert, its medical information may not always be accurate or current. Transparency of the chatbot model, ethics of exploiting user data, and bias in ChatGPT's algorithm training data are all issues that need to be addressed. Therefore, stakeholders must take responsibility and research ways to improve ChatGPT. This will eventually lead to the development of a human-like medical chatbot. The argument is also to properly investigate the hurdles to reaching this goal as soon as possible so that quality assurance systems and regulation norms can keep up with this disruptive technology (Chow et al., 2023). ChatGPT's usability and accessibility could boost academic production. ChatGPT may receive and generate copy in several languages, avoiding English-language constraints that might hinder publication for non-English speakers and democratizing knowledge dissemination. However, the capability of ChatGPT to generate misleading or erroneous text raises worries about scholarly misinformation. As shown by the COVID-19 infodemic, medical publishing misinformation can harm society. ChatGPT sometimes writes plausible sounding but wrong or illogical responses; interestingly, it addressed this possibility in its response to humans (Liebrenz et al., 2023).

Virtual assistants for patient health management are another critical use of ChatGPT in medicine. ChatGPT and other AI medical writing tools create ethical and legal problems despite their potential. These include copyright breaches, medico-legal issues, and transparent AI-generated content requirements. In conclusion, ChatGPT has several medicinal and therapeutic uses. These applications have various limitations and ethical issues, detailed along with their medical and healthcare prospects (Dave et al., 2023). ChatGPT is popularizing AI, especially among the public. The chatbot models were designed to aid human-to-human natural language conversation. It is a "statistical correlation machine" (correlation instead of causation). Thus, ChatGPT and other AI language models raise ethical issues like bias, privacy, and abuse. It highlights ChatGPT's ethical issues and application challenges. There are also practical instructions for ChatGPT stakeholders that may be used as checklists for ChatGPT apps. These commandment examples promote ChatGPT ethics (Zhou et al., 2023).

Some research shows the limitations of ChatGPT and other AI tools in healthcare, focusing on ethical issues, bias, data privacy, and the accuracy of AI-generated medical information. ChatGPT's performance on standardized assessments as a medical student suggests its use in medical education, radiology reporting, genetics research, data optimization, and discharge summaries. Tools should supplement human skills, not replace them. Despite promising applications, ChatGPT struggles with critical thinking and misleading references, requiring strict cross-verification. Transparency, accountability, and clear policies must address misuse, bias, blind trust, and privacy. AI-generated content evaluations and academic integrity are crucial. If used responsibly, AI can benefit healthcare, academia, and industry without compromising honesty or research quality. Effective and ethical AI deployment requires collaboration among developers, researchers, educators, and politicians. These efforts to safely harness AI's promise must include domain-specific tools, guidelines, regulations, and public discourse (Jeyaraman et al., 2023; Ray, 2023; Pathak, 2023).

2.4 Routine Treatment Using ChatGPT

ChatGPT writes exquisite comments on almost any topic. The possible consequences of this technology inspire wonder and anxiety. The Perelman School of Medicine Senior Vice Dean met with ChatGPT to discuss healthcare applications. Condensed but unedited comments from his interview follow. Several things must be examined before ChatGPT is used in routine treatment (Asch, 2023).

1. Data privacy and security: The sensitive nature of healthcare information necessitates stringent data privacy and security measures to ensure patient data is protected.
2. Regulation: Always ensure the safe and appropriate use of ChatGPT in healthcare. Healthcare organizations will be required to comply with various regulations, including HIPAA.
3. Data quality and quantity: To ensure ChatGPT can provide accurate and pertinent responses, it will need access to a large, diverse, high-quality dataset, particularly in the healthcare industry.
4. Integration with existing systems: ChatGPT must be integrated with existing healthcare systems, such as electronic health records, to be effective.
5. Human oversight: Although ChatGPT can automate specific duties, it is essential to Human oversight is needed to ensure the model's output is accurate and correct any mistakes.
6. Ethical considerations: Using ChatGPT in healthcare raises several ethical concerns, including bias and accountability, which must be addressed.

ChatGPT can shape marketing if ethical issues are addressed. We argue that ChatGPT-based solutions can help marketers create content faster and with comparable quality to humans. ChatGPT can also help marketers automate customer care, improve research, and understand customers. We examined the ethical implications and hazards for marketers, consumers, and other stakeholders necessary for ChatGPT-based marketing; doing so can revolutionize marketing while protecting stakeholders (Rivas & Zhao, 2023).

2.5 Exercise and Sport Using ChatGPT for Guidance

Even if the tool provides the correct information, it can produce errors and inconsistencies in sample-size calculations. This is something that should be taken into consideration, even though the employment of artificial intelligence tools contains enormous potential. It is hoped that the computation of sample sizes and other research activities will become more accurate as artificial intelligence technology grows and learns from humans' feedback. However, scientists need to exercise caution regarding the utilization of these techniques. Additionally, more complex and powerful versions of this technology, such as ChatGPT4, should be evaluated in subsequent research (Methnani et al., 2013).

ChatGPT became the focus of attention for academics all around the world. Over one hundred million people worldwide subscribe to this artificial intelligence (AI) language model, which has sparked many debates about its precision, its benefits, and the dangers it poses to the fields of research and education. Regarding legal precision, It has already been determined that linguistics, mathematics, and medicine are all evaluated. Most of the findings indicate that ChatGPT could Obtain a satisfactory grade in each area. On the other hand, its abilities in sports science and psychology have not yet been examined and evaluated. A more accurate performance might be achieved due to this general region's vast amount of information. Even so, the potential to result in severe errors, which teachers can avoid. ChatGPT became the focus of academics worldwide. This artificial intelligence (AI) language model has more than one hundred million users worldwide, resulting in many conversations regarding its accuracy, benefits, and dangers to education and science. Regarding legal precision, It has already been determined that linguistics, mathematics, and medicine are all evaluated. Most of the findings indicate that ChatGPT could Obtain a satisfactory grade in each area. On the other hand, its abilities in sports science and psychology have not yet been examined and evaluated. A more accurate performance might be achieved due to this general region's vast amount of information. Even so, Certain topics in the area associated with contentious research findings have the potential to result in severe errors, which teachers can avoid. and researchers were able to identify it fast (Szabo, 2023).

ChatGPT could design safe workout routines for diverse situations. However, AI-generated exercise regimens generally prioritized safety above training effectiveness and failed to address individual health problems and goals. ChatGPT's steady increases in training load and intensity were meant to benefit patients, but the model's ability to fine-tune its suggestions through continual engagement was lacking. Current AI technologies can supplement exercise prescriptions, especially for those without access to expensive professional counsel. AI technologies are not yet suggested to replace tailored, progressive, and health condition-specific prescriptions from healthcare and fitness professionals. More research is needed to integrate real-time physiological feedback and interactive AI models (Dergaa et al., 2024).

ChatGPT has the potential to offer acceptable individualized dietary advice and has several significant enhancements over the Food4Me algorithm. It still tends to generate recommendations that contain inconsistent and unpredictable errors. For instance, it may not provide accurate information regarding the intake of macro- or micronutrients. Now, people without nutrition knowledge are not recommended to rely on ChatGPT for tailored dietary suggestions. Nevertheless, ChatGPT continues to be a technique that shows promise and has the potential to become a dependable instrument for personal nutrition in the future with additional updates and fine-tuning implemented (Agne & Gedrich, 2024).

3. METHODOLOGY

A narrative summary accompanied this lengthy literature assessment. Narrative synthesis uses academic writing to summarize and explain synthesis outcomes. The qualitative research process includes design, data collecting, analysis, and report writing. Content analysis uses qualitative data from verbal, visual, or written sources to characterize certain phenomena and help conclude objectively. The flexible data analysis method is suitable for systematized qualitative reviews. Systematic qualitative assessors must adapt content analysis methodologies to highly ordered and contextualized sources to find knowledge and theory. (Limna et al., 2022; Jaipong et al., 2023; Lim, 2023; Kok, 2023; Siripipatthanakul & Phuangsuwan, 2024). Qualitative research shows how individuals or groups decide and act in each situation. It explains specific manners and why what was witnessed occurred when it did. In-depth information is necessary, and being able to communicate in both directions throughout the interview makes it easier to acquire extra facts. The researchers can ask questions outside the boundaries of the semi-structured surveys, which helps them collect data and follow up more effectively (Siripipatthanakul et al., 2022; Phuangsuwan et al., 2024).

The instrument's validity is the measurement that could measure what a researcher wants to measure. The instrument's reliability is the consistency of measurement (Siripipattanakul, 2011). The validity and reliability of the measurement must be approved. Thus, interview questions were based on purposive sampling scholarly papers; the secondary data in Scopus, Web of Science, and Google Scholar regarding related topics and keywords were used to develop the instrumentation (interview questions). Three experts in the healthcare field provided the reliability and validity of the interview questions using Item Objective Congruence (IOC) Analysis for the two interview questions. The results of IOC analysis, two questions, are practical and can be used in this study (IOC=1).

In this study, data was collected from twelve (12) ChatGPT users in the healthcare sector in Thailand using semi-structured interviews. The sample groups in this study were classified as (1) strategic planners, (2) healthcare providers, and (3) researchers.

The interview questions were based on the study of Limna et al. (2023) and are as follows.

1) What are ChatGPT's benefits and ethical concerns in Thailand's healthcare sector and hospitals?
2) What is the linkage between ChatGPT, healthcare knowledge, and research?

Ethical approval was not sought for the present study because this study is a qualitative interview and does not provide the names of respondents. Only gender, age, and duties were represented by respondents' demographics, with the date and time of interviews. The researchers obtained informed verbal consent one by one, and respondents could terminate participation at the time if they did not want to answer the interview questions. The criteria respondents are over 18 years old to avoid ethical issues, and no need to ask for consent forms from their parents. The researchers declare that there is no conflict of interest.

Secondary data collection and analysis were conducted between April 15, 2024, and July 15, 2024. The primary data collection, adopting interviews, was on July 17 and 18, 2024. Data analysis was conducted using content analysis. Plagiarism was using Grammarly and Turnitin. The results of plagiarism are 7% and 13%, respectively. Grammar was evaluated using Grammarly and proven by an English expert. Grammarly checks grammar, prevents plagiarism, and evaluates AI-generated content. The acceptable level of plagiarism and AI writing for a paper publication should be less than 15%. Turnitin was used to evaluate the similarity of content in online and internal sources to academic works from educational institutions. Turnitin's result should be less than 15% in plagiarism and AI writing.

4. RESULTS

This study used qualitative content analysis. ChatGPT, usage, healthcare industry, chatbots, and artificial intelligence (AI) were the critical terms (keywords) for the purposive sampling of secondary data. The scholarly papers in this study were selected (purposive sampling) from 2019 to 2024, mainly from 2023. There are 30 academic articles from valid sources, such as Google Scholar, Scopus, PubMed, MDPI, Web of Science, etc. The word cloud result is shown in Figure 1 (below).

Figure 1. Word Clouds Analysis (Author generated, August 9, 2024)

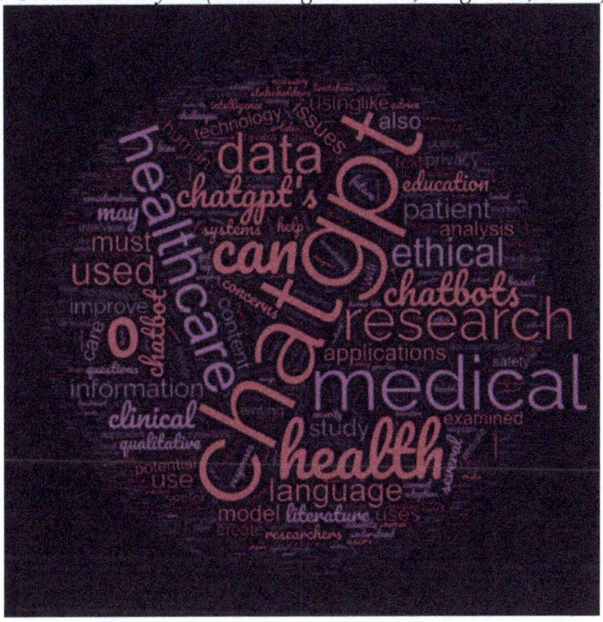

https://www.wordclouds.com/

The researchers adopted Grammarly and Turnitin for plagiarism checking. An English expert checked for grammar and typographical errors. Plagiarism is accepted for about 10% or less.

Figure 2. ChatGPT Results (Author generated, August 10, 2024)

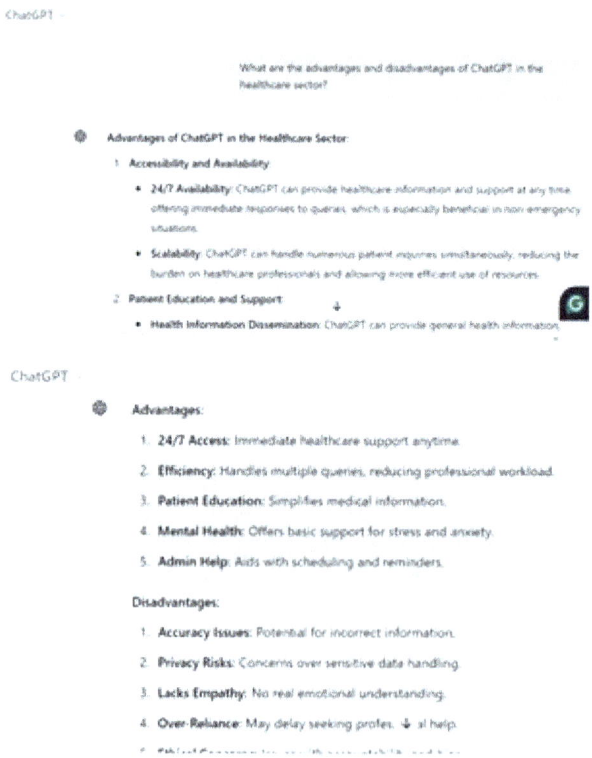

https://chatgpt.com/

Figure 3. Grammarly Evaluation Results (Author generated, August 29, 2024)

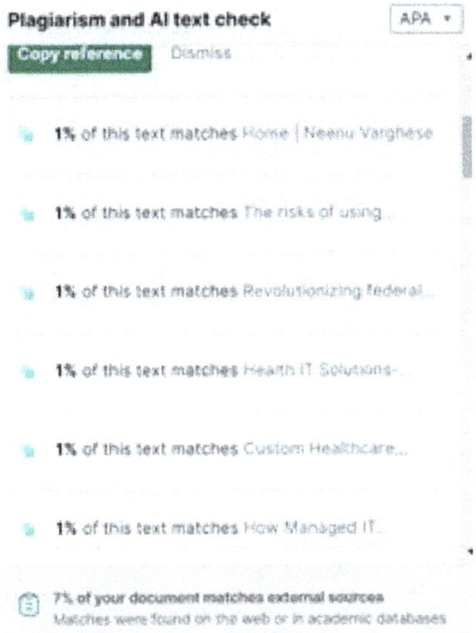

(Grammar and Plagiarism Evaluation using Grammarly)

Figure 4. Turnitin Evaluation Results (Author generated, August 14, 2024)

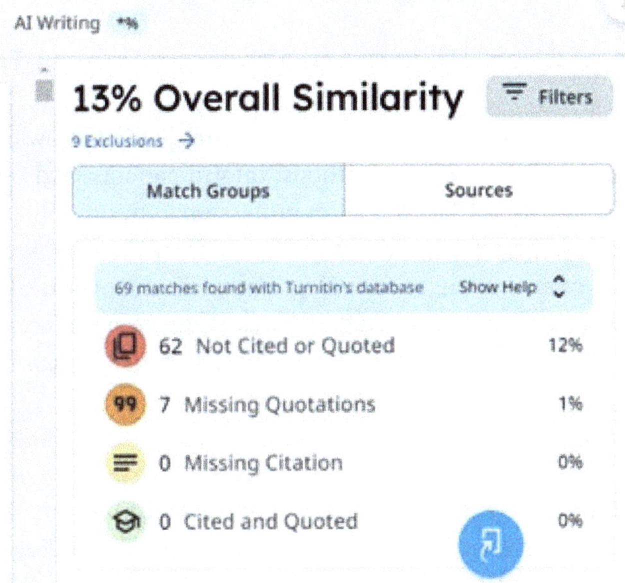

(Plagiarism and AI Writing evaluation using Turnitin)

Table 1. Respondents' Demographics

No.	*Gender*	*Age*	*Role*	*Date and time of interviews*
1	Male	32	Strategic Planner	July 17, 2024, at 3.16 pm
2	Male	45	Strategic Planner	July 17, 2024, at 4.15 pm
3	Female	41	Strategic Planner	July 17, 2024, at 15.16 pm
4	Female	43	Strategic Planner	July 17, 2024, at 4.17 pm
5	Male	48	Healthcare Provider	July 18, 2024, at 09:00 am
6	Male	36	Healthcare Provider	July 18, 2024, at 10:00 am
7	Female	43	Healthcare Provider	July 18, 2024, at 10:00 am
8	Female	43	Healthcare Provider	July 18, 2024, at 11:00 am
9	Male	51	Researcher	July 19, 2024, at 8.50 pm
10	Male	56	Researcher	July 19, 2024, at 9.10 pm
11	Female	37	Researcher	July 19, 2024, at 10:00 am
12	Female	48	Researcher	July 19, 2024, at 11:00 am

The respondents comprise three groups of respondents, as follows: the first group is the strategic planners (two males and two females), the second group is the healthcare providers (two males and two females), and the third group is the researchers (two males and two females).

The age was between 32 and 56 years old.

4.1 Benefits of ChatGPT in the healthcare sector in Thailand

Healthcare benefits from ChatGPT include better patient knowledge and communication. ChatGPT can answer questions, inform patients, and provide helpful information. In some cases, ChatGPT helps professionals by providing medical data. Many online tools help patients decide if they need medical or dental treatment. Language and communication, such as English and Thai, are crucial to well-being in ChatGPT humane discussions. ChatGPT can generate more accurate and reliable sources with more specific assessments based on the human intelligence of professionals.

"ChatGPT helps users provide advice on general healthcare, such as exercise and sports, that matches people with a systemic disease, such as hypertension and heart disease. Users can receive health consultations and advice without paying additional fees and could enhance their understanding of improving health-related technologies."

Respondent 1

"ChatGPT gives some medical information and advice related to general health care, such as exercise, proper diet, and reducing disease risk. ChatGPT helps

individually disseminate public information about epidemics, public health, and health-related questions".
Respondent 3
"ChatGPT can provide information about exercise science, sports strategy, nutrition, and injury prevention. Users can assess their sports and fitness routines."
Respondent 4
"ChatGPT increases the convenience of accessing medical services. It helps reduce waiting time for doctor appointments and other essential services that do not require a doctor's physical presence.
Respondent 6
"ChatGPT helps users create objectives, track progress, and stay motivated. It can give fitness plans, challenges, and encouraging remarks."
Respondent 8
"ChatGPT can suggest exercises or methods for overcoming fitness plateaus or sports problems. It helps focus, performance anxiety, and recovery from setbacks."
Respondent 10
"ChatGPT simulates sports and fitness talk, making it entertaining. It can cover fitness training trends and sports news. ChatGPT can help you achieve your goals regardless of your athletic abilities".
Respondent 11

4.2 Ethical Concerns of ChatGPT in the Healthcare Sector in Thailand

ChatGPT may improve healthcare personnel, education, and patient outcomes. Medical data privacy, ethics, and biases must be addressed. ChatGPT can significantly improve healthcare and medical knowledge if adequately studied and explored. Ethics, data protection, security, openness, and responsibility are needed to use ChatGPT ethically in healthcare. ChatGPT has many prospects in healthcare, but it must first overcome some challenges. ChatGPT can improve patient care, empower physicians, and advance medical knowledge by sharing information and lowering risks. ChatGPT can transform healthcare if adequately adopted and analyzed. The medical tool ChatGPT may change healthcare.

"Good information from ChatGPT can help individuals with health-related questions. It also supports medical studies and research by providing quality information that can be used in health research. However, ethical concerns need to be addressed.
Respondent 2
"Ethical issues among healthcare students and researchers need to be discussed. Even though ChatGPT is a machine learning model and gives some

good information. However, some information biases could be incurred. Copy and paste among users is unacceptable. Turnitin and Grammarly are artificial intelligence tools that can detect AI writing, and they should be less than 10% in high-quality papers.
Respondent 9
"In this digital era, Artificial Intelligence, ChatGPT, and Gemini are digital tools that could give users good ideas. However, copying ideas from these tools is a critical issue in education and any sector."
Respondent 12

4.3 The Linkage between ChatGPT, Healthcare Knowledge, and Research

While ChatGPT is not a clinical entity, it contributes to healthcare knowledge. Its information processing capabilities can summarize medical conditions, answer basic health questions, and support medical research. However, it is crucial to remember that it cannot replace the expertise of medical specialists; their validation of responses from credible sources is always necessary. ChatGPT's ability to digest medical literature, generate research ideas, and expedite data analysis for healthcare research is undeniable. However, it must work with human expertise to ensure accuracy and ethical consideration to be truly effective. The role of professionals in healthcare is irreplaceable, and ChatGPT is a tool that can enhance their work, not replace it.

"ChatGPT supports healthcare studies and research by providing guiding quality information that can be used in health research."
Respondent 5
"ChatGPT can guide good research topics in healthcare services. It can help users handle complex questions or conditions and refer them to be more efficient and accurate."
Respondent 7

5. DISCUSSIONS

ChatGPT's Benefits in the Healthcare Sector

The results support Javaid et al. (2023), Aydın & Karaarslan (2022), Muftić et al. (2023), Zaman (2023), Hosseini et al. (2023), Kalla & Smith (2023), Oviedo-

Trespalacios et al. (2023), Rasul et al. (2023), Sok & Heng (2023), Raj et al. (2023), Ong et al. (2023), and Rice et al. (2024), it could be discussed as follows;

ChatGPT, launched in November 2022, excels in several fields, including healthcare. It provides real-time, evidence-based recommendations and helps uncover drug interactions and therapy choices to improve clinical decision-making. AI-based chatbots that promote health, educate, and modify behavior are popular. Acceptance and incentive to utilize health chatbots need more investigation. ChatGPT is used in e-commerce, education, entertainment, finance, health, news, and productivity. It could boost consumer service efficiency. ChatGPT can assess medical reactions, but its limitations and faults require constant improvement and learning. ChatGPT's research on healthcare applications shows its potential and the need for caution and improvement. Several examples of ChatGPT or other AI technologies' expected effects on healthcare include better patient communication: ChatGPT can inform patients, answer questions, and repeat appointments or prescriptions. Improved clinical decision-making: ChatGPT analyzes a lot of medical data to help doctors diagnose and treat patients. Decisions may become more accurate and effective. ChatGPT can help doctors diagnose patients faster and more correctly by analyzing their symptoms and medical history and suggesting diagnoses. Many online tools help patients decide if they need medical help. ChatGPT's human-like discussion reminds users of the importance of language and communication to human well-being. Effective language allows patients and healthcare personnel to connect. Language models could improve therapy by helping patients communicate with healthcare practitioners and each other. For instance, simplifying language may help patients follow medical orders. Therefore, ChatGPT can be used to construct more accurate and reliable symptom monitors with more specific suggestions for the following measures.

ChatGPT, developed by OpenAI, is a potential medical tool with several uses. ChatGPT analyzes medical data to ease complex processes and improve patient care, clinical decision-making, and healthcare professional communication. The technology's ability to make human-like writing could change medical care. One of ChatGPT's most essential healthcare features is doctor advice. It analyzes medical literature, studies, and research to update clinicians. ChatGPT could diagnose medical conditions by assessing the patient's symptoms, medical history, ailments, and diseases, recommending therapies, and predicting results. Thus, more conscious judgments can improve patient health and results. ChatGPT may influence medical advice. The model's training data may show healthcare inequalities rather than demographic diversity. Prejudices must be eliminated for healthcare equity. ChatGPT has transformed healthcare despite these obstacles. This can improve patient care, productivity, and operations. ChatGPT lets doctors identify disease early, customize treatment, and remotely monitor patients. A large dataset trains ChatGPT to answer natural language queries and write like humans. GPT can treat disease, but it needs current medical data. Critical clinical applications benefit from medical dataset-trained NLP models. ChatGPT has medical potential, but privacy, ethics, and biases are difficulties. ChatGPT can provide individualized care and remote patient monitoring. However, patient self-treatment and AI-driven misinformation are risks. Debate and ambiguity surround ChatGPT incorporation in education, research, and healthcare. These sectors need rigorous analysis and a disciplined plan to reduce harm and boost profits. ChatGPT, an NLP-based healthcare system, improves patient outcomes and service delivery. ChatGPT is popular and clinically useful. ChatGPT improves clinical decision-making, cancer screening, and differential diagnosis lists. ChatGPT also gives accurate disease and medical information through intelligent question-answering. ChatGPT can generate clinical letters, radiology reports, medical notes, and discharge summaries, improving healthcare practitioners' efficiency and accuracy.

5.1 Ethical Concerns about ChatGPT

According to Sallam (2023), Temsah et al. (2023), Kong & Fu (2023), Choudhury & Shamszare (2023), Liebrenz et al. (2023), Chow et al. (2023), Asch (2023), Stahl & Eke, (2024), Hua et al. (2024), Zeb et al. (2024), Sidiropoulos & Anagnostopoulos, (2024); it could be discussed as follows.

ChatGPT in healthcare has the potential to aid with patient information, triage, mental health support, medical education, and administrative work. However, extensive testing and integration with the systems already in place will be required to be effective in a real-world healthcare setting in Thailand. In the healthcare field, ChatGPT brings ethical concerns such as privacy breaches, the possibility of receiving incorrect information, algorithmic prejudice, and weakening of the relationship between the physician and the patient. These concerns must be addressed appropriately to ensure that artificial intelligence is used responsibly and helpfully in the healthcare industry. The potential for ChatGPT to improve healthcare is very high; nevertheless, it is necessary to research its risks and advantages first. To maximize benefits while minimizing hazards, it is necessary to do a comprehensive analysis, maintain constant research, and take measures. Addressing patient self-treatment and AI-driven infodemics demands quickly communicating erroneous or misleading information. Ethical and secure ChatGPT use in medicine requires careful consideration of various problems. Patients' trust in ChatGPT and its capacity to reduce risk and improve disease prognosis determine its acceptability. ChatGPT needs substantial research to overcome healthcare limitations and hazards. ChatGPT could improve healthcare staff, education, and patient outcomes. Medical data privacy, ethics, and biases must be addressed. ChatGPT can significantly improve healthcare and medical knowledge if adequately used, examined, and explored. Ethical compliance, data protection, security, openness, and responsibility are required to use ChatGPT responsibly within the healthcare industry. The healthcare industry presents ChatGPT with several opportunities; however, it must first overcome a few obstacles. ChatGPT can enhance patient care, empower healthcare providers, and advance medical knowledge by disseminating information and reducing risks. If adequately deployed and evaluated, ChatGPT can revolutionize the healthcare industry. It is possible that the influential medical tool ChatGPT will revolutionize healthcare.

5.2 ChatGPT and Healthcare Knowledge and Research

The findings support Hosseini et al. (2023), Kalla & Smith (2023), Oviedo-Trespalacios et al. (2023), Rasul et al. (2023), Sok & Heng (2023), Raj et al. (2023), Ong et al. (2023), Chow et al. (2023), Asch (2023), Stahl & Eke (2024), Hua et al. (2024), Zeb et al. (2024), and Sidiropoulos & Anagnostopoulos, (2024); Phuang-suwan et al. (2025), that as follows;

Even though ChatGPT provides some knowledge of healthcare, it is not clinical. Information processing can produce summaries of medical issues, answer basic health inquiries, and support medical research. On the other hand, it cannot take the position of actual medical professionals, and its responses should always be checked with reputable establishments. ChatGPT might assist healthcare research by processing vast medical literature, generating research ideas, and accelerating data analysis. However, it must combine its skills with human expertise to guarantee accuracy and consider ethical issues. Ethics are paramount when using ChatGPT in the medical and healthcare fields. User data and privacy must be handled appropriately when maintaining patient confidentiality. Data biases can perpetuate healthcare disparities when constructing ChatGPT's algorithms. To achieve equal outcomes in healthcare, it is essential to address these misconceptions. In addition, ChatGPT may display content that is either inaccurate or deceptive. Statements made by AI may appear feasible, but they are either incorrect or unreasonable. The significance of human control is brought to light in the verification of ChatGPT data and the correction of inaccuracies. ChatGPT analyzes medical documents to improve patient care, clinical decision-making, and communication among healthcare professionals. This helps speed up complex processes and improve overall patient care. The simplicity of the use of ChatGPT has the potential to increase academic production and democratize the exchange of knowledge across languages. However, medical use's limitations and ethical concerns must be considered.

Future research fields include real-time monitoring and predictive analytics, precision medicine and tailored treatment, ChatGPT in telemedicine and distant health care, and health care system integration. ChatGPT helps doctors make better clinical decisions and treat patients. It has pros and cons. Researchers must evaluate its strengths and downsides. Some clinical ChatGPT research has identified hazards and challenges. It will advise and assist ChatGPT-like medical AI research.

The findings support Szabo (2023); Methnani (2023); Alanezi (2024); Willms & Liu (2024);

ChatGPT helps strategic planners, healthcare practitioners, and researchers quickly and easily obtain vital information. ChatGPT can provide knowledge with responses, support for suggestions, and valuable ideas from previous reviews, generate topic article ideas, and individually disseminate public information about epidemics, public health, and health-related questions. Exercise and sports advice can match systemic diseases. ChatGPT can also be used for healthcare research, planning, and answers. This helps people achieve goals. ChatGPT adoption in healthcare has challenges. Handling medical data can raise privacy concerns. Data security policies must protect personal data. Using transparent and objective AI programs and reliable data for reference are crucial ethical considerations.

5.3 Sustainable Development in Hospitals in Thailand Using ChatGPT

This study's result supports Namahoot (2024), who states that developing countries such as Thailand recognize that previous research has primarily focused on developed nations, especially regarding service quality, attitudes, technological acceptance, and service usage intentions. Furthermore, it analyzes the impact of service quality, attitude, and technological acceptability. Thirdly, it examines the influence of service quality on the intention to utilize ChatGPT, considering attitudes and technological adoption as mediating variables. Finally, it aims to compare the impact of significant and minor ChatGPT services in Thailand. The results of this study are anticipated to provide insights that can be generalized and implemented in other ASEAN nations, thereby improving the overall quality of life alongside the growing number of ChatGPT users for sustainable development in hospitals in Thailand by using ChatGPT.

6. CONCLUSIONS AND LIMITATIONS

ChatGPT solves complex difficulties in revolutionizing healthcare, including hospitals and clinics. ChatGPT could speed up medication development, enhance disease diagnosis through picture analysis, and enable personalized treatment plans. This system can generate human-quality text, improving patient education and communication. ChatGPT, still under development, could improve patient outcomes and transform healthcare. ChatGPT is a quick and valuable instructional tool that could change healthcare and other industries. Adopting ChatGPT in medicine is tricky. Privacy concerns require strict data privacy and security protocols for sensitive patient data. Before using their data, avoid ethical difficulties. Data biases in ChatGPT's algorithms may prolong healthcare inequities. Researchers must identify and eradicate these biases for equitable healthcare results. ChatGPT may produce irrational content. Human monitoring is essential to verify ChatGPT data accuracy, solve problems, and investigate ways to increase human-AI collaboration and build systems using both technologies. ChatGPT helps strategic planners, healthcare practitioners, and researchers quickly and easily obtain vital information. ChatGPT can provide knowledge with responses, support for suggestions, and valuable ideas from previous reviews, generate topic article ideas, and individually disseminate public information about epidemics, public health, and health-related questions. Exercise and sports advice can match systemic diseases. ChatGPT can also be used for healthcare research, planning, and answers. This helps people achieve goals. ChatGPT adoption in healthcare has challenges. Handling medical data can raise privacy concerns. Data security policies must protect personal data. Using transparent and objective AI programs and reliable data for reference are crucial ethical considerations.

Researchers acknowledge that this study's limitation is its small sample size, which consisted of 12 respondents. The limitation of this study is that Thailand was used as a case study. The findings could be explained only in Thailand and may not be explained in other countries. A broader population is recommended, and expansion to other countries for further studies due to the small sample size and geographical focus only in Thailand. A small sample size and lack of quantitative data hinder the study. Future studies should incorporate mixed methods (qualitative and quantitative) to increase the robustness of the findings. Further studies on how ethical issues, such as privacy concerns and AI biases, could affect the broader adoption of ChatGPT in healthcare, including hospitals and clinics, are also recommended.

7. IMPLICATIONS OF HEALTH PROMOTION

Assessing ChatGPT's healthcare and ethical concerns requires extensive investigation. It is necessary to assess its efficacy, healthcare consequences, and improvements. ChatGPT must be widely tested for efficacy, safety, and user acceptability in healthcare settings, including hospitals and clinics. Healthcare ChatGPT implementation must be ethical and legal. Technology can improve human activity, fitness, and sports while protecting personal data, openness, and accountability. More studies could lead to healthcare ChatGPT policies, best practices, and frameworks. This research can assist the healthcare community in using ChatGPT to reduce risks, ensure ethics, optimize benefits for professionals, patients, and medical knowledge, and guide preventative activities like sports and exercise. Sports and exercise enthusiasts can benefit from ChatGPT. Sports, exercise, and advice are included in ChatGPT. ChatGPT tweaks workouts and sports training to meet goals, fitness levels, and resources. Building strength, endurance, or a new sport step-by-step with ChatGPT. ChatGPT shares sports methods, nutrition, exercise science, and injury prevention. Sports and fitness routines are assessed. ChatGPT helps consumers create objectives, track progress, and stay motivated. It can recommend exercises, challenges, and inspiring phrases. ChatGPT offers exercises, methods, and solutions to fitness plateaus and sports obstacles. For performance anxiety, focus, and recovery after setbacks. Sports and fitness chat may be entertaining with ChatGPT. There can be sports news, training trends, fitness trivia, and quizzes. Information, support, and inspiration from ChatGPT improve fitness and sports. Regardless of your physical level, ChatGPT can help you achieve your goals.

Exercise and sports advice can match systemic diseases for sustainable development in hospitals. ChatGPT can also be used for healthcare research, planning, and answers. This helps people achieve goals. ChatGPT adoption in healthcare has challenges. Handling medical data can raise privacy concerns. Data security policies must protect personal data. Using transparent and objective AI programs and reliable data for reference are crucial ethical considerations. A small sample size and lack of quantitative data hinder the study. To explain correlations between factors, future studies should address these constraints and pursue more thorough statistical analysis, such as ChatGPT for exercise and sports. ChatGPT discusses sports, exercise, and guidance. It adapts workouts and sports training to goals, fitness, and resources. ChatGPT gradually builds strength, endurance, or a new sport.

8. RECOMMENDATIONS FOR FURTHER STUDIES

Further topics are suggested for expanding studies covering Artificial intelligence (AI), not only for ChatGPT in the healthcare sector for sustainable development goals (SDGs) and sustainability, such as:

1. Image Analysis: AI algorithms can quickly and accurately detect cancers, fractures, and diseases in medical images, including X-rays, MRIs, and CT scans. Generative AI can generate synthetic medical pictures for training, improving data privacy and availability.

2. Drugs Molecular Modeling: AI can model and analyze molecular interactions to find drugs.
3. Clinical Trial Optimization: AI accelerates drug development by optimizing trial design, patient recruiting, and data analysis.
4. Medical Personalization: AI can analyze patient data to discover patterns and anticipate illness risk, enabling customized treatment approaches. Genomic Analysis: AI can discover illness predispositions and inform therapy recommendations using genomic data.
5. Risk Assessment: AI can predict disease risk from patient data, enabling early therapies. Disease outbreak prediction: AI can anticipate disease outbreaks using epidemiological data, improving public health planning. For patient care and monitoring, AI-powered chatbots can provide support, answer inquiries, and organize appointments.
6. Remote Patient Monitoring: AI can evaluate wearable device data to monitor patient health and detect early decline.
7. Medical Record Management: AI can streamline data entry, coding, and claims processing.
8. Scheduling: AI-powered solutions can optimize appointment scheduling to cut wait times and improve patient satisfaction. Issues and Considerations AI has great potential but also difficulties.
9. Privacy and Security: These two terms are crucial. Addressing algorithmic bias is required to prevent healthcare inequities, and regulations must change to keep up with AI regarding privacy and security issues

The Future of Healthcare: AI developments in surgery, diagnostics, and drug delivery systems present a promising future in healthcare. AI may become essential for healthcare practitioners, improving patient outcomes and changing the industry. ChatGPT for sports and exercise is helpful for physical, emotional, and mental wellness.

REFERENCES

Agne, I., & Gedrich, K. (2024). Personalized dietary recommendations for obese individuals–A comparison of ChatGPT and the Food4Me algorithm. *Clinical Nutrition Open Science, 56*, 192–201. DOI: 10.1016/j.nutos.2024.06.001

Alanezi, F. (2024). Examining the role of ChatGPT in promoting health behaviors and lifestyle changes among cancer patients. *Nutrition and Health (Berkhamsted, Hertfordshire)*, 02601060241244563. PMID: 38567408

Ali, S. M., Appolloni, A., Cavallaro, F., D'Adamo, I., Di Vaio, A., Ferella, F., Gastaldi, M., Ikram, M., Kumar, N. M., Martin, M. A., Nizami, A.-S., Ozturk, I., Riccardi, M. P., Rosa, P., Santibanez Gonzalez, E., Sassanelli, C., Settembre-Blundo, D., Singh, R. K., Smol, M., & Zorpas, A. A. (2023). Development goals towards sustainability. *Sustainability (Basel), 15*(12), 9443. DOI: 10.3390/su15129443

Asch, D. A. (2023). An interview with ChatGPT about health care. *NEJM Catalyst Innovations in Care Delivery, 4*(2). https://catalyst.nejm.org/doi/full/10.1056/CAT.23.0043

Aydın, Ö., & Karaarslan, E. (2022). OpenAI ChatGPT generated literature review: Digital Twin in healthcare. *SSRN, 4308687*, https://papers.ssrn.com/sol3/papers.cfm?abstract_id=4308687. DOI: 10.2139/ssrn.4308687

Choudhury, A., & Shamszare, H. (2023). Investigating the Impact of User Trust on the Adoption and Use of ChatGPT: Survey Analysis. *Journal of Medical Internet Research, 25*, e47184. https://www.jmir.org/2023/1/e47184. DOI: 10.2196/47184 PMID: 37314848

Chow, J. C., Sanders, L., & Li, K. (2023). Impact of ChatGPT on medical chatbots as a disruptive technology. *Frontiers in Artificial Intelligence, 6*, 1166014. DOI: 10.3389/frai.2023.1166014 PMID: 37091303

Dave, T., Athaluri, S. A., & Singh, S. (2023). ChatGPT in medicine: An overview of its applications, advantages, limitations, prospects, and ethical considerations. *Frontiers in Artificial Intelligence, 6*, 1169595. DOI: 10.3389/frai.2023.1169595 PMID: 37215063

Dergaa, I., Saad, H. B., El Omri, A., Glenn, J., Clark, C., Washif, J., & Chamari, K. (2024). Using artificial intelligence for exercise prescription in personalised health promotion: A critical evaluation of OpenAI's GPT-4 model. *Biology of Sport, 41*(2), 221–241. DOI: 10.5114/biolsport.2024.133661 PMID: 38524814

Dhunnoo, P. (2023). ChatGPT In Healthcare: What Science Says. Artificial Intelligence in Medicine. https://medicalfuturist.com/chatgpt-in-healthcare-what-the-science-says/

García-Ramírez, Y., Campoverde, P., Díaz, F., Ortega, J., & Vásquez, J. (2024, Feb). Assessing Ethical Implications of ChatGPT in Higher Education: A Focus on Students. In *International Congress on Information and Communication Technology* (pp. 183–199). Springer Nature Singapore., https://link.springer.com/chapter/10.1007/978-981-97-3302-6_16 DOI: 10.1007/978-981-97-3302-6_16

George, A. S., & George, A. H. (2023). A review of ChatGPT AI's impact on several business sectors. *Partners Universal International Innovation Journal, 1*(1), 9–23. DOI: 10.5281/zenodo.7644359

Hosseini, M., Gao, C. A., Liebovitz, D. M., Carvalho, A. M., Ahmad, F. S., Luo, Y., . . . Kho, A. (2023). An exploratory survey about using ChatGPT in education, healthcare, and research. medRxiv, 2023-03.DOI: 10.1101/2023.03.31.23287979

Hua, S., Jin, S., & Jiang, S. (2024). The limitations and ethical considerations of ChatGPT. *Data Intelligence*, *6*(1), 201–239. DOI: 10.1162/dint_a_00243

Iftikhar, L. (2023). Docgpt: Impact of ChatGpt-3 on health services as a virtual doctor. *EC Paediatrics : Open Access*, *12*(1), 45–55.

Jaipong, P. (2023). Business Model and Strategy: A Case Study Analysis of TikTok. *Advance Knowledge for Executives, 2*(1), 1-18. https://papers.ssrn.com/sol3/papers.cfm?abstract_id=4335962

Javaid, M., Haleem, A., & Singh, R. P. (2023). ChatGPT for healthcare services: An emerging stage for an innovative perspective. *BenchCouncil Transactions on Benchmarks. Standards and Evaluations*, *3*(1), 100105. DOI: 10.1016/j.tbench.2023.100105

Jeyaraman, M., Ramasubramanian, S., Balaji, S., Jeyaraman, N., Nallakumarasamy, A., & Sharma, S. (2023). ChatGPT in action: Harnessing artificial intelligence potential and addressing ethical challenges in medicine, education, and scientific research. *World Journal of Methodology*, *13*(4), 170–178. DOI: 10.5662/wjm.v13.i4.170 PMID: 37771867

Kalla, D., & Smith, N. (2023). Study and Analysis of Chat GPT and its Impact on Different Fields of Study. *International Journal of Innovative Science and Research Technology*, *8*(3), 827–833. https://papers.ssrn.com/sol3/papers.cfm?abstract_id=4402499

Kok, S. L. (2023). A Strategic Cooperative Model: The Case of Islamic Financing Hub. *Advance Knowledge for Executives, 2*(1), 1-15. https://papers.ssrn.com/sol3/papers.cfm?abstract_id=4393073

Kong, D., Qi, J., & Fu, X. (2023). Would You Accept Doctor ChatGPT: An Empirical Study

Liebrenz, M., Schleifer, R., Buadze, A., Bhugra, D., & Smith, A. (2023). Generating Scholarly content with ChatGPT: Ethical challenges for medical publishing. *The Lancet. Digital Health*, *5*(3), e105–e106. DOI: 10.1016/S2589-7500(23)00019-5 PMID: 36754725

Lim, L. (2023). Digital Marketing Strategies: A Case of Charles & Keith. *Advance Knowledge for Executives, 2*(2), 1-11. https://papers.ssrn.com/sol3/papers.cfm?abstract_id=4426397

Limna, P., Jakwatanatham, S., Siripipattanakul, S., Kaewpuang, P., & Sriboonruang, P. (2022). A review of artificial intelligence (AI) in education during the digital era. *Advance Knowledge for Executives, 1*(1), 1-9. https://papers.ssrn.com/sol3/papers.cfm?abstract_id=4160798

Limna, P., Kraiwanit, T., Jangjarat, K., Klayklung, P., & Chocksathaporn, P. (2023). The use Of ChatGPT in the digital era: Perspectives on chatbot implementation. *Journal of Applied Learning and Teaching*, *6*(1), 1–11. DOI: 10.37074/jalt.2023.6.1.32

Limna, P., Siripipatthanakul, S., Siripipattanakul, S., & Auttawechasakoon, P. (2023). The UTAUT model explaining intentions to use telemedicine among Thai people during the COVID-19 pandemic: A qualitative study in Krabi, Thailand. *International Journal of Computing Sciences Research*, *7*, 1468–1486. DOI: 10.25147/ijcsr.2017.001.1.111

Liu, J., Wang, C., & Liu, S. (2023). Utility of ChatGPT in Clinical Practice. *Journal of Medical Internet Research*, *25*, e48568. https://www.jmir.org/2023/1/e48568/. DOI: 10.2196/48568 PMID: 37379067

Methnani, J., Latiri, I., Dergaa, I., Chamari, K., & Saad, H. B. (2023). ChatGPT for sample-size calculation in sports medicine and exercise sciences: A cautionary note. *International Journal of Sports Physiology and Performance, 1(aop), 1-5.* https://journals.humankinetics.com/view/journals/ijspp/18/10/article-p1219.xml

Muftić, F., Kadunić, M., Mušinbegović, A., & Abd Almisreb, A. (2023). Exploring Medical Breakthroughs: A Systematic Review of ChatGPT Applications in Healthcare. *Southeast Europe Journal of Soft Computing, 12*(1), 13-41. https://scjournal.ius.edu.ba/index.php/scjournal/article/view/252

Nadarzynski, T., Miles, O., Cowie, A., & Ridge, D. (2019). Acceptability of artificial intelligence (AI)-led chatbot services in healthcare: A mixed-methods study. *Digital Health, 5*, 2055207619871808. https://pubmed.ncbi.nlm.nih.gov/31467682/. DOI: 10.1177/2055207619871808 PMID: 31467682

Namahoot, K. S. (2024). Adoption and Impact of Chat-Gpt in Thailand: Analyzing Service Quality and Technology Acceptance Through a Structural Equation Modeling Approach. *SSRN, 4898056*, https://papers.ssrn.com/sol3/papers.cfm?abstract_id=4898056

Ong, H., Ong, J., Cheng, R., Wang, C., Lin, M., & Ong, D. (2023). GPT technology to help address longstanding barriers to care in free medical clinics. *Annals of Biomedical Engineering*, *51*(9), 1906–1909. DOI: 10.1007/s10439-023-03256-4 PMID: 37355478

Oviedo-Trespalacios, O., Peden, A. E., Cole-Hunter, T., Costantini, A., Haghani, M., Kelly, S., & Reniers, G. (2023). The risks of using ChatGPT to obtain common safety-related information and advice. *SSRN, 4346827*, https://papers.ssrn.com/sol3/papers.cfm?abstract_id=4346827

Pathak, A. (2023). Exploring Chatgpt: An Extensive Examination of its Background, Applications, Key Challenges, Bias, Ethics, Limitations, and Future Prospects. Applications, Key Challenges, Bias, Ethics, Limitations, and Future Prospects. https://papers.ssrn.com/sol3/papers.cfm?abstract_id=4499278

Phuangsuwan, P., Siripipatthanakul, S., Limna, P., & Pariwongkhuntorn, N. (2024). The Impact of Google Maps Application on the Digital Economy. Corporate and Business Strategy Review, 5(1), 192-203. https://papers.ssrn.com/sol3/papers.cfm?abstract_id=4785205

Phuangsuwan, P., Siripipatthanakul, S., Praesri, S., & Rakpathum, W. (2025). The Relationship between Good Governance and Organizational Performance through Mediating Role of Employee Satisfaction. *Journal of Governance and Regulation/ Volume, 14*(1).

Raj, R., Singh, A., Kumar, V., & Verma, P. (2023). Analyzing the potential benefits and use cases of ChatGPT as a tool for improving the efficiency and effectiveness of business operations. *Bench Council Transactions on Benchmarks. Standards and Evaluations*, *3*(3), 100140. DOI: 10.1016/j.tbench.2023.100140

Rasul, T., Nair, S., Kalendra, D., Robin, M., de Oliveira Santini, F., Ladeira, W. J., & Heathcote, L. (2023). The role of ChatGPT in higher education: Benefits, challenges, and future research directions. *Journal of Applied Learning and Teaching*, *6*(1), 41–56. DOI: 10.37074/jalt.2023.6.1.29

Ray, P. P. (2023). ChatGPT: A comprehensive review on background, applications, key challenges, bias, ethics, limitations and future scope. *Internet of Things and Cyber-Physical Systems*, *3*, 121–154. DOI: 10.1016/j.iotcps.2023.04.003

Rice, S., Crouse, S. R., Winter, S. R., & Rice, C. (2024). The advantages and limitations of using ChatGPT to enhance technological research. *Technology in Society*, *76*, 102426. DOI: 10.1016/j.techsoc.2023.102426

Rivas, P., & Zhao, L. (2023). Marketing with ChatGPT: Navigating the ethical terrain of GPT-based chatbot technology. *AI*, *4*(2), 375–384. DOI: 10.3390/ai4020019

Sallam, M. (2023, Mar). ChatGPT utility in healthcare education, research, and practice: Systematic review on the promising perspectives and valid concerns. *Health Care*, *11*(6), 887. DOI: 10.3390/healthcare11060887 PMID: 36981544

Shahsavar, Y., & Choudhury, A. (2023). User Intentions to Use ChatGPT for Self-Diagnosis and Health-Related Purposes: Cross-sectional Survey Study. *JMIR Human Factors*, *10*(1), e47564. https://humanfactors.jmir.org/2023/1/e47564. DOI: 10.2196/47564 PMID: 37195756

Sidiropoulos, D., & Anagnostopoulos, C. N. (2024). Applications, challenges and ethical issues of AI and ChatGPT in education. *arXiv preprint arXiv:2402.07907*. https://arxiv.org/abs/2402.07907

Siripipatthanakul, S. (2011). Development of a Model for Administration of Student Dental Health Promotion Work for Basic Education Schools in Thailand. *International Journal of Learning*, *17*(12), 137–150. DOI: 10.18848/1447-9494/CGP/v17i12/47373

Siripipatthanakul, S., Limna, P., Siripipattanakul, S., & Auttawechasakoon, P. (2022). The Impact of TPB Model on customers' intentions to buy organic foods: A qualitative study in Angsila-Chonburi, Thailand. *Psychology and Education Journal*, *59*(2), 419-434. https://papers.ssrn.com/sol3/papers.cfm?abstract_id=4109868

Siripipatthanakul, S., & Phuangsuwan, P. (2024). *Salutogenic Marketing in Preventive Dentistry: Leveraging Digital Technology for Preventive Dentistry*. IGI Global Publishing. DOI: 10.4018/979-8-3693-3872-8.ch009

Sok, S., & Heng, K. (2023). ChatGPT for education and research: A review of benefits and risks. *Cambodian Journal of Educational Research*, *3*(1), 110–121. DOI: 10.62037/cjer.2023.03.01.06

Sribanasarn, W., Kaewplang, S., Khotdee, M., Phumiphan, A., Sivanpheng, O., & Kangrang, A. (2025). Sustainable Development Goals for Education and Research in the Ranking of Green Universities of Mahasarakham University Advancing Sustainability: An Analysis of Education, Research, and University Operations In 2024. *Journal of Lifestyle and SDGs Review*, *5*(3), e04627–e04627. DOI: 10.47172/2965-730X.SDGsReview.v5.n03.pe04627

Stahl, B. C., & Eke, D. (2024). The ethics of ChatGPT–Exploring the ethical issues of an emerging technology. *International Journal of Information Management*, *74*, 102700. DOI: 10.1016/j.ijinfomgt.2023.102700

Szabo, A. (2023). ChatGPT is a breakthrough in science and education but fails a test in sports and exercise psychology.

Temsah, O., Khan, S. A., Chaiah, Y., Senjab, A., Alhasan, K., Jamal, A., & Senjab, A. M. (2023). Overview of early ChatGPT's presence in medical literature: Insights from a hybrid literature review by ChatGPT and human experts. *Cureus*, *15*(4), 1–7. https://pubmed.ncbi.nlm.nih.gov/37038381/. DOI: 10.7759/cureus.37281 PMID: 37038381

Vaishya, R., Misra, A., & Vaish, A. (2023). ChatGPT: Is this version good for healthcare and research? *Diabetes & Metabolic Syndrome*, *17*(4), 102744. DOI: 10.1016/j.dsx.2023.102744 PMID: 36989584

Washif, J., Pagaduan, J., James, C., Dergaa, I., & Beaven, C. (2024). Artificial intelligence in sport: Exploring the potential of using ChatGPT in resistance training prescription. *Biology of Sport*, *41*(2), 209–220. DOI: 10.5114/biolsport.2024.132987 PMID: 38524820

Willms, A., & Liu, S. (2024). Exploring the feasibility of using ChatGPT to create just-in-time adaptive physical activity mHealth intervention content: Case study. *JMIR Medical Education*, *10*, e51426. https://mededu.jmir.org/2024/1/e51426. DOI: 10.2196/51426 PMID: 38421689

Wu, X., Duan, R., & Ni, J. (2024). Unveiling security, privacy, and ethical concerns of ChatGPT. *Journal of Information and Intelligence*, *2*(2), 102–115. DOI: 10.1016/j.jiixd.2023.10.007

Yaraghi, N. (2023). *ChatGPT And Health Care: Implications For Interoperability And Fairness*. Health Affairs Forefront., DOI: 10.1377/forefront.20230605.938282

Zaman, M. (2023). ChatGPT for Healthcare Sector: SWOT Analysis. *International Journal of Research in Industrial Engineering*. DOI: 10.22105/riej.2023.391536.1373

Zeb, A., Ullah, R., & Karim, R. (2024). Exploring the role of ChatGPT in higher education: Opportunities, challenges, and ethical considerations. *The International Journal of Information and Learning Technology*, *41*(1), 99–111. DOI: 10.1108/IJILT-04-2023-0046

Zhou, J., Müller, H., Holzinger, A., & Chen, F. (2023). Ethical ChatGPT: Concerns, Challenges, and commandments. *arXiv preprint arXiv:2305.10646*. https://doi.org//arXiv.2305.10646DOI: 10.48550

Chapter 2
Sustainable Dentistry Using Artificial Intelligence (AI) for Digital Education and Business Among University Dental Hospitals

Supaprawat Siripipatthanakul
https://orcid.org/0000-0001-6671-2682
Bangkok Thonburi University, Thailand

Sorasun Rungsiyanont
Srinakharinwirot University, Bangkok, Thailand

Sutithep Siripipattanakul
https://orcid.org/0000-0002-5477-6723
Kasetsart University, Bangkhen, Thailand

ABSTRACT

This chapter demonstrates how digital technology and AI enhance individual dental care and learning. Digital dentistry tools are expanding opportunities for dental staff, practitioners, students, and patients. Due to the pandemic and the prevalence of contagious diseases, distance learning has become more efficient, accessible, and effective. This chapter presents a systematic study of Scopus, Web of Science

DOI: 10.4018/979-8-3693-9800-5.ch002

(WOS), and Google Scholar papers mainly from 2021 to 2025, employing purposive sampling, PRISMA criteria, and content analysis. Digital education, chat forums, and digital publications can engage instructors, students, and patients, boosting academic accomplishment, continuing education, and patient and community dental healthcare understanding based on knowledge and attitudes. Moreover, dental marketing with digital business provides fast, personalized services.

1. INTRODUCTION

Technologies drive digital education, collaborative advocacy, interventions for high-risk groups, and investments in digital infrastructure. It underscores the significance of comprehensive monitoring, research, and innovation. Future research should facilitate global collaboration, develop user-friendly digital solutions, and improve cost-effectiveness. It highlights the effectiveness of digital education in clinical health communication, influencing oral health education, practice, policies, and research. Digital education is scalable, accessible, and efficient for varied audiences, transcending the limitations of time and distance (Thapa, 2024).

Community-based dental education can enhance public health by improving the availability, affordability, accessibility, accommodation, and acceptability of dental services. Health literacy among students and the community, as well as clinical outcomes, may also be enhanced. The length of community-based education, along with rural and socioeconomic backgrounds, may affect students' preferred practice settings. It may help realign community-based education to benefit both communities and students, thereby enhancing access and mitigating health inequities. It is essential to evaluate results, encompassing students' intentions to practice, actual practice sites, and the acceptability, affordability, accommodation, and accessibility of services (Ayibuofu-Uwandi & Dyer, 2024).

In dentistry, dental departments at public hospitals, dental clinics, and university hospitals are swiftly integrating digital intelligence, encompassing both human and artificial intelligence, for digital dental education. Communication technology has the potential to enhance dentistry education and patient care. Virtual classrooms can enhance dental education. These tools enhance dental student autonomy and cultivate a digital culture via both synchronous and asynchronous learning modalities. Digital commerce promotes dentistry in marketing and dental education (Khurshid, 2023; Siripipatthanakul et al., 2024).

Inadequate resources, faculty, infrastructure, and technological access hinder dental education in developing nations. Certain issues present suggestions for enhancing dental education in specific areas. It is essential to have a framework in place to address the challenges in dental education in underdeveloped nations. Adequate infrastructure, faculty retention, community engagement, and technological integration are essential. Emphasis is placed on public-private partnerships, international collaboration, and the provision of ethical and culturally competent care. The initiatives and ongoing enhancements can facilitate greater accessibility, equity, and sustainability in dentistry education for low-income countries. These activities benefit dental students and, more importantly, the oral health of their communities. Given the significance of oral health to overall well-being, governments, educational institutions, healthcare organizations, and communities must collaborate to enhance dental education (Al-Worafi, 2024, a, b).

1.1 Research Objective

This systematic review utilizes the PRISMA methodology to delineate the principles of digital education in community dentistry in developing nations.

1.2 Research Question

What are the fundamental components of digital education in community dentistry and dental clinics in developing countries?

2. LITERATURE REVIEW

2.1 Sustainability Theory

Sustainability and sustainable development have emerged as significant concepts and objectives within both scientific and societal realms. Sustainability, associated with favorable long-term conditions, is an intrinsically practical endeavor in geography and other disciplines. However, a comprehensive description of fundamental concepts underpinning sustainability studies and applications has been absent. Several key concepts underscore the importance of choice, place, scale, systems, limits, change, and interconnected ideas related to sustainability. The rural context serves to exemplify fundamental principles of sustainability; however, these concepts are broadly applicable to endeavors and investigations aimed at enhancing environmental and social transformations within local, regional, and global systems influenced by human activities (Harrington, 2016; Phuangsuwan et al., 2023; Rakpathum et al., 2025).

2.2 Sustainable Development in University Dental Hospitals

Sustainable dentistry emphasizes providing underprivileged individuals with accessible, affordable, and preventive oral healthcare while supporting environmental, economic, and social sustainability. The education of dental students and practitioners in socially responsible practices is included in this, and it takes place within the context of a university hospital. Domains for intervention, including illness prevention, carbon footprint mitigation, and the management of plastics, nitrous oxide, and antibiotics, are examined. Resources are allocated to support teams in implementing sustainable practices (Fareed & Zafar, 2024; Hackley & Luca, 2024).

One of the primary goals is to reduce the inequities in oral health, while another is to include communities in oral hygiene education and to promote environmentally friendly dentistry practices (such as lowering the consumption of plastic and managing dental waste). Sustainable development encompasses three key components: social, economic, and environmental dimensions, with a focus on accessibility and affordability (Lee & Divaris, 2014; Huang & Chang, 2022).

2.3 New Strategic Model Employing the Digital Intelligence

In the 21st century, business models have experienced substantial alterations, particularly following the pandemic caused by the Coronavirus Disease 2019 (COVID-19). Currently, the normalization of the epidemic is slowing down the rapid development that has been occurring. Despite this, technological developments, such as artificial intelligence (AI), are inevitable and are reshaping economic growth paradigms from factor-driven systems to innovation-driven systems. A more in-depth investigation into the developments in business models and their impact on economic growth is warranted. When viewed from the perspective of labor entrepreneurship and innovation, innovative human capital leverages artificial intelligence (AI) and other scientific and technological advancements to support the transformation of the economic development model through innovation. Digital intelligence has the potential to contribute to an increase in both the marginal return and the production multiplier effect. This disrupts the traditional business paradigm, encouraging innovation and facilitating economic growth. During the period when the pandemic is returning to normal, the method addresses the problem of slow economic growth and accelerates the shift to a growth mode (Lv et al., 2024; Phuangsuwan & Rakpathum, 2024; a, b).

Since the 1950s, X-rays, digital imaging, and artificial intelligence (AI) have enabled dentists to diagnose oral health problems more effectively. Digital technology in strategic management for dental clinics and dentistry revolutionizes oral healthcare by enhancing efficiency, personalization, and accessibility of dental visits, as well as digital marketing, communications, and processes. Digital intelligence (business intelligence) in dentistry, dental clinics, marketing, and ethics may be related. Dental marketing and ethics encompass the ethical and transparent promotion of dental products, services, and research. All marketing communications must protect patient privacy. Dental clinics and researchers must prioritize patient safety, confidentiality, and informed consent to retain professional ethics and public confidence. AI-driven digital intelligence, also known as business intelligence, integrates emotional, social, and cognitive intelligence with human intelligence to enhance decision-making capabilities. Also called business intelligence. Artificial intelligence-supported dentists who employ digital intelligence for strategic management and dental diagnosis. Digital marketing and technology integration is a hot topic in digital intelligence research, which mixes artificial and human intelligence. Digital intelligence in dental clinics and dentistry is crucial for sustainable development (Siripipatthanakul et al., a & b).

2.4 Decisions Using Human Intelligence and Artificial Intelligence

The foundation of design and implementation is achieved through the application of human intelligence. Access to care, a lack of understanding, and the essential demand for ongoing professional development are some of the challenges present in community dentistry. Human intelligence is required to recognize these problems.

In light of the ability to analyze the problems and devise original solutions for decision-making, utilize digital education as a remedial measure. It is impossible to build successful digital educational tools and platforms for professionals, students, and patients without incorporating both creativity and innovation into the process. The creation of content that is not only intriguing but also engaging, user interfaces that are easy to use, and relevant learning experiences are all features that fall under this category. The application of digital tools to dentistry education and community outreach is being driven by human intelligence, which is propelling technology into the future. Human intelligence is required for both the development of digital education and its application. This intelligence is necessary for learning and adaptability. To make efficient use of these new technologies, both students and professionals need to acquire the necessary skills (John et al., 2025; Hsu et al., 2025).

It is the patient's responsibility to absorb and apply the information they have learned through digital media. When it comes to adapting teaching and learning strategies to their respective digital formats, human cognitive flexibility is considered necessary despite the proliferation of digital tools; effective communication remains of the utmost significance. Empathy and communication are two essential aspects. Empathy and the ability to communicate effectively are two of the most distinguishing characteristics of human intellect. These qualities are also crucial for the development of digital instructional materials that are sensitive to other cultures, easy to comprehend, and adapted to meet the specific needs of the community. It is essential to engage in strategic planning to develop a digital education program that is both sustainable and effective. It is essential to plan the infrastructure, training, content production, and assessment procedures to ensure the endeavor's long-term success. The foresight and planning that have been generated are a result of human intelligence. Human intelligence is essential for addressing the ethical concerns associated with the use of digital technology in education and healthcare (Meskó et al., 2024; Makda, 2025).

These implications include safeguarding personal information, ensuring equal access to information, and responsible data use. Digital platforms can more effectively transfer information generated by human specialists (such as dental professionals and educators) to a larger audience, which can increase the extent of knowledge. Digital platforms provide the opportunity to connect professionals, students, and even patients, facilitating collaborative learning and knowledge sharing.

2.5 Intelligent Design and Personalized Learning

Personal learning refers to the intelligent design of digital platforms that can accommodate a variety of learning styles and paces, thereby increasing educational efficiency. The process of analyzing data from digital learning platforms can provide insights into the efficiency of educational material and delivery, which in turn makes it possible for human-driven adjustments to be made. In essence, human intelligence is the driving force behind the conception, development, implementation, and assessment of using digital education to increase sustainable community dentistry within university hospitals. This is because digital education is inherently tied to human intelligence. To identify problems, develop solutions, learn and adapt to new technologies, communicate effectively, plan strategically, and handle ethical considerations, we utilize our cognitive abilities. The digital tools themselves are the result of our intelligence and were developed to enhance our power to either educate or provide care (Bhutoria, 2022; Strielkowski et al., 2025).

2.6 Digital Education in Dentistry

Dental education encounters various problems that substantially impact the training and readiness of prospective dental professionals. This article identifies the primary challenges and proposes potential strategies to address them. The swift progression of technology requires ongoing revisions to courses, including breakthroughs like digital imaging, CAD/CAM systems, and laser dentistry. Ensuring staff and student competence in these technologies requires a significant investment in training and resources. In conclusion, addressing these challenges requires curriculum reform, technological investment, enhanced clinical training opportunities, robust financial support systems, targeted mental health initiatives, and adaptability. Dental education encounters various problems that substantially impact the training and readiness of prospective dental professionals (Thomas, 2024).

To effectively improve oral health outcomes and access to care, the key components of digital education in community dentistry and dental clinics in low-income countries encompass several crucial features essential for enhancing oral health. An abbreviated version of these core concerns is presented in the following fashion:

2.6.1 Tele-Dentistry and Digital Communication

Through the utilization of tele-dental care, one of the most effective methods for reaching underserved communities in rural areas is to provide dental treatment. The utilization of digital communication tools enables the remote conduct of consultations, diagnosis, treatment arrangements, and follow-ups. For example, tele-dental care enables early screenings to be made more accessible in geographically isolated locations. This would eliminate the need for patients to travel significant distances in order to undergo preliminary evaluations. Instruction and literacy in digital technology are of the utmost importance (Shukla & Attar, 2025).

To achieve success, dental professionals and community health workers must be equipped with the necessary electronic skills. This includes the ability to utilize digital equipment, software, and online platforms for education, communication, and record-keeping. Within the realm of dentistry, training programs should concentrate equal attention on the technical aspects of these tools as well as the applications associated with them.

2.6.2 Mobile Health Applications (mHealth), and Digital Imaging

mHealth and digital imaging provide patients with information on the importance of maintaining good oral hygiene, remind them of their scheduled appointments, and collect data for community oral health surveys. People can take a more active role in managing their oral health when they use mobile health applications that are accessible to them. The abbreviation "EHRs" refers to Electronic Health Records. The use of digital record-keeping enables the improvement of patient information tracking and community health trends, while also enhancing efficiency and reducing errors. Having electronic health records stored in the cloud can be especially helpful for accessibility in various environments (Garg et al., 2025).

By enabling patients to identify the oral health problems they are experiencing, technologies such as digital radiography and intraoral cameras enhance diagnostic capabilities and facilitate easier communication between patients and their health-care providers. Additionally, the use of this technology facilitates patient education. Continuous learning opportunities can be made available to dental professionals who have access to online educational resources. These options include webinars, online courses, and digital libraries, among others. When it comes to locations where traditional educational institutions are difficult to access, this is especially true.

2.6.3 Accessibility and Affordability

The cost-effectiveness of the solutions should be given priority, and they should be adaptable to areas with relatively limited internet connectivity and infrastructure. This may necessitate the use of simpler technology or offline resources, depending on the specific situation. Educational content and digital technology must be tailored to the specific oral health concerns and cultural contexts of the communities being served, ensuring relevance to the local community's needs. It is essential to ensure that programs are designed to be self-sustaining, thereby guaranteeing their long-term viability. This can be accomplished by fostering the growth of local capabilities and distributing resources effectively (Renger et al., 2025).

2.6.4 Digital Education Benefits

Better access to dental care can be achieved through the use of tele-dentistry, which eliminates geographical boundaries. An example of improved quality of care is the use of digital tools to enhance the accuracy of diagnosis and treatment planning. Improvements in patient education and engagement can be made possible through the use of visual aids and easily accessible information. In the field of dentistry, the term "continuous professional development" refers to the process of providing dental practitioners with ongoing educational opportunities. Effective data collection and management are essential components of both community oral health programs and individual patient care. Defeating the following challenges: Making sure that everyone has equitable access to technology and internet connectivity is what we mean when we talk about the "digital divide." Not only does this include the cost of gear and software, but it also includes the cost of training (Khurshid, 2023).

Both individuals and healthcare professionals exhibit a significant amount of resistance to change. The provision of ongoing maintenance and assistance is what is indicated by the term "technical support." When it comes to dentistry and dental hospitals in developing countries, the fundamentals of digital education revolve around the utilization of digital tools that are easily accessible and inexpensive. These tools facilitate the enhancement of education, the improvement of communication, and ultimately the expansion of the scope and quality of oral healthcare treatment. To achieve this, it is essential to prioritize training, community relevance, and sustainable implementation.

2.7 Digital Business in University Dental Hospitals (Dentistry)

The term "digital business" refers to the utilization of various digital platforms and technologies to improve services, streamline operations, and facilitate easier engagement for patients and the community. For teaching, providing services, and conducting research, hospitals affiliated with universities can incorporate digital solutions. Listed below are some examples of digital tools that currently exist. There are platforms for tele-dental care that enable remote consultations to take place. Mobile applications are responsible for a variety of tasks, including appointment scheduling, reminders, and educational content related to oral health. Electronic health records, often referred to as EHRs, are being utilized to enhance the coordination of care. Diagnostics based on artificial intelligence and three-dimensional printing are being utilized in the sectors of orthodontics and prosthetics. Online learning modules are available for both students and community outreach (Hou, 2023; Plugmann, 2021).

University hospitals can reap benefits from education, as it enhances the curriculum for dentistry by combining digital skills and addressing environmental sustainability issues. Research enables the conduct of studies driven by data on patient habits and the effectiveness of digital care services provided to the community, thanks to the insights gained through research. Tele-dental care enables increased outreach and follow-up in rural and remote areas. Tele-dental treatment is becoming increasingly convenient. When a business is viable over the long term, it minimizes the quantity of resources utilized (such as paper and travel), and it encourages environmentally responsible habits. To achieve true sustainability, university dental hospitals must develop multidisciplinary programs that integrate public health, information technology, and dentistry. These programs should be integrated in order to achieve long-term sustainability. Additionally, they need to collaborate with organizations specializing in technology to offer innovative dental solutions. To address the specific requirements of the community, it is important to encourage community engagement in the development of digital tools. Specifically, this aligns with the United Nations' Sustainable Development Goals (SDGs). A high-quality education is one of the four Sustainable Development Goals that must be achieved. Infrastructure, innovation, and industry are all areas that require strengthening, which brings us to the ninth target of the Sustainable Development Goals agenda.

To improve the delivery of oral healthcare, promote fairness, strengthen training for dental professionals, and advance sustainable development, reducing inequalities is a necessary step. The future is undergoing a paradigm shift, and that movement is toward sustainable community dentistry in university hospitals that embrace digital business practices. This transition is occurring in the direction of the future. By leveraging technology and education, this integrated strategy ensures that university hospitals not only contribute to the provision of medical care but also to the empowerment of the communities that they serve. This is accomplished through the utilization of academic institutions.

2.8 Salutogenic Digital Marketing for Digital Business in Dentistry

Salutogenic digital marketing has the potential to enhance health and wellness rather than merely focusing on illness prevention in dentistry. Dentists and dental hygienists help individuals maintain oral health through prevention, education, and advanced technology—salutogenic advertising advocates for oral hygiene and preventive dentistry. Websites, mobile applications, and social media platforms can provide articles, videos, infographics, and interactive modules. Telemedicine enables patients to consult dentists remotely, promoting early intervention and preventive care. Conducting surveys, interviews, or focus groups is advisable to ascertain the impact of the study technique on patients' perceptions of outcomes (Siripipatthanakul & Phuangsuwan, 2024).

2.9 Google Maps for Digital Business in Dentistry

Google Maps is essential for helping customers navigate worldwide, a renowned destination. It encompasses detailed maps, sites of interest, and recommendations for accommodations, eating, and attractions. The Google Maps program facilitates the identification of businesses, reservation arrangements, and order execution for users. Moreover, Google Maps suggests nearby enterprises that may appeal to the user, depending on their location and preferences. It promotes user exploration of new enterprises and increases local expenditure through mobile commerce and regional suggestions. Google Maps has had a profound impact on the digital economy. It helps enterprises enhance visibility, engage with customers, and attract foot traffic to their physical locations. It enhances mobile commerce, offers local advice, and supports the tourism sector. Google Maps fosters economic growth in the digital sphere, boosts revenues, and enhances user experiences by connecting users with relevant companies and facilitating efficient navigation across all sectors (Phuangsuwan et al., 2024, c).

3. METHODOLOGY

3.1 Data Collection and Sampling

Purposive sampling, the PRISMA method, and content analysis based on scholarly papers indexed in Scopus, Web of Science (WOS), and Google Scholar were utilized in the systematic review. The review was conducted between 2021 and 2025. The keywords utilized in this search are as follows: community dentistry, digital intelligence, human intelligence, artificial intelligence (AI), digital technologies, sustainable development, sustainable management, and dental clinics. Through the utilization of the PRISMA Method, the content validity of the systematic review has been evaluated by three specialists. For analysis and interpretation in this chapter, only journal articles from respected academic institutions were chosen.

3.2 The Prisma Method and Data Analysis

The Prisma Method in this chapter was based on the study of Siripipatthanakul & Phuangsuwan (2024); Siripipatthanakul & Siripipattanakul (2025a,b, & c).

The PRISMA METHOD includes four steps as follows (Figure 1).

Step 1: ***Identifying the Problem*** - The early stage of entries can be identified through manual searches, literature databases, or other methods. This study's initial step consisted of random sampling, which was performed by randomly picking the topic matter. The associated article contains 188 papers.

Step 2: ***Screening:*** After eliminating duplicates, this phase displays the remaining records. At this stage, the titles and abstracts of acknowledged records are assessed for their relevance to the study's subject matter or objectives. The second phase involved the execution of purposeful sampling, which was achieved by selecting academic papers from Google Scholar, Scopus, and Web of Science (WOS). Forty-nine (49) articles were selected.

Step 3: ***Eligibility:*** This section outlines the quantity of research that may proceed following the initial screening. In this phase, essential information articles are assessed against established criteria to determine eligibility. A purposive sampling method was employed in the third phase, resulting in the selection of 30 papers suitable for a systematic review. The selected papers were based on terms from AI, Grammarly, Turnitin, and Word Cloud, primarily from 2021 to 2025.

Step 4: ***Inclusions:*** This stage represents the total number of studies included in the systematic review analysis. The eligibility prerequisites have been satisfied, and these studies are appropriate for future investigation. The flow graphic illustrates the amount of research stopped at each phase and the rationale behind the decision. Some of the most common reasons for exclusion are a lack of relevance to the research issue, an inadequate study design, an absence of appropriate data, or inclusion criteria. According to the PRISMA methodology, the fourth step was processed by three academic experts. They used content analysis to demonstrate that the systematic review contained accurate information.

Figure 1. PRISMA METHOD (Data Collection & Analysis).

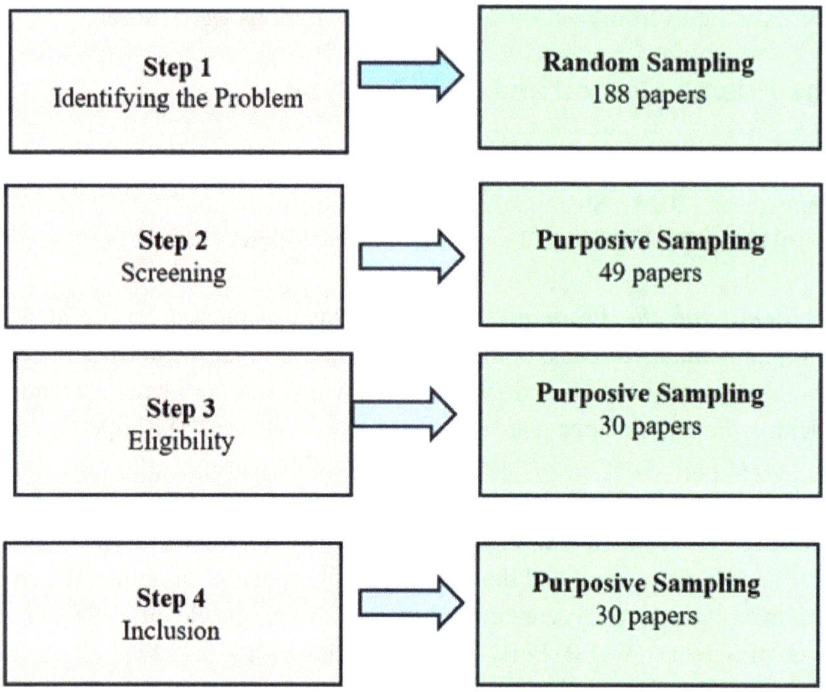

4. RESULTS

To avoid ethical problems caused by plagiarism and similarities with artificial intelligence. Grammatical analysis was performed on this chapter using Grammarly. Before a chapter is published, Grammarly is used to check for errors in grammar, plagiarism, and artificial intelligence similarity. Grammarly results show that the accuracy of grammar is over 95%, without ethical issue concerns. Three experts evaluated the content validity of this chapter.

Figure 2 shows a word cloud of the associated keywords in this chapter.

Figure 2. Word Cloud

https://www.wordclouds.com/ (June 16, 2025).

In the context of university dental hospitals, sustainable development through the utilization of artificial intelligence (AI) for digital education and business involves leveraging AI technologies to generate long-term value, efficiency, and a positive societal impact within these specialized healthcare and academic institutions. The purpose of this integration is to enhance the educational outcomes for dental staff, professionals, and students, while concurrently boosting the operational and financial viability of the hospitals through the implementation of digital transformation.

Sustainable development is the process of meeting the needs of the present without compromising the ability of future generations to meet their own needs. This indicates that for university dental hospitals, reducing waste, optimizing resource use (including energy and water), and promoting environmentally friendly practices in both clinical and educational settings are all key aspects of environmental sustainability. The function that artificial intelligence plays in data analysis can help discover areas that could use improvement, even though the direct influence of AI in this context may be indirect (for example, improving appointment scheduling to reduce patient travel or performing predictive maintenance on equipment to extend its lifespan). Ensuring that everyone has equal access to high-quality dental education and care, fostering a constructive learning and working environment, and making a positive contribution to the community's health are all aspects of social sustainability. The use of artificial intelligence has the potential to significantly democratize access to knowledge and personalize learning. In the context of economic sustainability, the maintenance of financial stability and growth, the optimization of operational expenses, and the generation of revenue to support teaching, research, and patient care missions come together. These issues are immediately addressed by the use of AI in digital business.

The term "artificial intelligence" (AI) can simulate human intelligence processes, which is what artificial intelligence (AI) refers to. The following are important artificial intelligence technologies that are relevant here: Algorithms that learn from data in order to generate predictions or judgments (for example, forecasting student performance or recognizing patterns in patient data) are referred to as machine learning (ML). The ability of computers to comprehend, interpret, and produce human language is referred to as natural language processing (NLP).

Examples of this include analyzing patient notes and producing educational content. The process of enabling computers to "see" and understand visual information (for example, analyzing dental X-rays or evaluating practical skills) is referred to as computer vision. Robotics is the automation of physical tasks (for example, in sterilization, although it is now less frequent in roles that include direct education or commercial processes). The process of determining the likelihood of future outcomes by analyzing past data through the application of statistical algorithms and machine learning techniques is referred to as predictive analytics.

In university dental hospitals, digital education refers to the use of digital tools and technologies to deliver, facilitate, and enhance the learning experience for dental students, residents, and participants in continuing education programs. Using AI, this can be revolutionized by Artificial intelligence algorithms that monitor student performance, learning styles, and progress to personalize educational content and offer specific resources, simulations, or clinical scenarios. This method is referred to as personalized learning paths. Because of this, every student can learn at their own appropriate pace and concentrate on areas where they have room for development.

Tutors powered by artificial intelligence can provide rapid feedback on practical skills (for example, using haptic feedback dental simulators with integrated AI analysis), answer queries, and assist students through challenging procedures, simulating the experience of having a one-on-one instructor. Artificial intelligence can automate the grading of written assignments, quizzes, and even practical examinations (for example, analyzing performance on virtual reality simulations or scanning dental models for accuracy). In addition to providing a consistent and objective evaluation, this frees up time for faculty members. Virtual Reality (VR) and Augmented Reality (AR) enrich these immersive learning environments by providing dynamic scenarios, variable difficulty levels, and performance analytics. This enables students to practice complex procedures in a safe, repeatable, and realistic setting. Artificial intelligence can sift through vast volumes of dental literature, research papers, and clinical recommendations to provide students and teachers with information that is both pertinent and up-to-date, thereby streamlining the process of evidence-based learning. Artificial intelligence can analyze vast datasets of student interactions, performance, and engagement to identify trends, predict at-risk students, and inform pedagogical improvements.

In the context of university dental hospitals, digital business refers to the utilization of digital technologies to optimize operating efficiency, enhance the patient experience, generate revenue, and support research activities. The function that AI plays in this context is essential for achieving sustainable economic growth and improving service delivery. Artificial intelligence can forecast patients who are likely to miss their appointments, optimize appointment slots to reduce wait times and increase clinic utilization, and automate appointment reminders, all of which contribute to increased efficiency and patient satisfaction. Predictive Maintenance of Equipment Artificial intelligence can monitor the functioning of dental equipment (such as imaging machines and dental chairs) and predict probable failures. This enables preventive maintenance to be performed, which in turn reduces costly breakdowns. AI is capable of evaluating billing data, identifying potential coding errors, predicting payment trends, and optimizing claims submissions, which has the potential to improve financial recovery and reduce administrative responsibilities. Revenue Cycle Management is a subfield of artificial intelligence. When it comes to marketing and patient acquisition, artificial intelligence can analyze demographic data and patient preferences, enabling the successful targeting of marketing campaigns, personalizing outreach, and attracting new patients. Artificial intelligence can forecast demand for dental supplies, optimize inventory levels, and manage procurement processes, all of which contribute to reducing waste and lowering costs. Artificial intelligence algorithms can recognize anomalous patterns in billing or claims, which may be indicative of fraudulent behavior. This helps to protect the hospital's financial integrity. Although it is not artificial intelligence in its purest form, artificial intelligence has the potential to enhance tele-dentistry by evaluating patient-submitted photographs or descriptions to assist in preliminary diagnosis or triage.

This would make care more accessible and efficient. Evaluation of Research Data: Artificial intelligence can accelerate dental research by analyzing vast datasets comprising patient records, clinical outcomes, and genomic information. This analysis can help identify disease trends, assess treatment efficacy, and detect potential medication interactions. The collaborative relationship between artificial intelligence (AI) in digital education and digital business makes a direct contribution to the long-term growth of university dental hospitals. Artificial intelligence-enhanced digital education yields dental professionals who are highly competent, flexible, and technologically literate. These professionals are better equipped to deliver high-quality care and drive innovation, ensuring the long-term sustainability of the dental workforce. Enhanced operating Efficiency: Artificial intelligence helps reduce operating expenses, minimize waste, and improve the overall efficiency of the hospital, all of which contribute to economic sustainability. This is accomplished by automating routine processes, improving resource allocation, and offering predictive insights. Insights driven by artificial intelligence in patient management and potentially clinical decision assistance (although this requires careful consideration of ethical and regulatory frameworks) have the potential to lead to more effective treatments and enhanced patient experiences. The production of better practitioners is another direct benefit of digital education, which also has a direct impact on patient care. Intelligence (AI) provides university dental hospitals with actionable insights from both educational and business data. It enables informed strategic planning and resource allocation for long-term growth and sustainability. The adoption of artificial intelligence positions university dental hospitals at the forefront of dental education and healthcare, attracting top talent (both students and faculty) and enabling them to develop innovative services and conduct groundbreaking research. This ensures that they remain relevant and competitive in a rapidly changing landscape. Therefore, artificial intelligence serves as a powerful enabler for university dental hospitals to accomplish their educational, clinical, and research goals more effectively and efficiently. This lays the groundwork for long-term growth and a continuous positive impact on dental health and education for many years to come.

5. DISCUSSIONS

Several key aspects, including energy consumption, material procurement, waste transportation and management, biodiversity preservation, and community engagement, influence the sustainable practices of dentistry. The implementation of sustainable development is essential to ensure that both the current generation and future generations have access to the fundamental necessities and a quality of life. Due to the ever-increasing costs, demands, and environmental impact, the delivery of modern healthcare is unsustainable. When it comes to setting environmentally friendly standards, dental experts and dentists consider the relationship between human health and the health of the Earth. Although there is a greater understanding of the phenomenon of global warming, there is a significant lack of information on how to become more environmentally friendly. This is despite a greater awareness of the phenomenon. There is a possibility that adopting more environmentally friendly practices will yield benefits, not just in terms of financial gain, but also in terms of reputation.

The chapter's findings support Duane et al. (2020) in that driver management is crucial for ecologically sustainable dentistry and carbon emission reduction. Sustainable societies must address current demands without compromising future needs. A sustainable world is becoming a global priority. Travel is responsible for the most carbon emissions and health problems in dentistry. Internally, reducing travel and energy consumption, as well as carefully selecting products and their disposal, can help lessen the impact. Bigger dental enterprises can positively impact their suppliers and the industry by purchasing from environmentally friendly companies. External drivers need policy, guidance, and study. Governments must rethink decontamination strategies for the environment. Consider planetary and public health when revising decontamination documents. Dental organizations must help these teams. Insurance companies and health care buyers should study dental provider sustainability strategies. Undergraduate and graduate students should study sustainability. Dental manufacturers could be advised on sustainable product production. Dentistry should prioritize changing goods or procedures that have a disproportionate negative impact on the environment by identifying hotspots or areas of high environmental contribution, utilizing other assessments like life cycle analysis. Dentistry should encompass single-use devices, chemicals, and products. Training students and developing sustainability centers is crucial to research capability.

The chapter supports Dormen & Özkan (2025) that the world is facing environmental challenges, making healthcare even more crucial. Dentistry has the potential to lead this revolution by impacting the global environment and shaping sustainable healthcare. Green dentistry includes eco-friendly methods. Green dentistry is an innovative approach that utilizes resources efficiently to minimize environmental impact and enhance patient safety. This method emphasizes waste management, energy efficiency, and digitalization. It is both an environmental necessity and an opportunity to enhance patient satisfaction, clinical management, and long-term economic sustainability. The sustainable dentistry methods from the history of green dentistry. It emphasizes educational programs and international collaborations to enhance the awareness of dentists and healthcare professionals. Environmentally friendly methods can change the entire healthcare system, not simply dentists or polyclinics. Success depends on raising sector knowledge of green transformation, implementing sustainable policies, and adopting practical solutions at the individual level. Innovative strategies should be employed in future studies to enhance the applicability of this framework. Innovation and mindful policy will lead to more sustainable and effective dental practices with less environmental impact.

This chapter supports the studies of Al-Worafi (2024a, b); educators in dentistry from underdeveloped countries play a crucial role in shaping the future of oral healthcare, despite the significant challenges they face. When it comes to oral healthcare, the dental education workforce in underdeveloped nations faces numerous challenges, innovations, and repercussions. An insufficient number of faculty members, inadequate resources, outdated curricula, research obstacles, and clinical training issues are some of the challenges that are faced. Some examples of innovative alternatives include faculty member training, global collaborations, telemedicine, public-private partnerships, community-based education, advocacy for legislation, and other similar initiatives. In addition to increasing local knowledge and advocating for legislative reforms, the initiatives work to expand access to dental care, reduce disparities in oral health, and promote oral health.

Phuangsuwan et al. (2025) note that excellent governance is one of the non-economic variables that can impact economic development. Consequently, community dentistry, dental departments at public hospitals, dental clinics, and university hospitals are rapidly integrating digital intelligence, which includes both human and artificial intelligence, for digital dental education.

The findings support Al-Emran et al. (2025), who suggest that service quality, system quality, and information quality significantly enhance user satisfaction. The utilization of Generative AI techniques is favorably correlated with user satisfaction. There is a beneficial impact of Generative AI on advancing societal sustainability. No substantial negative link was identified between privacy concerns and the utilization of Generative AI. Numerous theoretical contributions offer insights for diverse stakeholders involved in the development, implementation, and management of Generative AI technologies within educational contexts, including dentistry.

6. CONCLUSION

This chapter highlights that technology improvements in community dentistry education are improving the quality of dental care and education for individuals. Oral health education is evolving as a result of the integration of digital tools in dentistry education and practice, which simultaneously provides new opportunities for dental students, practitioners, and patients. Due to the pandemic and infectious diseases, it has become necessary to develop teaching strategies that are more efficient, accessible, and effective in order to achieve distance. According to the data, dental clinics and community dentistry practices are rapidly integrating digital intelligence, which includes both human and artificial intelligence. Education and individual dental treatment could both benefit from the implementation of communication technologies. Educational opportunities in dentistry can be enhanced by utilizing digital resources, such as virtual classrooms. By facilitating both synchronous and asynchronous learning, these tools encourage student autonomy and the development of a digital culture in the field of dentistry. Through the use of digital education, discussion forums, and digital books, it is believed that students and tutors can be engaged, which will ultimately lead to improved academic performance and the promotion of ongoing education.

The following are some of the ways this strategy benefits a wide range of stakeholders. To foster sustainable community dentistry, the implementation of digital education for dental professionals, dental students, and patients at university hospitals The introduction of digital education into community dentistry in university hospitals offers a significant contribution to the long-term viability of oral healthcare. This is accomplished by increasing the effectiveness of learning, broadening the scope of outreach, and reducing the amount of resources used. The following are some of the ways this strategy is advantageous to a wide range of stakeholders:

Figure 3. Conceptual Framework

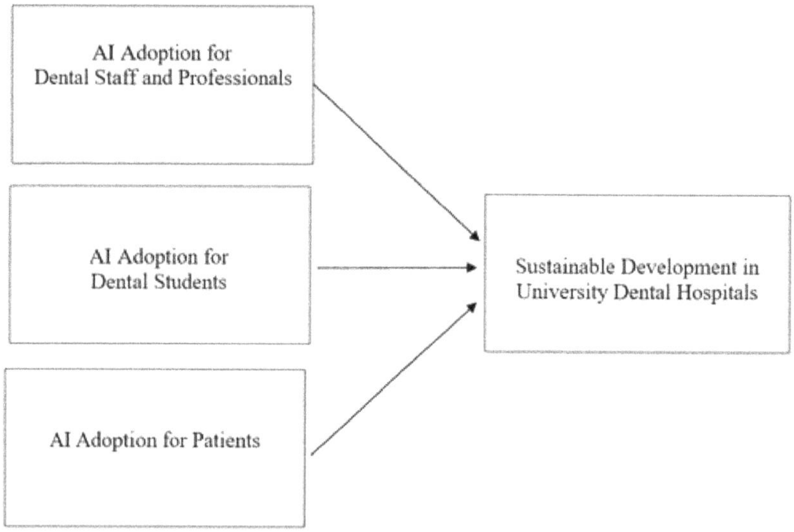

6.1 Digital Education Benefits for Dental Staff and Practitioners

1. For those working in the dental field (professionals, staff, and practitioners): Continuing Education: Professionals can sustainably upgrade their skills through the use of online modules and virtual workshops, which reduces the need for travel and printed materials.
2. Interprofessional Collaboration: The use of digital platforms facilitates collaboration among professionals in the fields of dentistry, medicine, and public health, enabling them to address community health holistically. Decision-Making That Is
3. Driven by Data: The use of digital records and analytics technologies has the potential to enhance care delivery and inform the community's needs.

6.2 Digital Education Benefits For Dental Students

1. The integration of e-learning with clinical practice, including films, simulations, and case-based learning, enables a more in-depth understanding while simultaneously reducing the environmental impact of traditional classroom resources.
2. Blended learning is recommended for dental students. Access to Remote Communities: Students are prepared for real-world community service by par-

ticipating in tele-dental projects that are integrated into the curriculum. These projects train students in digital outreach.

3. Sustainability Mindset: Incorporating sustainability principles (such as eco-friendly practices and waste reduction) into training from the very beginning can be achieved through the use of digital education.

6.3 Digital Education Benefits For Patients

1. Oral health literacy is particularly important for patients and the community. Mobile applications, video explainers, and digital consultations all contribute to increased awareness and the promotion of preventive care, particularly in underserved communities. Patients living in remote or rural areas can access medical information and advice without the need for in-person visits. This is referred to as accessibility. Interactive digital solutions support better oral hygiene habits and chronic disease management, leading to lasting behavioral changes.
2. Outcomes Regarding Sustainability: Reduces the amount of energy used, paper used, and travel required for traditional teaching and outreach. Equity is promoted by providing scalable education and services to marginalized and diverse groups, thereby promoting social justice.
3. Economic: Reduces expenses over the long term by promoting preventative education and early intervention of the disease. Through the use of digital education in sustainable community dentistry at university hospitals, access barriers can be bridged, capacity can be built among professionals and students, and communities can be empowered. It positions dental education and service delivery in a way that is more resilient, inclusive, and environmentally responsible, aligning with the broader objectives of sustainable development.

7. LIMITATIONS

In this chapter, a systematic qualitative review approach is employed, and some respondents may be omitted. There is a possibility of bias in selective scientific articles that are based on deliberate sampling, and they cannot be generalized. For this reason, it is recommended that a quantitative survey be conducted to inform further research based on probability sampling. A more comprehensive explanation, founded on the perspectives of stakeholders, can be obtained through the use of mixed methods, which include both quantitative and qualitative surveys. These approaches provide in-depth data that can be utilized for strategic planning and management. Since their research is a review paper, it is possible that it does not include a substantial correlation analysis between spending and carbon footprint, which serves as a proxy for sustainability. Education on sustainability should be incorporated into the Sustainable Development Goals (SDGs) for dental professionals working in hospitals and clinics, as well as for dental students who are in their undergraduate years. The incorporation of digital education into community dentistry in university hospitals makes a significant contribution to the sustainability of oral healthcare. The benefits of adopting digital education for dental professionals, dental students, and patients at university hospitals, in order to promote sustainable community dentistry, include enhanced learning efficiency, expanded outreach, and reduced resource consumption. Other benefits include the advancement of outreach. Therefore, it is recommended that further research be conducted on this topic.

8. FUTURE RESEARCH

8.1 Digital Education in Community Dentistry and Good Governance

Community dentistry in the long term is closely tied to effective governance and the implementation of digital education for professionals, dental students, and patients in university hospitals. Sustainable community dentistry emphasizes providing equitable dental healthcare, achieving long-term health outcomes, and utilizing resources efficiently. Not only can the implementation of digital education within university hospitals for dental professionals, students, and patients improve the quality of healthcare delivery, but it also closely corresponds with the principles of good governance. Sustainable community dentistry emphasizes providing healthcare and dental services that are easily accessible, reasonably priced, and centered on prevention for all populations. The dissemination of information and the provision of assistance for ongoing training through the utilization of digital education using online platforms, simulations, mobile applications, and e-learning. Transparency, accountability, involvement, responsiveness, efficiency, and inclusivity are all essential components of good governance in the administrative institutions' procedures.

8.1.1. Sustainable Dentistry Based on Digital Education

Transparency is one way in which it helps to achieve effective governance. Information on patient rights, treatment methods, and guidelines is made accessible to the general public through digital platforms. This ensures that dental professionals and students adhere to ethical standards and practices supported by appropriate evidence.

As a result, the quantity of misinformation to which patients and the community are exposed is reduced, and trust is established among both constituencies.

8.1.2. Continuous Growth

Two methods that can be utilized to document it are online modules and training logs. By providing patients with learning aids, they are able to better grasp the numerous treatment options available to them, which permits them to offer informed consent. This result makes it possible to provide support for professional responsibility and to encourage active participation from well-informed patients.

8.1.3. Process Participation

Community feedback methods, such as surveys and online forms, allow patients to voice their complaints and share their requirements. Collaboration is a process that involves students and professionals working together to achieve a common goal. Interprofessional education is an example of collaborative learning. It ensures stakeholders are included and stimulates community engagement.

8.1.4. The Use of Digital Tools and Attitudes

This technology makes real-time updates on health issues, such as recommendations on maintaining adequate dental hygiene during pandemics, possible. Educational chatbots or mobile apps can provide prompt answers to commonly asked questions (FAQs) for economically disadvantaged groups. The objective of this project is to increase accessibility and responsiveness to the community's needs.

8.2 Hospital Management for Effectiveness and Efficiency

In operation, it helps reduce the expenses and time associated with outreach and physical training programs. Provides the opportunity to scale education across huge populations while having a minimum impact on the environment. The result is that it encourages methods that are sustainable and efficient with resources in both education and care. Fairness and complete inclusion. It is possible to modify digital information to accommodate vulnerable groups, including the elderly, children, and individuals with disabilities. Through the use of mobile learning, dental literacy is promoted in groups that are either rural or have poor incomes. The outcome is that it improves the accessibility of oral health knowledge and services for all individuals. The adoption of digital education in university hospital-based community dentistry enables institutions to incorporate the fundamental principles of good governance, including openness, accountability, participation, and inclusivity, into their strategy for sustainable development. This integrated strategy not only enhances oral health outcomes but also strengthens the institution's legitimacy and its long-term impact on society.

9. IMPLICATION: ARTIFICIAL INTELLIGENCE EDUCATION STRATEGIES FOR FUTURE-PROOFING CURRICULUM DESIGN

Future-proofing curriculum design is centered on the incorporation of artificial intelligence tools and concepts into educational systems. The goal of these strategies is to better prepare students and institutions for the fast-changing future of work and learning. This set of tactics aims to ensure that educational programs remain relevant, adaptable, and aligned with the evolving advancements in technology and changing societal needs. A more organized explanation is as follows:

9.1. Integration of Artificial Intelligence Literacy Across Professions.

The goal is to make artificial intelligence a fundamental talent, comparable to digital literacy or critical thinking. Take action: Integrate principles of artificial intelligence (such as machine learning, data ethics, and algorithm bias) into a wide range of topics, not only STEM. Influence: Encourages students to think across disciplines and trains them to use artificial intelligence tools in a variety of industries.

9.2. Technologies for Adaptive Learning.

Using platforms powered by artificial intelligence, the goal is to personalize learning paths. To adapt training effectively, it is recommended to implement artificial intelligence systems that evaluate individual learning styles, pace, and progress. Influence: Increases student engagement, provides support for learners from varied backgrounds, and enhances outcomes.

9.3. Curriculum Co-Design Utilizing Artificial Intelligence Tools

It will benefit educators by leveraging AI to generate current and relevant information. Educators in dentistry should implement artificial intelligence for curriculum mapping, content suggestion, and alignment with future job trends (for example, through labor market analytics). Impact: Accelerates the process of curriculum revision and ensures that it is aligned with the requirements of the actual world.

9.4. An Emphasis on Human-Centered Artificial Intelligence and Ethics

Acquiring an understanding of and a conscientious methodology for utilizing artificial intelligence. Incorporate modules addressing the ethics of artificial intelligence, equity, transparency, and the societal impact of automation. This influence enhances researchers' and students' preparedness to make ethical decisions in AI-driven contexts by fostering critical awareness.

9.5. Educators' Opportunities for Professional Development

To achieve the goal of sustainable development, it should include providing them with AI tools and fostering a deeper understanding. Action should be taken to provide ongoing training in artificial intelligence technology, classroom applications, and ideas for curriculum design. Impact: Enables educators to confidently and meaningfully utilize artificial intelligence in their teaching. Fostering innovation and problem-solving is the objective of the Real-World Artificial Intelligence Project-Based Learning. The action involves incorporating hands-on artificial intelligence projects that address real-world challenges, such as building chatbots or analyzing databases.

Educators must enhance the readiness of stakeholders, including dental students, professionals, and patients, for future careers and entrepreneurial endeavors. Ongoing assessment of the curriculum using an AI application guarantees that educational programs stay efficient and adaptable. Utilize artificial intelligence methodologies to track student performance, engagement patterns, and the relevance of the curriculum. Effect: Facilitates curriculum enhancements informed by data, therefore elevating the overall quality of education. To ensure the curriculum remains relevant in an AI-driven future, it is imperative to provide students and educators with the requisite tools, mindsets, and ethical frameworks for success in an AI-transformed society. It is essential to reevaluate not only the content of our teaching but also the methods and rationale behind it, to ensure that education remains flexible, inclusive, and meaningful.

10. ACKNOWLEDGEMENT

The researchers acknowledge the collaboration between international universities, including Manipal GlobalNxt University, Malaysia; Bangkok Thonburi University, Thailand; Kasetsart University, Thailand; and Universitas Terbuka, Indonesia.

No competing interests, as stated by the researchers.

REFERENCES

Al-Emran, M., Abu-Hijleh, B., & Alsewari, A. A. (2025). Examining the impact of Generative AI on social sustainability by integrating the information system success model and technology-environmental, economic, and social sustainability theory. *Education and Information Technologies*, *30*(7), 9405–9426. DOI: 10.1007/s10639-024-13201-0

Al-Worafi, Y. M. (2024, a). Dentistry Education Workforce in Developing Countries. In *Handbook of Medical and Health Sciences in Developing Countries: Education, Practice, and Research* (pp. 1-16). Cham: Springer International Publishing. https://link.springer.com/referenceworkentry/10.1007/978-3-030-74786-2_176-1

Al-Worafi, Y. M. (2024, b). Dentistry Education Challenges in Developing Countries. In *Handbook of Medical and Health Sciences in Developing Countries: Education, Practice, and Research* (pp. 1-15). Cham: Springer International Publishing. https://link.springer.com/referenceworkentry/10.1007/978-3-030-74786-2_200-1

Ayibuofu-Uwandi, V., & Dyer, T. A. (2024). What are the public health benefits of community-based education in dentistry? A scoping review. *British Dental Journal*, 1–7. https://www.nature.com/articles/s41415-024-7908-4. DOI: 10.1038/s41415-024-7908-4 PMID: 39369154

Bhutoria, A. (2022). Personalized education and artificial intelligence in the United States, China, and India: A systematic review using a human-in-the-loop model. *Computers and Education: Artificial Intelligence*, *3*, 100068. DOI: 10.1016/j.caeai.2022.100068

Dormen, M., & Özkan, P. (2025). Sustainable Dental Approaches for the Environment and Human Health: A Traditional Literature Review. *HRU International Journal of Dentistry and Oral Research*, *5*(1), 51–58. DOI: 10.61139/ijdor.1649869

Duane, B., Stancliffe, R., Miller, F. A., Sherman, J., & Pasdeki-Clewer, E. (2020). Sustainability in dentistry: A multifaceted approach needed. *Journal of Dental Research*, *99*(9), 998–1003. DOI: 10.1177/0022034520919391 PMID: 32392435

Fareed, M. A., & Zafar, M. S. (2024). The Path to Sustainable Oral Healthcare to Foster Sustainability in Dentistry. *European Journal of Dentistry, 18*(03), 701–702. DOI: 10.1055/s-0044-1785187 PMID: 38744325

Garg, V., Kumar, H., Bansal, R., & Bhardwaj, A. (2025). Envisioning Digital Health Technology Innovations for 2025: Enhancing Digital Interventions in the Post-COVID-19 Era. In *Innovations in Healthcare Technologies in India: An Initiative of ICMR-CIBioD (Centre for Innovation and Bio-Design)* (pp. 1-17). Singapore: Springer Nature Singapore. https://link.springer.com/chapter/10.1007/978-981-97-0244-2_1

Hackley, D. M., & Luca, J. (2024). Sustainability in Dentistry: An Overview for Oral Healthcare Team Members. *Journal of the California Dental Association, 52*(1), 2422150. DOI: 10.1080/19424396.2024.2422150

Harrington, L. M. B. (2016). Sustainability theory and conceptual considerations: A review of key ideas for sustainability, and the rural context. *Papers in Applied Geography, 2*(4), 365–382. DOI: 10.1080/23754931.2016.1239222

Hou, M. (2023). Digital economy, enterprise digital transformation, and digital business model: Evidence from China. DOI: 10.1080/13602381.2023.2241762

Hsu, M. S., Yeh, C. L., Cheng, S. J., & Lin, C. P. (2025). Integrating digital technologies in dental technician education: A comparative study of national examination in Asian countries. *Journal of Dental Sciences, 20*(1), 28–35. DOI: 10.1016/j.jds.2024.10.017 PMID: 39873091

Huang, Y. K., & Chang, Y. C. (2022). Oral health: The first step to sustainable development goal 3. *Journal of the Formosan Medical Association, 121*(7), 1348–1350. DOI: 10.1016/j.jfma.2021.10.018 PMID: 34732302

John, J., Durward, C., Kruger, E., Mani, S. A., & Tennant, M. (2025). Dental Education Without Borders. In *Handbook of Dental Education Technology* (pp. 1–28). Springer., DOI: 10.1007/978-981-97-0275-6_3-1

Khurshid, Z. (2023). Digital dentistry: Transformation of oral health and dental education with technology. *European Journal of Dentistry, 17*(04), 943–944. https://www.thieme-connect.com/products/ejournals/abstract/10.1055/s-0043-1772674. DOI: 10.1055/s-0043-1772674 PMID: 37729928

Lee, J. Y., & Divaris, K. (2014). The ethical imperative of addressing oral health disparities: A unifying framework. *Journal of Dental Research, 93*(3), 224–230. DOI: 10.1177/0022034513511821 PMID: 24189268

Lv, B., Deng, Y., Meng, W., Wang, Z., & Tang, T. (2024). Research on digital intelligence business model based on artificial intelligence in post-epidemic era. *Management Decision, 62*(9), 2937–2957. https://www.emerald.com/insight/content/doi/10.1108/md-11-2022-1548/full/html. DOI: 10.1108/MD-11-2022-1548

Makda, F. (2025). Digital education: Mapping the landscape of virtual teaching in higher education–a bibliometric review. *Education and Information Technologies, 30*(2), 2547–2575. https://link.springer.com/article/10.1007/s10639-024-12899-2. DOI: 10.1007/s10639-024-12899-2

Meskó, B., Kristóf, T., Dhunnoo, P., Árvai, N., & Katonai, G. (2024). Exploring the Need for Medical Futures Studies: Insights From a Scoping Review of Health Care Foresight. *Journal of Medical Internet Research, 26*, e57148. https://www.jmir.org/2024/1/e57148/. DOI: 10.2196/57148 PMID: 39383528

Phuangsuwan, P. & Rakpathum, W. (2024). Social Media and Its Effect on Higher Education: A Review Article. Advance Knowledge for Executives. 3(2), No. 43, 1-11.

Phuangsuwan, P., Siripipatthanakul, S., Hadi, S., Suttipong, R., & Wattanakul, P. (2023). A Review of Sustainable Development Guidelines for Green Universities in Thailand. *Advance Knowledge for Executives, 2*(4), 1–11.

Phuangsuwan, P., Siripipatthanakul, S., Limna, P., & Pariwongkhuntorn, N. (2024). c). The impact of Google Maps application on the digital economy. *Corporate & Business Strategy Review, 5*(1), 192–203. DOI: 10.22495/cbsrv5i1art18

Phuangsuwan, P., Siripipatthanakul, S., Praesri, S., & Rakpathum, W. (2025). The Relationship Between Good Governance and Organizational Performance Through the Mediating Role of Employee Satisfaction. *Journal of Governance and Regulation, 14*(1), 100–108. DOI: 10.22495/jgrv14i1art9

Plugmann, P. (2021). Digitalization in dentistry. *Digitalization in Healthcare:* https://link.springer.com/chapter/10.1007/978-3-030-65896-0_6

Rakpathum, W., Siripipatthanakul, S., Phuangsuwan, P., & Charoenporn, C. (2025). Enhancing Sustainable Development Goals (SDGs) for Rural Tourism Communities: The Case of Mae Kampong Village, Chiang Mai, Thailand. *Journal of Lifestyle and SDGs Review, 5*(1), e04755–e04755. https://www.sdgsreview.org/LifestyleJournal/article/view/4755. DOI: 10.47172/2965-730X.SDGsReview.v5.n01.pe04755

Renger, F., Patzke, K., & Alrayes, M. (2025). Dental Care Models and their Contribution to Reducing Health Inequalities: A Public. *Health Perspectives*. DOI: 10.71123/jrnhc.v2.i1.25002

Reyazat, F. (2023). The New Path for Humanity. *Artificial Intelligence*.

Shukla, K., & Attar, A. M. (2025). Integration of dental patient-reported outcomes (dPROs) in tele dentistry to enhance patient-centered care: A scoping review. *The Journal of Evidence-Based Dental Practice*, *25*(1), 102084. DOI: 10.1016/j.jebdp.2024.102084 PMID: 39947782

Siripipatthanakul, S., Nyen Vui, C., & Phuangsuwan, P. (2024a). Strategic Management Adopting Digital Intelligence (Business Intelligence) for Dentistry and Dental Clinics. *Open Access Journal of Dental Sciences, 9*(1), 000388. https://papers.ssrn.com/sol3/papers.cfm?abstract_id=4739624

Siripipatthanakul, S., & Phuangsuwan, P. (2024). Salutogenic Marketing in Preventive Dentistry. In Leveraging Digital Technology for Preventive Dentistry (pp. 255-278). IGI Global. DOI: DOI: 10.4018/979-8-3693-3872-8.ch009

Siripipatthanakul, S., Phuangsuwan, P., Jaipong, P., & Pholphong, L. (2024). b). A Management Model for Leadership in Diversity and Equality Affecting Human Resource Satisfaction and Performance in Dentistry. *Journal of Dental Sciences*, 9(3), 000401. https://papers.ssrn.com/sol3/papers.cfm?abstract_id=4919825

Siripipatthanakul, S., & Siripipattanakul, S. (2025a). Rural Dental Health Transformation by Adopting Digital Technologies. *Transforming Dental Health in Rural Communities: Digital Dentistry*, 47-80. DOI: DOI: 10.4018/979-8-3693-7165-7.ch003

Siripipatthanakul, S., & Siripipattanakul, S. (2025b). Talent Management Ensuring the Safety and Cybersecurity in Schools. *Cultivating Creativity and Navigating Talent Management in Academia*, 383-402. DOI: DOI: 10.4018/979-8-3693-6880-0.ch018

Siripipatthanakul, S., & Siripipattanakul, S. (2025c). Online Gambling of Higher Education Learners. In *International Academic Transformations and Cross-Border Collaborations* (pp. 377–400). IGI Global Scientific Publishing.

Strielkowski, W., Grebennikova, V., Lisovskiy, A., Rakhimova, G., & Vasileva, T. (2025). AI-driven adaptive learning for sustainable educational transformation. *Sustainable Development (Bradford)*, *33*(2), 1921–1947. DOI: 10.1002/sd.3221

Thapa, P. P. (2024). Digital Education and Awareness for Oral Health: Exploration of Digital Tools and Educational Platforms to Promote Awareness About the Importance of Oral Health. In *Leveraging Digital Technology for Preventive Dentistry* (pp. 225–254). IGI Global. DOI: DOI: 10.4018/979-8-3693-3872-8.ch008

Thomas, A. (2024). Challenges in dental education. *Indonesian Journal of Prosthodontics*, *5*(1), 86–88. DOI: 10.46934/ijp.v5i1.268

KEY TERMS AND DEFINITIONS

Sustainable Development in Dentistry: Sustainable development prioritizes delivering accessible, affordable, and preventive oral healthcare to disadvantaged populations while promoting environmental, economic, and social sustainability. The instruction of dentistry students and practitioners in socially responsible practices occurs within the framework of a university hospital. A key objective is to mitigate disparities in oral health, while another is to engage communities in oral hygiene education and advocate for sustainable dental practices, including reducing plastic usage and managing dental waste.

Digital Education in Dentistry: Dental education faces various challenges that significantly impact the training and readiness of prospective dental professionals. This article identifies the primary challenges and proposes potential strategies to address them. The swift progression of technology requires ongoing revisions to courses, including breakthroughs like digital imaging, CAD/CAM systems, and laser dentistry. Ensuring staff and student competence in these technologies requires a significant investment in training and resources. In conclusion, addressing these challenges requires curriculum reform, technological investment, enhanced clinical training opportunities, robust financial support systems, targeted mental health initiatives, and adaptability. Dental education encounters various problems that substantially impact the training and readiness of prospective dental professionals.

Tele-Dentistry (Tele-Dental Care): Tele-dental care is an effective way to reach rural and impoverished communities. Digital communication tools enable remote consultations, diagnosis, treatment, and follow-up care. In remote areas, tele-dental treatment facilitates easier early screenings. Patients would no longer need to travel far for preliminary examinations. Digital literacy education is crucial.

Mobile Health Applications (mHealth) and Digital Imaging: Mobile applications could be used to educate patients about oral hygiene, remind them of appointments, and collect data for community oral health surveys. Mobile health apps help people manage their oral health more actively. “EHRs” stands for Electronic Health Records. Digital record-keeping improves patient tracking, community health trends, efficiency, and mistake reduction. Cloud-based electronic health records are valuable for accessibility in diverse settings.

Digital Business: Digital business is about using digital platforms and technologies to improve services, streamline operations, and involve patients and the community. University hospitals can use digital solutions for teaching, services, and research. Current digital tools are included here. Tele-dental platforms provide remote consultations. Mobile apps schedule appointments, notify users, and provide oral health education. Electronic health records (EHRs) improve care coordination.

Accessibility: Accessibility refers to the ease of obtaining or utilizing something, whereas affordability pertains to the cost or price of that object. Although something may be readily available, it may not be financially attainable for many individuals.

Affordability: Affordability refers to the ability to be afforded; inexpensiveness (cost-effectiveness). It differs from accessibility, as something that may be economically feasible yet not readily available to all individuals. Achieving equilibrium between accessibility and affordability is crucial for ensuring that products and services are accessible to a diverse population, regardless of their financial circumstances or physical capabilities.

Chapter 3
Sustainable Clinic Management Based on Practices and Human Resource Management (HRM)

Pongsakorn Limna
Pathumthani University, Ban Klang, Thailand

Sutithep Siripipattanakul
https://orcid.org/0000-0002-5477-6723
Kasetsart University, Bangkhen, Thailand

ABSTRACT

Human resource management (HRM) as a strategic driver of healthcare sustainability is examined in this systematic analysis of sustainable clinic management. The study employed data collection and analysis based on peer-reviewed publications from 2020 to 2025, sourced from Scopus, Web of Science, and Google Scholar, utilizing the PRISMA framework. The findings indicate that green human resource management (GHRM) and digital transformation are converging to bring operational sustainability initiatives and HRM strategies closer together. Electronic medical records, telemedicine, and virtual HR processes are helping clinics reduce environmental impact and boost efficiency. HRM also boosts employee engagement, diversity, well-being, and environmental responsibility. Sustainability and human capital development improve clinic resilience and long-term performance while

DOI: 10.4018/979-8-3693-9800-5.ch003

supporting global sustainability goals. The best practices and strategic advice for clinic administrators and policymakers wanting to implement sustainability across all levels of healthcare management.

1. INTRODUCTION

Sustainable clinic management is fundamentally grounded in the application of the Triple Bottom Line across all dimensions of a clinic's operations. This holistic approach aims not only to maintain financial viability but also to promote environmental stewardship, uphold social responsibility, and ensure ethical conduct, all while delivering high-quality patient care. Within this framework, the Human Resources (HR) department plays a pivotal role as a strategic enabler and driver of sustainability. Rather than functioning solely as an administrative unit, HR is essential in embedding sustainable values into the organization's culture, fostering employee engagement, and aligning workforce capabilities with long-term sustainability objectives. The effective implementation of sustainable practices in clinic operations depends on the synergy between well-designed procedures and an empowered, committed workforce. Operational initiatives—such as waste management, energy efficiency, green procurement, and community engagement—represent the visible aspects of sustainability. However, these initiatives yield meaningful impact only when supported by employees who are informed, motivated, and aligned with the clinic's sustainability mission. HR departments facilitate this alignment through strategic Human Resource Management (HRM) practices, including sustainability-focused recruitment and selection, targeted training and development, and performance management systems that integrate environmental and social responsibility metrics (Alim & Sulley, 2024; Bhati et al., 2023; Caylan, 2024; Papademetriou et al., 2025; Parzhanova, 2025; Popescu et al., 2024; Purwadi et al., 2024; Tunio, 2024; Vasileiou et al., 2024).

Recruiting candidates who value sustainability, conducting virtual interviews to minimize environmental impact, and providing ongoing education on sustainable practices are all essential initiatives within HRM. In addition, HR plays a central role in fostering a culture of accountability by forming green teams, recognizing and rewarding environmentally conscious behaviors, and ensuring that leadership consistently models sustainable values. The HR function also contributes significantly to social sustainability by supporting fair labor practices and advancing diversity, equity, and inclusion (DEI), while promoting employee well-being through initiatives that address mental health and work-life balance. These efforts not only enhance staff morale and retention but also create the conditions necessary for the successful implementation of environmentally and socially responsible operational practices.

Moreover, integrating sustainability into both clinical operations and HR strategy offers substantial benefits. Organizations that adopt this integrated approach are more likely to achieve cost savings through efficient resource utilization, enhance their reputation among patients and healthcare professionals, and improve health outcomes by fostering healthier, more engaged work environments. In doing so, they are also better positioned to navigate regulatory and environmental challenges, maintain resilience amid resource constraints, and make meaningful contributions to the well-being of their local communities (Balkhi et al., 2022; Gomes et al., 2024; Papademetriou et al., 2025; Parashakti et al., 2024; Sinsky et al., 2020).

Ultimately, sustainable clinic management goes beyond reducing environmental impact or improving efficiency—it recognizes that people are both drivers and beneficiaries of sustainability. By strategically engaging the HRM as a cornerstone of sustainable transformation, clinics can build resilient systems that support a healthier planet, foster equitable and inclusive care, and ensure long-term organizational success. This systematic review outlines practices and HRM strategies in clinics that contribute to sustainable development, emphasizing the vital interplay between operational initiatives and workforce engagement. The study contributes to the growing body of knowledge on sustainable healthcare management by synthesizing evidence-based approaches, offering practical guidance for clinic administrators, and highlighting the transformative role of HRM in achieving sustainability goals.

1.1 Research Objective

This systematic review aims to synthesize literature on HRM practices in clinical settings to identify strategies that support sustainable development within the healthcare sector.

1.2 Research Question

What are the essentials of practices and HRM in clinics for sustainable development?

2. LITERATURE REVIEW

2.1 Sustainability Theory and Sustainable Clinic Management

Sustainability theory is a comprehensive and evolving framework that explores how human societies can thrive over the long term without depleting natural resources, causing irreversible environmental harm, or compromising the well-being of future generations. Rooted in multidisciplinary scholarship—including ecology, economics, sociology, political science, ethics, and engineering—sustainability theory offers a valuable lens through which organizations, such as healthcare clinics, can evaluate and inform their operational and strategic decisions. A widely used conceptual model within this theory is the "Triple Bottom Line" (TBL), which emphasizes the integration of economic viability, social responsibility, and environmental stewardship (Alim & Sulley, 2024; Balay-Odao et al., 2024; Molero et al., 2021; Sajwani, 2024; Saruchera, 2025). In the context of healthcare, sustainable clinic management involves applying these principles across all aspects of operations and strategic planning—not as isolated green initiatives, but as an integrated approach that shapes policies, infrastructure, service delivery, and stakeholder engagement. Sustainable clinic management recognizes the interdependence of financial health, patient outcomes, staff well-being, and environmental impact. By adopting a systems-thinking perspective, clinics can address challenges holistically, ensuring that improvements in one area support broader organizational goals. This approach entails long-term thinking, stakeholder collaboration, and continuous innovation. Leadership commitment is crucial, as is embedding sustainability into governance structures, accountability systems, and organizational culture (Alamgir & Shan, 2023; Rashah et al., 2024; Tushar et al., 2023; Ugwu et al., 2025; Vasileiou et al., 2024; Verdonck & Verniers, 2024).

Key pillars of sustainable clinic management include strategic leadership and policy development, sustainable HRM, environmentally responsible operations, patient-centered care, financial resilience, and the integration of digital technologies. Clinics can reduce their ecological footprint by implementing energy efficiency measures, promoting water conservation, minimizing waste, and adopting sustainable procurement practices. At the same time, HR practices—such as green training, ethical recruitment, and employee well-being initiatives—support a culture of sustainability from within. Engagement with patients, communities, and regulators further enhances the clinic's role as a socially responsible institution. Overall, sustainability theory offers a foundational lens through which clinics can evolve into resilient, ethical, and high-performing organizations. By embedding sustainability in all dimensions of management, clinics are better positioned to provide high-quality care while contributing to environmental protection, social equity, and long-term organizational success (Balay-Odao et al., 2024; Bosco et al., 2024; Calabrese et al., 2023; Hameed et al., 2024; Mostepaniuk et al., 2023; Sepetis & Parlavantzas, 2025).

2.2 Human Resource Management (HRM) and Sustainability in the Healthcare Sector

HRM plays a pivotal role in advancing sustainability in the healthcare sector by embedding environmental, social, and economic principles into the management of people. This approach, often referred to as Sustainable Human Resource Management (SHRM) or Green Human Resource Management (GHRM), emphasizes the critical role that healthcare professionals play as agents of change. In a sector characterized by high environmental impact and pressing social challenges—such as staff burnout, workforce shortages, and the need for equitable care delivery—HRM becomes a key mechanism for driving sustainable transformation from within (Kailay et al., 2024; Kumi et al., 2025; Papademetriou et al., 2025). HRM contributes to sustainability across several dimensions. Environmentally, recruitment and training processes can be aligned with green values by attracting candidates who are committed to sustainability, utilizing paperless and digital systems, and providing education on waste reduction, energy conservation, and resource efficiency. Socially, HRM supports the well-being of the workforce by promoting mental health, work-life balance, safe working conditions, and inclusive, equitable practices. Initiatives that foster employee engagement—such as green recognition programs and feedback mechanisms—further integrate sustainable thinking into everyday behavior and organizational culture. Performance management systems can incorporate sustainability goals into employee evaluations, while incentive structures can reward environmentally and socially responsible actions, reinforcing accountability and continuous improvement. From an economic perspective, SHRM contributes to cost reduction by decreasing employee turnover, enhancing productivity, and streamlining workforce-related processes. Moreover, a demonstrated commitment to sustainability enhances organizational reputation and makes healthcare institutions more attractive to a new generation of professionals who prioritize social and environmental responsibility in their career choices (Eze & Francis, 2024; Faeni et al., 2025; Hussain et al., 2024; Koman et al., 2024; Liang & Li, 2024; Malik et al., 2021; Soekotjo et al., 2025).

However, integrating sustainability into HRM within the healthcare sector presents notable challenges. High-pressure work environments, ongoing staffing shortages, complex regulatory requirements, and resistance to organizational change can all hinder the adoption of sustainable practices. Furthermore, measuring the impact of HRM-driven sustainability initiatives remains challenging, and many such programs require significant upfront investments in training, infrastructure, or technology. Despite these obstacles, SHRM is increasingly recognized as a vital component in building a resilient and future-ready healthcare system. By aligning HR strategies with sustainability objectives, healthcare organizations can cultivate a workforce that is not only skilled and engaged but also actively contributes to the long-term well-being of the organization, its patients, the broader community, and the environment (Bornay-Barrachina et al., 2023; Faisal et al., 2023; Lu et al., 2025; Malik et al., 2024; Papademetriou et al., 2025; Ren et al., 2023).

2.3 Practices and Human Resource Management (HRM) for Sustainable Clinic Management

Practices and HRM for sustainable clinic management are fundamentally concerned with aligning day-to-day clinical operations and workforce initiatives with long-term sustainability objectives. This alignment is crucial for ensuring the long-term environmental, social, and economic performance of healthcare organizations (Campos-García et al., 2024; Kailay et al., 2024; Sarwar & Shahzad, 2024; Papademetriou et al., 2025). Sustainable practices in clinic management encompass a range of operational strategies designed to minimize environmental impact and improve efficiency. The transition to digital systems, such as electronic medical records (EMRs), has proven effective in reducing paper use, while telemedicine and digital appointment scheduling streamline service delivery and decrease the carbon footprint associated with patient visits. Additionally, energy and resource efficiency are also critical, as clinics increasingly adopt energy-efficient lighting and appliances, implement water conservation measures, and improve inventory management to prevent overstocking and the spoilage of medical supplies. Sustainable procurement practices further reinforce these efforts by prioritizing environmentally conscious and locally sourced vendors and purchasing recyclable and biodegradable materials. Waste reduction is another priority, involving comprehensive staff training on the segregation of general, hazardous, and medical waste, and encouraging the safe use of reusable instruments and protective equipment. Moreover, sustainable architectural and design elements, including natural lighting, effective ventilation, green spaces, and adequate insulation, contribute significantly to lowering energy consumption and enhancing the well-being of patients and staff (Akinola & Telukdarie, 2023; Dion et al., 2023; Dion & Evans, 2024; Hameed et al., 2024; Olawade et al., 2025; Read & Meath, 2025; Ullah et al., 2023).

HRM plays a pivotal role in embedding sustainability into the clinic's culture and practices. Building employee awareness and providing training on environmental regulations and eco-friendly practices are essential to fostering a workforce that is informed and motivated to contribute to sustainability goals. GHRM policies integrate sustainability considerations into job descriptions, performance evaluations, and incentive structures, while actively encouraging staff participation in environmental activities. In addition, HRM practices aimed at enhancing employee health and engagement—such as promoting work-life balance, supporting mental health, and offering flexible work arrangements—create a culture of accountability and shared responsibility for environmentally responsible behaviors. Inclusive and ethical practices are also integral to sustainable clinic management, ensuring non-discrimination, diversity, and equity in recruitment and promotion, while upholding safe working conditions and adhering to ethical labor standards. Identifying and empowering champions of sustainability within the organization fosters continuous improvement, innovation, and open feedback, all of which are essential for lasting success (Atalla et al., 2025; Ige-Olaobaju et al., 2025; Sarwar & Shahzad, 2024; Wu et al., 2021; Yoo, 2024). Integrating HRM with environmentally responsible operational practices enhances organizational effectiveness, boosts employee morale and retention, and strengthens the clinic's reputation and patient trust within the community. These initiatives directly support the United Nations Sustainable Development Goals (UNSDGs), particularly SDG 3 (Good Health and Well-being), SDG 8 (Decent Work and Economic Growth), and SDG 12 (Responsible Consumption and Production). In summary, HRM serves as the engine driving the human dimension of sustainability by embedding green objectives into both daily routines and the strategic vision of clinics committed to sustainable development (Ab & Wahyuni, 2023; Oberai & Anand, 2025; Papademetriou et al., 2025; Zournatzidou et al., 2025).

2.4 Synthesis of Related Research

Mousa and Othman (2020) investigated the extent to which GHRM practices are implemented in Palestinian healthcare organizations and how these practices influence sustainable performance. The study revealed that GHRM practices were implemented at a moderate level, with 'green hiring' and 'green training and involvement' identified as the most impactful. In contrast, 'green performance management and compensation' had the least influence. Despite moderate implementation, sustainable performance was reported at a relatively high level, particularly in terms of environmental outcomes. Structural equation modelling confirmed a positive relationship between GHRM practices and sustainability, with environmental sustainability showing the most substantial effect. The study offers valuable insights into the role of GHRM in developing countries and provides a practical framework to guide policymakers in enhancing sustainable performance through strategic HR initiatives.

Azizi et al. (2021) conducted a narrative review to explore the challenges and HRM strategies adopted by non-clinical organizations in response to the disruptions caused by the COVID-19 pandemic. Through a comprehensive analysis of academic databases, several key organizational challenges were identified, including economic shocks, health crises, shifts in social behavior, and operational difficulties. To address these issues, organizations implemented strategies focused on increasing flexibility, enhancing internal efficiency, strategic talent acquisition, and fostering innovation based on continuous organizational assessments. The study concluded that effectively applying these HRM strategies during the pandemic can lead to improved employee mental well-being, job satisfaction, productivity, motivation, and workplace health and safety, ultimately strengthening organizational resilience during times of crisis.

Mensah et al. (2023) investigated the relationship between GHRM practices and employee innovative work behaviour within the healthcare sector, focusing on Korle Bu Teaching Hospital in Ghana. The analysis revealed that specific GHRM practices—green training, green hiring, and green compensation—were significant predictors of employees' innovative work behaviour. These results indicate that effectively implementing environmentally focused HR practices can stimulate innovation among hospital staff. The study contributes to understanding how GHRM influences employee outcomes and recommends that organizations treat training as a strategic investment, prioritize recruiting individuals with strong environmental values, and design effective reward systems to reinforce green initiatives.

Correia et al. (2024) addressed the growing pressure on organizations—particularly in the healthcare sector—to balance economic development with environmental sustainability by fostering a culture of green innovation. In response to the increasing demand for environmentally responsible practices, the study emphasized the importance of GHRM in enhancing sustainable performance within healthcare institutions in Pakistan. The study aimed to examine how GHRM practices influence sustainable performance through the mediating role of green innovation, while also assessing the moderating effect of risk management on this relationship. Findings revealed that GHRM practices significantly contribute to sustainable performance when mediated by green innovation. Furthermore, risk management was found to play a moderating role, strengthening the impact of GHRM and green innovation on sustainability outcomes. The study offers practical implications for healthcare leaders and policymakers, suggesting that embedding GHRM within a broader green innovation strategy can serve as a proactive approach to managing environmental risk and achieving long-term sustainable performance.

Wang et al. (2024) examined the HRM practices of the world's top five hospitals through a comparative multi-case study approach. The research found that, despite variations in specific HRM frameworks, all hospitals demonstrated a strong commitment to cultivating organizational culture, supporting employee development, and aligning HR strategies with institutional goals. Key elements included sustainable talent management, comprehensive training programs, and robust welfare policies designed to enhance staff well-being and motivation. While compensation was within the mid-to-upper industry range, it was not directly linked to workload; instead, performance assessments focused on work quality and alignment with organizational values. The study provides valuable insights and a reference model for other hospitals aiming to enhance operational efficiency through strategic HRM integration.

3. METHODOLOGY

3.1 Data Collection

This study employed a systematic qualitative review to explore sustainable practices and HRM strategies in clinical settings. The review followed the PRISMA (Preferred Reporting Items for Systematic Reviews and Meta-Analyses) guidelines to ensure a transparent, comprehensive, and replicable research process. A purposive sampling strategy was employed to identify and select relevant academic literature that addresses explicitly sustainability, clinic management, and HRM practices. The sources were limited to peer-reviewed journal articles, scholarly papers, proceedings, books, book chapters, and editorial notes indexed in Scopus, Web of Science (WOS), and Google Scholar, covering the publication period from 2020 to 2025 to ensure the inclusion of current and emerging trends. The search strategy employed carefully selected keywords, including "sustainability," "HRM," "SHRM," "GHRM," "sustainable healthcare," "clinic management," and "environmental performance in clinics." Inclusion criteria required that articles explicitly discuss sustainability in clinical settings with a focus on HR strategies or operational practices. Studies of various methodological approaches—including conceptual, empirical, and review-based research—were considered eligible for inclusion.

According to the study of Asrifan et al. (2025), Siripipatthanakul, S., & Siripipattanakul (2025a, b, c), the PRISMA METHOD was adopted in this systematic review in four steps:

Step 1: ***Identifying the Problem*** - The early stage of entries can be identified through manual searches, literature databases, or other methods. This study's initial step consisted of random sampling, which was performed by randomly picking the topic matter. The associated article contains 288 papers.

Step 2: ***Screening:*** After eliminating duplicates, this phase displays the remaining records. At this stage, the titles and abstracts of acknowledged records are assessed for their relevance to the study's subject matter or objectives. The second phase involved the execution of purposeful sampling, which was achieved by selecting academic papers from Google Scholar, Scopus, and Web of Science (WOS). One hundred twenty-six (126) articles were selected in this step.

Step 3: ***Eligibility:*** This section outlines the quantity of research that may proceed following the initial screening. In this phase, essential information articles are assessed against established criteria to determine eligibility. A purposive sampling method was employed in the third phase, resulting in the selection of 72 papers suitable for a systematic review. The selected papers were based on terms from AI, Grammarly, Turnitin, and Word Cloud, primarily from 2021 to 2025.

Step 4: ***Inclusions:*** This stage represents the total number of studies included in the systematic review analysis. The eligibility prerequisites have been satisfied, and these studies are appropriate for future investigation. The flow graphic illustrates the amount of research stopped at each phase and the rationale behind the decision. Some of the most common reasons for exclusion are a lack of relevance to the research issue, an inadequate study design, an absence of appropriate data, or inclusion criteria. According to the PRISMA methodology, the fourth step was processed by three academic experts. They used content analysis to demonstrate that the systematic review contained accurate information.

3.2 Data Analysis

Following article selection, a qualitative content analysis was conducted to systematically extract and code thematic patterns across the literature. The analysis involved organizing and synthesizing findings related to sustainable operational strategies, HRM initiatives, and their impacts on clinical performance, workforce well-being, and alignment with sustainability goals such as the UN Sustainable Development Goals (UNSDGs. The objective was to identify recurring themes, innovative practices, and evidence of strategic integration between HRM and sustainability in healthcare environments. To support content analysis and enhance the visualization of dominant trends, a word cloud was generated using the online tool, simplewordcloud.com. This tool was used to transform the frequency of keywords and terms extracted from the reviewed literature into a visual representation. The word cloud highlighted the most prominent concepts associated with sustainable clinic management, providing an intuitive overview of the dataset and facilitating the identification of key focus areas in SHRM and operational practices. This methodological approach provided a rigorous foundation for understanding how clinics are incorporating sustainability into both human resource and operational systems, and how these practices contribute to environmental, social, and economic performance.

4. RESULTS

The systematic review revealed several key findings regarding the integration of sustainable practices and HRM in clinical settings between 2020 and 2025. Based on content analysis of the literature, the evidence highlights a growing convergence between operational sustainability efforts and HRM strategies. In addition, the analysis demonstrates that clinics increasingly recognize the strategic role of human capital—developed and managed through HRM—as essential to achieving long-term sustainability goals.

One of the most prominent findings of the review is that digital transformation is a foundational element of sustainable clinic management. Clinics widely adopted EMRs, telemedicine services, and digital appointment scheduling systems. These innovations have significantly contributed to environmental sustainability by minimizing paper consumption, reducing carbon emissions associated with patient travel, and lowering overall resource usage. Beyond environmental gains, these tools also enhanced administrative efficiency, improved access to care, and facilitated staff communication. Notably, digitalization extended into HRM functions—such as online recruitment processes and virtual training programs—which aligned operational efficiency with green HRM practices.

Environmentally sustainable operational practices were another dominant theme. Clinics implemented energy-efficient infrastructure (such as LED lighting and innovative HVAC systems), water conservation measures, and comprehensive waste management protocols—including the segregation of general, hazardous, and medical waste. Many clinics transitioned toward sustainable procurement practices by favoring recyclable, biodegradable, and locally sourced supplies. The adoption of green building design features, including improved insulation, natural lighting, and green spaces, contributed to both environmental conservation and enhanced patient and staff well-being. These efforts were most effective when coupled with staff training and internal communication that reinforced ecological responsibility.

The review identified HRM as a pivotal enabler in translating sustainability goals into organizational culture and daily practice. Clinics that adopted GHRM practices—such as environmentally aligned recruitment, sustainability-oriented job descriptions, and training on ecological practices—reported enhanced employee engagement and pro-environmental behavior. Performance management systems in these clinics incorporated sustainability metrics, and incentive programs were used to reward green initiatives. HR departments were also instrumental in forming "green teams" that led internal campaigns and innovation projects focused on sustainable improvement. These practices empowered staff to take ownership of sustainability initiatives, reinforcing a culture of shared accountability.

In addition to environmental initiatives, the findings highlighted the strong emphasis placed on social sustainability within HRM frameworks. Clinics implemented DEI strategies through inclusive hiring practices, anti-discrimination policies, and equitable promotion opportunities. Employee well-being programs were widespread, addressing physical and mental health through ergonomic design, access to counseling services, and promoting work-life balance. Flexible work arrangements—including hybrid schedules and adjustable shifts—contributed to increased job satisfaction and reduced burnout. Clinics that supported staff through wellness initiatives and inclusive leadership were more likely to retain employees and cultivate a collaborative, values-driven organizational culture.

The most successful sustainability outcomes were observed in clinics where HRM was fully integrated into operational planning. These clinics demonstrated a holistic approach, combining technological innovation with environmentally and socially responsible HR practices. This synergy enhanced the clinic's organizational resilience, regulatory compliance, and overall sustainability performance. Significantly, these clinics also contributed to achieving the UNSDGs, particularly SDG 3 (Good Health and Well-being), SDG 8 (Decent Work and Economic Growth), and SDG 12 (Responsible Consumption and Production).

To further illustrate the strategic role of HRM in supporting sustainability within clinical settings, Table 1 presents a summary of the key sustainable HRM practices identified in the reviewed literature, along with their associated organizational outcomes.

Table 1. Sustainable HRM Practices in Clinical Settings

HRM Dimension	Sustainable Practice	Outcomes Achieved
Recruitment and Selection	Hiring based on sustainability values, virtual interviews	Staff alignment with sustainability goals
Training and Development	Environmental awareness programs, digital learning modules	Improved staff knowledge and behavior
Performance Management	Evaluation based on sustainability key performance indicators	Accountability and performance enhancement
Employee Well-being	Mental health programs, ergonomic workspaces, flexible hours	Increased job satisfaction and retention
Diversity and Inclusion	Inclusive hiring practices, anti-discrimination policies	Stronger team cohesion and ethical workplace culture
Green Teams and Champions	Formation of internal sustainability committees	Innovation and shared responsibility

As presented in Table 1, the analysis identified six core dimensions of sustainable HRM practices. These practices reflect a deliberate effort by clinics to align workforce management with broader sustainability objectives. Recruitment and selection processes are increasingly emphasizing sustainability-minded candidates and incorporating digital interviewing to reduce their carbon footprint. Training and development initiatives focus on environmental awareness and integrating green values into clinical routines, utilizing online platforms to increase accessibility and reduce reliance on paper-based materials. Moreover, performance management systems incorporate sustainability-related Key Performance Indicators (KPIs), enabling clinics to measure and reward employee contributions to environmental and social objectives. Employee well-being is also prioritized, with clinics introducing mental health support, ergonomic work environments, and flexible scheduling to enhance job satisfaction and reduce burnout. Additionally, clinics adopt DEI strategies to ensure fair labor practices and promote a supportive workplace culture. The formation of green teams or appointing sustainability champions within the organization further strengthens internal engagement and facilitates continuous innovation. These findings underscore the strategic role of HRM as a driver of sustainable transformation, reinforcing its contribution to operational success and workforce resilience in the healthcare sector.

To complement the textual analysis, a word cloud was generated from the full text of the reviewed literature to visually represent the most frequently occurring terms associated with sustainable clinic management and HRM (Figure 1). The prominence of specific words in the cloud reflects their relative frequency and thematic centrality in the analyzed content.

Figure 1. Key Terms in Sustainable Clinic Management and HRM:

A Word Cloud Visualization (Source: Simple Word Cloud Generator, 2025)

As shown in Figure 1, the most dominant terms include “sustainability,” “practices,” “HRM,” “clinics,” “management,” and “environmental.” These keywords highlight the central focus of the systematic review—namely, integrating sustainability principles into clinical operations and human resource management systems. The frequent occurrence of terms such as “green,” “strategies,” “initiatives,” and “programs” suggests an emphasis on structured and proactive approaches to embedding sustainability across various domains of clinical management. In addition, the words “staff” and related terms, such as “workforce,” “job,” “well-being,” and “training,” highlight the critical role of human capital in driving and sustaining environmental and organizational performance. This finding is consistent with research indicating that employee engagement, professional development, and well-being initiatives are essential components of Green Human Resource Management (GHRM). Moreover, terms like “digital,” “performance,” “systems,” and “innovation” reflect the increasing digitization and technological transformation of clinical environments. These keywords support the conclusion that digital tools are foundational to operational efficiency and the success of sustainability initiatives, particularly in areas such as paperless systems, online recruitment, and virtual staff training. Notably, the presence of terms such as “culture,” “accountability,” “equity,” “diversity,” and “DEI” indicates that social sustainability and ethical labor practices are increasingly integral to clinic management. These findings further emphasize the interconnectedness of environmental, economic, and social dimensions within the broader sustainability agenda. The study's word cloud supports the findings of this review by visually illustrating the integrated and multi-dimensional approach that clinics are adopting. Additionally, it shows that sustainable clinic management is driven by a combination of environmental practices, digital solutions, and strategic HRM programs that collectively reinforce organizational performance, staff engagement, and ethical responsibility.

In summary, the findings highlight that sustainable clinic management is most effective when HRM is integrated as a strategic pillar. By aligning workforce strategies with environmental and social responsibility initiatives, clinics not only improve efficiency and reduce environmental harm but also cultivate a committed and empowered workforce. These integrated strategies are essential for building future-ready, ethical, and high-performing healthcare institutions.

5. DISCUSSIONS

The findings of this systematic review reveal a growing convergence between sustainable operational practices and HRM in clinical settings, supporting a shift toward integrated, future-ready healthcare systems. This aligns with existing literature that emphasizes the strategic role of HRM in embedding sustainability into organizational practices (Campos-García et al., 2024; Papademetriou et al., 2025; Popescu et al., 2024; Ren et al., 2023). Clinics are increasingly utilizing digital technologies, adopting green HRM practices, and promoting social equity and well-being—all of which are essential components of a holistic sustainability strategy.

A key insight from the review is the dual role of digital transformation in achieving both operational efficiency and environmental sustainability. The widespread adoption of EMRs, telehealth platforms, and virtual recruitment systems has contributed to significant reductions in paper consumption, energy use, and travel-related emissions. These findings are consistent with those of Akinola and Telukdarie (2023), who highlight digital innovation as a catalyst for sustainable transformation in healthcare. Furthermore, digital HRM tools such as online onboarding and e-learning modules support more efficient and eco-friendly personnel management (Back et al., 2022; Kumi et al., 2025), demonstrating how technology serves as a bridge between sustainability goals and human capital development.

The review also affirms the critical role of HRM in institutionalizing sustainability through green human resource practices. Recruitment strategies that prioritize sustainability values, along with performance management systems incorporating environmental and social metrics, help align individual behavior with organizational goals (Gomes et al., 2024; Liang & Li, 2024). In addition, the formation of green teams and the identification of sustainability champions within clinics promote a culture of shared responsibility and innovation (Kalogirou & Baumbusch, 2025; Soekotjo et al., 2025). This reflects the growing body of evidence suggesting that employees are more engaged and committed when they perceive their organization as environmentally and socially responsible (Faeni et al., 2025; Malik et al., 2021).

Equally significant is the integration of social sustainability within HRM frameworks. Many clinics in the reviewed literature adopted inclusive hiring practices, anti-discrimination policies, and flexible working arrangements to promote diversity, equity, and employee well-being. These findings reinforce earlier work by Eze and Francis (2024) and Kailay et al. (2024), who underscore the role of HRM in promoting work-life balance, mental health, and organizational commitment. By fostering supportive environments and addressing burnout risks, such practices not only contribute to improved job satisfaction but also reduce turnover and enhance long-term organizational resilience (Obeng & Atan, 2024; Stolarchuk et al., 2025).

Moreover, the alignment of HRM with the Sustainable Development Goals—particularly SDG 3 (Good Health and Well-being), SDG 8 (Decent Work and Economic Growth), and SDG 12 (Responsible Consumption and Production)—positions clinics as proactive agents of global health transformation. Clinics that integrate HRM into strategic planning demonstrate greater adaptability, enhanced regulatory compliance, and improved stakeholder trust, as supported by findings from Bosco et al. (2024) and Verdonck and Verniers (2024). These outcomes validate the claim that HRM is no longer a peripheral administrative function but a core strategic partner in sustainability transitions (Bornay-Barrachina et al., 2023).

Nonetheless, challenges persist. The literature and this review point to systemic barriers, including limited resources, staff resistance to change, and the complexity of quantifying the impact of sustainable HRM initiatives (Ramgolam et al., 2024; Ren et al., 2023). These constraints underscore the need for a more substantial leadership commitment, ongoing staff training, and the development of robust metrics to effectively assess sustainability outcomes. Clinics must also invest in capacity-building initiatives that empower HR departments to act as facilitators of sustainable transformation (Njah et al., 2021; Snowden et al., 2023; Willie, 2025).

This study reinforces the critical importance of HRM as a cornerstone of sustainable clinic management. Supported by prior research across diverse healthcare contexts, the evidence demonstrates that when empowered and aligned with sustainability objectives, HRM can drive transformative change, operationalize environmental and social values, and position clinics as ethical, adaptive institutions capable of navigating the evolving demands of the healthcare sector.

6. CONCLUSION

This chapter presents a systematic review of sustainable clinic management with a focus on human resource management (HRM) as a strategic driver of sustainability in healthcare settings. Utilizing the PRISMA framework, the study analyzed peer-reviewed articles published between 2020 and 2025 from Scopus, Web of Science, and Google Scholar. The findings reveal a growing convergence between operational sustainability initiatives and HRM strategies, particularly through the adoption of green human resource management (GHRM) practices and digital transformation. Clinics are increasingly leveraging electronic medical records, telemedicine, and virtual HR processes to reduce environmental impact and enhance efficiency. Simultaneously, HRM plays a pivotal role in promoting employee engagement, diversity, well-being, and environmental accountability. This integration of sustainable practices and human capital development not only supports compliance with global sustainability goals but also strengthens clinic resilience and long-term performance. The review contributes to the field by synthesizing current best practices and offering strategic insights for clinic administrators and policymakers seeking to embed sustainability across all levels of healthcare management.

This systematic review demonstrates that sustainable clinic management represents a transformative approach to healthcare delivery that fundamentally integrates environmental stewardship, social responsibility, and economic viability through strategic HRM. The analysis reveals that digital transformation, comprehensive environmental practices, and GHRM function as interconnected pillars supporting sustainable healthcare operations. The findings establish that HRM serves as the primary engine of sustainable transformation, with practices such as sustainability-oriented recruitment, environmental awareness training, performance management systems incorporating sustainability metrics, and employee well-being initiatives proving essential for creating organizational cultures that support long-term sustainability goals. Most significantly, the review demonstrates that the most successful sustainability outcomes occur when HRM is fully integrated into operational planning, creating synergistic relationships between technological innovation, environmental stewardship, and workforce engagement that contribute meaningfully to achieving the UNSDGs. For healthcare practitioners and policymakers, these findings provide compelling evidence that sustainable clinic management is not merely an operational consideration but a strategic imperative that enables healthcare organizations to achieve clinical excellence while building resilient systems that support environmental protection, social equity, and long-term organizational success. As the healthcare sector continues to face challenges related to climate change, resource scarcity, and health inequities, this research underscores that sustainable clinic management, anchored by strategic HRM practices and supported by comprehensive operational initiatives, represents a vital pathway for creating healthcare institutions that serve not only their immediate patients but also contribute to the well-being of communities and future generations.

In an era of environmental consciousness and resource depletion, sustainability has become a pervasive concern in virtually every sector, including healthcare. Sustainable clinic administration, mainly when assessed through best practices and effective HRM, provides a framework for healthcare practitioners to operate efficiently, ethically, and responsibly. This technique goes beyond regulatory compliance to integrate ecological, social, and economic aspects into clinic operations. Sustainable clinic management reduces environmental impact, maximizes resource efficiency, promotes social benefits, and ensures financial sustainability. This challenging goal requires a comprehensive approach that evaluates every action, from procurement to patient care, for its sustainability. This management uses energy efficiency, waste reduction, ethical sourcing, and community engagement. Energy use often contributes to a clinic's carbon footprint. Sustainability in this arena encompasses the use of LEDs, optimizing HVAC systems, utilizing solar panels whenever possible, and integrating innovative building technologies for energy monitoring and management. Low-flow fixtures, sterilization, and landscaping are essential for water conservation. Healthcare waste management is complicated due to the presence of harmful and contagious compounds. The hierarchy of sustainable practices includes source reduction, reuse of non-medical items, recycling of compatible materials (such as paper, plastics, and glass), and safe medical waste disposal through incineration with energy recovery or autoclaving. Sustainable clinic practices encompass procurement, supply chain management, and resource allocation. This means supporting suppliers who use ethical labor practices, employ sustainable production methods, and offer eco-friendly products. Clinics can purchase in bulk and opt for durable products to reduce packaging waste. Clinical facility design and development are vital. Sustainability practices, including the use of recycled materials, optimization of natural light and ventilation, and reduction of construction waste, can help reduce the clinic's environmental impact throughout its existence. However, the most advanced systems and environmentally friendly technology are only as efficient as their managers. HRM is essential to clinic sustainability. HRM is vital for integrating sustainability into business culture, not just supporting. Sustainable HRM practices aim to create an engaged, knowledgeable, and morally conscious workforce that promotes environmental and social responsibility. HRM helps clinics survive by recruiting and selecting. Clinics can recruit individuals who share their environmental and social goals by incorporating sustainability principles into job descriptions and interview processes. By teaching new hires about the clinic's sustainability efforts and their role in contributing to these efforts, onboarding and orientation programs help promote these values. Effective human resource management relies largely on training and development. Staff can learn energy efficiency, waste segregation, sustainable product use, and emergency readiness through regular training. Training can help workers identify and propose creative sustainability solutions by developing technical skills and a deep understanding of environmental issues and the clinic's impact. This ongoing educational environment encourages creativity and improvement. Performance management systems can include sustainability metrics. To do this, personnel must be evaluated on their environmental responsibility, waste reduction, and environmental activities, as well as their productivity. Incentives, public recognition, and job progression can reinforce good practices and promote sustainability. Recognition and incentives for sustainable activities can achieve this. Sustainable human resource management requires employee involvement and empowerment. Provide staff with opportunities to share their thoughts, engage in environmental committees, or lead sustainability activities, fostering a sense of ownership and dedication. When employees feel valued by their employer, they are more likely to seek out opportunities to improve and implement long-term solutions.

This grassroots approach to sustainability can inspire new ideas and enhance procedural compliance. Sustainable HRM prioritizes employee well-being and a positive work environment. This includes promoting work-life balance, fair wages and benefits, professional growth, and respect and inclusivity. A motivated staff is more productive, less likely to burn out, and more likely to embrace sustainable practices. This includes ensuring workplace safety, as well as the safe management of waste and the use of equipment. Communication is crucial to the sustainability goals of HRM. Informing staff of the clinic's sustainability goals, progress, and challenges keeps them interested. Regular updates, newsletters, and internal activities can promote sustainability and recognition. Leadership is crucial, demonstrating and promoting sustainability. HRM promotes workplace diversity, equity, and inclusion, boosting social sustainability. A diverse workforce improves decision-making and promotes inclusive patient care. Ethical labor standards, anti-discrimination laws, and equal grievance procedures create a fair workplace. Volunteering, health education, and sponsoring local businesses can also help clinics gain social license.

7. LIMITATIONS

The comprehensive qualitative review method employed in this study provided valuable insights but had some limitations. Purposive sampling was used to choose scientific papers, which may add selection bias and limit generalizability. Thus, the results focus on the views and circumstances in the literature rather than covering all clinical scenarios. Without actual data from direct respondents, interpretation and validation of identified trends are limited. Future research should employ probability-based sampling and quantitative methods, such as structured questionnaires, alongside qualitative methods, including interviews and focus groups, to overcome these limitations. These approaches would enhance the rigor, robustness, and applicability of the conclusions.

8. FUTURE RESEARCH

The findings of this review highlight several promising directions for future research. First, there is a clear need for quantitative studies to validate the qualitative themes identified and to statistically assess the relationships between sustainable practices and clinical performance outcomes. Approaches such as structured questionnaires, large-scale surveys, and inferential statistical analyses could provide measurable evidence on the effectiveness and impact of sustainability-oriented HRM strategies. Second, future studies should also examine the long-term financial implications of integrating sustainability into HRM practices. Such research would contribute to building a stronger economic case for sustainability investments in clinical settings and inform decision-makers about cost-effectiveness and return on investment. Moreover, there is significant value in conducting qualitative investigations, such as in-depth interviews, focus groups, and case studies, to explore the nuanced experiences of clinic staff and administrators in implementing sustainability initiatives. These methods would capture contextual variables and cultural factors that influence the success of sustainable clinic management. Ultimately, future research should investigate the scalability and adaptability of practical sustainability and HRM practices across diverse healthcare settings, including clinics of varying sizes, resource levels, and geographic regions. Comparative cross-case studies or mixed-methods designs would provide comprehensive insights into how sustainability models can be replicated, adapted, and sustained across varying organizational contexts.

9. IMPLICATION

The findings of this review carry important implications for healthcare leadership, policy development, and organizational strategy. Most notably, the identification of HRM as a strategic pillar in driving sustainable transformation necessitates a paradigm shift in how healthcare leaders perceive and utilize HR functions. Rather than serving merely as administrative support, HR departments should be positioned as strategic partners responsible for embedding sustainability across organizational processes. This transition requires targeted investment in HR capabilities, including professional development in sustainability principles and green management practices. From a policy perspective, integrating sustainability metrics into healthcare regulation and accreditation standards emerges as a critical recommendation. Policymakers are encouraged to incorporate environmental and social responsibility indicators into compliance frameworks, thereby institutionalizing sustainable practices within healthcare systems. Furthermore, the demonstrated link between employee well-being initiatives and broader sustainability outcomes suggests that policies promoting healthcare workforce welfare—such as mental health programs, flexible work arrangements, and diversity and inclusion efforts—can yield environmental and social co-benefits. The review also underscores the role of digital transformation as a key enabler of sustainability. This finding highlights the need for both public and private investment strategies in healthcare technology to consider not only clinical and operational efficiency but also environmental impact. Policy agendas and funding mechanisms should prioritize digital tools that reduce resource consumption, support virtual service delivery, and enhance organizational resilience.

The chapter offers practical and sustainable management advice for clinic managers and healthcare administrators. Sustainability should be integrated into organizational structures, rather than being a standalone effort. Sustainability initiatives must involve all employees in workforce development, seeing them as change agents and beneficiaries. Green teams and staff-led sustainability programs emphasize bottom-up innovation, while leadership engagement assures strategic alignment and long-term effect. Sustainability should be viewed as a strategic benefit, not merely a compliance requirement. Sustainable clinics are more likely to attract and retain talent, especially among healthcare professionals who respect environmental and social responsibility. Sustainability enhances an organization's reputation, boosts employee satisfaction, and fosters long-term competitiveness in a rapidly changing healthcare sector. Sustainable clinic management, supported by effective practices and strategic HRM, creates a more accountable and resilient healthcare system. A dedicated, knowledgeable, and empowered team supports and improves ecologically friendly activities. By integrating sustainability into all aspects of clinic operations and promoting environmental stewardship and social responsibility through effective human resource management, clinics can reduce their ecological footprint, optimize resources, improve their reputation, attract and retain top talent, and provide better, more ethical patient care for future generations. This comprehensive plan ensures the clinic operates economically while adhering to ethical and responsible practices, benefiting society and the environment.

10. ACKNOWLEDGEMENT

This study constitutes a collaborative effort between the International College of Pathumthani University and Kasetsart University. The authors hereby extend their sincere gratitude to the institutions for their invaluable support and encouragement throughout this work.

This study is not subject to competing interests, as stated by the authors.

REFERENCES

Ab, F., & Wahyuni, D. U. (2023). Implementation of green human resource management in improving environmental performance at hospital in Makassar. *Innovation Business Management and Accounting Journal*, *2*(3), 157–164. DOI: 10.56070/ibmaj.v2i3.52

Akinola, S., & Telukdarie, A. (2023). Sustainable digital transformation in healthcare: Advancing a digital vascular health innovation solution. *Sustainability (Basel)*, *15*(13), 10417. DOI: 10.3390/su151310417

Alamgir, W., & Shan, H. (2023). Clinical leadership and integration of triple bottom line for planetary health. *Life Sciences*, *4*(3), 180–181. DOI: 10.37185/LnS.1.1.439

Alim, M., & Sulley, S. (2024). Beyond healing: Embracing the triple bottom line approach in post-pandemic healthcare. *Cureus*, *16*(2), e54019. DOI: 10.7759/cureus.54019 PMID: 38476781

Asrifan, A., Siripipatthanakul, S., Alaqad, M. H., Saodi, S., & Sadaruddin, S. (2025). Managing Privacy and Security in Research: Effective Practices and Strategies. In *Privacy and Security Management Practices for Organizations* (pp. 151-182). IGI Global Scientific Publishing. DOI: DOI: 10.4018/979-8-3693-9720-6.ch006

Atalla, A. D. G., El-Ashry, A. M., & Khattab, S. M. K. (2025). Fostering eco-friendly excellence: Exploring the relationship between green human resource practices and organizational environmental performance as perceived by nurses: A cross-sectional study. *BMC Nursing*, *24*(1), 495. DOI: 10.1186/s12912-025-03097-7 PMID: 40335971

Azizi, M. R., Atlasi, R., Ziapour, A., Abbas, J., & Naemi, R. (2021). Innovative human resource management strategies during the COVID-19 pandemic: A systematic narrative review approach. *Heliyon*, *7*(6), e07233. DOI: 10.1016/j.heliyon.2021.e07233 PMID: 34124399

Back, D. A., Scherer, J., Osterhoff, G., Rigamonti, L., & Pförringer, D. (2022). Digital implications for human resource management in surgical departments. *European Surgery, 54*(1), 17–23. DOI: 10.1007/s10353-021-00709-9 PMID: 33936187

Balay-Odao, E. M., Colet, P. C., Almazan, J. U., Kuntuganova, A., Syzdykova, A., Kavashev, Z., Smagulova, M., Dauletkaliyeva, Z., Seidakhmetova, A., & Cruz, J. P. (2024). Environmental sustainability in healthcare: A qualitative study of the perspectives of nursing, medical and public health students in Kazakhstan. *Nurse Education in Practice, 76*, 103917. DOI: 10.1016/j.nepr.2024.103917 PMID: 38402830

Balkhi, B., Alshahrani, A., & Khan, A. (2022). Just-in-time approach in healthcare inventory management: Does it really work? *Saudi Pharmaceutical Journal : SPJ : the Official Publication of the Saudi Pharmaceutical Society, 30*(12), 1830–1835. DOI: 10.1016/j.jsps.2022.10.013 PMID: 36601508

Bhati, D., Deogade, M. S., & Kanyal, D. (2023). Improving patient outcomes through effective hospital administration: A comprehensive review. *Cureus, 15*(10), e47731. DOI: 10.7759/cureus.47731 PMID: 38021686

Bornay-Barrachina, M., Guerrero-Villegas, J., López-Fernández, M., & Ruiz-Rodríguez, M. (2023). Pressures for sustainability and strategic responses on employment relationships: The role of the HR manager. *European Research on Management and Business Economics, 29*(2), 100219. DOI: 10.1016/j.iedeen.2023.100219

Bosco, F., Di Gerio, C., Fiorani, G., & Stola, G. (2024). How to manage sustainability in healthcare organizations? A processing map to include the ESG strategy. *Journal of Public Budgeting, Accounting & Financial Management, 36*(5), 636–659. DOI: 10.1108/JPBAFM-04-2023-0065

Calabrese, M., Suparaku, S., Santovito, S., & Hysa, X. (2023). Preventing and developmental factors of sustainability in healthcare organisations from the perspective of decision makers: An exploratory factor analysis. *BMC Health Services Research, 23*(1), 797. DOI: 10.1186/s12913-023-09689-w PMID: 37491258

Campos-García, I., Alonso-Muñoz, S., González-Sánchez, R., & Medina-Salgado, M. S. (2024). Human resource management and sustainability: Bridging the 2030 agenda. *Corporate Social Responsibility and Environmental Management, 31*(3), 2033–2053. DOI: 10.1002/csr.2680

Caylan, S. (2024). Role of human resource management on strategic management. In Mızrak, F. (Ed.), *Trends, Challenges, and Practices in Contemporary Strategic Management* (pp. 51–69). IGI Global Scientific Publishing., DOI: 10.4018/979-8-3693-1155-4.ch003

Correia, A. B., Shahzad, M. F., Martins, J. M., & Baheer, R. (2024). Impact of green human resource management towards sustainable performance in the healthcare sector: Role of green innovation and risk management. *Cogent Business & Management, 11*(1), 1–21. DOI: 10.1080/23311975.2024.2374625

Dion, H., & Evans, M. (2024). Strategic frameworks for sustainability and corporate governance in healthcare facilities; Approaches to energy-efficient hospital management. *Benchmarking, 31*(2), 353–390. DOI: 10.1108/BIJ-04-2022-0219

Dion, H., Evans, M., & Farrell, P. (2023). Hospitals management transformative initiatives; Towards energy efficiency and environmental sustainability in healthcare facilities. *Journal of Engineering. Defence Technology, 21*(2), 552–584. DOI: 10.1108/JEDT-04-2022-0200

Eze, K. C., & Francis, J. (2024). Sustainability in healthcare: An investigation into dynamic employee recruitment, engagement and retention. *British Journal of Management and Marketing Studies, 7*(3), 31–49. DOI: 10.52589/BJMMS-B7DCYMNV

Faeni, D. P., Oktaviani, R. F., Riyadh, H. A., Faeni, R. P., & Beshr, B. A. H. (2025). Green human resource management and sustainable practices on corporate reputation and employee well-being: A model for Indonesia's F&B industry. *Environmental Challenges, 18*, 101082. DOI: 10.1016/j.envc.2025.101082

Faisal, M., Stanton, P., & Muchiri, M. (2023). Public healthcare in Pakistan: A people management solution? *Asia Pacific Journal of Human Resources, 61*(2), 462–482. DOI: 10.1111/1744-7941.12360

Gomes, D. R., Ribeiro, N., Gomes, G., Ortega, E., & Semedo, A. (2024). Green HRM's effect on employees' eco-friendly behavior and green performance: A study in the Portuguese tourism sector. *Sustainability (Basel), 16*(22), 10005. DOI: 10.3390/su162210005

Hameed, K., Naha, R., & Hameed, F. (2024). Digital transformation for sustainable health and well-being: A review and future research directions. *Discover Sustainability, 5*(1), 104. DOI: 10.1007/s43621-024-00273-8

Hussain, A., Umair, M., Khan, S., Alonazi, W. B., Almutairi, S. S., & Malik, A. (2024). Exploring sustainable healthcare: Innovations in health economics, social policy, and management. *Heliyon, 10*(13), e33186. DOI: 10.1016/j.heliyon.2024.e33186 PMID: 39027491

Ige-Olaobaju, A. Y., Ganiyu, I. O., Atiku, S. O., & Olarewaju, O. M. (Eds.). (2025). *Advances in ethical work climate and employee well-being*. IGI Global Scientific Publishing., DOI: 10.4018/979-8-3693-8819-8

Kailay, M., Paposa, K. K., & Chhibber, P. (2024). Employee well-being as a mediating variable in sustainable human resource management, organizational commitment, and job satisfaction of healthcare professionals: A structural equation modeling approach. *International Journal of Healthcare Management*, •••, 1–14. DOI: 10.1080/20479700.2024.2405327

Kalogirou, M. R., & Baumbusch, J. (2025). Examining Canadian hospitals' support for planetary health through the implementation of green teams and sustainability offices. *Journal of Healthcare Leadership*, *17*, 269–284. DOI: 10.2147/JHL.S517669 PMID: 40525086

Koman, G., Boršoš, P., & Kubina, M. (2024). Sustainable human resource management with a focus on corporate employee recruitment. *Sustainability (Basel)*, *16*(14), 6059. DOI: 10.3390/su16146059

Kumi, E., Amoako, G. K., Appiah, T., & Dartey-Baah, K. (2025). The impact of digital transformation on organisational dynamics, HR practices, and wellbeing in Ghana's healthcare sector: A social exchange perspective. *Future Business Journal*, *11*(1), 64. DOI: 10.1186/s43093-025-00449-2

Liang, X., & Li, J. (2024). Sustainable human resource management and employee performance: A conceptual framework and research agenda. *Human Resource Management Review*, *35*(2), 101060. DOI: 10.1016/j.hrmr.2024.101060

Lu, M. K., Moslehpour, M., Lin, P. K., & Chen, T. W. (2025). Impact of sustainable HRM practices on employee well-being in health organizations: The mediating role of perceived organizational support. *American Journal of Health Behavior*, *49*(2), 78–92. DOI: 10.5993/AJHB.49.2.8

Malik, A., Nguyen, M., Budhwar, P., Chowdhury, S., & Gugnani, R. (2024). Leveraging high-performance HRM practices and knowledge sharing for managing technological and social change in emerging market healthcare providers. *Technological Forecasting and Social Change*, *205*, 123463. DOI: 10.1016/j.techfore.2024.123463

Malik, S. Y., Hayat Mughal, Y., Azam, T., Cao, Y., Wan, Z., Zhu, H., & Thurasamy, R. (2021). Corporate social responsibility, green human resources management, and sustainable performance: Is organizational citizenship behavior towards environment the missing link? *Sustainability (Basel)*, *13*(3), 1044. DOI: 10.3390/su13031044

Mensah, L. E., Shukla, S., & Iqbal, H. F. (2023). Green human resource management practices and employee innovative behaviour: Reflection from Ghana. *IIMBG Journal of Sustainable Business and Innovation*, *1*(1), 58–74. DOI: 10.1108/IJSBI-02-2023-0002

Molero, A., Calabrò, M., Vignes, M., Gouget, B., & Gruson, D. (2021). Sustainability in healthcare: Perspectives and reflections regarding laboratory medicine. *Annals of Laboratory Medicine*, *41*(2), 139–144. DOI: 10.3343/alm.2021.41.2.139 PMID: 33063675

Mostepaniuk, A., Akalin, T., & Parish, M. R. (2023). Practices pursuing the sustainability of a healthcare organization: A systematic review. *Sustainability (Basel)*, *15*(3), 2353. DOI: 10.3390/su15032353

Mousa, S. K., & Othman, M. (2020). The impact of green human resource management practices on sustainable performance in healthcare organisations: A conceptual framework. *Journal of Cleaner Production*, *243*, 118595. DOI: 10.1016/j.jclepro.2019.118595

Njah, J., Hansoti, B., Adeyami, A., Bruce, K., O'malley, G., Gugerty, M. K., Chi, B. H., Lubimbi, N., Steen, E., Stampfly, S., Berman, E., & Kimball, A. M. (2021). Measuring for success: Evaluating leadership training programs for sustainable impact. *Annals of Global Health*, *87*(1), 63. DOI: 10.5334/aogh.3221 PMID: 34307066

Obeng, H. A., & Atan, T. (2024). Understanding turnover intentions: The interplay of organizational politics, employee resilience, and person-job fit in Ghana's healthcare sector. *Sustainability (Basel)*, *16*(22), 9980. DOI: 10.3390/su16229980

Oberai, H., & Anand, I. (2025). Unifying green HRM with sustainable development goals: Ways to develop capabilities and skills. In Tripathi, V., Rastogi, S., & Singh, N. (Eds.), *Implementing ESG Frameworks Through Capacity Building and Skill Development* (pp. 237–260). IGI Global Scientific Publishing., DOI: 10.4018/979-8-3693-6617-2.ch011

Olawade, D. B., Popoola, T. T., Egbon, E., & David-Olawade, A. C. (2025). Sustainable healthcare practices: Pathways to a carbon-neutral future for the medical industry. *Sustainable Futures : An Applied Journal of Technology, Environment and Society*, *9*, 100783. DOI: 10.1016/j.sftr.2025.100783

Papademetriou, C., Anastasiadou, S., Belias, D., & Ragazou, K. (2025). Integrating sustainability into human resource management: Building a greener workforce for the future. *Sustainability (Basel)*, *17*(3), 1113. DOI: 10.3390/su17031113

Parashakti, R. D., Febrian, W. D., Tarmizi, A., Satria, E., Hikmah Perkasa, D., & Yuliana, L. (2024). The role of green human resource management: Analysis of organizational culture, innovation and leadership. *Dinasti International Journal of Education Management and Social Science*, *6*(1), 475–485. DOI: 10.38035/dijemss.v6i1.3436

Parzhanova, A. (2025). Human resource management – Sustainable practices. *Edelweiss Applied Science and Technology*, *9*(1), 1100–1110. DOI: 10.55214/25768484.v9i1.4325

Popescu, C. R., Martínez-Falcó, J., Marco-Lajara, B., Sánchez-García, E., & Millán-Tudela, L. (Eds.). (2024). *Building sustainable human resources management practices for businesses*. IGI Global Scientific Publishing., DOI: 10.4018/979-8-3693-1994-9

Purwadi, P., Widjaja, Y. R., Junius, J., & Mahmudah, N. (2024). Strategic human resource management in healthcare: Elevating patient care and organizational excellence through effective HRM practices. *Golden Ratio of Data in Summary*, *4*(2), 236–241. DOI: 10.52970/grdis.v4i2.540

Ramgolam, G., Ramphul, N., & Chittoo, H. (2024). Sustainable human resource management—A systematic literature review and directions for future research. *Journal of the Knowledge Economy*, •••, 1–38. DOI: 10.1007/s13132-024-02273-5

Rashah, R. A. S. A., Al Rashah, K. A. H., Al Rashah, S. M. R., Saleh, I. A., Al Shaiban, M. A., Alrashah, M. A., & Al Musharraf, N. H. N. (2024). Comprehensive review of sustainability practices, innovation, and resource management in healthcare. *Journal of Ecohumanism*, *3*(8), 5457–5466. DOI: 10.62754/joe.v3i8.5245

Read, J., & Meath, C. (2025). A conceptual framework for sustainable evidence-based design for aligning therapeutic and sustainability outcomes in healthcare facilities: A systematic literature review. *HERD*, *18*(1), 86–107. DOI: 10.1177/19375867241302793 PMID: 39655601

Ren, S., Cooke, F. L., Stahl, G. K., Fan, D., & Timming, A. R. (2023). Advancing the sustainability agenda through strategic human resource management: Insights and suggestions for future research. *Human Resource Management*, *62*(3), 251–265. DOI: 10.1002/hrm.22169

Sajwani, R. A. (2024). Sustainability in healthcare practice. In Al Marri, K., Mir, F.A., David, S.A., Al-Emran, M. (eds), *BUiD Doctoral Research Conference 2023. Lecture Notes in Civil Engineering* (vol. 473). Springer. DOI: 10.1007/978-3-031-56121-4_25

Saruchera, F. (2025). Sustainability: A concept in flux? The role of multidisciplinary insights in shaping sustainable futures. *Sustainability (Basel)*, *17*(1), 326. DOI: 10.3390/su17010326

Sarwar, A., & Shahzad, S. (2024). Fostering sustainability in the healthcare organization through green HRM practices: The mediation analysis of perceived organizational support. *Employee Relations*, *46*(8), 1666–1688. DOI: 10.1108/ER-07-2023-0368

Sepetis, A., & Parlavantzas, I. (2025). Circular economy behavior and sustainable healthcare. *Circular Economy and Sustainability*, 1–23. DOI: 10.1007/s43615-025-00601-8

Sinsky, C. A., Biddison, L. D., Mallick, A., Dopp, A. L., Perlo, J., Lynn, L., & Smith, C. D. (2020). Organizational evidence-based and promising practices for improving clinician well-being. *NAM Perspectives*, 1–15. DOI: 10.31478/202011a PMID: 35291739

Siripipatthanakul, S., & Siripipattanakul, S. (2025a). Talent Management Ensuring the Safety and Cybersecurity in Schools. *Cultivating Creativity and Navigating Talent Management in Academia*, 383-402. DOI: 10.4018/979-8-3693-6880-0.ch018

Siripipatthanakul, S., & Siripipattanakul, S. (2025b). Online Gambling of Higher Education Learners. In *International Academic Transformations and Cross-Border Collaborations* (pp. 377–400). IGI Global Scientific Publishing., DOI: 10.4018/979-8-3373-0508-0.ch01

Siripipatthanakul, S., & Siripipattanakul, S. (2025c). Rural Dental Health Transformation by Adopting Digital Technologies. *Transforming Dental Health in Rural Communities: Digital Dentistry*, 47-80. DOI: DOI: 10.4018/979-8-3693-7165-7.ch003

Snowden, B., Lahiri, S., Dutton, R., & Morton, L. (2023). Achieving and sustaining change through capacity building train-the-trainer health initiatives in low-and middle-income countries: A systematic review. *The Journal of Continuing Education in the Health Professions*, *43*(2), 96–103. DOI: 10.1097/CEH.0000000000000458 PMID: 36215155

Soekotjo, S., Sosidah, , Kuswanto, H., Setyadi, A., & Pawirosumarto, S. (2025). A conceptual framework for sustainable human resource management: Integrating ecological and inclusive perspectives. *Sustainability (Basel)*, *17*(3), 1241. DOI: 10.3390/su17031241

Stolarchuk, C., Kumar, P., Lionis, C., Anastasaki, M., Conde, M. G., Chowdhury, M., & Awankem, B. (2025). Optimizing healthcare delivery: Strategies for workforce retention and resource allocation. *Journal of Surgical Specialties and Rural Practice*, *6*(1), 3–8. DOI: 10.4103/jssrp.jssrp_7_25

Tunio, R. (Ed.). (2024). *Intersecting human resource management and organizational culture for environmental sustainability*. IGI Global Scientific Publishing., DOI: 10.4018/979-8-3693-2699-2

Tushar, S. R., Moktadir, M. A., Kusi-Sarpong, S., & Ren, J. (2023). Driving sustainable healthcare service management in the hospital sector. *Journal of Cleaner Production*, *420*, 138310. DOI: 10.1016/j.jclepro.2023.138310

Ugwu, C. N., Ugwu, O. P. C., Alum, E. U., Eze, V. H. U., Basajja, M., Ugwu, J. N., Ogenyi, F. C., Ejemot-Nwadiaro, R. I., Okon, M. B., Egba, S. I., & Uti, D. E. (2025). Sustainable development goals (SDGs) and resilient healthcare systems: Addressing medicine and public health challenges in conflict zones. *Medicine*, *104*(7), e41535. DOI: 10.1097/MD.0000000000041535 PMID: 39960902

Ullah, Z., Nasir, A. R., Alqahtani, F. K., Ullah, F., Thaheem, M. J., & Maqsoom, A. (2023). Life cycle sustainability assessment of healthcare buildings: A policy framework. *Buildings (Basel, Switzerland)*, *13*(9), 2143. DOI: 10.3390/buildings13092143

Vasileiou, A., Sfakianaki, E., & Tsekouropoulos, G. (2024). Exploring sustainability and efficiency improvements in healthcare: A qualitative study. *Sustainability (Basel)*, *16*(19), 8306. DOI: 10.3390/su16198306

Verdonck, P., & Verniers, I. (2024). Environmental sustainability in healthcare: Managerial concerns and solutions. *Baillière's Best Practice and Research in Clinical Anaesthesiology*, *38*(4), 379–385. DOI: 10.1016/j.bpa.2025.03.006

Wang, X., Wang, R. S., Qin, X., Huang, Y. N., Chiu, H. C., & Wang, B. L. (2024). Exploring human resource management in the top five global hospitals: A comparative study. *Frontiers in Public Health*, *11*, 1–10. DOI: 10.3389/fpubh.2023.1307823 PMID: 38249385

Willie, M. M. (2025). Strategies for enhancing training and development in healthcare management. *Advances in Human Resource Management Research*, *3*(1), 44–59. DOI: 10.60079/ahrmr.v3i1.408

Wu, A., Roemer, E. C., Kent, K. B., Ballard, D. W., & Goetzel, R. Z. (2021). Organizational best practices supporting mental health in the workplace. *Journal of Occupational and Environmental Medicine*, *63*(12), e925–e931. DOI: 10.1097/JOM.0000000000002407 PMID: 34840320

Yoo, D. Y. (2024). Eco-leadership in action: Integrating green HRM and the new ecological paradigm to foster organizational commitment and environmental citizenship in the hospitality industry. *Sustainability (Basel)*, *16*(20), 9044. DOI: 10.3390/su16209044

Zournatzidou, G., Ragazou, K., Sklavos, G., & Sariannidis, N. (2025). Linking HRM with sustainability: Achieving the goals of the 2030 agenda. In K. Ragazou, A. Garefalakis, C. Papademetriou, & A. Samara (Eds.), *Sustainability Through Green HRM and Performance Integration* (pp. 281-304). IGI Global Scientific Publishing. DOI: 10.4018/979-8-3693-5981-5.ch012

KEY TERMS AND DEFINITIONS

Sustainable Clinic Management: Sustainable clinic management is fundamentally grounded in the application of the Triple Bottom Line across all dimensions of a clinic's operations. This holistic approach aims not only to maintain financial viability but also to promote environmental stewardship, uphold social responsibility, and ensure ethical conduct, all while delivering high-quality patient care.

Sustainability Theory: Sustainability theory is a comprehensive and evolving framework that explores how human societies can thrive over the long term without depleting natural resources, causing irreversible environmental harm, or compromising the well-being of future generations. Rooted in multidisciplinary scholarship—including ecology, economics, sociology, political science, ethics, and engineering—sustainability theory offers a valuable lens through which organizations, such as healthcare clinics, can evaluate and inform their operational and strategic decisions.

Key Pillars of Sustainable Clinic Management: Key pillars of sustainable clinic management include strategic leadership and policy development, sustainable HRM, environmentally responsible operations, patient-centered care, financial resilience, and the integration of digital technologies.

Human Resource Management (HRM): HRM plays a pivotal role in advancing sustainability in the healthcare sector by embedding environmental, social, and economic principles into the management of people. This approach, often referred to as Sustainable Human Resource Management (SHRM) or Green Human Resource Management (GHRM), emphasizes the critical role that healthcare professionals play as agents of change.

Green Human Resource Management (GHRM): GHRM policies integrate sustainability considerations into job descriptions, performance evaluations, and incentive structures, while actively encouraging staff participation in environmental activities. In addition, HRM practices aimed at enhancing employee health and engagement—such as promoting work-life balance, supporting mental health, and offering flexible work arrangements—create a culture of accountability and shared responsibility for environmentally responsible behaviors.

Sustainable Practices in Clinic Management: Sustainable practices in clinic management encompass a range of operational strategies designed to minimize environmental impact and improve efficiency. The transition to digital systems, such as electronic medical records (EMRs), has proven effective in reducing paper use, while telemedicine and digital appointment scheduling streamline service delivery and decrease the carbon footprint associated with patient visits.

Chapter 4
Sustainable Private Hospitals Based on Prices, Services, and Facilities

Parichat Jaipong
https://orcid.org/0000-0002-9249-3169
Manipal GlobalNxt University, Nilai, Malaysia

Chok Nyen Vui
https://orcid.org/0000-0002-7447-2073
Manipal GlobalNxt University, Kuala Lumpur, Malaysia

ABSTRACT

Sustainable private hospitals reconcile profitability with environmental responsibility and social equality by incorporating sustainable principles throughout pricing, services, and facilities. This chapter employed the PRISMA METHOD for systematic review analysis. The findings show that entails delivering value-based treatment and transparent pricing, giving comprehensive services that prioritize preventive care and patient education, and constructing and managing facilities with a focus on energy efficiency, waste minimization, and a healthy environment. Sustainable private hospitals reduce environmental impact and operational expenses while simultaneously enhancing reputation and promoting long-term community welfare, thereby attracting patients and ensuring financial sustainability.

DOI: 10.4018/979-8-3693-9800-5.ch004

1. INTRODUCTION

Several aspects of private hospitals contribute to their sustainability, including energy conservation, procurement, transportation, waste management, biodiversity conservation, and community involvement. Sustainable development ensures that current and future generations have access to the fundamental necessities and quality of life (Dion & Evans, 2024). Modern healthcare delivery is unsustainable due to increasing costs, rising demands, and its environmental impact. Healthcare professionals and managers consider environmentally friendly standards and recognize the connection between human health and the health of the Earth. However, despite increased awareness of global warming, a significant dearth of information remains on how to become more ecologically friendly. (Leal Filho et al., 2023; Dion & Evans, 2024).

More sustainable practices have rewards, both financially and in terms of reputation. Spending and carbon footprint are closely connected and serve as a proxy for sustainability. The Sustainable Development Goals (SDGs) should include instruction on sustainability for healthcare professionals working in hospitals, as well as for other stakeholders. In 2015, all UN member states accepted the 2030 Agenda for Sustainable Development, which established 17 Sustainable Development Goals (SDGs). The SDGs aim for "peace and prosperity for people and the planet," while combating climate change and preserving oceans and forests. The SDGs link environmental, social, and economic responsibility, prioritizing sustainability. Healthcare providers, hospital professionals, and clinical professionals are encouraged to explore "Sustainable Development for Hospitals and Clinics" and contribute to all related research areas. However, from the perspective of hospital or clinic customers, they can participate in this Book by sharing their viewpoints. Sometimes, researchers do not use the term 'patients' but instead use 'customers,' based on management theories integrated with sustainability concepts (Chiu & Fong, 2023; Candio, 2024).

Traditional hospital and clinic services were based on theories such as the Parasuraman Model (tangibility, reliability, responsiveness, assurance, and empathy), The 7Ps Model (people, price, place, product, physical evidence, promotion, and process), the 4Ps (product, price, place, promotion). The 4Cs Model (customer value, cost, convenience, and communication), the Siripipattthanakul Model in 2022 (prices, facilities, and services), and HRM (such as 4Ms, man, money, material, and management; or diversity and equality, or leadership, etc.). (Siripipatthanakul, 2020; Siripipatthanakul, 2021; Siripipatthanakul, 2022). Digital intelligence can be applied to HRM and digital marketing, such as salutogenic digital marketing, in the fields of medicine and dentistry (Siripipatthanakul & Phuangsuwan, 2024).

Improving private hospitals and clinics could use these factors and focus on two sections: (1) customer outcomes, such as customer satisfaction and loyalty, and (2) employee outcomes, such as employee satisfaction and loyalty. The factor that influences customer loyalty is customer satisfaction regarding prices, services, and facilities. Moreover, the factor that influences employee and organizational performance is employee satisfaction with private healthcare human resource management (HRM) strategies. However, to accomplish the SDGs in this digital era, contemporary studies must incorporate concepts of sustainability that are integrated with digital technology or digital intelligence, which could improve sustainable private hospitals.

1.1 Research Question

What are the essentials of prices, services, and facilities affecting sustainable development in hospitals?

1.2 Research Objective

This chapter outlines the key aspects of prices, services, and facilities that impact sustainable development in hospitals, employing a systematic review (the PRISMA Method) and thematic analysis.

2. LITERATURE REVIEW

When it comes to hospitals, sustainable development involves striking a balance between economic, social, and environmental factors to ensure long-term viability and patient-centered care. When there is an emphasis placed on costs, services, and facilities, these aspects have a direct influence on the level of satisfaction experienced by patients and indirectly encourage patient loyalty.

2.1. Prices (Economic Sustainability)

Pricing that is both affordable and transparent fosters equity and accessibility, particularly for vulnerable populations. Pricing that is fair increases patient trust, particularly when it is combined with the patient's perception of value. It is possible that discontent and a reluctance to return could be the result of excessive or unclear costs. Sustainable hospitals manage their costs effectively in order to preserve quality without placing an undue burden on their patients. A reasonable pricing structure has a significant impact on customer satisfaction and loyalty. It enhances customer pleasure and fosters long-term partnerships by creating a perception of fairness (Siripipatthanakul, & Chana, 2021; Siripipatthanakul, 2022).

Customer satisfaction and loyalty are factors that influence prices, which in turn affect the potential for long-term profitability. In contrast, satisfaction is a more inclusive concept (personal). It is influenced by customer perceptions of service quality, product quality, price, and the situation, as well as personal factors (Djakarta et al., 2024). Additionally, it elucidates the relationship between price and customer satisfaction. Prices are considered flexible due to their ability to fluctuate in response to market developments. Including competitive prices in the market. Pricing is designed to generate revenue and sustain the organization; however, it may prove challenging to accomplish this objective amid stiff competition. Additionally, numerous objectives necessitate price determination, such as maximizing current profit, achieving maximum market share, and product-quality leadership, among others. Customer satisfaction is contingent upon price perceptions. One of the primary factors that contributes to the recognition and trust of products within the broader community is their quality. Consumers must also evaluate the quality of the service or product to be satisfied (Cahaya et al., 2023). In a restricted sense, price refers to the amount charged for a product or service. Price, taken more broadly, refers to the amount of money charged for a good or service. In a broader sense, the price is the sum of all the resources that customers contribute to obtain or utilize products or services. According to Ilyas and Mustafa (2022), the majority of customers are somewhat price-sensitive and prioritize other factors, including quality and trustworthiness.

Furthermore, price and cost can impact a hospital's quality of care in various ways. Furthermore, several critical design characteristics may impact the relationship between the quality of care and cost or price. Classifying the results based on predefined key attributes is therefore essential. Price fluctuations may also influence the quality of the hospital in various ways. Initially, the institutional learning effects of a price increase may result in a higher quality of care if hospitals increase their volume (Siciliani, 2014). Furthermore, increases in prices may permit hospitals to allocate additional funds (i.e., resources) toward service provision, which could potentially enhance the quality of care. Nevertheless, hospitals may be unable or unwilling to adjust their volume or resource input to maximize profits, resulting in a price change that does not affect the quality of care. When process measures are evaluated rather than outcome measures, the proportion of positive associations between cost/price and the quality of care is greater. Process measures may be more responsive to fluctuations in a hospital's cost or price and more indicative of the factors within the hospital's control than outcome measures (Jamalabadi et al., 2020). A reference pricing (RP) payment system has been suggested as a means of better aligning incentives and controlling the increasing costs of healthcare. This system encourages patients to utilize providers that charge lower prices. Reference pricing has been implemented for pharmacy benefits and has recently been extended to healthcare procedures. In addition, the availability of price and quality information has improved in recent years; however, many health services still lack transparency regarding their prices and quality. Numerous quality metrics are publicly accessible for a specific healthcare provider (Nassiri et al., 2022). Reference pricing offers several evident benefits. Proponents argue that it provides patients with the opportunity to choose a price-conscious provider while still offering access to a wide range of options. Additionally, the most expensive providers may be compelled to lower their prices to preserve their market share among price-sensitive patients (Nassiri et al., 2022).

Furthermore, prices can serve as an indicator of customer loyalty. A competitive price that caters to a wide range of demographics can lead to customer satisfaction. This satisfaction will foster customer loyalty, as consumers are more likely to make repeat purchases. If a consumer's expectations are reasonable, loyalty will be established when they are satisfied with the product or service. When consumers are content with a product, they develop loyalty. Consumer satisfaction is the result of the relationship between their expectations and the emotions they experience after consuming a product or service. Consumers are more likely to recommend products or services to others or use them again when they are satisfied (Sudirjo et al., 2023). The design of the chosen value will result in satisfaction, which is the feeling derived from comparing the actual performance of products or services received to what was expected. We can also understand customer satisfaction as a state in which the customer has either met or surpassed their expectations. Consumer satisfaction refers to the consumer's reaction to the discrepancy between their initial level of interest and the actual performance experienced after use (Behera et al., 2020). Customer satisfaction yields numerous advantages, including a harmonious relationship between the company and its customers (Luu, 2020). Consumer satisfaction provides a more solid foundation for repurchase. This fosters customer loyalty growth. This leads to the development of profitable word-of-mouth recommendations. The company's reputation is improving in the eyes of consumers, and there is potential for increased profit.

2.2 Services (Social Responsibility)

The provision of services, also known as social sustainability, encompasses clinical excellence, administrative support, responsiveness, and empathy. A significant factor in determining patient satisfaction is the provision of patient-centered care, which includes efficient communication and brief waiting periods. As part of the hospital's commitment to social responsibility, ethical procedures and ongoing service improvement are both important components. The impact of superior services on satisfaction and loyalty fosters the creation of trust and emotional connection, which in turn leads to increased patient retention and positive word-of-mouth. The general standard of perfection or superiority of a company's services is known as service quality. It entails fulfilling or surpassing customer expectations through various service delivery components, including reliability, responsiveness, assurance, empathy, and tangibles. The accuracy and promptness of service, the competence and behavior of employees, the effectiveness of problem resolution, and the overall customer experience are all factors that are used to evaluate service quality. Customer Satisfaction: Customer fulfillment is the perception that the goods or services received have met the customer's expectations (Siripipatthanakul, 2022; Singh et al., 2023).

Perceived service quality can be regarded as a mediating factor that promotes "satisfaction" and even enhances "intention," "retention," and "loyalty" in response to sensory stimuli. This theoretical perspective is substantiated by groundbreaking research that has verified the correlation between sensory appeal and brand loyalty, which is induced by satisfaction. A hospital's healthcare services are evaluated based on patient satisfaction, which is considered a critical criterion. Patient participation is a fundamental aspect of medical services, as the perceived quality of the service is influenced by the patient's symptoms and treatment course, which is a prerequisite for successful patient satisfaction. Analogous research has also indicated that the perception of medical services and patient satisfaction are two fundamental factors essential for enhancing service quality and the brand image of public hospitals (Tran et al., 2025). It measures the degree of satisfaction or joy that a customer experiences after engaging with a business. Satisfied customers feel that their needs and wants have been met or exceeded, and they see value in the products or services they received. Customer loyalty is influenced by various factors, including service quality, and is characterized by repeat purchase behavior, a higher customer lifetime value, and a significant contribution to the profitability and growth of the business. The quality of service influences customer satisfaction. Customers' requirements are promptly satisfied when they continue to receive personalized and timely assistance. Additionally, customer loyalty is contingent upon the quality of service. Customers who receive exceptional service are significantly more likely to maintain their association with an organization over time. They develop into devoted supporters who make subsequent purchases and endorse the organization to others (Siripipatthanakul, 2020; Siripipatthanakul, 2022; Singh et al., 2023).

Health services are valued for their ability to meet patients' needs. Consumer satisfaction has become increasingly significant as a quality indicator in numerous public sector services. The concept of quality of care, which is derived from patient satisfaction, pertains to the fulfillment of individual expectations and experiences, resulting in the identification of the service as qualitatively adequate (Alibrandi et al., 2023). Certain Asian studies have investigated the quality of outpatient services and patient satisfaction in private healthcare facilities by analyzing data obtained through questionnaires that assessed various aspects of healthcare. This dimension is associated with aspects such as clinic accessibility and basic facilities, including cleanliness, as well as staff professionalism, reliability, and ability to handle emergencies (Lescher & Sirven, 2019). The service has evolved from a simple delivery of services to individuals to one that is entirely patient-led, catering to the needs and desires of each individual. Patients seldom utilize technical quality information when selecting between hospitals; instead, they are more inclined to rely on subjective evaluations (such as word-of-mouth), and patient satisfaction serves as a proxy for these evaluations. The objective of logistic regression estimation is to determine the critical factors that must be considered when formulating strategies to enhance the quality of healthcare. Patients are empowered during this process, as they can express their satisfaction and actively participate in suggesting the dimensions that need to be improved to enhance the service (Alibrandi et al., 2023).

To satisfy the community's requirements, service innovation must be implemented, and patients and switchers must not abandon the hospital for other facilities. In the present day, patients prioritize healing when they visit the hospital; however, hospital services, which are advocates for the medication process, are acutely concerned. Sari et al. (2019) assert that hospitals lacking the necessary equipment to provide services will face competitive disadvantages in the market. The hospital's health services must be satisfactory to patients to encourage them to return. Riyanto (2018) has established a strong correlation between service quality and customer satisfaction. Customers will experience a sense of security and loyalty as a result of the high-quality service they receive. The hospital's ability to endure changes in the current environment is contingent upon the quality of its services. The quality of the service is perceived as good and satisfactory if it is received or felt as expected, according to Marnovita (2020). Patient satisfaction with the hospital's service delivery is evaluated through the concept of reliability. To augment the quantity of patient visits, both inpatient and outpatient, it is necessary to analyze patient satisfaction with hospital services (Utami et al., 2022).

The community now requires high-quality health services to ensure that health facilities are responsive to the health concerns of all members. To achieve the Sustainable Development Goals (SDGs), the third point of access to quality and equitable health services, it is imperative to enhance the quality of health services by strengthening facilities (Habibie et al., 2017). Hospital logistics is a sequence of operational design, planning, and implementation that encompasses the control of service activities, inventory management, and replenishment of goods in the provision of general and specialist patient health services (Moons et al., 2019). Customer service quality is the discrepancy between their expectations of service and their assessment of the service they receive. When the customer's expectations fall short of their perception of the service they receive, it is a welcome surprise. Customers will feel satisfied when their expectations and the way they perceive the service they receive align. Nevertheless, the customer is dissatisfied with the service when the customer's expectations exceed the perception of the service they receive (Ali et al., 2021b). The complexity of the issue of hospital service quality is not solely attributed to environmental factors and limited resources; it also results from discrepancies in perceptions among service users, healthcare professionals, and the government (Endeshaw, 2021). Patient satisfaction is a phenomenon that arises from the difference between the perceived service and the expected service. Furthermore, service quality is influenced by two primary factors: perceived service (the service received) and expected service (the service that was expected). If the service quality falls short of expectations, the patient will perceive it as unsatisfactory or inadequate. Consequently, the service's quality is contingent upon the provider's capacity to consistently meet the expectations of its users (Upadhyai et al., 2019). The level of patient satisfaction results from the performance of health services, which patients compare to their feelings. Patients will experience satisfaction when the quality of health services they receive meets or surpasses their expectations. Assessing patient satisfaction is beneficial for enhancing the quality of service. It is designed to assess the quality of service to enhance it. A wealth of critical data will be collected during the assessment of patient satisfaction, serving as a benchmark for activities designed to enhance the quality of service. Service quality and patient satisfaction are the primary factors that hospitals can leverage to enhance their business image, particularly private hospitals, and to promote profit growth (Ali et al., 2021a).

2.3. Facilities (Environmental Sustainability)

A hospital's dedication to well-being is reflected in the cleanliness, safety, and accessibility of its infrastructure (for example, green spaces, ventilation, and digital systems). The implementation of sustainable design principles, such as energy efficiency and waste minimization, not only enhances the patient experience but also aligns with broader environmental objectives. Facilities that are both contemporary and pleasant contribute to an increased sense of quality and safety. The impact of well-maintained facilities on happiness and loyalty is significant, as they lead to positive experiences that contribute to contentment and a desire to return (Siripipatthanakul, 2022; Chaiprakarn, 2022).

To enhance the quality of life in their community's environment, hospitals are obligated to provide quality and affordable health services (Gusti, Ardana, and Gede, 2014). The hospital's interior design is consistent with relevant standards. The Natural concept has the potential to create a natural and refreshing environment that is beneficial to all individuals, including patients, medical personnel, non-medical staff, and hospital visitors (Puspitasari et al., 2017). The selection of interior facilities in a hospital is expected to facilitate the circulation of health and administrative service delivery flows, while also transforming the intimidating image of the hospital into a welcoming environment by fostering a comfortable atmosphere and a sense of security for space users (Aljunid et al., 2020). The opportunity to meet in person is also a critical factor that must be taken into account, under the characteristics of the activities that must be conducted without compromising the hospital's security and confidentiality requirements. Additionally, there are expansive waiting areas and pathways that provide direct and indirect access to the lobby from other areas. The quality of the hospital's adaptation to the diverse needs and demands of its visitors can be evaluated through the use of such an interior design model (Aljunid et al., 2020). The primary determinant of satisfaction in health services is the presence of healing, as well as the quality of service provided by friendly, polite staff and the completeness of facilities, in addition to the quality of the results achieved in overcoming health problems. Furthermore, the physical hospital directly correlates with the quality of medical services. A well-designed building will not only offer the wearer comfort, but it will also influence the level of utilization, which in turn will contribute to the healing process of patients and employee performance. A high-quality building will also guarantee the implementation of medical service procedures. The hospital's health services are expected to be optimized by implementing the concept within its interior, in addition to enhancing the quality of service (Exposto et al., 2023). Therefore, the focus is on the comfort aspect. The dimensions of the space and the ceiling height are essential for determining the concept of the selected space. Additionally, past experiences, comments from relatives, and information from various media sources can influence customer expectations. Satisfied customers tend to remain with the organization for an extended period, exhibit reduced price sensitivity, and provide favorable feedback. Although health services have consistently delivered the same level of service to all patients, the degree of satisfaction may vary (Supartiningsih, 2017).

"Everything that is physical equipment and is provided by service vendors to support consumer convenience" is the definition of facilities. To ascertain service facilities, it is necessary to evaluate the facility indicator, which comprises numerous components. This term, "space designer," encompasses interior and architectural planning, including the placement of furniture and equipment within the room, the design of circulation flow, and other factors, such as the placement of meeting rooms, which must be accounted for in addition to their capacity (Wulansari et al., 2022). Subsequently, graphic messages were a critical component of a facility, and they were associated with the following elements: visual appearance, placement, selection of physical form, color selection, lighting, and sign form selection for specific purposes. Furthermore, partial consideration or planning, which encompasses elements such as textures, colors, and proportions, must be taken into account, combined, and enhanced to elicit intellectual and emotional responses from the user or viewer (Wulansari et al., 2022).

Thus, hospitals not only fulfill their ethical and environmental responsibilities by incorporating sustainable practices in pricing, service delivery, and facility management, but they also create an environment that fosters holistic care. This alignment results in increased patient satisfaction, which in turn fosters patient loyalty. It is a crucial component of long-term hospital success and a significant factor in community trust.

3. METHODOLOGY

To organize the information known about the practical aspects of curriculum, assessment, student experience, educational leadership, and educational technologies in a manner that is reproducible, valid, and understandable, systematic literature reviews provide a mechanism. Nevertheless, published reviews frequently convey a description of the knowledge included in the sample of studies as being based on a rigorous process. This is because reviews are reviews, regardless of whether they are poorly worded or have methodological flaws. Following evidence synthesis best practices, this study outlines five key areas where writers often fail: developing scoped, answer-oriented processes, including PRISMA flow diagrams and clear inclusion/exclusion criteria; and using trustworthy and replicable data sources; developing scoped, answerable, and aligned research questions; developing transparent, valid, and replicable search strategies using Boolean logic, truncation, and multiple databases; developing systematic screening and selection processes, including PRISMA flow diagrams and clear inclusion/exclusion criteria; and using trustworthy and replicable data sources.

According to the modified PRISMA method by Asrifan et al. (2025), Siripipatthanakul, S., & Siripipattanakul (2025a, b, c), the PRISMA METHOD was adopted in this systematic review in four steps:

Step 1: ***Identifying the Problem*** - Early entries can be found by manual searches, literature databases, or other ways. Randomly selecting the topic was the first step in this investigation. The linked article has 388 papers.

Step 2: ***Screening*** - This phase displays the remaining records after duplicates have been removed. At this stage, acknowledged record titles and abstracts are evaluated for relevance to the study's topic or goals. The second phase comprised purposeful sampling of academic papers from Google Scholar, Scopus, and Web of Science. This phase chose 97 articles.

Step 3: ***Eligibility -*** This section outlines the amount of research that is possible after screening. Essential information articles are evaluated for eligibility in this step. In Phase Three, 56 papers were selected for systematic evaluation using purposive sampling. The selected papers used AI, Grammarly, Turnitin, and Word Cloud terminology from 2021 to 2025.

Step 4: ***Inclusions:*** This stage shows the total systematic review analysis studies. These studies meet eligibility requirements for future research. The flow graphic shows how much research was discontinued at each point and why. Lack of relevance to the research subject, poor study design, lack of data, or inclusion criteria are common causes for exclusion. The fourth phase was processed by three academic experts using PRISMA. Content analysis proved the systematic review was accurate.

4. RESULTS

4.1 Conceptual Model for Sustainable Private Hospitals

Figure 1. The Conceptual Model

Table 1. Factors or Determinants

Models/ Components	Founders	References
Service Quality Model (tangibility, responsiveness, reliability, assurance, empathy)	Parasuraman Model	Zeithaml, B., & Parasuraman (1996). Siripipatthanakul (2021); Kanyama et al. (2022)
Hospitality Management Model (prices, services, facilities)	Siripipatthanakul Model (Dr. Ake's Model)	Siripipatthanakul,(2022); Siripipattanakul et al. (2022); Chaiprakarn, S. (2022)
7Ps Model (product, process, price, physical evidence, people, promotion, place)	Booms & Bitner	Siripipatthanakul & Puttharak (2021);
4Ps Model (product, price, promotion, place)	Jerry McCarthy & Phil Kotler	The model of Jerry McCarthy & Phil Kotler.
4Cs Model (cost, convenience, communication, customer)	Bob Lauterborn	The model of Bob Lauterborn.

Table 2. Mediator

Models/ Components	Founders	References
Customer Satisfaction Or patient satisfaction	Not Applicable	Siripipatthanakul (2020) Siripipatthanakul(2022); Siripipattanakul et al. (2022); Chaiprakarn, S. (2022)

Table 3. The Outcome Variable

Models/ Components	Founders	References
Customer Loyalty (or Behavioral Intention or patient loyalty)	Not Applicable	Siripipatthanakul (2020) Siripipatthanakul,(2022); Siripipattanakul et al. (2022); Chaiprakarn, S. (2022)

4.2 Word Clouds

Figure 2. Word Clouds

https://www.wordclouds.com/ (July 3, 2025)

4.3 Plagiarism Result

Three experts have validated the content of this chapter. Moreover, grammar was proved using Grammarly (premium version) and confirmed by an English expert. The appropriateness of grammar is more than 95% (excluding references), and plagiarism is 4%. Thus, this chapter is suitable for publication.

5. DISCUSSIONS

Increasing public awareness of the significance of health has an impact on the provision of health services by hospitals. To sustain their business, hospitals must implement an effective strategy to attract new customers and retain existing ones, thereby offering high-quality health services. The hospital is a healthcare institution that serves the community, and its characteristics are influenced by the community's socio-economic life, technological advancements, and the development of health-care science. Consequently, the hospital must continue to provide high-quality, affordable services to ensure that the district achieves the highest level of health (Apria et al., 2023).

The right business strategy for hospitals, particularly private, profit-oriented healthcare service providers, has been necessitated by intense competition and technological advancements. This strategy must consider the factors that can drive consumer loyalty and satisfaction. They are aware that a sustainable relationship between brands and customer loyalty requires more than just satisfaction, as evidenced by the assertion that efforts to cultivate customer loyalty are not solely focused on consumer satisfaction or dissatisfaction with the products or services they have acquired. In this instance, the success of service provider institutions is contingent upon good relationships with patients, who are the customers. Manthiou et al. define brand love as the emotional attachment of passionate consumers who are satisfied with a trading name. Several product or service elements, such as extraordinary quality, self-representing identity, positive influence obtained, natural fit, intrinsic appreciation, and emotional attachment to thoughts due to frequent use of services, can be used by consumers to find brand love (Apria et al., 2023).

The hospital is a location where service providers operate, and the services they offer must be capable of meeting the desires and requirements of customers. This phenomenon is because the services are essentially intangible and do not generate any ownership rights; instead, they can only be perceived as a taste or impression by the customer. This illustrates that pricing is one of the factors that contribute to dissatisfied customers. When the price of a product or service is reasonable in comparison to the value it provides, customers are more likely to be satisfied. The customer will move to a competitor if they are unhappy with the service they receive from the company. These actions will result in a decrease in sales, which will further diminish the firm's profits and could even lead to a loss (Mursyid et al., 2022).

The healthcare industry is placing a significant emphasis on patient satisfaction and quality of service, and this issue is being incorporated into their strategic planning process. Patients' perceptions of specific healthcare organizations' services, along with patient loyalty and word of mouth, influence the hospital's image and profitability. Additionally, healthcare professionals were compelled to identify the primary factors contributing to patient satisfaction in order to enhance healthcare services and assist service providers in reducing the time and money spent on addressing patient complaints due to the increasing expectations of service quality (Mgaya et al., 2024). Developing and maintaining positive relationships with patients is crucial for attaining the highest level of patient satisfaction. This goal can be achieved by delivering exceptional care that consistently surpasses or meets patients' expectations. Service quality is determined by how well and accurately customers' needs and wants are met. The service quality is acceptable and satisfactory when it is received or perceived as expected. The quality of service is considered an ideal standard when it meets or exceeds customer expectations (Mursyid et al., 2022).

Hospitals are responsible for enhancing health services to facilitate recovery and healing, with a focus on patient satisfaction and comfort. The primary determinant of satisfaction in health services is the presence of healing, as well as the quality of service provided by friendly, polite staff and the completeness of facilities, in addition to the quality of the results achieved in overcoming health problems. Hospitals, as part of the healthcare system, have a responsibility to enhance the quality of patient care by providing comprehensive facilities and delivering timely, accurate services. To ensure patient satisfaction, it is imperative to implement higher standards for the maintenance of hospital services, which encompass the quality of health services and facilities, to satisfy patients or the community. If the health services provided or the facilities offered meet the expectations of new patients, they will experience satisfaction. Therefore, patient satisfaction is a measure of the emotions generated by the comparison between the performance of health services and the patient's expectations (Exposto et al., 2023).

It is crucial to enhance the quality of the services provided, as service quality can be an effective strategy for gaining a competitive edge. Patient satisfaction can be fostered by the enhancement of service quality, which in turn will encourage patients to continue utilizing the hospital's services in the future. Hospitals, as healthcare facilities, play a critical role in the advancement of health. Andarini (2020) posits that patient satisfaction is influenced by service quality. Such an outcome indicates that the hospital's services are of high quality, which will result in patient satisfaction. In addition to enhancing the quality of service, hospitals must also take into account the facilities they provide. By establishing a high-quality facility, hospitals can bolster the quality of their services. Additionally, the quality of services offered by existing facilities and the prices that patients can afford to pay can be used to determine patient satisfaction. These are all factors that can contribute to patient satisfaction with hospital services (Itasia, 2021, and Perceka, 2020).

Furthermore, patient satisfaction was an evaluation or assessment that determined whether the selected service met or exceeded expectation after it was used. Patients were consumers of a service provided by a health company, such as a hospital (Wulansari et al., 2022). The quality of the service is perceived as good and satisfactory if the service received or felt is as expected, according to Marnovita (2020). These five dimensions of service quality—physical evidence, reliability, responsiveness, assurance, and empathy—will enhance customer trust and loyalty when implemented in the business environment. Satisfaction is significantly influenced by all components of service quality, according to some researchers. Nevertheless, it is not always the case that all service quality dimensions have the same impact on patient satisfaction (PS), patient loyalty (PL), word of mouth (WOM), and behavioral intention (BI) (AlOmari, 2022). Furthermore, patient satisfaction was significantly positively impacted by the initial impression of the service, clinical care, nurse care, quality of communication, housekeeping, food services, and overall service experience. Additionally, priority should be given to expenditures on enhancing cleaning practices, as is the case with medical equipment and medications. The clinical facilities were the most dissatisfying area, as half of the respondents believed that the medical equipment was outdated and that there were insufficient beds, which created a negative impression. In a previous study, we demonstrated that the tangible dimension was instrumental in compensating for deficiencies in other service quality dimensions (AlOmari, 2020).

Jerome McCarthy, a marketing professor from the United States, initially developed the concept of the "4 Ps" of marketing.

In 1960, McCarthy proposed a model consisting of four Ps. In 1981, Booms and Bitner modified this model to include 7Ps in order to cater to the requirements of the service sector. The term "sustainable hospitals" refers to healthcare facilities that operate in a manner that minimizes their negative impact on the environment, maximizes the positive social results, and ensures the long-term economic viability of the facility in terms of sustainability. The concept of "going green" encompasses a more comprehensive approach to the provision of medical care than just "going green."

The following is an explanation of hospitals that are sustainable in terms of their prices, services, and facilities: Prices, Services, and Facilities of Hospitals That Are Financially Sustainable.

5.1. Prices (Economic Sustainability)

The goal of sustainable hospitals is to achieve financial longevity and cost-effectiveness, not just for the hospital itself but also for patients and the healthcare system as a whole. Frequently, this entails...

Efficiency in Energy Use & Cost Reductions Due to Increased Productivity: There is a significant reduction in operational expenses when investments are made in energy-efficient lighting (LEDs), intelligent heating and cooling systems, and renewable energy sources (solar panels, geothermal). It is common knowledge that hospitals consume a significant amount of energy; thus, these savings can be tremendous.

Recycling and Waste Reduction: The implementation of comprehensive waste management programs, which include recycling, composting, and the reprocessing of single-use medical devices in situations where it is safe and practical, results in a significant reduction in the costs associated with disposal. Due to the substantial amount of waste generated by hospitals, this sector presents an essential opportunity for financial gain. To reduce water usage and associated utility bills, water conservation measures such as the use of low-flow fixtures, adequate irrigation, and rainwater harvesting are implemented. A higher value and lower long-term costs can be achieved through sustainable procurement by selecting suppliers who place a priority on sustainability and provide environmentally friendly products (for example, recycled content and non-toxic materials). This can be accomplished by reducing the amount of money spent on hazardous material handling or by extending the lifespan of items. When it comes to optimizing resource use, streamlining processes, avoiding redundant tests and procedures, and enhancing inventory management can lead to significant cost savings by reducing the amount of material used and the amount of waste produced. Sustainable hospitals develop a more resilient financial future by lowering their reliance on fluctuating fossil fuel prices and avoiding environmental hazards. This allows for long-term economic viability. Additionally, they can attract financial backing and investment from organizations that prioritize environmental, social, and governance (ESG) factors. The value-based healthcare approach emphasizes enhancing patient outcomes about the expenses incurred in providing medical care. The integration of cost-effectiveness and high-quality care is a hallmark of sustainable hospitals. This is typically accomplished through preventative care, early diagnosis, and efficient care pathways that limit the need for more expensive and intensive treatments. A reduction in regulatory penalties can be achieved by adhering to environmental standards and implementing preventive measures to minimize pollution. This can help avoid expensive fines and litigation.

5.2. Services (Social Sustainability and Patient Outcomes)

Sustainable hospitals take into account the health and happiness of its patients, employees, and the community at large, while also ensuring that they provide comprehensive medical care of the highest possible standard.

Increased Quality of Care and Health for Patients: The use of non-toxic building materials, the improvement of indoor air quality, and the expansion of access to natural light and green areas can all contribute to a healthier environment, which in turn can speed up the recovery process for patients, reduce stress, and increase overall patient satisfaction.

Reduced Exposure to Harmful Substances: A safer atmosphere for patients and staff can be created by minimizing the use of hazardous chemicals and materials in cleaning, medical procedures, and building maintenance. Community Health: Hospitals contribute to cleaner air and water in the communities surrounding them by reducing their environmental footprint. This, in turn, leads to improved public health outcomes and may also result in a decrease in the incidence of diseases associated with environmental factors. Resilience: Sustainable hospitals are better equipped to deal with environmental catastrophes and natural disasters, ensuring that patients continue to receive care even in the event of catastrophic events.

Improved Staff Satisfaction and Retention: Emphasizing staff well-being, which may include healthier work conditions, access to green spaces, and a commitment to ethical practices, can lead to increased staff morale, reduced rates of burnout, and lower turnover rates. As a result, this has the potential to enhance the quality of care. The goal of sustainable healthcare is to eliminate health disparities by ensuring that environmental benefits are shared across all communities, particularly vulnerable groups, who are frequently disproportionately affected by environmental pollution. Equitable access to care is one of the ways that sustainable healthcare works to achieve this goal. The adoption of telemedicine, robotics, and other digital health solutions can minimize the need for patients to travel, thereby reducing emissions. Additionally, this can increase efficiency, which in turn makes healthcare more accessible and potentially less expensive. Prevention and Wellness: Emphasizing preventive care and health promotion can help keep individuals healthy and out of hospitals, thereby reducing the overall demand for treatments that require significant resources.

5.3. Infrastructure (including environmental sustainability and infrastructure)

Both the physical infrastructure and the operational features of a hospital are significant to the hospital's capacity to remain operational over time. Incorporating passive solar design, appropriate insulation, and efficient heating, ventilation, and air conditioning systems to reduce energy consumption exemplifies energy-efficient design in green building design and construction. In the context of construction and remodeling, the term “sustainable materials” refers to the utilization of materials that are supplied locally, recyclable, rapidly renewable, and low in volatile organic compound (VOC) content. Implementing water-saving technologies, such as rainwater harvesting, greywater recycling, and efficient landscaping, is an example of these technologies. Infrastructure for waste management entails the design of facilities designated explicitly for waste segregation, recycling, and composting trash. Solar panels, wind turbines, and geothermal systems installed on-site are examples of renewable energy integration. These systems are designed to minimize reliance on fossil fuels and reduce carbon emissions. Advanced Waste Management Systems: This encompasses technological advancements, such as microwave sterilization for medical waste, as well as initiatives to facilitate the use of single-use plastics and other items. Recycling is just one component of this system. The use of water-efficient medical equipment, water-saving water meters, and leak detection systems is a critical component of efficient water systems. The utilization of native plants, the reduction of water-intensive lawns, and the creation of green spaces that promote biodiversity and offer therapeutic benefits are all examples of sustainable landscaping. Innovative building technologies utilize sensors and data analytics to optimize energy and water usage, monitor indoor air quality, and enhance operational efficiency. Transportation solutions include encouraging environmentally responsible commuting for both employees and patients (for example, providing bike storage, charging stations for electric vehicles, and incentives for public transportation) and optimizing the hospital's fleet of cars. In essence, sustainable hospitals are not only concerned with environmental protection; they also represent a fundamental shift in the way healthcare is delivered. The goal of these hospitals is to establish a system that is economically viable, socially responsible, and environmentally conscious, benefiting both the current generation and future generations.

6. CONCLUSIONS

This notion emphasizes that for a hospital to be sustainable, it must take into consideration the interconnection of its financial viability (prices), the quality and accessibility of its offers (services), and the environmental and operational efficiency of its infrastructure (facilities). For the sake of this discussion, sustainability is not limited to the concept of ecological "greenness," but rather encompasses the idea of long-term viability across economic, social, and environmental dimensions. This is how each component contributes to the whole.

Sustainable private hospitals strike a balance between affordability, high-quality services, and efficient facilities, ensuring long-term viability and patient satisfaction. By harmonizing competitive pricing with superior care and contemporary facilities, these hospitals enhance accessibility while maintaining profitability. Investments in sustainable technologies, digital infrastructure, and patient-centric services reduce environmental impact while enhancing operational efficiency. This methodology promotes sustainability by integrating economic performance with social responsibility and environmental stewardship.

6.1. Prices (Sustainability of the Global Economy)

Affordability and Fair Pricing: To remain in business, hospitals must have pricing models that enable patients to receive medical care without placing them in a difficult financial position. It is possible that this could incorporate tiered pricing, transparent billing, or programs that provide financial aid. By ensuring the hospital can cover its operational costs, invest in improvements, and remain financially sustainable in the long term, cost-effectiveness can be achieved through efficient pricing. Having pricing that is both competitive and fair, while also reflecting the value of the services being offered, is what this means. It does not necessarily mean having the lowest costs. income Generation for Reinvestment: Hospitals are able to reinvest in better facilities, advanced technology, and staff training when they generate sufficient income through pricing. This helps to ensure the institution's continued quality and viability over the long term.

6.2. Accessibility and Equity Services (Social Sustainability)

Sustainable hospitals prioritize offering services that are both affordable and easily accessible to all members of the community, regardless of their socioeconomic status or proximity to the hospital. This encompasses efforts such as outreach campaigns, telemedicine, and care that is sensitive to cultural norms. By providing high-quality services, patients can achieve better outcomes, which in turn fosters trust and ensures that the hospital remains a vital and valued resource for the community. Providing patients with access to a wide range of essential services can help limit their need to seek medical attention elsewhere, thereby contributing to the hospital's role as a central pillar of community health. Community well-being benefits sustainable hospitals, which often extend their services beyond direct medical and dental care to address the broader determinants of health in their community. These determinants include health education, prevention programs, and partnerships aimed at addressing social issues.

6.3. Infrastructure Facilities (Environmental sustainability perspective)

Efficient resource use is achieved through the design and operation of sustainable facilities, which aim to minimize the consumption of energy, water, and other resources. This encompasses water-saving fixtures, waste reduction programs, and energy-efficient lighting, as well as heating, ventilation, and air conditioning (HVAC) systems. Environmental impact reduction involves minimizing pollution as much as possible, handling waste in an environmentally responsible manner (particularly medical waste), and potentially utilizing renewable energy sources. Efficiency in Operations: Well-designed and well-maintained facilities contribute to the effective delivery of services, which in turn reduces operating costs and improves workflow for workers. This may include the utilization of technology, the optimization of layouts, and the efficient management of supply chains. Resilience sustainable facilities are often designed to be more resistant to environmental changes and disturbances, ensuring that patients continue to receive care even when the environment is subject to change. The following are the primary objectives of a hospital that is committed to sustainable development based on these three pillars: Take care of your finances so that you can continue to serve the community. Provide high-quality, easily accessible, and equitable services to improve the community's health. Perform your operations in a manner that is both resource-efficient and ecologically friendly. For hospitals to maintain their long-term sustainability and have a positive impact on the communities they serve, they must strike a balance and integrate all three categories.

7. IMPLICATION

A lack of a systematic way to price self-pay treatments is the private hospitals' most significant challenge. Pricing decisions often depend on legacy or gut emotion rather than strategy and evidence. This means stakeholders rely on intuition and historical pricing lists without considering patient value and market trends. Mergers and acquisitions of hospital sites complicate such difficulties. Branch processes mainly depend on local skills, pricing, and profitability interests. Private hospitals compete with each other and do not share best practices. Transparency and structure in self-pay pricing can have immediate and long-term economic benefits. Price levels do not accurately reflect the value of the process and provider, or local differences across sites, due to the lack of a clear self-pay pricing policy. Private healthcare has historically been a prominent component of the healthcare system. In contrast to public healthcare, private systems do not depend on public financing or governmental restrictions. They function autonomously through direct payments, insurance, and employer-sponsored plans. Although the private health system may not suit everyone, executives, employers, and corporate leaders typically opt for it due to its customization, superior quality, and efficiency. These represent merely the surface of the system's advantages. The incorporation of concierge healthcare services has transformed the private healthcare sector into a premium, customized medical experience, featuring on-demand physician access, care coordination, and targeted preventive health initiatives for busy professionals. This guide to private healthcare systems will explore its structure, advantages, and prospects. Expedited access to specialists, personalized care, and innovative therapies are among the numerous benefits of private healthcare systems. Nonetheless, they possess disadvantages, particularly regarding accessibility and cost. Understanding the private healthcare system, including its providers, cost structures, and additional features, is essential for making an informed decision. One of the most effective methods to optimize private healthcare benefits is to integrate them with concierge medicine services. They provide round-the-clock global access to credentialed physicians, customized health plans, care coordination, and additional services. Thus, the customer (patient) satisfaction with the services, prices, and facilities of private hospitals is crucial for their survival in the competitive environment and sustainable development in this sector.

8. LIMITATIONS AND RECOMMENDATIONS

This chapter presents a systematic review of previous studies in thematic analysis examining customer (patient) satisfaction and loyalty about prices, services, and facilities. This analysis may not include respondents. Thus, questionnaire surveys and interviews are recommended for further studies to set the appropriate strategies. Research could benefit the healthcare sector in both the private and public sectors.

REFERENCES

Ali, B. J., Gardi, B., Othman, B. J., Ahmed, S. A., Ismael, N. B., Hamza, P. A., Aziz, H. M., Sabir, B. Y., Sorguli, S., & Anwar, G. (2021a). Hotel service quality: The impact of service quality on customer satisfaction in hospitality. *International Journal of Engineering Business Management*, *5*(3), 14–28. DOI: 10.22161/ijebm.5.3.2

Ali, B. J., Saleh, P. F., Akoi, S., Abdulrahman, A. A., Muhamed, A. S., Noori, H. N., & Anwar, G. (2021b). Impact of service quality on the customer satisfaction: Case study at online meeting platforms. *International Journal of Engineering Business Management*, *5*(2), 65–77. DOI: 10.22161/ijebm.5.2.6

Alibrandi, A., Gitto, L., Limosani, M., & Mustica, P. F. (2023). Patient satisfaction and quality of hospital care. *Evaluation and Program Planning*, *97*, 102251. DOI: 10.1016/j.evalprogplan.2023.102251 PMID: 36806007

Aljunid, S. S., Huda Mohamad Shukri, N. N., Mohd Taib, M. Z., & Samah, Z. A.Shariffah Syafiqah AljunidNurul Nabilah Huda Mohamad ShukriMohd Zafrullah Mohd TaibZanariah Abu Samah. (2020). Determinants of Patient Satisfaction on Interior Design Quality of Public Hospitals in Malaysia. *Malaysian Journal of Public Health Medicine*, *20*(2), 233–241. DOI: 10.37268/mjphm/vol.20/no.2/art.800

AlOmari, F. (2020). Measuring Gaps in Healthcare Quality Using SERVQUAL Model: Challenges and Opportunities in Developing Countries. *Measuring Business Excellence*. DOI: 10.1108/MBE-11-2019-0104

AlOmari, F. (2022). The mediating role of hospital image: The impact of care cost and service quality on patient satisfaction. *Journal of Innovation in Business and Economics*, *6*(01), 1–16. DOI: 10.22219/jibe.v6i01.18475

Andarini, R. (2020). The Influence of Services Quality to Patients Satisfaction at National Brain Center Hospital. *Institutional Repository of* Bakrie University. https://repository.bakrie.ac.id/4383/

Asrifan, A., Siripipatthanakul, S., Alaqad, M. H., Saodi, S., & Sadaruddin, S. (2025). Managing Privacy and Security in Research: Effective Practices and Strategies. In *Privacy and Security Management Practices for Organizations* (pp. 151-182). IGI Global Scientific Publishing. DOI: 10.4018/979-8-3693-9720-6.ch006

Behera, R. K., Gunasekaran, A., Gupta, S., Kamboj, S., & Bala, P. K. (2020). Personalized digital marketing recommender engine. *Journal of Retailing and Consumer Services*, *53*, 101799. https://doi.org/https://doi.org/10.1016/j.jretconser.2019.03.026. DOI: 10.1016/j.jretconser.2019.03.026

Cahaya, Y. F., Siswanti, I., Putra, Y. M., & Pattiwael, A. C. (2023). Contributions to Customer Satisfaction from Product Quality, Promotion and Price. *Journal of Economics. Finance and Management Studies*, *6*(6), 2434–2440.

Candio, P. (2024). *Sustainability and Corporate Performance in Health Care.* Springer., DOI: 10.1007/978-3-031-63985-2

Chaiprakarn, S. (2022). The Impact of Prices, Services and Facilities on Customer Satisfaction at Drug Stores in Thailand. *PROCEEDING: Volume 1 No. 2 2023*, 304.

Chiu, W. K., & Fong, B. Y. F. (2023). Environmental, social and governance and sustainable development in healthcare. *Recent trends of research and education in ESG and sustainability*, 99-112. https://doi.org/DOI: 10.1007/978-981-99-1564-4

Crawford, J. (2025). Systematic Literature Reviews: Why I Rejected Your Review. *Journal of University Teaching & Learning Practice*, *22*(2). DOI: 10.53761/10vb5076

Dion, H., & Evans, M. (2024). Strategic frameworks for sustainability and corporate governance in healthcare facilities; approaches to energy-efficient hospital management. *Benchmarking*, *31*(2), 353–390. DOI: 10.1108/BIJ-04-2022-0219

Djakaria, H., Yani, D. A., Wibowo, T. S., & Iswadi, U. (2024). Effect of Price, Location, And Service Quality on onsumer Satisfaction.b 5(1), 548–558. https://journal.yrpipku.com/index.php/msej/article/view/4074/2289

Endeshaw, B. (2021). Healthcare service quality-measurement models: A review. *Warasan Wichai Witthayasat Kanphaet*, *35*(2), 106–117. DOI: 10.1108/JHR-07-2019-0152

Exposto, L. A. S., Mulyati, M. I., Magno, J., & Carvalho, M. (2023). Choosing Service Facilities In The Hospital Interior To Increase Patient Satisfaction. *Asian Journal of Healthy and Science*, *2*(5), 213–224. DOI: 10.58631/ajhs.v2i5.46

Gusti, O. I., Ardana, N., & Gede, A. A. (2014). Interior Lobi Rumah Sakit yang Didesain Berdasarkan Kebijakan Sistem Pelayanan. *Jurnal Seni Dan Pendidikan Seni*, 1–10.

Habibie, W. L., Hardjosoekarto, S., & Kasim, A. (2017). Health reform in Indonesia towards sustainable development growth (Case study on BPJS Kesehatan, health insurance in Indonesia). *Review of Integrative Business and Economics Research*, *6*(3), 375–383. http://buscompress.com/journal-home.html

Hussey, P. S., Wertheimer, S., & Mehrotra, A. (2013). The association between health care quality and cost: A systematic review. *Annals of Internal Medicine*, *158*(1), 27–34. DOI: 10.7326/0003-4819-158-1-201301010-00006 PMID: 23277898

Ilyas, G. B., & Mustafa, H. (2022). Price, Promotion, and Supporting Facilities on Customer Satisfaction. *Golden Ratio of Marketing and Applied Psychology of Business, 2*(1), 01-11.

Jamalabadi, S., Winter, V., & Schreyögg, J. (2020). A systematic review of the association between hospital cost/price and the quality of care. *Applied Health Economics and Health Policy, 18*(5), 625–639. DOI: 10.1007/s40258-020-00577-6 PMID: 32291700

Kanyama, J., Nurittamont, W., & Siripipatthanakul, S. (2022). Hotel service quality and its effect on customer loyalty: The case of Ubon Ratchathani, Thailand during COVID-19 Pandemic. *Journal of Management in Business. Health Care Education, 1*(2), 1–20. https://papers.ssrn.com/sol3/papers.cfm?abstract_id=4004388

Leal Filho, W., Lisovska, T., Fedoruk, M., & Taser, D. (2023). Medical waste management and the UN Sustainable Development Goals in Ukraine: An assessment of solutions to support post-war recovery efforts. *Environmental Challenges, 13*, 100763. DOI: 10.1016/j.envc.2023.100763

Lescher, M., & Sirven, N. (2019). Healthcare quality, patients' satisfaction, and hospital incentives in France. Revue d' ´economie politique. *Dalloz, 129*, 525–551.

Luu, T. T. (2020). Linking authentic leadership to salespeople's service performance: The roles of job crafting and human resource flexibility. *Industrial Marketing Management, 84*, 89–104. https://doi.org/https://doi.org/10.1016/j.indmarman.2019.06.002. DOI: 10.1016/j.indmarman.2019.06.002

Marnovita. 2020. Hubungan kualitas pelayanan dengan kepuasan pelanggan. *Jurnal Ilmiah Psikologi* 8(1):100-106.

Mgaya, T. W., & Gwahula, R. (2024). The Effect of Service Quality on Customer Satisfaction at St. Joseph Referral Hospital-Peramiho, Tanzania. *European Journal of Theoretical and Applied Sciences, 2*(2), 223–233. DOI: 10.59324/ejtas.2024.2(2).19

Moons, K., Waeyenbergh, G., & Pintelon, L. (2019). Measuring the logistics performance of internal hospital supply chains – A literature study. *Omega, 82*, 205–217. DOI: 10.1016/j.omega.2018.01.007

Mursyid, P., Maidin, A., & Syamsuddin, S. (2022). The influence of price, service quality and relationship marketing on patient satisfaction in the outpatient installation of the haji hospital, South Sulawesi province. *Journal of Asian Multicultural Research for Medical and Health Science Study, 3*(2), 59–68. DOI: 10.47616/jamrmhss.v3i2.292

Nassiri, S., Adida, E., & Mamani, H. (2022). Reference pricing for healthcare services. *Manufacturing & Service Operations Management*, *24*(2), 921–937. DOI: 10.1287/msom.2021.0986

Perceka, A. L. (2020). Quality of Nursing Services with Patient Satisfaction in the Emergency Room at RSUD Dr. Slamet Garut. *Scientific Journal of Public Administration*, *6*(2). DOI: 10.21776/ub.jiap.2020.006.02.14

Puspitasari, D. A., Anggraeni, A. W., & Rachmaniyah, N. (2017). 140321-ID-desain-interior-ruang-inap-dan-fasilitas. *Jurnal Sains Dan Seni ITS, 6*(1).

Putri, I. Ivana. (2021). The Relationship between Nurse Performance and Patient Satisfaction in an Inpatient Room. *Faculty of Health Repository Sari Mulia University*.http://repository.unism.ac.id/id/eprint/2010

Singh, V., Sharma, M. P., Jayapriya, K., Kumar, B. K., Chander, M. A. R. N., & Kumar, B. R. (2023). Service quality, customer satisfaction and customer loyalty: A comprehensive literature review. *Journal of Survey in Fisheries Sciences*, *10*(4S), 3457–3464.

Siripipattanakul, S., Siripipatthanakul, S., Limna, P., & Auttawechasakoon, P. (2022). Determinants of hotels' customer loyalty during the COVID-19 pandemic in Thailand. *Journal of Management Information and Decision Sciences*, *25*(4), 1–14. https://papers.ssrn.com/sol3/papers.cfm?abstract_id=4118267

Siripipatthanakul, S. (2020). Service Quality, Patient Satisfaction and Patient Loyalty in the Private Dental Care Sector: A Case of Smile Family Dental Clinic. *Graduate School of Advanced Technology Management* (Doctoral dissertation, ASSUMPTION UNIVERSITY OF THAILAND).

Siripipatthanakul, S. (2021). Service quality, patient satisfaction, word-of-mouth, and revisit intention in a dental clinic, Thailand. [IJTSRD]. *International Journal of Trend in Scientific Research and Development*, *5*(5), 832–841. https://papers.ssrn.com/sol3/papers.cfm?abstract_id=3910239

Siripipatthanakul, S. (2022). *Determinant Factors Influencing Patient Satisfaction and Patient Loyalty at Dental Clinics in Laem Chabang, Thailand* (Doctoral dissertation, Doctoral Dissertation (DBA), Manipal GlobalNxt University, Malaysia).

Siripipatthanakul, S., & Chana, P. (2021). Service marketing mix (7Ps) and patient satisfaction in clinics: A review article. [IJTSRD]. *International Journal of Trend in Scientific Research and Development*, *5*(5), 842–850.

Siripipatthanakul, S., & Phuangsuwan, P. (2024). Salutogenic Marketing in Preventive Dentistry. In *Leveraging Digital Technology for Preventive Dentistry* (pp. 255–278). IGI Global., DOI: 10.4018/979-8-3693-3872-8.ch009

Siripipatthanakul, S., & Puttharak, S. (2021). Marketing mix analysis in private dental healthcare service sector. [IJTSRD]. *International Journal of Trend in Scientific Research and Development*, *5*(5), 827–831. https://papers.ssrn.com/sol3/papers.cfm?abstract_id=3910242

Siripipatthanakul, S., & Siripipattanakul, S. (2025a). Talent Management Ensuring the Safety and Cybersecurity in Schools. *Cultivating Creativity and Navigating Talent Management in Academia*, 383-402. DOI: 10.4018/979-8-3693-6880-0.ch018

Siripipatthanakul, S., & Siripipattanakul, S. (2025b). Online Gambling of Higher Education Learners. In *International Academic Transformations and Cross-Border Collaborations* (pp. 377–400). IGI Global Scientific Publishing., DOI: 10.4018/979-8-3373-0508-0.ch01

Siripipatthanakul, S., & Siripipattanakul, S. (2025c). Rural Dental Health Transformation by Adopting Digital Technologies. *Transforming Dental Health in Rural Communities: Digital Dentistry*, 47-80. DOI: 10.4018/979-8-3693-7165-7.ch003

Siripipatthanakul, S., & Vui, C. N. (2021). A conceptual review on the mediating effect of patient satisfaction towards patient loyalty in the dental practice in Thailand. *International Journal of Behavioral Analytics*, *1*(2), 1–16.

Sudirjo, F., Violin, V., Abdullah, A., & Iswahyudi, M. S. (2023). The Effect of Promotion, E-Service Quality and Price on Customer Satisfaction and Its Implication on Loyalty of Tokopedia Customers. *JEMSI (Jurnal Ekonomi, Manajemen, dan Akuntansi)*, *9*(5), 1724-1728.

Supartiningsih, S. (2017). Kualitas Pelayanan an Kepuasan Pasien Rumah Sakit: Kasus Pada Pasien Rawat Jalan. *Jurnal Medicoeticolegal Dan Manajemen Rumah Sakit*, *6*(1), 9–15. DOI: 10.18196/jmmr.6122

Tran, V. A., Tran, Q. N., Doan, H. M., La, G. L., Vu, T. D., & Pham, T. H. (2025). How sensory marketing affects perceived service quality and customer satisfaction: Study in Vietnam public hospitals. *Journal of Health Organization and Management*, *39*(4), 568–583. DOI: 10.1108/JHOM-03-2024-0125 PMID: 39657827

Upadhyai, R., Jain, A. K., Roy, H., & Pant, V. (2019). A review of healthcare service quality dimensions and their measurement. *Journal of Health Management*, *21*(1), 102–127. DOI: 10.1177/0972063418822583

Wulansari, R., & Pratama, M. S. R. (2022). The Influence of Services Quality and Facilities on Patient Satisfaction at Wijaya Kusuma Hospital Lumajang, East Java. *Adpebi International Journal of Multidisciplinary Sciences*, *1*(1), 166–174. DOI: 10.54099/aijms.v1i1.254

Zeithaml, V. A., Berry, L. L., & Parasuraman, A. (1996). The behavioral consequences of service quality. *Journal of Marketing*, *60*(2), 31–46. DOI: 10.1177/002224299606000203

KEY TERMS AND DEFINITIONS

Sustainable Development: Sustainable development aims to meet present demands without compromising future needs. Sustainable development is to create a civilization where living conditions and resources meet human needs without harming the planet. Sustainable development balances economic, environmental, and social needs.

Sustainability: Sustainable development is closely aligned with the concept of sustainability, which is inherently normative in nature. UNESCO delineated a distinction between the two concepts: "Sustainability is frequently perceived as a long-term objective (i.e., a more sustainable world), whereas sustainable development pertains to the various processes and pathways to attain it."

Sustainability Dimensions: Sustainability often encompasses three dimensions: environmental, economic, and social. Numerous definitions underscore the environmental aspect. This may encompass addressing significant environmental issues, such as climate change and biodiversity decline. The concept of sustainability can inform decisions at all levels, from global to individual. A pertinent concept is sustainable development, which is often used interchangeably with the terms. UNESCO delineates the two concepts as follows: "Sustainability is frequently perceived as a long-term objective (i.e., a more sustainable world), whereas sustainable development pertains to the various processes and pathways to attain it."

Private Hospitals: A private hospital is not government-owned, encompassing both for-profit and non-profit institutions. Funding is provided by patients ("self-pay"), insurers, or foreign embassies. Private hospitals are typically integrated, to varying extents, into most healthcare systems globally.

Prices: "Price" occasionally denotes the amount of money solicited by a seller for products or services, rather than the final payment sum. In business, the desired amount is sometimes referred to as the offer price (or selling price), while the actual payment is termed the transaction price (or exchanged price). Private hospital prices are generally higher compared to public hospitals, owing to the use of superior medical technologies, reduced wait times, individualized treatment, and upscale amenities. Expenses fluctuate significantly depending on geographic location, area of expertise, and services rendered, with charges typically including consultations, diagnostics, pharmaceuticals, and inpatient care.

Private Hospital Services: Service is described as the act of assisting or performing tasks for another individual, typically for compensation or in return for something else. It involves providing assistance, support, or advice to others and is often aimed at fulfilling a particular need or want of the person being served. Typical instances of service encompass delivering medical care or dental services as a healthcare provider in the private hospital sector. Private hospital services encompass specialist medical treatment, advanced diagnostic procedures, elective surgical interventions, wellness initiatives, and round-the-clock emergency care. They frequently offer reduced wait times, personalized therapy, and enhanced amenities to promote patient comfort.

Private Hospital Facilities: Private hospital facilities often feature modern patient rooms, recovery rooms, operation rooms, dental department, advanced surgical devices, intensive care units (ICUs), diagnostic laboratories, imaging centers (including MRI and CT scans), pharmacies, waiting areas, parking facilities, restrooms, air conditioning systems, and other essential amenities. They focus on comfort, privacy, and high-tech medical support.

Patient Satisfaction: Patient satisfaction refers to the degree of contentment patients experience regarding the care, services, and overall experience provided by a healthcare facility, such as a hospital. It encompasses elements such as communication, quality of treatment, wait times, staff conduct, and comfort, which affect loyalty and the hospital's image.

Patient Loyalty: Patient loyalty refers to the probability of patients seeking subsequent care from the same hospital or healthcare provider. It is established via constant quality service, trust, happy experiences, and robust patient-provider connections.

Sustainable Development Goals (SDGs): The Division for Sustainable Development Goals (DSDG) within the United Nations Department of Economic and Social Affairs (UNDESA) offers substantial support and capacity-building for the Sustainable Development Goals (SDGs) and associated thematic areas, including water, energy, climate, oceans, urbanization, transport, science and technology, the Global Sustainable Development Report (GSDR), partnerships, and Small Island

Developing States. DSDG is crucial in assessing the UN system-wide execution of the 2030 Agenda and in conducting advocacy and outreach initiatives on the SDGs. To actualize the 2030 Agenda, widespread ownership of the SDGs must convert into a robust commitment from all stakeholders to execute the global objectives. DSDG seeks to promote this engagement.

Chapter 5
Healthcare Digitization and Sustainability of Penang Healthcare Providers:
A Case of Medical Tourism

Seng Loong (Stanley) Kok
https://orcid.org/0009-0006-0997-7960
Manipal GlobalNxt University, Gelugor, Malaysia

Patcharavadee Sriboonruang
https://orcid.org/0000-0002-2171-2387
Kasetsart University, Bangkok, Thailand

ABSTRACT

This chapter describes how Malaysian healthcare providers in Penang promote ESG-aligned sustainability through digital solutions. Digitalization improves operational efficiency, environmental performance, and patient-centered care, according to stakeholder theory, institutional theory, and the resource-based view. Digital tools like EMRs, AI-assisted diagnostics, blockchain-based records, and telemedicine platforms can improve healthcare delivery and system resilience, according to a PRISMA analysis of policy initiatives, institutional practices, and ESG principles. The findings show that Penang's healthcare providers encourage lowering of ecological footprints and administrative redundancies. The study identified technological inequalities, data governance challenges, and regulatory control difficulties, despite

DOI: 10.4018/979-8-3693-9800-5.ch005

achieving promising results. ESG performance, ethical digital stewardship, and cross-border health regulations need improvement. Policymakers, administrators, and global health strategists use the insights to promote sustainable digital health.

1. INTRODUCTION

1.1 Digitization on Medical Healthcare Sustainability

The impact of digitalisation and Environmental, Social, and Governance (ESG) considerations is increasingly complex and multi-dimensional, shaping the industry's sustainability, ethical responsibilities, operational efficiency, and firm performance; and healthcare is no exception (Kalia & Aggarwal, 2023; Leung & You, 2023; Leogrande, 2024). In 2020, the global COVID-19 pandemic became the catalytic force in accelerating digital transformation across global healthcare systems (Golinelli et al., 2020; Bhambere et al., 2021), prompting healthcare institutions to revamp service delivery through the lens of safety, scalability, and sustainability.

The digital transformation during the pandemic extended beyond administrative functions. Contactless technologies were integrated with automated appointment scheduling, symptom tracking, and EMR interoperability, enhancing both operational efficiency and patient satisfaction (Gendy & Yuce, 2022; Yadav, 2024). In Malaysia, due to social distancing protocols and the requirement to minimize physical contact and reduce nosocomial transmission risks, the rapid deployment of contactless registration systems, digital triage tools, and remote monitoring platforms was facilitated (Wang et al., 2021). These innovations were not merely responsive measures but marked a paradigm shift toward resilient, patient-centered care models (Tabeje & Klien, 2021; Lee & Lee, 2021).

In the context of sustainability, the integration of digitization into medical healthcare systems is increasingly recognized as a cornerstone of sustainable development, offering a multidimensional framework that addresses environmental stewardship, economic efficiency, and social equity (Faggini et al., 2018; Bvuchete et al., 2022). At the environmental level, digital health technologies such as electronic health records (EHRs), telemedicine platforms, AI-assisted diagnostics, and Internet of Medical Things (IoMT) devices significantly reduce the carbon footprint of healthcare delivery (Daniel-Watanabe et al., 2024; Man et al., 2024). These are achieved by minimizing paper usage, optimizing energy consumption in clinical operations, and reducing patient and provider travel through the use of virtual consultations. Digitization contributes to lower greenhouse gas emissions and more sustainable resource utilization.

Economically, digitization enhances the sustainability of healthcare systems by streamlining administrative processes, reducing redundancies, improving operational efficiency, and enabling data-driven decision-making (Adeniran et al., 2024; Ng'andu & Haabazoka, 2024).

Real-time monitoring and predictive analytics enable early diagnosis and preventative care, reducing costly interventions and hospital readmissions. Resource limits in low- and middle-income nations require creative healthcare delivery, making these efficiencies important.

From a social sustainability perspective, digital healthcare fosters inclusivity by expanding accessibility and equity to healthcare across geographic, socioeconomic, and demographic boundaries (Heaslip & Holley, 2023; Jerjes & Harding, 2024). Mobile health applications and telehealth services have the potential to enable patients in remote or underserved areas to receive timely medical attention, thereby narrowing health disparities (Snoswell et al., 2023). Furthermore, digital platforms support health literacy and patient engagement, enabling individuals to take a more active role in managing their health. Dobrovolska & Kolomiiets (2024) suggest the importance of integrating digital technologies into the healthcare sector to increase its efficiency and accessibility.

While digitalisation has its positive impact on both environmental sustainability and social responsibility, it also at the same time imposes challenges such as interoperability issues, regulatory constraints, and ethical considerations, requiring a balance between technological efficiency and patient-centered care (Menvielle et al., 20217; Kwiatkowska & Skórzewska-Amberg, 2019; Oră tean et al., 2022). As digital healthcare requires adherence to stringent regulatory frameworks and ethical principles, patient data security and privacy, and AI-driven decision-making transparency are pivotal to governance considerations (Jawad, 2024; Pisarenco & Pisarenco, 2024). Compliance with global standards ensures the digitalisation innovations in healthcare are implemented professionally and responsibly, fostering confidence and trust among stakeholders, and preventing infringement of sensitive data (Gao, 2024; Prastyanti & Sharma, 2024).

Thus, digitization and sustainability in healthcare imply a paradigm shift toward more resilient, equitable, and ecologically responsible systems. In global healthcare agendas like the UN Sustainable Development Goals (SDGs), digital innovation is seen as a catalyst and conduit for universal healthcare inclusivity and long-term systemic sustainability.

1.2 Penang Healthcare Providers Overview

Penang is Southeast Asia's largest medical tourism destination due to its sophisticated and strategically integrated medical healthcare sector. The region has many governmental and internationally approved private hospitals that offer a wide range of services. Advanced diagnostics, minimally invasive operations, reproductive therapies, and chronic disease management are backed by cutting-edge medical technology and multilingual healthcare experts.

The robustness of Penang's healthcare ecosystem provides a solid foundation for Penang's success as a leading medical tourism hub in Southeast Asia, attracting international patients primarily from Indonesia, China, and Singapore. In 2025, the Malaysia Healthcare Travel Council (MHTC) indicates that Penang contributes nearly 40.7% of Malaysia's total healthcare travel revenue (Seraj, 2025). The growth of Penang's medical tourism industry is underpinned by coordinated efforts from the Penang Centre of Medical Tourism (PMED), which facilitates cross-sectoral collaboration among hospitals, wellness centers, and government agencies.

This institutional support enhances the patient experience by streamlining access to care, ensuring quality assurance, and promoting Penang's unique value proposition—affordable, high-quality medical services within a culturally rich and tourist-friendly environment. Various studies have highlighted key determinants of medical tourist satisfaction in Penang, including service quality dimensions such as tangibles, assurance, and responsiveness, as well as the mediating role of perceived value in shaping patient loyalty and destination image (Nazem & Mohamed, 2015; Abdullah et al., 2019; Vashu et al., 2021; Yong et al., 2021).

As leading institutions like RUMC and Universiti Sains Malaysia develop professional training in medical informatics and AI-driven diagnostics, Penang's healthcare providers are increasingly aligning with global trends in digital health and precision medicine. Penang's competitive edge in regional healthcare is strengthened by training quality, technology innovation, and strategic governance, contributing to its goal of becoming a global medical tourism hub.

2. LITERATURE REVIEW

2.1 Theoretical Lenses on ESG Frameworks in Healthcare Sustainability

Originally conceptualized within the domain of responsible investment and corporate social responsibility (Friede et al., 2015; Eccles et al., 2014), the ESG framework has transcended into a salient paradigm for evaluating organizational sustainability, accountability, and ethical stewardship. Given the multi-faceted nature of the ESG framework, there is no singular theoretical perspective that offers a comprehensive explanation of ESG dynamics, especially in the healthcare context.

To explain ESG origin, implementation, and impact, academic studies often use stakeholder, institutional, resource-based, legitimacy, and dynamic capacities theories. These approaches acknowledge the relationship between internal capabilities, external pressures, stakeholder engagement, and institutional legitimacy. This integrative paradigm is vital for fostering scholarly investigation and evidence-based ESG policies in healthcare systems worldwide.

Within the healthcare sector, ESG theory functions not only as a diagnostic lens for institutional performance but also as a strategic mechanism for navigating stakeholder expectations, regulatory shifts, and systemic transformation. Furthermore, ESG theory has evolved into a strategic lens through which healthcare organizations assess their long-term viability in the face of environmental, social, and regulatory pressures (Sepetis et al., 2024; Leung et al., 2023).

To advance theoretical grounding in this domain, it is essential to critically examine the foundational theories that underpin ESG conceptualizations and assess their applicability and limitations in healthcare provider contexts.

2.1.1 Stakeholder Theory

In stakeholder theory, Freeman (1984) suggests that the legitimacy and sustainability of an organization are contingent upon its ability to balance the competing interests of diverse stakeholders. In the context of healthcare, stakeholders include patients, healthcare workers, regulators, insurers, and community actors. This theoretical argument is consistent with the social and governance dimensions of ESG, as it emphasizes inclusive stakeholder engagement and decision-making, institutional transparency, and ethical accountability within healthcare systems (Mitchell et al., 1997; Donaldson & Preston, 1995). However, it is criticised for its operational ambiguity and the conflict of interests between stakeholders when reconciling heterogeneous stakeholder claims, especially in resource-constrained settings (Jensen, 2002). While it is not a comprehensive theory in management studies, it nevertheless provides a means of combining ethical questions with complex operational environments and encapsulating details within a general vision.

2.1.2 Institutional Theory

The institutional theory framework (DiMaggio & Powell, 1983) can be used to conceptualize ESG adoption as a function of the pressures exerted by regulatory bodies, professional norms, and peer institutions, which are categorized as coercive, mimetic, and normative. Schellenberg et al. (2018) highlight that the approach is commonly adopted in conjunction with other theoretical perspectives and has considerable predictive power to determine the model outcome (Canabal & White, 2008). Within the healthcare sector, the proliferation of sustainability certifications, benchmarking protocols, and ESG reporting norms reflects institutional isomorphism (Greenwood et al., 2011; Leung et al., 2023). While this theory elucidates patterns of ESG diffusion, it has been critiqued for overstating conformity and underemphasizing the agency and innovation of healthcare leaders responding proactively to ESG imperatives.

2.1.3 Resource-Based View (RBV)

Barney (1991) advocates the importance of firm-specific resources in achieving and sustaining competitive advantage Barney (1991) further suggests these resources must be valuable, rare, imperfectly imitable, and imperfectly substitutable to acquire a sustainable competitive advantage, which is often referred to as VRIO: Value, Rarity, Inimitability, and Organizational support. Amit and Schoemaker (1993) define a resource as "stocks of available factors that are owned or controlled by the firm," which can be tangible and intangible. Amit and Schoemaker (1993) further expand the concept of resources to capability, defined as the firm's ability to utilize its resources "to effect a desired end." Under the RBV lens, ESG capabilities are viewed as valuable, rare, inimitable, and non-substitutable assets that can enhance organizational performance. In healthcare, ESG-enabling resources, such as green infrastructure, digital health systems, and governance competencies, are increasingly viewed as strategic differentiators (Hart, 1995; Sepetis et al., 2024). However, RBV has been critiqued for insufficiently engaging with external institutional and stakeholder dynamics, potentially rendering it less adaptable to sectors characterized by public accountability and complex regulatory environments.

2.1.4 Legitimacy Theory

Legitimacy theory offers a sociological and organizational framework that explains how entities, particularly corporations, strive to align their actions with societal norms, values, and expectations to maintain public approval and ensure continued operation, especially in the context of corporate social responsibility (Eliwa et al., 2021). Aerts and Cormier (2009) argue that organisations can make strategic choices to alter their legitimacy status and cultivate resources through corporate actions by adapting their activities and changing perceptions. Legitimacy theory posits that organizations undertake ESG initiatives to align with evolving societal values and secure continued social acceptance (Suchman, 1995; Bani-Khaled et al., 2025). This perspective is particularly pertinent to healthcare providers, whose public trust and moral legitimacy are intrinsically linked to transparency and responsiveness. However, legitimacy theory is often criticised for instrumentalism, particularly in contexts where ESG practices tend to be adopted as reputational signals or "greenwashing" mechanisms (Cho et al., 2015).

2.1.5 Dynamic Capabilities Theory (DCT)

DCT, often applied together with RBV theory (Shan et al., 2019; Pulka & Tijjani, 2023; Mataruka et al., 2024) suggests firms need to acquire the lasting dynamic capability to adapt to environmental changes and achieve a competitive advantage (Teece et al., 1997; Xu et al., 2017; Shan et al., 2019). Under the DCT lens, it can be adopted to explore how healthcare organizations can develop, integrate, and reconfigure ESG-related competencies in response to environmental volatility, social expectations, and technological change. This approach offers a comprehensive explanation in the context of climate resilience, pandemic preparedness, and digital transformation (Fan et al., 2024; Ishaq et al., 2024; Xi et al., 2024). Nevertheless, empirical operationalization of dynamic capabilities in ESG-specific healthcare contexts remains an under-researched area.

2.2 ESG Frameworks Applications in Healthcare Sustainability

The application of Environmental, Social, and Governance (ESG) theory in the healthcare sector has gained popularity as a multi-dimensional framework for evaluating institutional sustainability, ethical governance, and stakeholder value creation. Recent research trend suggests that ESG implementation in healthcare has evolved from a mere reporting requirement to a strategic imperative that impacts clinical outcomes, operational efficiency, and firm competitive advantage (Chiu & Fong, 2023; Candio, 2024; Pratici et al., 2025).

In the healthcare context, ESG frameworks are increasingly important to assess how providers align their operations with broader societal goals, such as the United Nations Sustainable Development Goals (SDGs), especially SDG 3 (Good Health and Well-being) and SDG 13 (Climate Action) (Consolandi et al., 2020; Leung et al., 2023; Chiu & Fong, 2023), Sepetis et al. (2024) propose an integrated ESG-Digital Transformation model that links ESG metrics with digital health adoption to enhance institutional adaptability and sustainable finance.

Sustainable development could be improved based on knowledge, attitudes, and practices (Siripipatthanakul, S., & Siripipattanakul, 2025, a, b).

2.2.1 Environmental Dimension: Operationalizing Green Healthcare

The healthcare system has a considerable ecological footprint, accounting for approximately 4.4% of global carbon emissions (Pichler et al., 2019). Key strategies include energy-efficient infrastructure, waste reduction, and digitalization to minimize paper use and travel-related emissions (Purohit et al., 2021; Wolf et al., 2022; Leung et al., 2023; Selvakumar et al., 2025). However, critical reviews caution that digital health solutions, such as AI and blockchain, may contribute to increased carbon emissions, including e-waste and energy consumption by data centers (Cao et al., 2023; Sharma & Dash, 2023; Zheng et al., 2023).

2.2.2 Social Dimension: Equity, Access, and Workforce Well-being

ESG's social aspect often refers to equitable access to care, patient safety, and workforce resilience. Digital health platforms, telemedicine, and multilingual interfaces have been shown to narrow the gap of healthcare disparities and improve patient engagement (Grieco-Page et al., 2021; Tan-McGrory et al., 2022; Ch et al., 2025). However, scholars also caution that persistent digital divides, especially among multi-ethnic populations and the elderly who are less technology literate, may impair efforts toward inclusivity in ESG-aligned healthcare systems (Whitehead et al., 2023; Solomou et al., 2025; Gallegos-Rejas et al., 2025).

Since the onset of COVID-19, healthcare frontliners have faced a complex web of well-being challenges and continue to do so in its aftermath (Cordoba, 2021). Studies indicate these challenges include prolonged psychological distress, emotional burnout, understaffing, and the strain of digital transition, which signify inadequate institutional support and systemic resource inequities (Konttila et al., 2019; O'Donnell et al., 2023; Sipos et al., 2024). These phenomena underscore a critical need for inclusive governance, equitable resource distribution, and trauma-informed policies that prioritize the well-being of frontline workers as a cornerstone of healthcare sustainability (Buchan & Perfilieva, 2015; Gray et al., 2020; Ahmad et al., 2023).

2.2.3 Governance Dimension: Ethical Stewardship and Data Integrity

Governance issues in ESG often relate to institutional transparency, data privacy and protection, and ethical leadership (Camilleri, 2024; Zahari et al., 2024; Akinsola, 2025). In the healthcare context, this includes compliance with data privacy regulations (such as the General Data Protection Regulation (GDPR)), cybersecurity protocols, and the responsible deployment of emerging technologies (Fatehi et al., 2020; Tully et al., 2020; Javaid et al., 2023). Adoption of Blockchain and

AI has gained traction as governance tools that can enhance auditability, consent management, and algorithmic accountability (Asit et al., 2023; Akther et al., 2025; Leiva & Castro, 2025).

Nevertheless, considerable studies also highlight the challenges in regulatory harmonization and ESG literacy gap among healthcare administrators, which may hinder effective implementation (Furtner et al, 2023; Ilori et al, 2023; Pesqueira et al., 2025). Scholars advocate for healthcare-specific ESG frameworks and integrated reporting mechanisms to ensure alignment with clinical, operational, and ethical standards (Leung et al., 2023; Bakker, 2025; da Silva et al., 2025).

3. METHODOLOGY

3.1 Data Collection

Data were collected from valid sources in Scopus, Web of Science, and Google Scholar, which were published online primarily between 2021 and 2025 in the English version, using purposive sampling. The related topics and keywords in this chapter, including digitalization of healthcare, sustainability, healthcare providers, environmental responsibility, social responsibility, and governance responsibility, were used for paper selection.

3.2 Data Analysis

Thematic analysis and content analysis were adopted; moreover, a systematic analysis using the PRISMA method was conducted. Based on the study of Siripipatthanakul (2025), Asrifan et al. (2025), Hadi et al. (2025), Siripipatthanakul & Siripipattanakul (2025); the process of data selection by purposive sampling using the keywords and publications in 2021-2025.

4. RESULTS

4.1 Conceptual Framework

Figure 1. Conceptual Framework

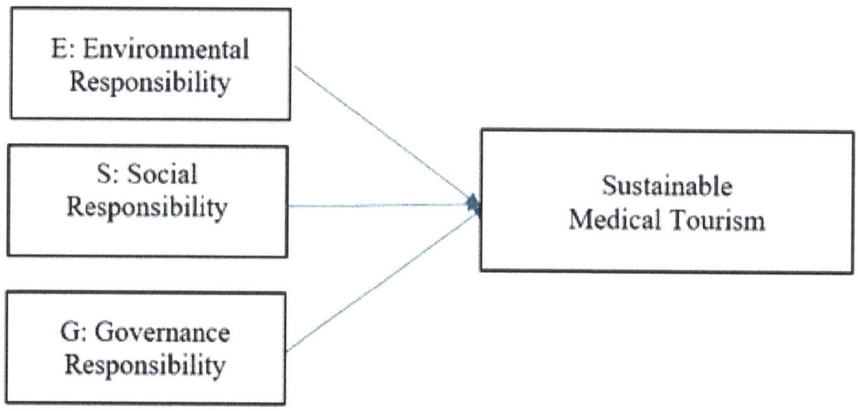

4.2 Word Clouds

Figure 2. Word Clouds

(https://www.wordclouds.com/) (July 4, 2025)

4.3 Table 1

Table 1. Major Healthcare Providers in Penang and Their Online Registration Systems

Healthcare Provider	Type	Online Registration Application
Penang General Hospital	Public	MySejahtera Portal
Seberang Jaya Hospital	Public	MySejahtera Portal
Balik Pulau Hospital	Public	MySejahtera Portal
Gleneagles Penang	Private	Gleneagles MyHealth360 Malaysia
Island Hospital	Private	Island Hospital Appointment System
Loh Guan Lye Specialists Centre	Private	Loh Guan Lye Online Appointment Booking
Sunway Medical Centre Penang	Private	Sunway Medical Penang Mobile App
Pantai Hospital Penang	Private	Pantai Hospital App Portal

continued on following page

Table 1. Continued

Healthcare Provider	Type	Online Registration Application
KPJ Penang Specialist Hospital	Private	KPJ Cares App Portal
Adventist Hospital	Private	Penang Adventist App Portal
Mount Miriam Cancer Hospital	Private	Mount Miriam Online Appointment Portal (WhatsApp)
Hospital Lam Wah Ee	Private	Hospital Lam Wah Ee Online Portal
Georgetown Specialist Hospital	Private	Georgetown Specialist Hospital Appointment Portal (WhatsApp)
Bagan Specialist Centre	Private	Bagan Specialist App Portal
Northern Heart Hospital Penang	Private	Northern Health Hospital Online Appointment Portal

Source: Author created, 2025

4.4 Grammarly Result

Grammarly (premium version) was employed to check grammar and plagiarism. The results show that the appropriateness of grammar is 97%, and plagiarism is 1%. The chapter's contents have been tested and validated by three experts. The final version has been proofread for English by an expert.

5. DISCUSSIONS

5.1 Digital Transformation in Penang's Healthcare Sector: Strategic Integration, Operational Innovation, Policy Alignment, and Competitive Advantage

Penang's healthcare sector shows how digital innovation and healthcare delivery may be used together to modernize Malaysia's health system in line with the 12th Malaysia Plan and JENDELA. Online registration systems at Penang's public and private healthcare facilities are a structural change that improves patient-centered care, institutional efficiency, and systemic resilience.

5.1.1 Digitalisation of Healthcare System - Institutional Adoption in Malaysia

Prior to the COVID-19 Pandemic, the development of healthcare digitalization in Malaysia was considered moderate. During the Covid 19 Pandemic, a cross agencies collaboration between National Security Council (NSC), the Ministry of Health

(MOH), the Malaysian Administrative Modernisation and Management Planning Unit (MAMPU), the Malaysian Communications and Multimedia Commission (MCMC) and the Ministry of Science and Technology (MOSTI), introduced a critical component of Malaysia's digital health transformation - the MySejahtera application (BERNAMA, 2020). Initially launched in 2020 as a pandemic response tool (Othman & Babulal, 2020), MySejahtera has since evolved into a multi-functional digital health platform that supports a wide range of services, including vaccination scheduling, digital health records, infectious disease tracking, and appointment booking with public healthcare providers (Onn, 2022). Ever since, private sector healthcare providers have introduced their respective applications, both web-based and mobile platforms.

As illustrated in Table 1, public hospitals such as Penang General Hospital, Seberang Jaya Hospital, and Balik Pulau Hospital utilize the national MySejahtera Portal, which integrates appointment scheduling, vaccination records, and health screening data. Private healthcare providers such as Island Hospital, Gleneagles Penang, Pantai Hospital, and Sunway Medical Centre have developed and enhanced their platforms and capabilities that offer features such as multilingual interfaces and AI-assisted devices (Siemens-Healthineers, 2025).

5.1.2 Operational and Strategic Implications

The digitalization of patient registration and service delivery has yielded measurable improvements in healthcare operations. In February 2025, the Ministry of Health Malaysia (MOH) reported that the implementation of cloud-based clinical management systems in public clinics, including those in Penang, has reduced average patient waiting times from three hours to under 30 minutes (BERNAMA, 2025a). These systems also have the potential to support real-time analytics for resource allocation, enabling dynamic scheduling of medical personnel and optimization of diagnostic equipment usage (Kelvin-Agwu et al., 2024).

The adoption of enterprise resource planning (ERP) systems integrated with AI modules to manage complex supply chains, ensure regulatory compliance, and enhance patient data security is increasing in importance in the Healthcare industry (Bialas et al., 2023; Mhaskey, 2024, 2025). These systems are advantageous in managing perishable medical inventories, aligning with evolving medical regulations, and reducing wastage. The use of AI-powered logistics and document management tools has also improved transparency and accountability in clinical governance (Mourya et al., 2024).

5.1.3 Policy and Infrastructure Readiness

Penang's digital healthcare development is supported by institutional commitment and investments. Under the JENDELA initiative, the national connectivity masterplan, the Malaysian Communications and Multimedia Commission (MCMC) has prioritized internet connectivity upgrades in public hospitals, including Penang General Hospital, to address in-building coverage gaps and enable 5G deployment (BERNAMA, 2025b). These upgrades enable the effective implementation of telemedicine, remote diagnostics, and cloud-based health informatics.

It is also noted that the RM18.9 million allocation under Budget 2025 for the digital transformation of 100 public health clinics, including several in Penang, underscores the federal government's commitment to institutionalizing digital health as a public good (MalayMail, 2025). This initiative includes the rollout of electronic medical records (EMR) systems and the establishment of Wellness Hubs that emphasize preventive care and health literacy.

5.2 Competitive Advantages of Digitalization in Penang's Healthcare Sustainability and Medical Tourism Ecosystem

Penang's healthcare sector has undergone a digital makeover, making it a regional leader in smart healthcare delivery and a top destination for foreign medical tourists. The three competitive advantages of operational efficiency, patient-centric digital experiences, and strategic worldwide positioning support this transition.

5.2.1 Enhancing Operational Efficiency through AI and ERP Integration

Digitalization has enabled Penang's healthcare providers to streamline operations, reduce redundancies, and improve clinical governance. The integration of Enterprise Resource Planning (ERP) systems with Artificial Intelligence (AI) modules has enabled hospitals to automate administrative workflows, manage medical inventories, and ensure real-time regulatory compliance (Bialas et al., 2023; Mhaskey, 2024, 2025).

According to Ong (2025), the implementation of ERP systems in Penang hospitals offers improved resource planning, staff scheduling, and supply chain management, reducing overstocking and shortages through AI-powered demand forecasting.

These technologies also reduce data breaches and ensure compliance with Malaysia's Personal Data Protection Act by restricting access to sensitive patient data. In Sunway Medical Centre Penang (SMCP) and Gleneagles Hospital, AI-assisted radiology, robotic surgery, and hybrid imaging technologies have reduced diagnostic turnaround times and improved surgical precision. This operational agility may enhance clinical outcomes and save costs, making Penang's healthcare offerings more competitive for domestic and foreign patients.

5.3 Improving Patient Accessibility and Experience through Digital Platforms

Penang's healthcare providers have embraced patient-facing digital applications that enhance accessibility, personalization, and continuity of care. These include multilingual appointment systems, mobile health apps, and teleconsultation platforms.

Public hospitals, such as Penang General Hospital and Seberang Jaya Hospital, are integrated with the MySejahtera and MyHealth Portal systems, allowing patients to schedule appointments, access vaccination records, and receive health alerts digitally.

Private institutions, such as Island Hospital and Gleneagles Penang, offer e-appointment systems, AI-powered triage, and real-time treatment updates, which improve transparency and reduce patient anxiety (Shrivastava & Song, 2022; Chouhan et al., 2023).

The government's investment of RM18.9 million in 2025 to digitize 100 public clinics, including several in Penang, has reduced average waiting times from three hours to under 30 minutes, significantly improving patient satisfaction (MalayMail, 2025).

These innovations align with the social dimension of ESG, promoting inclusivity and health equity by extending digital services to rural and underserved populations.

5.3.1 Attracting Foreign Patients through Digital Readiness and Global Integration

Penang's medical tourism competitiveness depends on its digital readiness. Online registration solutions provide pre-arrival coordination, bilingual communication, and transparent pricing, which builds international patients' trust. Digital tools reduce paper use, patient travel through teleconsultations, and healthcare facility energy consumption, supporting sustainability goals. Penang's healthcare digitization is a multifaceted plan that integrates national policy, operational excellence, and global sustainability imperatives using technology. This concept can be used by other places to modernize healthcare while improving equity, efficiency, and environmental responsibility.

Penang's digital maturity has become a cornerstone of its medical tourism strategy, attracting patients from ASEAN (especially Indonesia). The Malaysian Healthcare Travel Council (MHTC) reported in 2024 that digital tools, including e-visa processing, telemedicine for pre-operative and post-operative consultations, and the adoption of digital health technologies, have enhanced Penang's appeal to international patients by simplifying logistics and building trust (The Malaysian Reserve, 2024). These capabilities not only generate foreign revenues but also stimulate local economic development through job creation, infrastructure investment, talent development, and knowledge transfer.

Strategic planning based on top, middle, and bottom-level community participation is crucial for stakeholders in sustainable development in organizations, including hospitals and clinics. (Phuangsuwan et al., 2025).

5.3.2 Strategic Enhancements: Toward Resilient and Responsible Digital Health

To operationalize ESG-aligned digital transformation, healthcare institutions must embrace strategic innovations that are not only technologically advanced but also ethically grounded and contextually adaptive.

i. AI-Driven Predictive Diagnostics: The Potentials and Pitfalls

Recent literatures suggest that Artificial Intelligence (AI) is redefining diagnostic paradigms by revolutionising early disease detection through the analysis of complex, high-dimensional data from imaging, genomics, and electronic health records (EHRs) (Knevel & Liao, 2023; Kuo, 2023; George et al., 2023; Aamir et al., 2024; Parija & Poddar, 2024; Moglia et al., 2025). Studies have demonstrated AI's capacity to outperform traditional diagnostic methods in areas such as radiology, dermatology, and oncology (Mirbabaie et al., 2021; Sadr et al., 2025; Sadeghi et al., 2025; Thomas & Leon, 2025).

Despite the enormous potential of AI adoptions in healthcare, the rapid advancement and integration of AI have provoked skepticism about how society perceives, accepts, and regulates this emerging force. Public perception plays a critical role in shaping the adoption, ethical deployment, and long-term sustainability of AI technologies (Moch, 2023). While the promises of AI evoke hope for a brighter and more equitable future, concerns about algorithmic bias, transparency, and regulatory oversight persist, and job automation has led to cautious optimism (Victor et al., 2025).

Hence, in the absence of robust governance, AI may inadvertently reinforce health disparities or produce false positives that burden healthcare systems (Goktas & Grzybowski, 2025; Sharma et al., 2025). Thus, future strategies must prioritize human-AI collaboration, regulatory harmonization, and continuous model retraining using real-world data.

ii. Blockchain Integration for Patient Records: Addressing the Patient Data Protection and Privacy

Blockchain technologies leverage distributed ledger that provides secure and efficient storage, management, and transmission of data over a decentralized network, which offer to ensure transparency and immutability, addressing long-standing challenges in data security, interoperability, and patient autonomy (Doria, 2025; Rathore et al., 2025; Mijwil et al., 2025).

Eren et al. (2025) highlighted that the primary concerns regarding Blockchain adoption are data sovereignty and jurisdictional compliance. Regulations such as the General Data Protection Regulation (GDPR) in the European Union and the Health Insurance Portability and Accountability Act (HIPAA) in the United States impose stringent requirements on data storage, access, and privacy, which may conflict with the immutable nature of blockchain. Furthermore, its decentralized nature raises concerns regarding data retrieval rights and the right to be forgotten.

Moreover, scalability and energy efficiency remain critical barriers, as blockchains are known for their high energy consumption due to mining processes that require substantial computational power (Eren et al., 2025; Niranjana et al., 2025; Raja et al., 2025)—increasing their carbon footprint. For instance, public blockchains like Ethereum are resource-intensive, prompting a shift toward permissioned or hybrid models that balance decentralization with operational feasibility.

iii. Expansion of Telemedicine Services: Toward HealthCare Inclusivity

Telemedicine has transitioned from a pandemic-era necessity to a strategic pillar of modern healthcare (Sophia, 2025). It enhances access, reduces hospital congestion, and supports chronic disease management, particularly in underserved regions (Saharkhiz et al., 2024; Shankar et al., 2024; Gherman et al., 2025), which suggests virtual consultations can maintain care quality while reducing costs and environmental impact. It offers scalable, patient-centered solutions that align with ESG goals by reducing emissions, optimizing resource use, and enhancing care continuity.

Nevertheless, the sustainability of telemedicine depends on resolving structural and regulatory challenges. These include information infrastructure, e-commerce, legal and ethical considerations, security, health infrastructure, standards, laws, and regulations (Hadian et al., 2024). Moreover, digital inequities, such as limited broadband access in rural regions and low digital literacy, threaten to exacerbate health disparities if left unaddressed (Haimi et al., 2024).

6. CONCLUSION

In Penang, Malaysia, digital healthcare apps have transformed sustainability, operational excellence, and competitive positioning for healthcare providers. Based on ESG theory and multi-theoretical frameworks, including stakeholder, institutional, and resource-based perspectives, the findings show that digitalization improves environmental stewardship through paperless systems, social equity through telemedicine and multilingual access, governance through blockchain and AI, and competitive advantage. The strategic integration of digital tools like MySejahtera, EMR systems, and AI-assisted diagnostics in Penang public and commercial healthcare institutions improves efficiency, patient happiness, and worldwide appeal. The connection of Penang's healthcare digitization with JENDELA and the 12th Malaysia Plan shows how regional innovation may assist national and global sustainability goals, including the SDGs. The digital revolution also boosts medical tourism competitiveness. Penang's technologically developed healthcare ecosystem can help other jurisdictions upgrade their health systems by improving transparency, decreasing administrative friction, and encouraging pre-arrival coordination.

ESG-based sustainable medical tourism improves healthcare through ethical travel and development. Sustainable medical tourism emphasizes green hospital infrastructure, energy efficiency, and carbon reduction in healthcare and hospitality. International patients should travel green. Healthcare facilities should use renewable energy. Managing biological waste is important. Neighbors should save water and reduce pollution. Medical tourism hospitals and wellness centers are using LEED-certified building methods, telemedicine to reduce travel, and new climate policies with local governments. Sustainable medical tourism fosters healthcare equity, fair labor, and community inclusion. Health literacy, culturally sensitive care for various patient populations, and preventing medical tourism from expanding the gap between wealthy medical travelers and underserved local communities are needed. Training, fair compensation, local healthcare workers' engagement in the global healthcare ecosystem, and partnerships between private clinics, NGOs, and local health authorities to co-create accessible treatment pathways are also needed for social sustainability. It promotes patient rights, safety, satisfaction, pricing transparency, quality, and ethical service. Medical tourism should benefit locals and fund schools, clinics, and cleanliness. Third ESG component governance promotes medical tourism transparency, accountability, and regulatory compliance. Effective governance ensures medical tourism providers fulfill international accreditation standards, ethical business practices, and data privacy and patient confidentiality laws. Anti-corruption, responsible marketing, and international medical, pharmaceutical, and cross-border insurance laws are needed. Patients, local communities, hospital professionals, environmental campaigners, and government regulators must work together to create inclusive policies and long-term goals for sustainable medical tourism governance. Governments and businesses must report ESG performance using measurable metrics and third-party audits. Over time, ESG-aligned medical tourism builds community trust, environmental protection, and operational integrity. As global health crises, climate change, and inequality intensify, medical tourism promotes global solidarity, health equity, and responsible development. Malaysia and other Asian nations are studying ESG ways to relate medical tourism growth to SDG 3 (Good Health and Well-being), SDG 8 (Decent Work and Economic Growth), and SDG 13 (Climate Action). They encourage healthcare, tourism, transit, and environmental cooperation. Thus, ESG-certified sustainable medical tourism supports cleaner, greener healthcare travel, inclusive and ethical care, advantages for tourists and host communities, legitimacy, accountability, and long-term profitability. A strategic vision and practical implementation of green innovation incentives, sustainability management capacity building, and ESG principles in medical education and tourist planning are needed to shift medical tourism toward ESG. ESG-driven medical tourism improves global health and sustainability by respecting global boundaries, promoting social fairness, and upholding ethical governance.

7. LIMITATIONS

While this research provides a robust conceptual exploration of digital healthcare applications in Penang, several limitations of this study are acknowledged:

Scope and Geographic Specificity: The study primarily focuses on Penang-based institutions, which may limit its generalizability to other Malaysian states or lower-resource settings with different technological maturity levels.

Data Source Constraints: The study primarily draws on secondary data, policy documents, and theoretical literature. Primary data collection (e.g., interviews or surveys with healthcare administrators and patients) could have provided richer insights.

Technological Innovation and Trends: Given the rapid pace of digital health innovation, some platforms and technologies discussed may evolve or be superseded, which could affect the longitudinal applicability of findings.

Regulatory Analysis: The governance discussion draws on national frameworks; however, a detailed legal or cross-border policy analysis of ESG compliance (e.g., interoperability, data sovereignty) is beyond the scope of the current study.

8. FUTURE RESEARCH RECOMMENDATION

To expand on the current findings and address these limitations, suggest future studies could focus:

Conduct Comparative Case Studies between digitally advanced and under-served states in Malaysia or across ASEAN to examine how regional contexts shape ESG-aligned digital adoption.

Explore Patient-Centered Outcomes through primary research, including patient satisfaction, perceived trust in digital tools, and the role of health literacy in digital adoption.

Assess the Carbon Footprint and Lifecycle Impacts of digital infrastructure used in healthcare, including e-waste management and green data center practices.

Examine Cross-Border Governance Mechanisms and legal interoperability challenges associated with digital health platforms used by international patients, especially in the context of medical tourism.

Develop and validate ESG Performance Metrics explicitly tailored for healthcare providers to operationalize sustainability indicators within clinical and administrative settings.

9. RESEARCH IMPLICATIONS

This chapter describes how Penang, Malaysian healthcare providers use digital healthcare applications to promote ESG-aligned sustainability. Stakeholder theory, institutional theory, and the resource-based view are used to examine how digitalization improves operational efficiency, environmental performance, and patient-centered care. A thematic analysis of policy initiatives, institutional practices, and ESG (Environment, Social, and Governance) principles shows that digital tools like EMRs, AI-assisted diagnostics, blockchain-based records, and telemedicine platforms can improve healthcare delivery and system resilience. Penang's healthcare providers show that digital transformation can improve healthcare equity and competitiveness in medical tourism while reducing ecological footprints and administrative redundancies. Despite promising results, the study highlights technical disparity, data governance, and regulatory supervision. We recommend improving ESG performance measures, ethical digital stewardship, and cross-border health policy. The findings advance sustainable digital health discourse and provide policymakers, administrators, and global health strategists with practical advice.

REFERENCES

A., Siripipatthanakul, S., Alaqad, M. H., Saodi, S., & Sadaruddin, S. (2025). Managing Privacy and Security in Research: Effective Practices and Strategies. In *Privacy and Security Management Practices for Organizations* (pp. 151-182). IGI Global Scientific Publishing. DOI: 10.4018/979-8-3693-9720-6.ch006

Aamir, A., Iqbal, A., Jawed, F., Ashfaque, F., Hafsa, H., Anas, Z., Oduoye, M. O., Basit, A., Ahmed, S., Abdul Rauf, S., Khan, M., & Mansoor, T. (2024). Exploring the current and prospective role of artificial intelligence in disease diagnosis. *Annals of Medicine and Surgery (London)*, *86*(2), 943–949. DOI: 10.1097/MS9.0000000000001700 PMID: 38333305

Abdullah, A. R., Cheah, S., Mulia, V. B., & Abdul Fatah, I. A. (2019). *Factors attracting Indonesian medical tourists to Penang. African Journal of Hospitality, Tourism and Leisure* (Special Edition). GCBSS.

Adeniran, I. A., Efunniyi, C. P., Osundare, O. S., & Abhulimen, A. O. (2024). Data-driven decision-making in healthcare: Improving patient outcomes through predictive modeling. Engineering Science & Technology Journal, 5(8).

Aerts, W., & Cormier, D. (2009). Media legitimacy and corporate environmental communication. *Accounting, Organizations and Society*, *34*(1), 1–27. DOI: 10.1016/j.aos.2008.02.005

Ahmad, N., Ullah, Z., Ryu, H. B., Ariza-Montes, A., & Han, H. (2023). From corporate social responsibility to employee well-being: Navigating the pathway to sustainable healthcare. *Psychology Research and Behavior Management*, *16*, 1079–1095. DOI: 10.2147/PRBM.S398586 PMID: 37041962

Akinsola, K. (2025). Legal Compliance in Corporate Governance Frameworks: Best Practices for Ensuring Transparency, Accountability, and Risk Mitigation. Accountability, and Risk Mitigation.

Akther, A., Arobee, A., Adnan, A. A., Auyon, O., Islam, A. S. M., & Akter, F. (2025). Blockchain As a Platform For Artificial Intelligence (AI) Transparency. arXiv preprint arXiv:2503.08699.

Amit, R., & Schoemaker, P. J. (1993). Strategic assets and organisational rent. *Strategic Management Journal*, *14*(1), 33–46. DOI: 10.1002/smj.4250140105

Asif, R., Hassan, S. R., & Parr, G. (2023). Integrating a blockchain-based governance framework for responsible AI. *Future Internet*, *15*(3), 97. DOI: 10.3390/fi15030097

Bakker, B. (2025). Reporting Challenges of the Social Dimension ESG in Healthcare (Master's thesis, University of Twente).

Bani-Khaled, S., Azevedo, G., & Oliveira, J. (2025). Environmental, social, and governance (ESG) factors and firm value: A systematic literature review of theories and empirical evidence. *AMS Review*, 1–33. DOI: 10.1007/s13162-025-00303-2

Barney, J. B. (1991). Firm resources and sustained competitive advantage. *Journal of Management*, *17*(1), 99–120. DOI: 10.1177/014920639101700108

BERNAMA. (2020). "MySejahtera application to assist in monitoring COVID-19". Bernama. https://web.archive.org/web/20210622100036/https://www.bernama.com/en/general/news_covid-19.php?id=1833998. Retrieved 3 July 2025.

BERNAMA. (2025a). Shorter waiting times at government clinics nationwide praised. Bernama. https://www.bernama.com/bm/news.php?id=2389636

BERNAMA. (2025b).Seven Hospitals Identified for Internet Upgrades - Teo. https://www.bernama.com/en/general/news.php?id=2382174

Bhambere, S., Abhishek, B., & Sumit, H. (2021). Rapid digitization of healthcare—A review of COVID-19 impact on our health systems. *Int. J. All Res. Educ. Sci. Methods*, *9*, 1457–1459.

Bialas, C., Bechtsis, D., Aivazidou, E., Achillas, C., & Aidonis, D. (2023). Digitalization of the healthcare supply chain through the adoption of enterprise resource planning (ERP) systems in hospitals: An empirical study on influencing factors and cost performance. *Sustainability (Basel)*, *15*(4), 3163. DOI: 10.3390/su15043163

Buchan, J., & Perfilieva, G. (2015). *Making progress towards health workforce sustainability in the WHO European region*. World Health Organization.

Bvuchete, M., Grobbelaar, S., & Eeden, J. V. (2022). Digitalisation and sustainable supply chain strategy: An instrument for improving efficiencies in the public healthcare sector. *International Journal of Learning and Change*, *14*(5-6), 559–587. DOI: 10.1504/IJLC.2022.126422

Camilleri, M. A. (2024). Artificial intelligence governance: Ethical considerations and implications for social responsibility. *Expert Systems: International Journal of Knowledge Engineering and Neural Networks*, *41*(7), e13406. DOI: 10.1111/exsy.13406

Canabal, A., & White, G. O.III. (2008). Entry mode research: Past and future. *International Business Review*, *17*(3), 267–284. DOI: 10.1016/j.ibusrev.2008.01.003

Candio, P. (2024). Evolution of ESG and Corporate Performance in Health Care. In *Sustainability and Corporate Performance in Health Care: ESG Implications for the European Industry* (pp. 67–83). Springer Nature Switzerland. DOI: 10.1007/978-3-031-63985-2_4

Cao, Z., Zhou, X., Wu, X., Zhu, Z., Liu, T., Neng, J., & Wen, Y. (2023). Data center sustainability: Revisits and outlooks. *IEEE Transactions on Sustainable Computing*.

Ch, A. S., Pervaiz, F., Nawaz, H., Rafiq, S., Bibi, Y., Almagharbeh, W. T., & Mobeen, M. (2025). Health Equity In Telemedicine: Addressing Disparities In Digital Healthcare Access-A Narrative Review-S. *Insights-Journal Of Life And Social Sciences, 3*(2), 56–62. DOI: 10.71000/rw9xsy20

Chiu, W. K., & Fong, B. Y. F. (2023). Recent trends of research and education in ESG and sustainability. In *Environmental, social and governance and sustainable development in healthcare* (pp. 99–112). Springer Nature Singapore. DOI: 10.1007/978-981-99-1564-4_7

Chiu, W. K., & Fong, B. Y. F. (2023). SDG 3 and ESG—Linkage and the Way Forward. In *Environmental, Social and Governance and Sustainable Development in Healthcare* (pp. 113–116). Springer Nature Singapore. DOI: 10.1007/978-981-99-1564-4_8

Cho, C. H., Michelon, G., Patten, D. M., & Roberts, R. W. (2015). CSR disclosure: The more things change…? *Accounting, Auditing & Accountability Journal, 28*(1), 14–35. DOI: 10.1108/AAAJ-12-2013-1549

Chouhan, A. S., Jain, A., Jain, S., & Gupta, P. (2023). Maximizing Efficiency and Minimizing Wait Times: A Case Study on the Use of Technology to Streamline Patient Appointments. *International Journal of Knowledge Based Computer Systems, 11*(1).

Consolandi, C., Phadke, H., Hawley, J., & Eccles, R. G. (2020). Material ESG outcomes and SDG externalities: Evaluating the health care sector's contribution to the SDGs. *Organization & Environment, 33*(4), 511–533. DOI: 10.1177/1086026619899795

Cordoba, L. E. (2021). Well-being and mental health of healthcare workers before, during, and after COVID-19. *Salud Mental, 44*(5), 211–214. DOI: 10.17711/SM.0185-3325.2021.027

da Silva, A. F., Carreira, F., & Cepêda, C. (2025). Does Corporate Governance Impact ESG Performance Reporting in Healthcare? In *Environmental, Social, Governance and Digital Transformation in Organizations* (pp. 51–72). Springer. DOI: 10.1007/978-3-031-86079-9_3

Daniel-Watanabe, L., Moore, R., England, N. H. S., Tongue, B., & Royston, S. (2024). What is the Carbon Footprint of Digital Healthcare?

DiMaggio, P. J., & Powell, W. W. (1983). The iron cage revisited: Institutional isomorphism and collective rationality in organizational fields. *American Sociological Review*, *48*(2), 147–160. DOI: 10.2307/2095101

Dobrovolska, O., & Kolomiiets, S. (2024). The Impact of Digitalisation on Social Determinants of Public Health. *Health Economics and Management Review*, *5*(3), 128–142. DOI: 10.61093/hem.2024.3-09

Donaldson, T., & Preston, L. E. (1995). The stakeholder theory of the corporation: Concepts, evidence, and implications. *Academy of Management Review*, *20*(1), 65–91. DOI: 10.2307/258887

Doria, M. (2025). The Application of Blockchain Technology in Securing Electronic Health Records Blockchain for Healthcare Data Security. 324-1.

Eliwa, Y., Aboud, A., & Saleh, A. (2021). ESG practices and the cost of debt: Evidence from EU countries. *Critical Perspectives on Accounting*, *79*, 102097. DOI: 10.1016/j.cpa.2019.102097

Eren, H., Karaduman, Ö., & Gençoğlu, M. T. (2025). Security challenges and performance trade-offs in on-chain and off-chain blockchain storage: A comprehensive review. *Applied Sciences (Basel, Switzerland)*, *15*(6), 3225. DOI: 10.3390/app15063225

Faggini, M., Cosimato, S., Nota, F. D., & Nota, G. (2018). Pursuing sustainability for healthcare through digital platforms. *Sustainability (Basel)*, *11*(1), 165. DOI: 10.3390/su11010165

Fan, Z., Long, R., & Shen, Z. (2024). Regional digitalization, dynamic capabilities and green innovation: Evidence from e-commerce demonstration cities in China. *Economic Modelling*, *139*, 106846. DOI: 10.1016/j.econmod.2024.106846

Fatehi, F., Hassandoust, F., Ko, R. K., & Akhlaghpour, S. (2020). General data protection regulation (GDPR) in healthcare: Hot topics and research fronts. In Digital Personalized Health and Medicine (pp. 1118-1122). IOS Press.

Freeman, R. E. (1984). *Strategic management: A stakeholder approach*. Pitman.

Furtner, D., Hutas, G., Tan, B. J. W., & Meier, R. (2023). Journey from an enabler to a strategic leader: Integration of the medical affairs function in ESG initiatives and values. *Pharmaceutical Medicine*, *37*(6), 405–416. DOI: 10.1007/s40290-023-00485-9 PMID: 37464231

Gallegos-Rejas, V. M., De Guzman, K. R., Kelly, J. T., Smith, A. C., & Thomas, E. E. (2025). Strategies to improve telehealth access for culturally and linguistically diverse communities: A systematic review. *Journal of Public Health (Oxford, England)*, fdaf030. DOI: 10.1093/pubmed/fdaf030 PMID: 40106706

Gao, R. Y. (2024). The diffusion of a US trade-based approach to international personal data transfers and its implications for national data privacy regulations. *International Data Privacy Law*, *14*(4), 352–376.

Gendy, M. E. G., & Yuce, M. R. (2022). Emerging technologies used in health management and efficiency improvement during different contact tracing phases against COVID-19 pandemic. *IEEE Reviews in Biomedical Engineering*, *16*, 38–52. DOI: 10.1109/RBME.2022.3219433 PMID: 36331632

George, A. H., Shahul, A., & George, A. S. (2023). Artificial intelligence in medicine: A New way to diagnose and treat disease. *Partners Universal International Research Journal*, *2*(3), 246–259.

Gherman, A., Andrei, D., Popoiu, C. M., Stoicescu, E. R., Levai, M. C., Stoian, I. I., & Bloancă, V. (2025). Multidisciplinary Telemedicine in Healthcare During and After the COVID-19 Pandemic: A Narrative Review. *Life (Chicago, Ill.)*, *15*(5), 783. DOI: 10.3390/life15050783 PMID: 40430210

Goktas, P., & Grzybowski, A. (2025). Shaping the future of healthcare: Ethical clinical challenges and pathways to trustworthy AI. *Journal of Clinical Medicine*, *14*(5), 1605. DOI: 10.3390/jcm14051605 PMID: 40095575

Golinelli, D., Boetto, E., Carullo, G., Nuzzolese, A. G., Landini, M. P., & Fantini, M. P. (2020). Adoption of digital technologies in health care during the COVID-19 pandemic: Systematic review of early scientific literature. *Journal of Medical Internet Research*, *22*(11), e22280. DOI: 10.2196/22280 PMID: 33079693

Gray, B. J., Bright, D., Bolton, S., & Davies, A. R. (2020). Towards a healthy and sustainable workforce for the future. Public Health Wales. www. nati o nalar chives. gov. uk/doc/open-gover nment-licen ce/versi on/3.

Greenwood, R., Raynard, M., Kodeih, F., Micelotta, E. R., & Lounsbury, M. (2011). Institutional complexity and organizational responses. *The Academy of Management Annals*, *5*(1), 317–371. DOI: 10.5465/19416520.2011.590299

Grieco-Page, H., Black, C. J., Berent, J. M., Gautam, B., & Betancourt, T. S. (2021). Beyond the pandemic: Leveraging rapid expansions in US telemental health and digital platforms to address disparities and resolve the digital divide. *Frontiers in Psychiatry*, *12*, 671502. DOI: 10.3389/fpsyt.2021.671502 PMID: 34421669

Hadi, S., Purnasari, E., Hidayat, R., Lukitaningsih, A., Kirana, K. C., & Siripipatthanakul, S. (2025). Challenges and Management Practices in Protecting Employee Personal Data in the Digital Era. In Privacy and Security Management Practices for Organizations (pp. 89-116). IGI Global Scientific Publishing. DOI: DOI: 10.4018/979-8-3693-9720-6.ch004

Hadian, M., Jelodar, Z. K., Khanbebin, M. J., Atafimanesh, P., Asiabar, A. S., & Dehagani, S. M. H. (2024). Challenges of implementing telemedicine technology: A systematized review. *International Journal of Preventive Medicine*, *15*, 8. DOI: 10.4103/ijpvm.ijpvm_48_23 PMID: 38563036

Haimi, M., Goren, U., & Grossman, Z. (2024). Barriers and challenges to telemedicine usage among the elderly population in Israel in light of the COVID-19 era: A qualitative study. *Digital Health*, *10*, 20552076241240235. DOI: 10.1177/20552076241240235 PMID: 38550265

Hart, S. L. (1995). A natural-resource-based view of the firm. *Academy of Management Review*, *20*(4), 986–1014. DOI: 10.2307/258963

Heaslip, V., & Holley, D. (2023). Ensuring digital inclusion. *Clinics in Integrated Care*, *17*, 100141. DOI: 10.1016/j.intcar.2023.100141

Ilori, O., Lawal, C. I., Friday, S. C., Isibor, N. J., & Chukwuma-Eke, E. C. (2023). A framework for Environmental, Social, and Governance (ESG) auditing: Bridging gaps in global reporting standards. *International Journal of Social Science Exceptional Research*, *2*(1), 231–248. DOI: 10.54660/IJSSER.2023.2.1.231-248

Ishaq, S., Hoang, T. G., Tanveer, U., Hoang, T. H., & Truong, H. Q. (2024). Transformative capabilities of MedTech organizations in driving circularity in the healthcare industry: Insights from multiple cases. *Journal of Cleaner Production*, *446*, 141370. DOI: 10.1016/j.jclepro.2024.141370

Javaid, M., Haleem, A., Singh, R. P., & Suman, R. (2023). Towards insighting cybersecurity for healthcare domains: A comprehensive review of recent practices and trends. *Cyber Security and Applications*, *1*, 100016. DOI: 10.1016/j.csa.2023.100016

Jawad, L. A. (2024). Security and privacy in digital healthcare systems: Challenges and mitigation strategies. *Abhigyan*, *42*(1), 23–31.

Jensen, M. C. (2002). Value maximization, stakeholder theory, and the corporate objective function. *Business Ethics Quarterly*, *12*(2), 235–256. DOI: 10.2307/3857812

Jerjes, W., & Harding, D. (2024). Telemedicine in the post-COVID era: Balancing accessibility, equity, and sustainability in primary healthcare. *Frontiers in Digital Health*, *6*, 1432871. DOI: 10.3389/fdgth.2024.1432871 PMID: 39233772

Kalia, D., & Aggarwal, D. (2023). Examining impact of ESG score on financial performance of healthcare companies. *Journal of Global Responsibility*, *14*(1), 155–176. DOI: 10.1108/JGR-05-2022-0045

Kelvin-Agwu, M. C., Adelodun, M. O., Igwama, G. T., & Anyanwu, E. C. (2024). Strategies for optimizing the management of medical equipment in large healthcare institutions. *Strategies (La Jolla, Calif.)*, *20*(9), 162–170.

Knevel, R., & Liao, K. P. (2023). From real-world electronic health record data to real-world results using artificial intelligence. *Annals of the Rheumatic Diseases*, *82*(3), 306–311. DOI: 10.1136/ard-2022-222626 PMID: 36150748

Konttila, J., Siira, H., Kyngäs, H., Lahtinen, M., Elo, S., Kääriäinen, M., Kaakinen, P., Oikarinen, A., Yamakawa, M., Fukui, S., Utsumi, M., Higami, Y., Higuchi, A., & Mikkonen, K. (2019). Healthcare professionals' competence in digitalisation: A systematic review. *Journal of Clinical Nursing*, *28*(5-6), 745–761. DOI: 10.1111/jocn.14710 PMID: 30376199

Kuo, C. L. (2023). *Revolutionizing healthcare paradigms: The integral role of artificial intelligence in advancing diagnostic and treatment modalities. International Microsurgery Journal.* IMJ.

Kwiatkowska, E. M., & Skórzewska-Amberg, M. (2019). Digitalisation of healthcare and the problem of digital exclusion. *Central European Management Journal*, *27*, 48–63.

Lee, S. M., & Lee, D. (2021). Opportunities and challenges for contactless healthcare services in the post-COVID-19 Era. *Technological Forecasting and Social Change*, *167*, 120712. DOI: 10.1016/j.techfore.2021.120712 PMID: 33654330

Leiva, V., & Castro, C. (2025). Artificial intelligence and blockchain in clinical trials: Enhancing data governance efficiency, integrity, and transparency. *Bioanalysis*, *17*(3), 161–176. DOI: 10.1080/17576180.2025.2452774 PMID: 39844748

Leogrande, A. (2024). Integrating ESG Principles into Smart Logistics: Toward Sustainable Supply Chains.

Leung, T. C. H., & You, C. S. X. (2023). ESG application in sustainable development of the healthcare industry. In *Environmental, Social and Governance and Sustainable Development in Healthcare* (pp. 47–64). Springer Nature Singapore. DOI: 10.1007/978-981-99-1564-4_4

Leung, T. C. H., & You, S. X. (2023). Environmental, Social and Governance (ESG) of Listed Companies in the Healthcare Industry of Hong Kong. In *Gaps and Actions in Health Improvement from Hong Kong and Beyond: All for Health* (pp. 421–436). Springer Nature Singapore. DOI: 10.1007/978-981-99-4491-0_28

Mainardes, E. W., Alves, H., & Raposo, M. (2011). Stakeholder theory: Issues to resolve. *Management Decision*, *49*(2), 226–252. DOI: 10.1108/00251741111109133

MalayMail. (2025). Health Ministry says RM18.9m allocated for digital transformation of 100 public health clinics nationwide. MalayMail. 8 February 2025. Retrieved 3 July 2025 from https://www.malaymail.com/news/malaysia/2025/02/08/health-ministry-says-rm189m-allocated-for-digital-transformation-of-100-public-health-clinics-nationwide/166001

Man, L. C., Lin, Y., Pang, G., Sanderson, J., & Duan, K. (2024). Digitalization to achieve greener healthcare supply chain. *Journal of Cleaner Production*, *463*, 142802. DOI: 10.1016/j.jclepro.2024.142802

Mataruka, L., Zishiri, C., Muzurura, J., Mkumbuzi, W. P., & Garatsa, C. (2024). Enhancing Performance of Zimbabwean Service-based Firms through Digital Transformation and Sustainable Competitive Advantage: A Structural Equation Analysis. *African Journal of Commercial Studies*, *5*(1), 7–20. DOI: 10.59413/ajocs/v5.i1.2

Menvielle, L., Audrain-Pontevia, A. F., & Menvielle, W. (Eds.). (2017). *The digitization of healthcare: new challenges and opportunities*. DOI: 10.1057/978-1-349-95173-4

Mhaskey, S. V. (2025). Optimizing healthcare distribution: The role of enterprise resource planning systems.

Mijwil, M. M., Aljanabi, M., Abotaleb, M., Shukur, B. S., Al Sailawi, A. S. A., Bala, I., Hiran, K. K., Doshi, R., & Dhoska, K. (2025). Exploring the Impact of Blockchain Revolution on the Healthcare Ecosystem: A Critical Review. *Mesopotamian Journal of CyberSecurity*, *5*(1), 78–89. DOI: 10.58496/MJCS/2025/006

Mirbabaie, M., Langer, M., Hofeditz, L., & Frowerk, J. (2025). AI'll Be There: Challenges and Opportunities in the AI-Supported Doctor-Patient Relationship.

Mitchell, R. K., Agle, B. R., & Wood, D. J. (1997). Toward a theory of stakeholder identification and salience: Defining the principle of who and what really counts. *Academy of Management Review*, *22*(4), 853–886. DOI: 10.2307/259247

Moch, E. (2023). The Industrial Revolution of Artificial Intelligence: A New Era of Automation and Innovation. *International Journal of Public Administration Management and Economic Development*, *8*(2), 1–12. DOI: 10.60026/ijpamed.v8i2.104

Moglia, V., Johnson, O., Cook, G., de Kamps, M., & Smith, L. (2025). Artificial intelligence methods applied to longitudinal data from electronic health records for prediction of cancer: A scoping review. *BMC Medical Research Methodology*, *25*(1), 24. DOI: 10.1186/s12874-025-02473-w PMID: 39875808

Mourya, A., Jobanputra, B., & Pai, R. (2024). AI-powered clinical trials and the imperative for regulatory transparency and accountability. *Health and Technology*, *14*(6), 1071–1081. DOI: 10.1007/s12553-024-00904-0

Nazem, G., & Mohamed, B. (2015). Understanding medical tourists' perception of private hospital service quality in Penang Island. *Asian Culture and History*, *8*(1), 100–111. DOI: 10.5539/ach.v8n1p100

Ng'andu, D., & Haabazoka, L. (2024). A Study of the Effect of Health Records Digitalization on Healthcare Facility Operational Efficiency. *Open Journal of Business and Management*, *12*(2), 1135–1157. DOI: 10.4236/ojbm.2024.122060

Niranjana, J., Daniel, E., Durga, S., & Kathiresan, V. (2024) Enhancing Storage Efficiency for Health Data Records through Block chain-Based Storj Mechanism. In Proceedings of the 2024 3rd International Conference on Intelligent Technologies, Control, Optimization, and Signal Processing, Krishnankoil, 14–16; pp. 1–7. DOI: 10.1109/INCOS59338.2024.10527538

O'Donnell, S., Quigley, E., Hayden, J., Adamis, D., Gavin, B., & McNicholas, F. (2023). Psychological distress among healthcare workers post COVID-19 pandemic: From the resilience of individuals to healthcare systems. *Irish Journal of Psychological Medicine*, *40*(3), 508–512. DOI: 10.1017/ipm.2022.35 PMID: 35938227

Ong, R. (2025). How Are AI and ERP Systems Reshaping Healthcare in Penang, Malaysia? Multiable. https://multiable.com.my/2025/06/25/how-are-ai-and-erp-systems-reshaping-healthcare-in-penang-malaysia/

Onn, Y. (2022). MySejahtera services to include booking for hospital, clinic appointments. NST Online. https://www.nst.com.my/news/nation/2022/12/865062/mysejahtera-services-include-booking-hospital-clinic-appointments Retrieved 3 July 2025.

Oră tean, R., Sava, R., & Mărginean, S. (2022). Measuring Healthcare Digitalisation In The European Union: Trends And Challenges. *Revista Economica (Sibiu)*, *74*(4), 64–74. DOI: 10.56043/reveco-2022-0038

Othman, N., & Babulal, V. (2020). MySejahtera app disseminates COVID-19 information. NST Online. https://www.nst.com.my/news/nation/2020/04/583117/mysejahtera-app-disseminates-COVID-19-information

Parija, S. C., & Poddar, A. (2024). Artificial intelligence in parasitic disease control: A paradigm shift in health care. *Tropical Parasitology*, *14*(1), 2–7. DOI: 10.4103/tp.tp_66_23 PMID: 38444798

Pesqueira, A., Fitzgerald, J., Kurman, P. A., Jaimes, S. D. G., Curado, J., & Gianico, S. (2025). Balancing Ethical, Data Privacy, and Security Dimensions in Blockchain-Based Healthcare Governance: Aligning With ESG Principles. Navigating Privacy, Innovation, and Patient Empowerment Through Ethical Healthcare Technology, 1-38.

Phuangsuwan, P., Siripipatthanakul, S., Siripipattanakul, S., & Jaipong, P. (2025). The Impact of Community Participation in Sustainable Learning Resource Development: A Case of Bangkok, Thailand. *Sustainability (Basel)*, *17*(10), 4620. DOI: 10.3390/su17104620

DOI: 10.3390/su17104620

Pichler, P. P., Jaccard, I. S., Weisz, U., & Weisz, H. (2019). International comparison of health care carbon footprints. *Environmental Research Letters*, *14*(6), 064004. DOI: 10.1088/1748-9326/ab19e1

Pisarenco, C., & Pisarenco, S. (2024). Digitalisation of Health Data: Impact on Patient-Centredness and Safety. Buletinul Academiei de Ştiinţe a Moldovei. Ştiinţe Medicale, 80(3), 139-143.

Prastyanti, R. A., & Sharma, R. (2024). Establishing Consumer Trust Through Data Protection Law as a Competitive Advantage in Indonesia and India. Journal of Human Rights. *Culture and Legal System*, *4*(2), 354–390. DOI: 10.53955/jhcls.v4i2.200

Pratici, L., Salvatore, F. P., Fanelli, S., Zangrandi, A., & Milone, M. (2025). Using ESG paradigm as a basis for social reporting in nonprofit organizations: Evidence from cases in healthcare. *Management Decision*, *63*(2), 586–609. DOI: 10.1108/MD-10-2023-2012

Pulka, B. M., & Tijjani, T. S. (2023). Revisiting resource-based view of a firm: A conceptual framework. Sustainable Governance, Citizenship and National Development, 707.

Purohit, A., Smith, J., & Hibble, A. (2021). Does telemedicine reduce the carbon footprint of healthcare? A systematic review. *Future Healthcare Journal*, *8*(1), e85–e91. DOI: 10.7861/fhj.2020-0080 PMID: 33791483

Raja, J., Ashish, A., Boianapalli, S., & Rashid, S. Z. (2025). Blockchain Technology in Supply Chain Management Enhancing Transparency and Efficiency. In ITM Web of Conferences (Vol. 76, p. 02011). EDP Sciences. DOI: 10.1051/itmconf/20257602011

Rathore, N., Kumari, A., Patel, M., Chudasama, A., Bhalani, D., Tanwar, S., & Al-abdulatif, A. (2025). Synergy of AI and Blockchain to Secure Electronic Healthcare Records. *Security and Privacy*, *8*(1), e463. DOI: 10.1002/spy2.463

Sadeghi, T. S., Ourang, S. A., Sohrabniya, F., Sadr, S., Shobeiri, P., & Motamedian, S. R. (2025). Performance of artificial intelligence on cervical vertebral maturation assessment: A systematic review and meta-analysis. *BMC Oral Health*, *25*(1), 187. DOI: 10.1186/s12903-025-05482-9 PMID: 39910512

Sadr, H., Nazari, M., Khodaverdian, Z., Farzan, R., Yousefzadeh-Chabok, S., Ashoobi, M. T., Hemmati, H., Hendi, A., Ashraf, A., Pedram, M. M., Hasannejad-Bibalan, M., & Yamaghani, M. R. (2025). Unveiling the potential of artificial intelligence in revolutionizing disease diagnosis and prediction: A comprehensive review of machine learning and deep learning approaches. *European Journal of Medical Research*, *30*(1), 1–36. DOI: 10.1186/s40001-025-02680-7 PMID: 40414894

Saharkhiz, M., Rao, T., Parker-Lue, S., Borelli, S., Johnson, K., & Cataife, G. (2024). Telehealth expansion and Medicare beneficiaries' care quality and access. *JAMA Network Open*, *7*(5), e2411006–e2411006. DOI: 10.1001/jamanetworkopen.2024.11006 PMID: 38739388

Schellenberg, M., Harker, M. J., & Jafari, A. (2018). International market entry mode–a systematic literature review. *Journal of Strategic Marketing*, *26*(7), 601–627. DOI: 10.1080/0965254X.2017.1339114

Selvakumar, P., Muralidharan, V., Kumar, G. S., Kumar, D. S., Anand, T., & Manjunath, T. C. (2025). Reducing the Carbon Footprint in Healthcare. *Journal of Environmental Nanotechnology*, *14*(1), 453–463. DOI: 10.13074/jent.2025.03.2511154

Sepetis, A., Rizos, F., Pierrakos, G., Karanikas, H., & Schallmo, D. (2024). A sustainable model for healthcare systems: The innovative approach of ESG and digital transformation. In Healthcare (Vol. 12, No. 2, p. 156). mdpi.

Seraj, Z. (2025). Klang Valley takes medical tourism crown from Penang. MalayMail. https://www.malaymail.com/news/malaysia/2025/02/17/klang-valley-takes-medical-tourism-crown-from-penang/165936.

Shan, S., Luo, Y., Zhou, Y., & Wei, Y. (2019). Big data analysis adaptation and enterprises' competitive advantages: The perspective of dynamic capability and resource-based theories. *Technology Analysis and Strategic Management*, *31*(4), 406–420. DOI: 10.1080/09537325.2018.1516866

Shankar, D. S., Li, Z. I., Hoberman, A. R., Blaeser, A. M., Gonzalez-Lomas, G., & Youm, T. (2024). Patient Satisfaction with Postoperative Telemedicine Versus In-Office Visits Following Primary Hip Arthroscopy: A Prospective Observational Study Before and During the COVID-19 Pandemic. *Telemedicine Journal and e-Health*, *30*(2), 464–471. DOI: 10.1089/tmj.2023.0157 PMID: 37585554

Sharma, P., & Dash, B. (2023). The digital carbon footprint: Threat to an environmentally sustainable future. *SSRN*.

Sharma, R., Soni, G., & Sethia, S. (2025). Bias and Ethical Concerns in Generative AI-driven Medical NLP Models. Available at *SSRN* 5255346. DOI: 10.2139/ssrn.5255346

Shrivastava, U., & Song, J. (2022). Digitization and public trust in health system during COVID pandemic. In *Trust and Digital Business* (pp. 177–187). Routledge. DOI: 10.4324/9781003266525-16

Siemens-Healthineers. (2025). Gleneagles Hospital Penang Introduces Southeast Asia's First SOMATOM Pro.Pulse Dual Source CT Scanner. https://www.siemens-healthineers.com/en-my/press-room/press-features/first-somatom-pro-pulse-gleneagles-penang

Sipos, D., Goyal, R., & Zapata, T. (2024). Addressing burnout in the healthcare workforce: Current realities and mitigation strategies. *The Lancet Regional Health. Europe*, *42*, 42. DOI: 10.1016/j.lanepe.2024.100961 PMID: 39070752

Siripipatthanakul, S. (2025) *Privacy and Security Management Practices for Organizations*, *2025*, 1–306.

Siripipatthanakul, S., Limna, P., Siripipattanakul, S., & Phuangsuwan, P. (2025). Modelling Problem-Based Learning, Student Satisfaction, and Effectiveness Among Higher Education Students in Thailand. In *International Academic Transformations and Cross-Border Collaborations* (pp. 311–332). IGI Global Scientific Publishing.

Siripipatthanakul, S., & Siripipattanakul, S. (2025a). Rural Dental Health Transformation by Adopting Digital Technologies. *Transforming Dental Health in Rural Communities: Digital Dentistry*, 47-80. DOI: DOI: 10.4018/979-8-3693-7165-7.ch003

Siripipatthanakul, S., & Siripipattanakul, S. (2025b). Oral Healthcare Knowledge, Attitude, and Practice (KAP) of Primary School Students in Rural Areas Using Digital Technologies. In *Transforming Dental Health in Rural Communities: Digital Dentistry* (pp. 141-172). IGI Global Scientific Publishing.

Snoswell, C. L., Chelberg, G., De Guzman, K. R., Haydon, H. M., Thomas, E. E., Caffery, L. J., & Smith, A. C. (2023). The clinical effectiveness of telehealth: A systematic review of meta-analyses from 2010 to 2019. *Journal of Telemedicine and Telecare, 29*(9), 669–684. DOI: 10.1177/1357633X211022907 PMID: 34184580

Solomou, T., Mappouras, S., Kyriacou, E., Constantinou, I., Antoniou, Z., Canciu, I. C., Neophytou, M., Lantos, Z., Schizas, C. N., & Pattichis, C. S. (2025). Bridging language barriers in healthcare: A patient-centric mobile app for multilingual health record access and sharing. *Frontiers in Digital Health, 7*, 1542485. DOI: 10.3389/fdgth.2025.1542485 PMID: 40041125

Sophia, E. (2025). Adoption of Teleradiology during the COVID-19 Pandemic: Opportunities and Challenges in the UAE Healthcare System.

Suchman, M. C. (1995). Managing legitimacy: Strategic and institutional approaches. *Academy of Management Review, 20*(3), 571–610. DOI: 10.2307/258788

Tan-McGrory, A., Schwamm, L. H., Kirwan, C., Betancourt, J. R., & Barreto, E. A. (2022). Addressing virtual care disparities for patients with limited English proficiency. *The American Journal of Managed Care, 28*(1). PMID: 35049259

Tebeje, T. H., & Klein, J. (2021). Applications of e-health to support person-centered health care at the time of COVID-19 pandemic. *Telemedicine Journal and e-Health, 27*(2), 150–158. DOI: 10.1089/tmj.2020.0201 PMID: 32746750

Teece, D., Pisano, G., & Shuen, A. (1997). Dynamic Capabilities and Strategic Management. *Strategic Management Journal, 18*(7), 509–533. DOI: 10.1002/(SICI)1097-0266(199708)18:7<509::AID-SMJ882>3.0.CO;2-Z

The Malaysian Reserve. (2024). Malaysia's advanced healthcare attracts international patients. The Malaysian https://themalaysianreserve.com/2024/06/04/malaysias-advanced-healthcare-attracts-international-patients/

Thomas, T. S. P., & Leon, L. (2025). Artificial Intelligence in Health and Well-Being: Advancing Diagnostics, Personalized Medicine, and Global Health Initiatives. In Smart Healthcare, Clinical Diagnostics, and Bioprinting Solutions for Modern Medicine (pp. 39-62). IGI Global Scientific Publishing.

Tully, J., Selzer, J., Phillips, J. P., O'Connor, P., & Dameff, C. (2020). Healthcare challenges in the era of cybersecurity. *Health Security, 18*(3), 228–231. DOI: 10.1089/hs.2019.0123 PMID: 32559153

Vashu, D., Masri, R., Huei, C. T., & Lee, K. C. S. (2021). Destination image as a healing destination among medical tourists: An exploratory case study of Penang, Malaysia. *ABAC Journal, 41*(2), 156–176.

Victor, O., Ugochukwu, S., Macdonald, N., & Ebuka, M. (2025). Public Perception of Artificial Intelligence and Its Role in Achieving the Sustainable Development Goals.

Wang, Q., Su, M., Zhang, M., & Li, R. (2021). Integrating digital technologies and public health to fight Covid-19 pandemic: Key technologies, applications, challenges and outlook of digital healthcare. *International Journal of Environmental Research and Public Health*, *18*(11), 6053. DOI: 10.3390/ijerph18116053 PMID: 34199831

Whitehead, L., Talevski, J., Fatehi, F., & Beauchamp, A. (2023). Barriers to and facilitators of digital health among culturally and linguistically diverse populations: Qualitative systematic review. *Journal of Medical Internet Research*, *25*, e42719. DOI: 10.2196/42719 PMID: 36853742

Wolf, R. M., Abramoff, M. D., Channa, R., Tava, C., Clarida, W., & Lehmann, H. P. (2022). Potential reduction in healthcare carbon footprint by autonomous artificial intelligence. *NPJ Digital Medicine*, *5*(1), 62. DOI: 10.1038/s41746-022-00605-w PMID: 35551275

Xi, M., Liu, Y., Fang, W., & Feng, T. (2024). Intelligent manufacturing for strengthening operational resilience during the COVID-19 pandemic: A dynamic capability theory perspective. *International Journal of Production Economics*, *267*, 109078. DOI: 10.1016/j.ijpe.2023.109078

Xu, G., Wu, Y., Minshall, T., & Zhou, Y. (2017). Exploring the Innovation Ecosystems Across Science, Technology and Business: A Case of 3D Printing in China. *Technological Forecasting and Social Change*. DOI: 10.1016/j.techfore.2017.06.030

Yadav, S. (2024). Transformative frontiers: A comprehensive review of emerging technologies in modern healthcare. *Cureus*, *16*(3), e56538. DOI: 10.7759/cureus.56538 PMID: 38646390

Yakin, A., Khang, A., Muthmainnah, M., Elngar, A. A., Siripipatthanakul, S., & Limna, P. (2025). Unraveling the Quantum Robotics Influence: Transforming Social Interaction for the Future. In The Quantum Evolution (pp. 349-372). CRC Press.

Yong, S. P., Goh, Y. N., Ting, M. S., & Lunyai, J. (2021). Revisit intention for medical services: An investigation on Penang as a medical tourism hub. *Malays J Consum Fam Econ*, *26*, 127–157.

Zahari, A. I., Said, J., Muhamad, N., & Ramly, S. M. (2024). Ethical culture and leadership for sustainability and governance in public sector organisations within the ESG framework. *Journal of Open Innovation*, *10*(1), 100219. DOI: 10.1016/j.joitmc.2024.100219

Zheng, R., Wu, G., Cheng, Y., Liu, H., Wang, Y., & Wang, X. (2023). How does digitalization drive carbon emissions? The inverted U-shaped effect in China. *Environmental Impact Assessment Review*, *102*, 107203. DOI: 10.1016/j.eiar.2023.107203

Chapter 6
Sustainable Development Based on Mobile Apps for Translation, Management, and Digital Marketing in Clinics

Sutithep Siripipattanakul
https://orcid.org/0000-0002-5477-6723
Kasetsart University, Bangkhen, Thailand

Parichat Jaipong
https://orcid.org/0000-0002-9249-3169
GlobalNxt University, Kuala Lumpur, Malaysia

Penpim Phuangsuwan
https://orcid.org/0000-0003-2371-7998
University of Phayao, Bangkok, Thailand

ABSTRACT

Numerous studies show that mobile apps improve clinic services. They inform patients of diagnoses, treatment plans, and pricing, service, and facility options. The systematic review detects plagiarism using Word Cloud and Grammarly. The English versions of Google Scholar, Web of Science (WOS), and Scopus databases use AI writing similarity checks to examine scientific article material from 2021 to 2025. Mobile apps boost management, communication, and marketing, but they also increase patient outcomes and organizational performance in dental clinics. This technique could minimize healthcare utilization and clinic management costs using

DOI: 10.4018/979-8-3693-9800-5.ch006

mobile apps for translation, management, and digital marketing. Medical professionals and patients have various commercial mobile app options. However, mobile app resource costs and low user adoption make cost-benefit analysis problematic.

1. INTRODUCTION

In recent decades, the rapid advancement of digital technology has prompted significant changes across virtually every aspect of human activity, including the healthcare sector. These innovations have had a significant impact on the health sector. The phrase "digital health" has emerged as an all-encompassing concept that encompasses not only the data gathered electronically but also the technical and communication infrastructures and applications involved in the healthcare ecosystem. Digital health is undergoing revolutionary changes that are transforming the fields of medicine, biomedical science, and health care. These changes are redefining and reengineering the tools that are required to create a better future (Abernethy et al., 2022; Oke & Sibomana, 2025). Extensive scientific data demonstrate that mobile health (mHealth) applications can enhance quality of life, alleviate symptoms, and restore health for patients. Besides enhancing patients' health outcomes, mHealth applications reduce healthcare utilization and the financial burdens associated with illness management. Now, patients and healthcare practitioners possess numerous options among commercially accessible mHealth applications. Nevertheless, the elevated resource expenditures and minimal user uptake of mHealth applications render the cost-benefit connection contentious (Rowland et al., 2020; An et al., 2023).

Recently, there has been an increase in the focus on sustainable innovations in healthcare due to the growing necessity for more efficient and cost-effective healthcare systems. Adopting telemedicine, which can improve patient outcomes and reduce healthcare costs, is one solution in the realm of technology and digital health solutions. The quality of healthcare services has been improved while healthcare expenditures have been reduced through the use of digital health technologies. Another area in which innovation has been beneficial is the development of new healthcare management techniques and policies. These policies and measures are intended to enhance the quality of healthcare services, reduce costs, and increase access to healthcare services (Alami et al., 2020; Hussain et al., 2024). The adoption of healthcare sustainability innovations that address unsustainable behaviors is uncommon, despite their availability. A novel set of behaviors, routines, and ways of working that are directed at improving health outcomes, efficiency, cost-effectiveness, or users' experiences and that are implemented by planned and coordinated actions are referred to as innovations in healthcare settings. Surveys indicate that healthcare professionals are enthusiastic about addressing climate change and environmental issues; however, they perceive substantial variation in the sustainability of healthcare practices (Kotcher et al., 2021; Rajagopalan et al., 2023).

Given the increasing demand for healthcare services that are more accessible, of higher quality, and affordable, it is imperative to develop long-term solutions to the industry's intricate challenges. Innovative health economics, social policy, and management are necessary to deliver high-quality, affordable, and accessible services in the emerging healthcare sector. Sustainable healthcare solutions are indispensable as the global population ages and expands. Sustainable healthcare innovation has the potential to address the challenges of changing demographics, increasing healthcare expenditures, and the prevalence of chronic illnesses. A comprehensive approach that integrates technical advancements, evidence-based research, and teamwork is necessary for the achievement of successful health outcomes and long-term healthcare systems. Numerous initiatives have advocated for sustainable healthcare innovations, including those that aim to reduce expenses and improve accessibility (Hussain et al., 2024). By eliminating stacks of paper that contain employee files and applications, contemporary organizations can conserve both time and space in the workplace. Mobile applications have penetrated every aspect of life, particularly in the business sector, as communication technology continues to expand and become more prevalent (Rakshit et al., 2021). The integration of technology into human resource management has resulted in a significant transformation of its business processes (Bratton et al., 2021). The transformation of human resource management (HRM) into digital HRM is a result of the integration of technology into its business processes. Digital transformation is a change in the manner in which companies employ digital technologies to establish new digital business models that enable them to generate and capitalize on additional value. The smartphone and electronic application markets have experienced substantial growth, prompting them to expedite the development of electronic applications. Building an application can offer enterprises an infinite number of growth opportunities, as the majority of consumer activity is currently conducted through applications—the primary advantages of developing an online application for businesses (Uzkurt et al., 2023).

The advancement of sustainable development in clinics can be facilitated by mobile applications centered on translation, management, and digital marketing. Translation applications dismantle linguistic obstacles, facilitating inclusive communication with a varied patient demographic. Management applications optimize processes, minimize paper use, and enhance resource efficiency, fostering environmental and economic sustainability. Digital marketing applications assist clinics in engaging communities, promoting preventative care, and enhancing service accessibility, thus fostering social sustainability. Collectively, these mobile instruments promote egalitarian, efficient, and environmentally sustainable clinical operations. Integrating technology into daily operations enables clinics to attain sustainability objectives while enhancing patient experience and operational resilience in a progressively digital healthcare environment.

1.1 Research Objective

This chapter explains the sustainable development for clinics based on mobile app adoption, mainly for mobile applications centered on translation, management, and digital marketing.

1.2 Research Question

What are the benefits of sustainable development for clinics based on mobile app adoption for mobile applications centered on translation, management, and digital marketing?

2. LITERATURE REVIEW

Utilizing digital tools to enhance the effectiveness, accessibility, and environmental responsibility of healthcare is an essential component of sustainable growth in clinics through mobile applications. Through the use of digital scheduling, remote monitoring, and electronic prescriptions, mobile applications can potentially eliminate the need for paper records, reduce trip emissions thanks to telemedicine, and optimize resource management. These innovations support the following three important pillars of sustainability:

2.1 Clinic Management and Environmental Sustainability

This reduces the company's carbon footprint by reducing the use of paper and travel. Digital records and remote consultations also reduce energy consumption and waste.

Social, environmental, cost, and accessibility are all aspects of healthcare sustainability. Healthcare is a substantial contributor to carbon emissions and is required to mitigate its environmental impact. To be socially sustainable, healthcare systems must address health inequities, socioeconomic determinants of health, and patient empowerment (Wang et al., 2024). Sustainable health economics, social policy, and management developments are required to satisfy the global healthcare demand. These principles included reducing the environmental impact of individual practices; choosing medications and equipment that are better for the environment when it is safe to do so; cutting down on waste and unnecessary use of resources, medications, and equipment; teaching formal education about environmental sustainability; including environmental sustainability in anesthesia research and quality improvement programs; leading environmental sustainability efforts in local organizations; and working with industry to improve environmental sustainability. In the outpatient setting, solid waste (defined as discarded materials such as paper, plastics, glass, and food waste) is a tangible starting point for waste reduction, as it contributes to a substantial percentage of the waste identified in audits (US Environmental Protection Agency, 2024).

Paper products are also a significant contributor to the waste generated in the ambulatory setting, particularly in pediatric clinics, where families are typically provided with vaccine information sheets during each well-child visit. One practice replaced individual vaccine information sheets with a single sheet that included quick response (QR) codes that connected to the information provided by the Centers for Disease Control and Prevention. Ultimately, the authors replaced their handout with a single laminated sheet in each examination room, with paper copies available only upon parental request (Yun et al., 2023). According to the authors, this modification led to the reduction of paper consumption by nearly 80,000 sheets. This initiative resulted in heightened awareness of sustainability practices and motivated employees to advocate for supplementary measures in the clinic. Clinics that offer travel medicine services, which typically necessitate a diverse array of vaccines, may find paper reduction appealing. However, routine printing of potentially lengthy after-visit summaries can also incorporate this approach. Furthermore, the use of smartphones and tablets to securely and digitally fax patient documentation and charts can reduce paper waste and eliminate the electronic waste generated by the operation of fax machines, fax servers, and the server rooms that support them. Further, reducing energy consumption is an additional method of reducing waste in the clinic. Purchasing products that have a reduced environmental impact is a critical step. The Electronic Product Environmental Assessment Tool (EPEAT) assists in the identification of environmentally preferable electronic products that are required in clinics, including TVs, printers, and desktops. When purchasing new equipment and resources, this list can be cross-referenced (Earth911, 2024).

Clinic management that prioritizes environmental sustainability emphasizes the effective utilization of resources, minimization of waste, and implementation of eco-friendly practices. Essential practices encompass the implementation of digital systems to reduce paper consumption, the utilization of energy-efficient equipment, the responsible management of biological waste, and the advocacy of sustainable construction standards. Sustainable procurement and water conservation are prioritized as well. These approaches not only diminish the clinic's environmental impact but also improve public health and organizational efficacy. By incorporating sustainability into everyday operations, clinics advance global environmental objectives while enhancing patient trust and operational efficiency. This proactive strategy fosters enduring resilience and accountable healthcare service provision.

2.2 Clinic Management and Social Sustainability

Access to healthcare is increased, particularly in underserved or rural areas, which contributes to social sustainability. Through the use of apps, patients can receive ongoing care, health education, and reminders, all of which contribute to their long-term overall well-being.

Sustainable healthcare delivery necessitates innovative methodologies that optimize population health and mitigate socioeconomic determinants of health. Social, economic, and environmental components must be integrated into interdisciplinary healthcare delivery systems. Telemedicine and digital health technologies have the potential to enhance the accessibility of healthcare in rural or underserved regions and minimize patient travel. One solution is the utilization of digital technology, as digital health platforms can enhance patient engagement and self-management. At the same time, telemedicine and remote monitoring can decrease the number of in-person visits. Moreover, electronic health records and mobile health applications are sustainable healthcare innovations that have the potential to enhance patient satisfaction and health outcomes (Hussain et al., 2024).

Recently, public health systems have been gradually transitioning to a more comprehensive approach, which is based on the concept of One Health (One Health Global, 2022). This method acknowledges the link between human and animal health and the health of their ecosystems. This innovative method is capable of withstanding and overcoming the new challenges that the healthcare system must confront, including environmental threats. So, according to the 2030 Agenda for Sustainable Development's Sustainable Development Goals (SDGs), health systems should start to include environmental and social sustainability in their focus on patient outcomes, fairness, and financial stability. In healthcare, social sustainability often means ensuring that everyone has equal access to care, which is part of universal health coverage, and that the community is actively involved in health decisions and prevention efforts. The population's role and collective action are particularly prominent in the context of preventive care. Empowering and enabling the community to assume responsibility for its health and ecosystem is a critical component of healthcare service planning (Pennucci et al., 2022).

Clinic management and social sustainability emphasize equitable healthcare access, community engagement, and staff well-being. Key elements include inclusive patient services, culturally sensitive care, and support for vulnerable populations. Ensuring fair labor practices, continuous staff training, and a safe, respectful work environment enhances employee satisfaction and service quality. Clinics also strengthen social sustainability by collaborating with local organizations, promoting health education, and fostering trust within the community. These efforts build strong social ties, reduce health disparities, and create a more inclusive and resilient healthcare system that prioritizes people's well-being alongside organizational goals.

2.3 Clinic Management and Economic Sustainability

Integrating mobile applications into clinic operations reduces operational expenses by optimizing clinic workflows, lowering the number of missed appointments, and boosting patient adherence to treatment. Additionally, efficient systems lead to more effective resource allocation. Clinics can operate more sustainably, improve patient care, and support broader health and environmental goals under the Sustainable Development Goals (SDGs) by integrating mobile applications into their operations.

Healthcare innovations have the potential to enhance the efficacy and efficiency of healthcare delivery while simultaneously reducing costs. Research indicates that the implementation of new technology and innovations in healthcare may improve patient outcomes while simultaneously reducing costs (Moreno et al., 2022). Consequently, the implementation of sustainable innovations in healthcare may lead to improved outcomes and cost savings. The study demonstrated that improved health outcomes may be achieved through the implementation of favorable social policies and affordable healthcare. According to research, health outcomes may be enhanced by universal healthcare and other social policies that prioritize healthcare access. Consequently, we propose that the effective adoption of long-term innovations in healthcare may be facilitated by social policies that prioritize healthcare access and cost. The adoption of sustainable technologies in healthcare may be facilitated by effective management practices (Hussain et al., 2024). In addition to environmental sustainability, ethical sustainability necessitates that AI ensure equitable access to healthcare resources and not exacerbate existing disparities (Van, 2021). In order to prevent the amplification of biases or the generation of detrimental downstream effects, such as misinformation or discriminatory treatment paths, AI tools must be designed and validated. A forward-thinking, strategic approach is necessary to meet the demand for patient-centered, equitable, and trustworthy solutions as AI becomes more integral to healthcare. The future is contingent upon the development of robust partnerships among developers, clinicians, policymakers, and ethicists, as well as the promotion of global standards and adaptive regulatory models. The emphasis must transition from reactive measures to proactive frameworks that anticipate emerging challenges, promote sustainability, and guarantee that AI-driven care remains both clinically valuable and ethically grounded (Goktas & Grzybowski, 2025).

Clinic management and economic sustainability emphasize financial efficiency, long-term viability, and value-oriented healthcare services. Strategies encompass optimizing resource allocation, implementing cost-efficient technology, and enhancing processes to minimize waste and expenditures. Diversifying revenue streams, including the provision of specialist services or telemedicine, fortifies income stability. Transparent financial planning and performance evaluation provide accountability and informed decision-making. Investing in preventive care and patient retention enhances cost-efficiency. Clinics can sustain profitability by harmonizing pricing with quality, thereby providing accessible treatments. Economic sustainability fosters ongoing enhancement, resilience amid economic volatility, and the capacity to reinvest in superior patient care and infrastructure.

2.4 Human Resource (HR) Development by Adopting Mobile Apps

Through the implementation of mobile applications for Human Resource Development (HRD), firms can enhance the efficiency, personalization, and scalability of their HR processes. This includes the training, management, and engagement of their staff.

2.4.1 Clinic Staff Training

Continual learning and skill enhancement are two of the most important advantages. Mobile device applications enable users to access training modules, tutorials, and microlearning content on the go. Employees can learn at their own pace, fostering lifelong learning and skill development.

The increasing number of mobile devices has resulted in significant advancements in mobile communications, such as 5G technology, mobile applications, data and video, voice, storage capacity, and personalization. Information systems (IS) and information technology (IT) are indispensable for the operation and efficiency of organizations, to establish data frameworks that satisfy business requirements and facilitate all business operations (Kamar et al., 2023). Additionally, training activities are implemented to enhance employees' efficiency, knowledge, skills, and attitudes toward specific tasks. They must ascertain the training requirements of their subordinates, implement suitable methodologies and techniques, and assess the efficacy of the training. The process of career path planning entails the coordination of the organization's employees' career advancements, with a particular emphasis on training, promotion, and transfer. It necessitates the identification of the individual's strengths and weaknesses. The utilization of mobile applications in HRM and the impact of these applications on organizational performance have been the subject of numerous studies (Setyaningrum & Muafi, 2022). There is an impact of a mobile HR application on employee engagement and work satisfaction. There is a positive correlation between the use of the mobile application and increased levels of employee engagement and job satisfaction. Various factors impact adoption, such as perceived utility, usability, and compatibility with users' job-related responsibilities. The survey also revealed that employees were more inclined to utilize a mobile application if they perceived it to be user-friendly and practical (Kaur & Kaur, 2022).

Iakovets (2022) identified a positive correlation between the utilization of mobile applications and increased levels of job satisfaction and productivity among employees. Furthermore, mobile applications influence the learning and development of employees. The study found a positive correlation between the use of the mobile application and increased levels of staff learning and development. The survey also revealed that the mobile application facilitated staff access to training and development materials, resulting in enhanced skills and knowledge.

2.4.2 Organizational Performance Management

Real-time performance tracking, utilizing analytics, enables applications to monitor progress, offer rapid feedback, and pinpoint areas of weakness in performance. As a result, data can inform HR decisions, and individualized development plans can be created.

After downloading and utilizing their applications, they can acquire a wealth of information about their customers, including their preferences, geographical location, and peak activity times. Enterprises can also rapidly acquire actionable insights from users by conducting an in-app survey, analyzing user reviews in app stores, or utilizing analytics tools. This enables them to identify areas for improvement in product quality, services, and other aspects. Therefore, the development of an HR management app or any other online application offers various advantages to businesses, such as enhancing customer loyalty, saving time, space, and money, and acquiring valuable insights that can be used to improve the quality of their products and services. The strong correlation between strategic HRM and business performance necessitates the widespread application of human resource management (HRM) techniques within an organization (Easa et al., 2021). There has been a growing emphasis on implementing innovative HRM technologies and methodologies within organizations (Vrontis et al., 2022). The objective of these tools and techniques is to foster a healthy work environment, enhance business productivity, and cultivate a positive work culture. The successful integration of the latest HRM technology is undoubtedly a crucial factor in achieving business success and competitiveness in the contemporary world (Kaur et al., 2022). This procedure encompasses the activities and tasks that constitute a job, including its description, determination of responsibilities, appropriate design, and specification of the individual who occupies it. Human resource planning is the process of determining the organization's requirements for the types and quantities of workers. The procedure involves comparing the demand for workers, the available workforce, and the net deficit to determine the organization's workforce requirements and any resulting deficit. The process of selection and appointment involves identifying potential employees in the labor market and subsequently screening candidates through job applications, tests, personal interviews, and other methods to ensure that the most suitable candidate is appointed to the appropriate position (Kaur & Kaur, 2022).

2.4.3 Staff Engagement

Enhanced Engagement and Communication: Push notifications, interactive features, and social learning tools are all helpful in maintaining employee engagement. Communication applications also simplify the process of disseminating HR policies and changes. Travel, printing, and logistics costs are reduced when mobile learning is used instead of traditional workshops. This results in cost-effective training. The fact that it can be scaled across regions makes it particularly beneficial for hybrid or remote workforce groups. According to accessibility and sustainability, mobile apps not only ensure that all employees, especially those working in remote places, have equal access to growth opportunities, but they also encourage paperless and environmentally friendly human resource operations. Organizations can update training, empower employees, and cultivate a culture of continuous growth by utilizing mobile applications in human resource development (HRD). This is accomplished while simultaneously encouraging sustainability, efficiency, and inclusivity (Luo, 2024; Nabivi, 2025).

Technology can be responsibly managed and developed in a way that improves the engagement of healthcare professionals and promotes positive reactions to it. The significance of engagement has been investigated in the context of general technology, including mobile applications and virtual reality. However, this is the first study to investigate how responsible technology principles enhance the attitudes, satisfaction, and usage intentions of healthcare practitioners, to the best of our knowledge. Additionally, we investigate whether "techno-overload" mitigates the impact of responsible technology principles on employee engagement, which in turn influences their attitudes, satisfaction, and technology usage intentions. Responsible AI signals and outcomes are connected by employee engagement. In IS contexts, employee engagement has been extensively investigated due to its significance as a determining factor in the adoption of IT (Wang et al., 2023). People employ and express themselves physically, cognitively, or emotionally during role performances during engagement. The level of engagement of employees will determine their acceptance or resistance to technical changes, such as the adoption of new technology or innovation (Braganza et al., 2020). The key to successful technological implementation is the involvement of highly engaged employees. In the healthcare sector, employee engagement with technology is defined as the extent to which healthcare practitioners are enthusiastic about the integration of AI into their systems. The extent of employee engagement is contingent upon the advantages they derive from organizational resources, which encompass information (or signals) regarding their responsibilities, enabling them to understand the expectations and strategies for success. Using effective internal communication and training, technology can offer guidance on how to operate and exploit systems fully, responsibly, and ethically. The knowledge acquired through this engagement process will lead to a greater understanding of the technology usage of employees (Wang et al., 2023).

2.5 Translation Mobile Apps (Translator) for Clinics' Staff

Utilizing translation mobile apps in clinics directly supports staff effectiveness and organizational performance, particularly in cases where patient populations are multilingual or diverse.

2.5.1 Communication and Appointments in Clinics

A translator leads to increased employee performance. When communicating with patients who speak different languages, clinicians and staff members can use translation applications to convey their messages more correctly. Miscommunication is reduced, which saves time and reduces the number of errors. Enhances staff confidence in handling patients from diverse backgrounds without requiring an in-person interpreter. Consequently, workers experience more confidence and decreased stress, resulting in increased job satisfaction and productivity (Squires, 2018).

2.5.2 Patient Experience Improvement

Patient experience directly correlates to a stronger organizational reputation. Clear communication enhances patients' trust, safety, and overall satisfaction. Positive experiences also result in better evaluations, more patient retention, and greater relationships with the community. As a consequence, the clinic develops a more responsive and inclusive service model, which enhances its brand image and gives it an advantage over its competitors. Customers can access fundamental information and frequently asked questions without the need to contact a support or service center through electronic applications. Some even permit the use of IVR or chatbots instead of human support centers, which results in a reduction in service costs and the waste of time and money. Mobile applications are optimized for smaller screen sizes, which facilitates their use and scanning by visual inspection. Companies invest significant resources in developing and enhancing their brand, as well as cultivating customer loyalty. Online applications can provide a significant advantage in establishing loyalty programs and demonstrating the business's professionalism, ensuring it is always accessible to customers from any location (Abdeldayem et al., 2024).

2.5.3. Operational efficiency and Reducing Costs in Clinics

Mobile app translation reduces the need for third-party human interpreters for routine encounters. Enables a reduction in waiting time and speeds up appointment times. The result is that the clinic's total efficiency and cost-effectiveness are improved accordingly. Supports the development of human resources and training. Staff members can benefit from using language tools for training in cultural competency and interactions across languages. Provides staff with opportunities to develop their abilities in adaptive communication and lifelong learning. The use of translation apps in clinics enables staff members to communicate more effectively, reducing obstacles to care and improving the overall quality of service. Consequently, this leads to improved staff performance, increased patient satisfaction, and improved organizational outcomes that align with the goals of inclusive and sustainable healthcare (Al Shamsi, 2020; Ahrens & Elias, 2023).

Digital technology is expected to impact the cost structures of businesses significantly. Additionally, these developments enable organizations to operate with reduced errors and increased efficiency. Environmentally friendly healthcare technologies have the potential to enhance health outcomes, reduce costs, and encourage sustainability. Compared to paper-based systems, electronic health records enhance patient outcomes, reduce medical errors, and enhance care coordination, all while reducing costs. Telemedicine, like other digital health technologies, has the potential to improve health outcomes, reduce healthcare costs, and increase access to healthcare in underserved regions (Xinxin et al., 2024). Advancements in healthcare that are both cost-effective and feasible are possible. Sustainable healthcare innovations have the potential to reduce healthcare costs by increasing effectiveness, reducing waste, and attenuating the burden of diseases that can be prevented (Hussain et al., 2024).

3. METHODOLOGY

3.1 Systematic Review, The PRISMA method

The PRISMA (Preferred Reporting Items for Systematic Reviews and Meta-Analyses) method is a standardized framework used to guide transparent and comprehensive reporting in systematic reviews and meta-analyses. It involves four key phases: identification, screening, eligibility, and inclusion, often illustrated through a flow diagram. PRISMA ensures clarity in literature search strategies, inclusion/exclusion criteria, data extraction, and result synthesis. It promotes methodological rigor and reproducibility by requiring detailed documentation of sources and decision-making processes. Widely used in health and social sciences, PRISMA enhances the quality and credibility of evidence-based research by helping researchers synthesize findings systematically and transparently (Siripipatthanakul & Phuangsuwan, 2024).

The PRISMA method was used for meta-analysis following the studies of According to the modified PRISMA method by Asrifan et al. (2025); Hadi et al. (2025); Siripipatthanakul & Siripipattanakul (2025a, b, c), the PRISMA METHOD was adopted in this systematic review in four steps:

Step 1: ***Identifying the Problem*** - Manual searches, literature databases, or other techniques can be used to find early entries. Randomly selecting the topic was the initial stage in this inquiry. The linked article has 779 papers.

Step 2: ***Screening*** - This phase involves identifying the residual records after eliminating duplicates. At this stage, recognized record titles and abstracts are assessed for their pertinence to the study's subject or objectives. The second phase involved intentional sampling of scholarly articles from Google Scholar, Scopus, and Web of Science. This phase selected 98 items.

Step 3: ***Eligibility*** - This section outlines the extent of the study that is feasible after screening. In this phase, essential information articles are assessed for eligibility. In Phase Three, 41 papers were selected for systematic examination through a process of selective sampling. The chosen papers employed AI, Grammarly, Turnitin, and Word Cloud terminology from 2021 to 2025.

Step 4: ***Inclusions*** - This step presents a comprehensive analysis of systematic review research. These studies fulfill the criteria for subsequent research. The flowchart illustrates the extent of research discontinuation at each stage and the reasons behind it. Common reasons for exclusion include irrelevance to the research topic, inadequate study design, insufficient data, or inappropriate inclusion criteria. The fourth step was conducted by three academic experts utilizing PRISMA. The content analysis confirmed the accuracy of the systematic review.

3.2 Content Validity and Analysis

The use of mobile applications has been shown to improve the quality of services provided in clinics, according to a substantial body of research evidence. They engage in conversation with patients to explain diagnosis, treatment plans, and decision-making processes concerning costs, services, and facilities. Word Cloud and Grammarly are the tools the researchers use to check for plagiarism, as stated in the systematic review. Moreover, artificial intelligence-based writing similarity checking is utilized to analyze content derived from academic publications, primarily between 2021 and 2025, and solely in the English language form, as found in the databases Scopus, Web of Science (WOS), and Google Scholar.

The chapter contents have been validated for content analysis by three experts in healthcare, business, and management, by the recommendation of Siripipatthanakul et al. (2024) and Phuangsuwan et al. (2024).

4. RESULTS

Extensive scientific data demonstrate that mobile applications can enhance the quality of services in clinics. They communicate with patients to explain diagnoses, treatment plans, and choice decisions regarding prices, services, and facilities. According to the systematic review, the researchers use Word Cloud and Grammarly to detect plagiarism. Additionally, AI writing similarity checking is utilized to analyze content based on scholarly papers, primarily from 2021 to 2025, in the English version of Google Scholar, Web of Science (WOS), and Scopus databases. The findings suggest that, in addition to enhancing management, communication, and marketing, the adoption of mobile applications can improve patient outcomes and organizational performance in dental clinics. This approach could help managers reduce healthcare utilization and the financial burdens of human resource management. Patients and healthcare practitioners possess many options among commercially accessible mobile applications. Nonetheless, the substantial resource expenditures and limited user uptake of mobile applications render the cost-benefit analysis contentious.

4.1 Conceptual Framework

Figure 1. Conceptual Framework

4.2 Grammarly Result

According to Yakin et al. (2025); Siripipatthanakul & Siripipattanakul (2025b &c); Siripipatthanakul et al. (2025); Phuangsuwan et al. (2025); the academic papers is necessary to be checked grammar and plagiarism using AI or software. This study employed Grammarly and the results show that the appropriate of grammar is over 90% and without plagiarism.

4.3 Word Clouds

Figure 2. Word Cloud

https://www.wordclouds.com/ (July 19, 2025)

5. DISCUSSIONS

Using the prior reasoning as a foundation, let us concentrate on how particular mobile app features, such as translation, appointment scheduling, and digital marketing, contribute to the long-term growth of clinics. The utilization of mobile applications for translation, management, and digital marketing provides clinics with numerous sustainability advantages. Translation applications augment communication and inclusivity, hence enhancing patient care. Management applications enhance operational efficiency, minimize documentation, and maximize resource utilization, thereby promoting environmental and economic sustainability. Digital marketing applications enhance outreach, elevate health awareness, and draw patients, fostering social sustainability. These applications also diminish the necessity for physical goods and in-person visits, hence reducing carbon footprints. In summary, mobile app adoption enhances operational efficiency, patient satisfaction, and long-term sustainability, connecting clinic operations with contemporary digital and environmental objectives.

Artificial intelligence and digital technology are practical for clinic management in several ways to enhance management, communication, and marketing. Adopting mobile applications can improve patient outcomes and organizational performance in dental clinics.

5.1. Social Sustainability for Equity in Clinics

The characteristics of the translation through the incorporation of translation capabilities into a clinic's mobile application can eliminate linguistic barriers, resulting in improved accessibility and inclusivity. The ability to comprehend health information, appointment specifics, and communicate more effectively with healthcare practitioners is made possible for individuals who are not native speakers of the language. Through the provision of more equitable access to healthcare services, this directly contributes to the promotion of social sustainability. Enhanced Patient Understanding and Adherence: When patients can comprehend medical instructions and information in the language that they prefer, they are more likely to stick to treatment programs, which ultimately results in improved health outcomes. The overall health and happiness of the community are improved as a result of this. Accurate translation helps to reduce the likelihood of misunderstandings occurring during consultations and while orders are being given, which ultimately results in an improved level of safety and efficiency in the delivery of medical care.

5.2. Economic and Social Sustainability for Management in Clinics

Management of Appointments by using of clinic resources, such as staff time and consultation rooms, can be optimized through the utilization of mobile applications that include appointment management systems (booking, rescheduling, and reminders). This results in improved efficiency in resource allocation. Because of this, the number of people who do not show up is decreased, processes are streamlined, and efficiency is improved, all of which contribute to economic sustainability. Improved Patient Convenience (Social) to improve patient convenience and satisfaction, online appointment scheduling and management should be made as simple as possible. Patients who receive reminders are more likely to keep their appointments, which results in improved continuity of care. Both the overall patient experience and the social sustainability of the organization are improved as a result of this. Automating appointment scheduling and reminders lessens the administrative strain on clinic staff, freeing them up to focus on other responsibilities and perhaps cutting operational expenses. This is an economic benefit related to the reduction of administrative costs.

5.3. Environmental, Social, and Economic Sustainability Using Digital Marketing

Mobile applications have the potential to serve as a platform for digital marketing initiatives that aim to reach specific patient demographics with pertinent health information, preventative care campaigns, and clinic updates. By doing so, community health literacy can be improved, and proactive healthcare seeking can be encouraged, both of which contribute to increasing social sustainability. Digital marketing through a clinic's app may be more cost-effective than traditional marketing tactics. This is because digital marketing is more efficient than traditional marketing. It improves the efficiency of marketing expenditures and contributes to the long-term viability of the economy by enabling focused campaigns and measurable results.

Mobile apps can help establish stronger patient relationships, promoting loyalty and encouraging patients to return for additional appointments. This is beneficial to both the long-term viability of the clinic and the continuous care of the patient. When these three functionalities—translation, appointments, and digital marketing—are incorporated into the mobile app strategy of a clinic, they have a synergistic impact that contributes to the advancement of sustainable development. Wider reach and inclusivity for Society are achieved through translation, broadening the clinic's reach to various demographics. Effective digital marketing educates these populations about the services available to them. Efficient operations and patient contentment (Economic and Social) by streamlined appointment management improve both efficiency and patient contentment, which contributes to both the economic and social elements of the situation. Better health outcomes can be achieved through community engagement, improved communication through translation, and targeted health information delivered via digital marketing, ultimately leading to a healthier community.

This is a social aspect of well-being. For the record: The primary way in which translation helps in the maintenance of social sustainability is by fostering inclusiveness and equitable access. In addition to improving economic sustainability through increased efficiency, appointment management also improves social sustainability through increased convenience. Economic sustainability is supported by digital marketing through cost-effective promotion, and social sustainability is supported by digital marketing through the dissemination of health information and the engagement of the community. Through the deliberate implementation of these mobile app features, clinics can shift toward a more sustainable model that is economically feasible, socially ethical, and ecologically conscientious (as was emphasized in the previous comment through less paperwork and travel).

5.4 Privacy and Security in Clinic Management for Sustainability

The findings support Siripipatthanakul (2025); Asrifan et al. (2025); Hadi et al. (2025) that the digital revolution has helped firms streamline operations and handle vast amounts of data, such as customer, health, and financial information. It is vulnerable to cyberterrorism. Cyberattacks can cause identity theft, financial theft, and data misuse. To reduce damages, firms must protect cloud environments and create data breach policies. Privacy and security management practices for organizations is useful how data privacy, environmental, and labor laws affect corporate strategy and management and benefits corporate executives, managers, cybersecurity specialists, data scientists, professionals, researchers, scholars, academicians, and more on online marketplaces, remote working, and cyber terrorism.

6. CONCLUSIONS

6.1 Mobile Applications for Dental Clinics:

Mobile applications for dental clinics augment patient care, optimize operations, and promote communication. These applications include functionalities such as online appointment scheduling, treatment notifications, virtual consultations, and access to dental records. Clinics facilitate efficient scheduling, inventory management, billing, and real-time patient engagement. Patients gain advantages from convenience, prompt updates, and tailored oral health recommendations. Specific applications incorporate AI-driven diagnostics and tele-dentistry services, facilitating remote care and follow-up consultations. Mobile applications enhance clinic efficiency, elevate patient contentment, and facilitate contemporary, technology-oriented dental office management following digital health trends.

6.2 Mobile Apps for Clinic Management:

Mobile apps for managing clinics make administrative tasks easier and better for patients. They make it easier to schedule appointments online, access electronic medical records (EMR), pay bills, and keep track of inventories. These apps make it easier for staff and patients to talk to one other in real time, cut down on paperwork, and automate routine tasks. Features like electronic prescriptions, teleconsultations, and ways for patients to give feedback improve the quality of care and encourage more people to use the service. Management of the clinic can keep an eye on things from a distance to make sure they run well and respond quickly. Integrating with cloud-based platforms makes sure that data is safe and easy to get to. Mobile apps make clinics run better, boost productivity, and improve the patient experience by making healthcare management easier and smarter.

6.3 Sustainable Development for Clinics:

Sustainable development in clinics emphasizes providing healthcare with reduced environmental effect, fostering social responsibility, and guaranteeing economic sustainability. This includes energy-efficient infrastructure, trash minimization, and the utilization of environmentally sustainable materials. It encompasses equal access to healthcare, patient-centered services, and the well-being of staff. Digitization, including electronic health records and telemedicine, decreases paper consumption and improves efficiency. It promotes economically efficient approaches that uphold service quality. Community involvement and health education are also pivotal. Sustainable clinics seek to enhance health outcomes while conserving resources for future generations through cohesive environmental, social, and economic initiatives.

6.4 Mobile Apps for Translation:

Translation mobile applications are essential in healthcare facilities for eliminating language barriers between personnel and patients. These applications provide real-time translation of text, audio, and images, facilitating effective communication during consultations, diagnoses, and treatment explanations. They accommodate various languages and frequently use medical terminology to guarantee precision. Translation applications promote patient comprehension, satisfaction, and safety by enabling clear, culturally attuned interactions. They also aid in handling varied patient demographics and enhance inclusion. Translation applications enhance healthcare delivery, mitigate misconceptions, and assist clinics in offering accessible, high-quality care to multilingual populations.

6.5 Mobile apps for Digital Marketing in Clinics:

Mobile apps for digital marketing in clinics empower healthcare providers to engage with patients, promote services, and build brand visibility. These apps enable targeted campaigns through push notifications, email marketing, social media integration, and loyalty programs. Clinics can share updates, health tips, promotional offers, and appointment reminders directly to users' devices, enhancing engagement and retention. Built-in analytics help track user behavior, optimize marketing strategies, and improve ROI. They also support patient reviews and feedback, strengthening trust and reputation. Overall, digital marketing apps modernize outreach efforts, attract new patients, and maintain continuous communication, driving growth and competitive advantage in healthcare services.

The findings suggest that, in addition to improving communication and marketing, as well as patient outcomes, adopting mobile applications to enhance organizational performance in clinics could help dental clinic managers reduce healthcare utilization and the financial burdens associated with human resource management. Patients and healthcare professionals have a wide variety of options available to them, including mobile applications that are available for commercial use. Despite this, the cost-benefit analysis is complicated by the significant resource costs and low consumer acceptance of mobile applications. Besides enhancing communication and marketing, improving patient outcomes, it is suggested that adopting mobile applications to improve the organizational performance of clinics could help dental clinic managers reduce healthcare utilization and the financial burdens of human resource management. Patients and healthcare practitioners possess many options among commercially accessible mobile applications. Nonetheless, the substantial resource expenditures and limited user uptake of mobile applications render the cost-benefit analysis contentious. In the context of clinics adopting mobile apps, sustainable development refers to the utilization of these technologies in a manner that not only enhances the delivery of healthcare and the outcomes of that delivery but also ensures the clinic's long-term survival and the beneficial influence it has on the community and the environment. This requires taking into consideration economic, social, and environmental factors, which is known as the "triple bottom line" approach. Increasing the availability of healthcare and improving access to it (Social Sustainability), Mobile applications have the potential to promote patient engagement by facilitating contact between patients and doctors through the use of secure messaging, appointment reminders, and access to medical records. This, in turn, can lead to improved adherence to treatment programs and improved health outcomes. By way of illustration, a patient can receive a reminder for their medication through the application.

According to telehealth & remote monitoring applications, it is possible to conduct virtual consultations, remotely monitor chronic illnesses (such as blood sugar levels or heart rate), and provide timely interventions. This is especially beneficial for patients who live in remote places or who have mobility limitations. As a result, access to medical treatment is increased, and the need to travel is decreased. Mobile apps have the potential to expedite appointment booking, rescheduling, and cancellations, hence reducing wait times and enhancing the overall patient experience. This can be accomplished through efficient appointment scheduling and management. The clinic's resources are also maximized as a result of this. Access to Health Information and Education Clinics can use mobile applications to give patients trustworthy health information, educational materials, and individualized guidance, thereby boosting health literacy and preventative treatment.

Utilizing the clinic's operations to their full potential (economic sustainability). The use of mobile applications can automate operations such as patient registration, form completion, billing, and insurance claims, freeing up staff time and reducing administrative costs. As an illustration, patients can electronically fill out intake paperwork prior to their scheduled visit. Secure communication capabilities in clinic apps can increase coordination among healthcare personnel, which can lead to more efficient workflows and improved patient care. The streamlining of communication procedures among staff members can accomplish this. The usage of resources inside the clinic can be optimized through efficient management, which can result in cost savings. Telehealth features have the potential to lower the costs associated with in-person consultations—enhancements to Billing and Payment Procedures. Mobile applications have the potential to make billing more transparent, promote online payment methods, and lessen the administrative load associated with managing payments.

Contributing to the long-term sustainability of the environment through paperwork reduction. The digitization of patient records, prescriptions, and communication through mobile applications results in a considerable reduction in the requirement for paper, which contributes to the preservation of the environment. Telehealth consultations have the potential to reduce the carbon footprint associated with patients and staff commuting to and from the clinic. Considerations to make regarding obstacles to sustainable adoption clinics need to handle various hurdles in order to achieve sustainable adoption of mobile applications, although the benefits are significant: The concept of digital literacy refers to the process of ensuring that all patients, even those who are elderly or have limited digital literacy, can efficiently utilize the apps. Training and user-friendly design are two potential solutions to this problem.

Data security and privacy are essential to implement stringent security measures in order to safeguard patient information and preserve confidence. It is vital to comply with rules such as the Health Insurance Portability and Accountability Act (HIPAA) in the United States or other standards of a similar nature. Integration with Preexisting Systems: To prevent data silos and ensure effective workflows, the mobile application must be able to interact seamlessly with the Electronic Health Records (EHR) and other existing systems at the clinic. The cost of Development and maintenance clinics needs to consider both the original investment and the ongoing costs of app development, upgrades, and technical support. Accessibility refers to the action of ensuring that the application is accessible to those who have disabilities. Agreement with the Sustainable Development Goals (also known as

SDGs). The implementation of mobile applications in medical clinics, including the following, can directly and indirectly contribute to several of the Sustainable Development Goals of the United Nations:

It is possible to achieve the Sustainable Development Goal as follows;

To improve Sustainable Development Goal 3 (SDG 3): Good Health and Well-being by strengthening patient participation, encouraging preventative care, and improving access to healthcare.

To improve SDG 9: Industry, Innovation, and Infrastructure by utilizing technology to enhance the delivery of healthcare, this goal can be achieved.

To improve Sustainable Development Goal 12 by responsible consumption and production; such as reduce paper consumption and minimize travel.

Sustainable development for clinics through the adoption of mobile apps requires a holistic approach that takes into consideration the long-term impact on patient care, clinic operations, and the environment. Clinics can achieve greater efficiency, improve health outcomes, and contribute to a more sustainable future by carefully considering the use and management of these technologies, providing translation services, scheduling appointments, and promoting sustainable development through the use of mobile applications. The explanation of digital marketing includes Translation, appointment scheduling, and digital marketing, all of which are included in the sustainable development of mobile apps for medical clinics.

7. IMPLICATIONS

Clinics based on mobile applications offer sustainable development and adoption for children. In terms of environmental, social, and economic aspects, the use of mobile applications in medical facilities has the potential to make a substantial contribution to sustainable development. Maintaining a healthy environment involves utilizing mobile applications for appointment scheduling, electronic health records (EHRs), prescriptions, and educational materials, which minimizes the amount of paper required, thereby reducing the amount of trash and deforestation that occurs. The integration of telehealth elements into mobile applications enables remote consultations, thereby decreasing the carbon footprint associated with transporting patients and staff to the clinic impact on reduced travel. Apps can assist in managing inventories, tracking equipment maintenance, and optimizing energy consumption within the clinic, thereby enhancing efficient resource management.

7.1 Sustainable social development:

Enhancing accessibility could be done by mobile applications, which have the potential to broaden the scope of healthcare services to include populations that are geographically dispersed or underserved by providing access to information, consultations, and monitoring. Enhanced Patient Engagement: Apps enable patients to take a more active part in their health by providing them with features such as appointment reminders, prescription tracking, access to health records, and educational content. As a result, this may result in improved health outcomes.

7.2 Better Communication:

Mobile apps facilitate seamless communication between patients and healthcare practitioners, enhancing the coordination of care and patient satisfaction. Apps can be created to cater to varied populations by including features such as support for several languages and accessibility options.

7.3 Maintaining a Sustainable Economy:

The digitization of procedures through mobile applications can result in a reduction in administrative costs (such as printing and mailing), an increase in the efficiency of appointment scheduling (this will minimize the number of patients who do not show up), and the possibility of a reduction in hospitalizations through remote monitoring and early intervention. Mobile applications have the potential to streamline workflows for physicians and staff, enabling them to manage their time and resources more efficiently. This results in increased efficiency. The incorporation of telehealth capabilities into mobile applications has the potential to open up new channels for delivering services and generating income. Through the promotion of environmental responsibility, the enhancement of social fairness and patient well-being, and the support of economic efficiency, the implementation of mobile applications in medical clinics is, in essence, under the aims of sustainable development.

8. LIMITATIONS AND RECOMMENDATIONS

This chapter represents a systematic review using the PRISMA method and may not include respondents. Thus, questionnaire or interview surveys are recommended for further studies.

9. ACKNOWLEDGEMENTS

This chapter is a systematic review and does not include respondents. Thus, an ethical approval committee is not required in this study. The authors declare that there is no conflict of interest.

REFERENCES

Abdeldayem, M. M., Aldulaimi, S. H., & Al-Kaabi, H. (2024). Exploring essential features for developing a human resource management mobile application: Insights from the Middle East. *International Journal of Engineering Business Management*, *16*, 18479790241275306. DOI: 10.1177/18479790241275306

Abernethy, A., Adams, L., Barrett, M., Bechtel, C., Brennan, P., Butte, A., Faulkner, J., Fontaine, E., Friedhoff, S., Halamka, J., Howell, M., Johnson, K., Long, P., McGraw, D., Miller, R., Lee, P., Perlin, J., Rucker, D., Sandy, L., & Valdes, K. (2022). The promise of digital health: Then, now, and the future. *NAM Perspectives*, *2022*(22), 10–31478. https://pmc.ncbi.nlm.nih.gov/articles/PMC9499383/. DOI: 10.31478/202206e PMID: 36177208

Ahrens, E., & Elias, M. (2023). Effective communication with linguistically diverse patients: A concept analysis. *Patient Education and Counseling*, *115*, 107868. DOI: 10.1016/j.pec.2023.107868 PMID: 37480794

Al Shamsi, H., Almutairi, A. G., Al Mashrafi, S., & Al Kalbani, T. (2020). Implications of language barriers for healthcare: A systematic review. *Oman Medical Journal*, *35*(2), e122. https://pmc.ncbi.nlm.nih.gov/articles/PMC7201401/. DOI: 10.5001/omj.2020.40 PMID: 32411417

Alami, H., Rivard, L., Lehoux, P., Hoffman, S. J., Cadeddu, S. B. M., Savoldelli, M., Samri, M. A., Ag Ahmed, M. A., Fleet, R., & Fortin, J. P. (2020). Artificial intelligence in health care: Laying the foundation for responsible, sustainable, and inclusive innovation in low-and middle-income countries. *Globalization and Health*, *16*(1), 52. https://link.springer.com/article/10.1186/s12992-020-00584-1. DOI: 10.1186/s12992-020-00584-1 PMID: 32580741

An, Q., Kelley, M. M., Hanners, A., & Yen, P. Y. (2023). Sustainable development for mobile health apps using the human-centered design process. *JMIR Formative Research*, *7*, e45694. DOI: 10.2196/45694 PMID: 37624639

Asrifan, A., Siripipatthanakul, S., Alaqad, M. H., Saodi, S., & Sadaruddin, S. (2025). Managing Privacy and Security in Research: Effective Practices and Strategies. In *Privacy and Security Management Practices for Organizations* (pp. 151-182). IGI Global Scientific Publishing. DOI: DOI: 10.4018/979-8-3693-9720-6.ch006

Braganza, A., Chen, W., Canhoto, A., & Sap, S. (2020). Productive employment and decent work: The impact of AI adoption on psychological contracts, job engagement and employee trust. *Journal of Business Research*. Advance online publication. DOI: 10.1016/j.jbusres.2020.08.018 PMID: 32836565

Bratton, J., Gold, J., Bratton, A., & Steele, L. (2021). *Human resource management.* Bloomsbury Publishing.

Earth911 (2024). Earth911 recycling search https://search.earth911.com..

Easa, N. F., & Orra, H. E. (2021). HRM practices and innovation: An empirical systematic review. *International Journal of Disruptive Innovation in Government, 1*(1), 15–35. DOI: 10.1108/IJDIG-11-2019-0005

Goktas, P., & Grzybowski, A. (2025). Shaping the future of healthcare: Ethical clinical challenges and pathways to trustworthy AI. *Journal of Clinical Medicine, 14*(5), 1605. DOI: 10.3390/jcm14051605 PMID: 40095575

Hadi, S., Purnasari, E., Hidayat, R., Lukitaningsih, A., Kirana, K. C., & Siripipatthanakul, S. (2025). Challenges and Management Practices in Protecting Employee Personal Data in the Digital Era. In *Privacy and Security Management Practices for Organizations* (pp. 89–116). IGI Global Scientific Publishing., DOI: 10.4018/979-8-3693-9720-6.ch004

Hussain, A., Umair, M., Khan, S., Alonazi, W. B., Almutairi, S. S., & Malik, A. (2024). Exploring sustainable healthcare: Innovations in health economics, social policy, and management. *Heliyon, 10*(13), e33186. DOI: 10.1016/j.heliyon.2024.e33186 PMID: 39027491

Iakovets, A. (2022). BalogMand ˇZidekK. The use of mobile application for sustainable development of SMEs in the context of industry 4.0. *Applied Sciences (Basel, Switzerland), 13*(1), 429. DOI: 10.3390/app13010429

Kamar, K., Lewaherilla, N. C., Ausat, A. M. A., Ukar, K., & Gadzali, S. S. (2022). The influence of information technology and human resource management capabilities on SMEs performance. *International Journal of Artificial Intelligence Research, 6*(1.2), 1.

Kaur, D., & Kaur, R. (2022). Elucidating the role of gender differences via TAM in e-recruitment adoption in India: A multi-group analysis using MICOM. *The Bottom Line (New York, N.Y.), 35*(2/3), 115–136. DOI: 10.1108/BL-11-2021-0104

Kotcher J, Maibach E, Miller J, et al. Views of health professionals on climate change and health: a multinational survey study. Lancet Planet Health 2021; 5: e316e23

Kruk, M. E., Gage, A. D., Arsenault, C., Jordan, K., Leslie, H. H., Roder-DeWan, S., Adeyi, O., Barker, P., Daelmans, B., Doubova, S. V., English, M., García-Elorrio, E., Guanais, F., Gureje, O., Hirschhorn, L. R., Jiang, L., Kelley, E., Lemango, E. T., Liljestrand, J., & Pate, M. (2018). High-quality health systems in the Sustainable Development Goals era: Time for a revolution. *The Lancet. Global Health, 6*(11), e1196–e1252. DOI: 10.1016/S2214-109X(18)30386-3 PMID: 30196093

(2023)... *Kybernetes*. DOI: 10.1108/K-08-2022-1189

Luo, J. (2024, Nov). Validating the impact of gamified technology-enhanced learning environments on motivation and academic performance: enhancing TELEs with digital badges. In *Frontiers in Education* (Vol. 9, p. 1429452). Frontiers Media SA. https://www.frontiersin.org/journals/education/articles/10.3389/feduc.2024.1429452/full

Moreno Serrano, R., & Ocampo-Corrales, D. B. (2022). The ability of European regions to diversify in renewable energies: The role of technological relatedness. *Research Policy, 51*(5), 104508. DOI: 10.1016/j.respol.2022.104508

Nabivi, E. (2025). The Role of Social Media in Green Marketing: How Eco-Friendly Content Influences Brand Attitude and Consumer Engagement. [measurements.]. *Sustainability (Basel), 2025*(17), 1965. DOI: 10.3390/su17051965

Oke, G. I., & Sibomana, O. (2025). Adoption of Digital Health Technology in Nigeria: A Scoping Review of Current Trends and Future Directions. *Advances in Public Health, 2025*(1), 4246285. DOI: 10.1155/adph/4246285

One health global. (n.d.) https://www.who.int/health-topics/one-health#tab=ta

Pennucci, F., De Rosis, S., Murante, A., & Nuti, S. (2022). Behavioural and social sciences to enhance the efficacy of health promotion interventions: Redesigning the role of professionals and people. *Behavioural Public Policy, 6*(1), 13–33. DOI: 10.1017/bpp.2019.19

Phuangsuwan, P., Siripipatthanakul, S., Chaiprakarn, S., & Rakpathum, W. Muthmainnha, Pariwongkhuntorn, N., & Wattanakul, P. (2024, Jun). Sustainable Development Adopting Artificial Intelligence (AI) in Marketing and Consumer Behaviour Analysis. In *International Conference on Data Analytics & Management* (pp. 569-587). Singapore: Springer Nature Singapore. https://link.springer.com/chapter/10.1007/978-981-96-3372-2_39

Phuangsuwan, P., Siripipatthanakul, S., Siripipattanakul, S., & Jaipong, P. (2025). The Impact of Community Participation in Sustainable Learning Resource Development: A Case of Bangkok, Thailand. *Sustainability (Basel)*, *17*(10), 4620. https://www.mdpi.com/2071-1050/17/10/4620. DOI: 10.3390/su17104620

Rajagopalan, S., Pronovost, P., & Al-Kindi, S. (2023, Jun). Implementing a sustainability framework in healthcare: a three-lens framework. In *Healthcare* (Vol. 11, No. 13, p. 1867). MDPI. https://www.mdpi.com/2227-9032/11/13/1867

Rakshit, S., Islam, N., Mondal, S., & Paul, T. (2021). Mobile apps for SME business sustainability during COVID-19 and onwards. *Journal of Business Research*, *135*, 28–39. DOI: 10.1016/j.jbusres.2021.06.005 PMID: 34751197

Rowland, S. P., Fitzgerald, J. E., Holme, T., Powell, J., & McGregor, A. (2020). What is the clinical value of mHealth for patients? *NPJ Digital Medicine*, *3*(1), 4. https://www.nature.com/articles/s41746-019-0206-x. DOI: 10.1038/s41746-019-0206-x PMID: 31970289

Setyaningrum, R. P., & Muafi, M. (2022). The role of digital HRM: contribution to the improvement of business sustainability. In: *International Conference on Business and Technology*. Cham: Springer International Publishing, pp. 840–848. DOI: 10.1007/978-3-031-26953-0_78

Siripipatthanakul, S. (2025). *Privacy and Security Management Practices for Organizations*. IGI Global Scientific Publishing. DOI: 10.4018/979-8-3693-9720-6

Siripipatthanakul, S., Limna, P., Siripipattanakul, S., & Phuangsuwan, P. (2025). Modelling Problem-Based Learning, Student Satisfaction, and Effectiveness Among Higher Education Students in Thailand. In *International Academic Transformations and Cross-Border Collaborations* (pp. 311–332). IGI Global Scientific Publishing., DOI: 10.4018/979-8-3373-0508-0.ch013

Siripipatthanakul, S., & Phuangsuwan, P. (2024). Salutogenic Marketing in Preventive Dentistry. In *Leveraging Digital Technology for Preventive Dentistry* (pp. 255–278). IGI Global. DOI: 10.4018/979-8-3693-3872-8.ch009

Siripipatthanakul, S., Phuangsuwan, P., & Limna, P., Muthmainnha, Siripipattanakul, S., Vui, C. N., & Jaipong, P. (2024, Jun). Artificial Intelligence (AI) Influencing Sustainable Governance: Governance Adopting AI. In *International Conference on Data Analytics & Management* (pp. 551-568). Singapore: Springer Nature Singapore.

Siripipatthanakul, S., & Siripipattanakul, S. (2025a). Oral Healthcare Knowledge, Attitude, and Practice (KAP) of Primary School Students in Rural Areas Using Digital Technologies. In *Transforming Dental Health in Rural Communities: Digital Dentistry* (pp. 141-172). IGI Global Scientific Publishing. DOI: 10.4018/979-8-3693-7165-7.ch006

Siripipatthanakul, S., & Siripipattanakul, S. (2025b). Rural Dental Health Transformation by Adopting Digital Technologies. *Transforming Dental Health in Rural Communities: Digital Dentistry*, 47-80. DOI: 10.4018/979-8-3693-7165-7.ch003

Siripipatthanakul, S., & Siripipattanakul, S. (2025c). Talent Management Ensuring the Safety and Cybersecurity in Schools. *Cultivating Creativity and Navigating Talent Management in Academia*, 383-402. DOI: 10.4018/979-8-3693-6880-0.ch018

Squires, A. (2018). Strategies for overcoming language barriers in healthcare. *Nursing Management, 49*(4), 20–27. DOI: 10.1097/01.NUMA.0000531166.24481.15 PMID: 29528894

US Environmental Protection Agency. (2024, 16 Jul) Criteria for the definition of solid waste and solid and hazardous waste exclusions.. https://www.epa.gov/hw/criteria-definition-solid-waste-and-solid-and-hazardouswaste-exclusions.

Uzkurt C, Ekmekcioglu EB, Ceyhan S, et al. Digital technology use of SMEs during the COVID-19 pandemic in Turkey: mobile applications' role on motivation and job performance.

Van Wynsberghe, A., & Sustainable, A. I. (2021). AI for sustainability and the sustainability of AI. [CrossRef]. *AI and Ethics, 1*(3), 213–218. DOI: 10.1007/s43681-021-00043-6

Vrontis, D., Christofi, M., Pereira, V., Tarba, S., Makrides, A., & Trichina, E. (2022). Artificial intelligence, robotics, advanced technologies and human resource management: A systematic review. *International Journal of Human Resource Management, 33*(6), 1237–1266. DOI: 10.1080/09585192.2020.1871398

Wang, W., Chen, L., Xiong, M., & Wang, Y. (2023). Accelerating AI adoption with responsible AI signals and employee engagement mechanisms in health care. *Information Systems Frontiers, 25*(6), 2239–2256. DOI: 10.1007/s10796-021-10154-4

White SM, Shelton CL, Gelb AW, (2022) Principles of environmentally-sustainable anaesthesia: a global consensus statement from the World Federation of Societies of Anaesthesiologists. Anaesthesia; 77: 201e12

Xinxin, C., Umair, M., Rahman, S., & Alraey, Y. (2024). RETRACTED: The potential impact of digital economy on energy poverty in the context of Chinese provinces. *Heliyon, 10*(9), e30140. Advance online publication. DOI: 10.1016/j.heliyon.2024.e30140 PMID: 38707298

Yakin, A., Khang, A., Muthmainnah, M., Elngar, A. A., Siripipatthanakul, S., & Limna, P. (2025). Unraveling the Quantum Robotics Influence: Transforming Social Interaction for the Future. In *The Quantum Evolution* (pp. 349-372). CRC Press.

Yu, M., Wang, Y., & Umair, M. (2024). Minor mining, major influence: Economic implications and policy challenges of artisanal gold mining. *Resources Policy, 91*, 104886. DOI: 10.1016/j.resourpol.2024.104886

Yun, Y. M., Kirby, C., Bob, N., Calabria, C., Hernandez, A., Cook, B., Krolczyk, J., & Jee, S. H. (2023). Promoting sustainability practices in the outpatient pediatric setting. *The Yale Journal of Biology and Medicine, 96*(2), 261–265. DOI: 10.59249/VCAH6394 PMID: 37396977

KEY TERMS AND DEFINITIONS

Mobile Applications for Dental Clinics: Dental clinic mobile apps improve patient care, operations, and communication. These apps allow online appointment scheduling, treatment notifications, virtual consultations, and dental record access. Clinics streamline scheduling, inventory, billing, and patient involvement. Patients benefit from convenience, rapid updates, and personalized oral health advice. Some applications use AI-driven diagnostics and tele-dentistry for remote care and follow-ups. Mobile apps improve clinic efficiency, patient satisfaction, and digital health-based dental office administration.

Mobile Apps for Clinic Management: Clinic management mobile apps increase administrative and patient care. They enable online appointment scheduling, EMR access, billing, and inventory management. These apps enable real-time patient-staff communication, reduce paperwork, and automate routine tasks. Electronic prescriptions, teleconsultations, and patient feedback improve service quality and participation. Clinic administration may monitor operations remotely, ensuring efficiency and reaction. Integration with cloud systems secures and simplifies data access. Mobile apps improve clinic operations, efficiency, and patient experience by simplifying and managing healthcare.

Sustainable Development for Clinics: Clinics should limit their environmental impact, promote social responsibility, and ensure economic sustainability. This includes energy-efficient infrastructure, garbage reduction, and eco-friendly materials. It includes staff well-being, patient-centered treatment, and equal healthcare access. Electronic health records and telemedicine save paper use and boost efficiency. Service quality is maintained using cost-effective methods. Community engagement and health education are crucial. Through integrated environmental, social, and economic measures, sustainable clinics improve health and preserve resources for future generations.

Systematic Review, The PRISMA method: PRISMA is a standardized paradigm for transparent and complete systematic review and meta-analysis reporting. It includes identification, screening, eligibility, and inclusion, usually shown in a flow diagram. PRISMA clarifies literature search, inclusion/exclusion, data extraction, and result synthesis. It requires source and decision-making documentation to ensure methodological rigor and reproducibility. PRISMA helps health and social scientists integrate findings methodically and publicly, improving evidence-based research.

Mobile Apps for Translation: Healthcare workers need translation smartphone apps to communicate with patients. These apps translate text, audio, and graphics in real time, making consultations, diagnoses, and treatment explanations easier. They employ medical terminology in multiple languages to ensure accuracy. Translation software enable clear, culturally appropriate interactions, improving patient comprehension, satisfaction, and safety. They improve inclusiveness and manage diverse patient demographics. Translation software improve healthcare delivery, reduce misconceptions, and help clinics provide high-quality, multilingual treatment.

Mobile apps for Digital Marketing in Clinics: Clinic mobile apps for digital marketing let providers communicate with patients, promote services, and develop brand awareness. These apps use push notifications, email marketing, social network integration, and loyalty programs to target campaigns. Clinics can send updates, health recommendations, promotions, and appointment reminders to users' devices to boost engagement and retention. Built-in analytics track user activity, optimize marketing, and boost ROI. Supporting patient evaluations and feedback builds trust and reputation. Digital marketing apps update outreach, attract new patients, and keep communication going, helping healthcare services expand and compete.

Chapter 7
Online Purchase Intentions Among Healthy Drink Consumers:
A Sustainable Healthcare Sector Model

Parichat Jaipong
https://orcid.org/0000-0002-9249-3169
Manipal GlobalNxt University, Nilai, Malaysia

ABSTRACT

Healthy drink products have been gaining popularity among consumers worldwide due to the environmental and health benefits they offer. According to the trend of healthy drink consumption, the industry has flourished and expanded into various consumer product and service categories. To explore purchasing behavior related to healthy drink products, this study applied the theory of planned behavior (TPB), a method for predicting consumer behavior that has been widely used in various research areas in recent years, based on the studies using the PRISMA method. Based on the literature review, the TPB model (attitude, subjective norms, and perceived behaviour control) that incorporates E-WOM and perceived value was examined in this study to predict online purchase intentions among Thai consumers of healthy drinks. The study also shows TPB factors and perceived value significantly direct the effect on purchase intention in healthy drink products. The results can be applied to any related healthy products industry and used to develop a strategy for customer intention.

DOI: 10.4018/979-8-3693-9800-5.ch007

1. INTRODUCTION

Healthy drinks are beverages specifically designed to deliver essential nutrients, vitamins, and minerals, making them an attractive option for individuals seeking to enhance their overall well-being. A well-balanced diet is essential for maintaining optimal health. Nonetheless, our rapid lifestyles often hinder the acquisition of all necessary nutrients exclusively through our standard meals. The emergence of health drinks has provided a convenient and efficient solution to this nutritional gap. Adhering to a balanced diet and regulating daily caloric consumption can bolster immunity (Gangwar et al., 2023). The trend of healthy eating was gaining popularity among consumers seeking nutritious food alternatives. Health considerations significantly influenced the experience of food consumption. Health consciousness profoundly influenced the extent to which individuals were equipped to adopt healthy behaviors autonomously. A prevalent notion to consider was an individual's readiness to participate in activities that could impact their health, referred to as health consciousness. Health-conscious consumers exhibited heightened awareness and concern regarding the preservation of their well-being. Another dietary alternative that can help individuals limit their daily caloric intake is nutritious beverages. A balanced diet that incorporates all essential nutrients is an additional advantage of healthy eating. Consuming a selection of nutritious beverages may enhance self-esteem, improve physical fitness, and promote overall health. Individuals must adhere to a balanced diet to meet all their body's nutritional requirements. These specialized beverages deliver concentrated nutrients that fulfill the body's specific needs (Sugajski et al., 2023; Gangwar et al., 2023). It is essential to consider individual nutritional needs and goals when selecting a healthy beverage. Moreover, healthy living has become increasingly popular globally, including in Thailand. Thai consumers are now more concerned with health and environmental issues than they were in the past. These concerns were driving their pursuit of superior, healthier products (Photcharoen et al., 2020). Health was becoming vital to Thais. They endeavored to maintain a healthy lifestyle and were vigilant regarding their consumption. Thai individuals consume health-promoting foods to safeguard against significant health issues. Furthermore, they focused on their dietary intake to improve their quality of life. Consumer expenditure has increased due to an escalating trend among consumers to adopt healthier lifestyles (Mintel, 2021). Consumers increasingly favored nutritious products due to their convenience. The authors (Fleseriu et al., 2020) examined the benefits of consuming nutritious food and beverages, as well as their potential effects on individuals. The consciousness of personal health influenced the consumption of nutritious beverages. Health-conscious consumers may purchase this product for its potential benefits in supporting overall health and boosting immunity (Watanabe et al., 2020). Moreover, there was an increasing conviction that this enterprise had evolved into the world's preeminent health-focused market, attributed to the rising demand for a broader range of health products. The study concentrated on healthy beverage products marketed to Thai consumers, despite the availability of numerous healthful items in the market today. Numerous models have been employed in studies examining the factors that influence online purchasing behavior, with the Theory of Planned Behavior (TPB) serving as a prominent example. The Theory of Planned Behavior (TPB) has gained recognition and is commonly employed in research to predict users' intended applications and specific behaviors. This research investigated purchase intention in Thailand's healthy beverage market, focusing on factors including attitude, perceived behavioral control, subjective norms, electronic word-of-mouth, and perceived value.

1.1 Research Objective

This chapter systematic review about the relationship between the consumer behaviour variables: consumer attitudes, subjective norms, perceive behavior control, e-WOM on perceived value of health drink products, the relationship of these variables with purchase intention and the mediating role of perceived value with the help on the components of TPB model and E-WOM, which influenced online purchase intentions to Thai healthy drinks consumption among online consumers.

1.2 Research Question

What is the theoretical model to explain the relationship between consumer behaviours of online consumers in healthy drinks consumption in Thailand regarding the TPB model, E-WOM, and perceived value?

2. LITERATURE REVIEW

Consumer behaviors of online consumers regarding healthy drink consumption in Thailand, as influenced by the TPB model, E-WOM, and perceived value. The expansion of the health food industry has been swift. As a result, consumers have shifted their attention to healthcare and developed a greater concern for dietary habits. Many researchers have shown interest in and conducted studies on the behaviour of consuming healthy drinks:

2.1 Attitude

Personal attitudes are crucial factors alongside health and security considerations (He and Tian, 2023). An individual's attitude toward it directly affects their intention to engage in the behavior. The greater the intention, the more suitable the action and demeanor. The objective of all independent variables was to correlate with an appropriate attitude rather than to predict actual behavior. Ajzen posited that the majority of outcomes from appropriate behaviors are positive; conversely, inappropriate actions may yield adverse results. Behavioral beliefs and attitudes toward behavior constitute the two components of attitudes. Consumer perceptions of global brands have long captivated scholars of consumer behavior (Junaid et al., 2022). Ethnocentric consumers demonstrate a collectivist orientation, acquiring information via interpersonal communication, which influences their purchasing decisions based on emotions and brand loyalty. Conversely, cosmopolitan consumers exhibit individualism, obtaining information from media and peers, which influences their purchasing decisions (Shanbhogue & Ranjith, 2024). Consumer perceptions of a brand can be categorized as either positive or negative. A positive brand attitude leads to favorable brand evaluations and an improved brand image, while a negative attitude diminishes consumer assessments and brand perception (Liang et al., 2024). Consumers typically associate symmetry or asymmetry with brand excitement and assess this perceived relationship about their self-concept. Celebrity-specific traits influence consumers; thus, it is crucial to investigate how these traits affect attitudes. Consumers' brand perceptions are shaped by their prior experiences, which in turn influence their purchasing intentions. Purchase intentions can serve as a dependable indicator of actual purchasing behavior. A firm intention to purchase does not always guarantee a transaction; however, it is generally acknowledged that individuals who express a clear intent to buy are more likely to finalize the purchase (Talwar et al., 2021). The employment of celebrity influences as a traditional marketing tactic hinges on the premise that influencing consumer perceptions of products fosters a more positive attitude, subsequently linked to a heightened intention to purchase (Dalziel & De Klerk, 2021). The viewpoints, concepts, and inclinations of millennial consumers fluctuate based on their interaction with social media influences. Further study offers substantial and novel insights at the intersection of influencer marketing, online reviews, brand equity, and consumer behavior. We begin by enhancing the growing body of research on the influence of influencer characteristics, particularly beauty, on consumer sentiments (Casalo et al., 2020). Behavioral beliefs were characterized as personal convictions that supported specific behavioral outcomes. An individual's attitude toward their actions can be characterized by the associated feelings they experience when executing their behavior, which may be positive or negative. Behavioural posits that recognizing and evaluating the consequences of particular actions form an attitude. Favorable outcomes generally fostered a positive disposition toward the action, while unfavorable outcomes engendered a negative attitude toward the behavior. It was generally accurate, provided one assumed that the decision would yield a favorable result. Utomo et al. (2021) found that the attitudes and awareness of business owners substantially affected their intentions to adopt products.

2.2 Subjective Norms

Subjective norms encompass diverse perspectives, typically from authoritative individuals or entities, that can influence an individual's decision, including their purchasing intention. Subjective norms refer to individuals' perceptions of how their peers and groups would evaluate them based on their specific behaviors. Operationally, subjective norms are fundamentally different from personal norms. Personal norms refer to an individual's moral values that influence their behavior, whereas subjective norms pertain to the behaviors that others expect and wish for individuals. Subjective norms evaluated the societal pressures influencing individuals to either participate in or refrain from particular behaviors (Husain et al., 2021; Yarmohammadi et al., 2023). Subjective norms refer to individuals' perceptions of how their peers and groups would evaluate them based on their specific behaviors. Operationally, subjective norms are fundamentally different from personal norms. Personal norms refer to an individual's moral values that influence their behavior, whereas subjective norms pertain to the behaviors that others expect and wish for individuals. In this study, a subjective norm is defined as the conviction that significant individuals in the customers' lives expect them to assist in facilitating environmentally sustainable purchases and desire them to behave under this expectation. Recent studies indicate a positive correlation between subjective norms and entrepreneurial intention (Ahmed et al., 2020). The theory of planned behavior posits that an individual's objective is closely linked to their attitudes toward the behavior. Behavioral attitudes may be associated with normative perspectives (also referred to as subjective norms) due to their reliance on similar information. Subjective norms refer to an individual's perception of the beliefs held by social reference groups regarding the acceptability of engaging in a specific behavior. As these opinions become increasingly favorable, they garner greater support from the social group, resulting in an enhancement of self-efficacy. Subjective norms shape an individual's self-concept, affect their beliefs about self-efficacy, and ultimately influence the likelihood of developing specific intentions. Numerous empirical studies have examined the relationship between subjective norms and entrepreneurial intention. Consequently, numerous studies have demonstrated that environmentally beneficial actions can be influenced by individual and social factors. Subjective norms and customers' internally oriented beliefs and attitudes may have a significant impact. The subjective norm is contingent upon the reference group considered pertinent by the client, which may change over time. This contribution may help assess the degree to which stable or unstable predictors of pro-environmental behaviors influence green customer citizenship behaviors. Adherence to subjective norms is contingent upon an individual's apprehension of social pressure or the receipt of guidance on appropriate or beneficial conduct within a social group. Consumers may solicit assistance from others when uncertain about the ramifications of a particular action. Social pressure can be encountered by various stakeholders, including friends, family, and other members of society (Setiawan et al., 2021). The subjective norm may also affect pro-environmental perspectives. Evidence suggests that subjective norms, including the expectations of educators, peers, and institutions, may positively affect attitudes toward Internet usage. The subjective norm regarding mobile data service usage has been shown to influence attitudes toward these services positively. A positive and substantial correlation has been demonstrated between subjective norm and pro-environmental attitude. The subjective norm influences the creation of private profiles, the dissemination of personal information, the acceptance of unknown individuals as friends on social networks, and the adoption of strategies to counteract online hatred. Furthermore, subjective norms from the immediate social environment and familial teachings may affect an individual's food purchasing choices, portion sizes consumed, and perceptions regarding food waste. Subjective norms are a variable in the Theory of Planned Behavior (TPB) that delineate the social influences individuals perceive from various sources, such as parental guidance, the perspectives of close friends and family, and the prevailing social norms within their community. Such effects can significantly influence the decision-making process, particularly in relation to responsible consumption and minimizing food waste. The impact of attitude in moderating the connection between subjective norms and responsible food waste behavior was also apparent. Individuals with a more optimistic perspective and a greater propensity to adhere to their own sustainable living principles were more inclined to take action (Elshaer et al., 2021).

2.3 Perceive Behavior Control

Perceived Behavioral Control elucidates how individuals assess their capacity to determine the ease or difficulty of a specific behavior. This element was incorporated into the original TRA model to enhance its predictive efficacy uniformly across various contexts and to encompass non-volitional dimensions of behavior. PBC examined the effects of external variables, including location, timing, and labeling. External factors may affect a consumer's purchasing decisions, potentially serving as advantages or disadvantages. "Perceived behavioral control" denotes the capacity to execute a specific activity under both favorable and adverse conditions. Factors including availability, cost, location, or timing may affect the perceived sense of behavioral control. Although attitude and subjective norms were associated with behavioral intention, perceived behavioral control had a direct effect on behavioral intention. Perceived behavioral control influenced an individual's intent. It may be characterized as an individual's evaluation of their performance capability. Perceived behavioral control is acknowledged as a significant determinant of intention. This construct relates to an individual's viewpoint, ability, competence, and agency in action. Individuals possessing an elevated sense of perceived behavioral control believe they can execute a specific activity at any location and at any time. Studies in various contexts have demonstrated a significant relationship between perceived behavioral control and intended behavior. Research indicates that perceived behavioral control has a positive effect on intended behavior (Panwanitdumrong & Chen, 2021). Furthermore, perceived behavioral control refers to an individual's cognitive assessment of their capability and motivation to engage in a particular behavior. It encompasses their conviction that they can overcome obstacles such as cost, time, and willingness. Perceived behavioral control, as articulated by Kurniawan et al. (2022), refers to the degree to which an individual can influence their behavior, particularly in circumstances that are controllable with sufficient effort and resources. Perceived behavioral control significantly and positively affected the intention to diminish self-littering on the mountain. Perceived behavioral control affected littering behavior. Tuhin et al. (2022) asserted that attitude influences the relationship between personal norms and behavioral intentions in the context of consumer purchasing behavior. Perceived behavioral control is a subjective evaluation that considers past experiences and foresees current obstacles, thereby affecting attitudes and subjective norms related to a behavior. The greater the control over a behavior, the more intense the intention to perform that action or attain a desired result. Kurniawan (2022) posits that augmented opportunities for an individual are associated with elevated challenges and an improved perception of behavioral control. An essential element to examine in order to comprehend the mechanisms affecting consumer behavioral intentions is perceived control within the realm of e-commerce. Furthermore, perceived value constitutes the consumer's holistic assessment of the products or services they have utilized, gauged by their perception of the value obtained. A standard measure for evaluating perceived value is the relationship between price and quality. Improvements could be achieved by reducing the expenses associated with acquiring and utilizing the products or services (tangible perceived value) and by enhancing the benefits for the individual. Perceived behavioral control denotes consumers' ability to overcome barriers before initiating a behavior or action. Perceived behavioral control has a substantial effect on intention, as widely recognized. This construct relates to a person's perception, capability, and regulation of their actions. Studies across diverse contexts have demonstrated a significant correlation between intended behavior and perceived behavioral control. Panwanitdumrong and Chen (2021) have confirmed that perceived behavioral control positively influences intended behavior. Moreover, perceived behavioral control escalates with the potential for success, despite an increase in the number of obstacles. Another study corroborates this, illustrating a positive correlation between perceived behavioral control and behavioral intention. Consumers' intentions were positively influenced by perceived behavioral control. A supplementary study suggested that consumers' perceived behavioral control has a substantial effect on their intentions to acquire environmentally sustainable products.

2.4 Electronic Word of Mouth

Electronic word-of-mouth (e-WOM) has emerged as a highly advantageous source of information for consumers. Online assessments and reviews can profoundly influence consumer purchasing decisions and affect a business's profitability. Recent research indicates a robust correlation between favorable electronic word-of-mouth (eWOM) and the intention to repurchase. Consumers who offer positive evaluations of a product or service are often more predisposed to return and make additional purchases from the same brand or establishment. E-WOM was a crucial marketing tool that significantly influenced consumer choices. Experts indicate that 76% of consumers presently trust peer recommendations. Consumers increasingly depended on word-of-mouth communications to assess product satisfaction. Furthermore, social influence refers to the degree to which an individual perceives that members of their social circle, including family, friends, or other significant individuals, have an impact on their behavior. It substantially influenced an individual's purchasing decision. The perceived quality of a product or service substantially affects the intention to produce favorable electronic word of mouth (eWOM). Perceived quality refers to the subjective assessment a consumer makes of a product or service's quality, influenced by their perceptions and experiences. It is a vital factor in the purchasing decision-making process, influencing consumer attitudes and behaviors. Recent research (Jain et al., 2023) highlights the importance of perceived quality in shaping consumers' online experiences, as shared through electronic word-of-mouth (eWOM). The perceived quality substantially influences the intention to produce favorable electronic word-of-mouth (eWOM). When consumers perceive a product or service as superior, they are more likely to share this positive experience with potential buyers. A consumer who obtains a product and experiences outstanding quality or performance may be motivated to share this positive experience through online reviews or social media. Positive assessments arising from favorable electronic word-of-mouth intentions have a significant impact on overall brand perception. Consumers emphasize online reviews and ratings in their decision-making process. Batjo et al. (2022) investigate the correlation between perceived quality and electronic word-of-mouth (eWOM). In a competitive business environment, customers' perceptions of a product or service's pricing can significantly influence their purchasing decisions and their subsequent sharing of that experience via electronic word-of-mouth (eWOM). The perception of price can significantly affect the intention to produce positive electronic word-of-mouth. When consumers perceive that a product or service offers outstanding value for the price paid, they are more likely to share this positive experience with other consumers online. A consumer who discovers a favorable offer or perceives substantial discounts may be motivated to express their satisfaction through positive reviews or endorsements on social media platforms. Madi et al. (2024) assert that perceived quality has a significant influence on the intention to disseminate positive electronic word-of-mouth (eWOM). When consumers perceive a product or service as high quality, they are more likely to share their positive experiences with other prospective purchasers. A consumer who obtains a product and encounters outstanding quality or performance may be motivated to disseminate this favorable experience via online reviews or social media platforms. Positive electronic word-of-mouth intent fosters favorable assessments that substantially affect a brand's overall perception. There is a correlation between perceived quality and electronic word-of-mouth (eWOM). E-WOM is a contemporary phenomenon that has become crucial for the exchange of information among social media users. Online ratings, evaluations, and recommendations from peers and influencers have a significant influence on purchasing decisions. Camilleri et al. (2022) assert that electronic word-of-mouth (E-WOM) influences consumer purchasing decisions. A separate study indicates a notable shift in consumers' purchasing focus following an increase in the volume of electronic word-of-mouth (E-WOM). The execution of promotional strategies via electronic word-of-mouth on social media is considerably more efficacious due to its ability to reach a wider audience. Electronic word of mouth can profoundly impact consumers' purchasing decisions. As consumers encounter more electronic word-of-mouth, its impact on purchase intention intensifies. Harmful user-generated content may deter potential customers, while positive information fosters trust and enhances credibility. The perceived value was the primary determinant in forecasting customers' preferences and behavioral intentions (Molinillo et al., 2021).

2.5 Perceived Value

The concept of perceived value has attracted considerable attention from various consumer behavior researchers, with their interest in this domain increasing daily. The notion of perceived value relates to the degree to which a consumer believes that acquiring a product would be advantageous to them. The perceived value was established during the pre-purchase stage of the purchasing decision process. Customer perceived value (CPV) refers to "the consumer's holistic assessment of a product's utility, based on their perceptions of the received items and the value derived from them." It involved assessing the consumer's input relative to the advantage gained. Sure, researchers have criticized the prior definition of perceived value, considering it overly restrictive in scope. The precise value is defined as a multidimensional construct that includes perceived price, benefits, quality, and cost. According to Roh et al. (2022), perceived value may encompass affective, social, epistemic, and conditional dimensions. Furthermore, values serve as the benchmarks by which consumers evaluate their preferences. Consumer assessments and preferences are dictated by their perceptions of value. Consumers prioritize the satisfaction of their paramount desires when acquiring and utilizing brand products. Customer assessments and preferences are the determinants of perceived value. Perceived value is a crucial determinant of repurchase intention, as evidenced by the current literature. Customer satisfaction is directly proportional to the perceived value of the company's services. A positive and significant correlation exists between perceived value and word-of-mouth (WoM). The perceived value, defined as the consumer's assessment of a product or service, fundamentally impacts the exchange transaction. Perceived value is the perceptual difference between the quality, benefits, and utility consumers obtain and the price and sacrifices they incur. The perceived value was obtained during the pre-purchase stage of the purchasing decision process. Perceived value has a significant influence on behavioral responses (Cotarelo et al., 2021; Mimoun et al., 2022; Pereira et al., 2023). The perceived value was the primary determinant in forecasting consumers' behavioral intentions and preferences. The perceived value of a brand has a significant influence on the decision to purchase a product. From the consumer's viewpoint, perceived value highlights the various benefits of a product. Moreover, some studies suggested that perceived value was a precursor to purchasing behavior. Previous empirical research has indicated that perceived value positively influences purchase intention, examining the determinants of perceived value and their impact on the intention to purchase organic food. Padungyos et al. (2020) define perceived value as a consumer's assessment of goods or services, predicated on the belief that the value received corresponds to the costs incurred. The value of an outcome escalates when it satisfies the client's desires, needs, and expectations. Moreover, perceived value is the difference between how a potential client assesses all costs and all benefits. Perceived value is the ratio of the benefits recognized by clients to the resources they have expended or consumed to achieve a result. Perceived value refers to the assessment of user consumption and expenditure in relation to the benefits derived from the resulting outcome, considering both what is received and what is sacrificed. The perception of value also escalates.

Consequently, an elevated perception of value correlates with an increase in satisfaction, whereby the perceived value in a restaurant is evaluated based on the time and money invested relative to the experience provided to customers. Companies employ diverse marketing components, such as advertising, sales personnel, and the Internet, to elevate the perceived value of their products in consumers' perceptions through effective communication. Guerra-Tamez et al. (2020) assert that customer satisfaction is directly proportional to the perceived value of the company's services.

2.6 Purchase Intention

Businesses must first identify the factors that affect customers' purchase intentions to cultivate lasting relationships and convert them into loyal patrons. Purchase intention denotes the probability of a consumer acquiring a specific product or service in the future, or their readiness to do so. Purchase intention, also referred to as a purchase plan, reflects a consumer's subjective inclination to acquire goods or services and serves as a crucial indicator of their needs or preferences for specific items. Customers often make emotional decisions prior to making a purchase, and these decisions can predict their future behavior and purchasing choices. This framework was essential for consumer research, as purchase intention was based on examining the correlation between buyer behavior and intentions. Setiawan et al. (2022) define purchase intention as a consumer's intent to obtain a particular product and the quantity needed within a specified timeframe. Consumers evaluate a product before deciding to purchase, which subsequently cultivates an interest in acquiring it. Concerning the likelihood that consumers will opt to acquire a product following its assessment. Assessment procedure. Purchase interest is a stage in which consumers evaluate alternatives before reaching a purchasing decision. Purchasing intention refers to consumer behavior characterized by a desire to acquire products. This curiosity may arise from the experience of using, consuming, and assessing the product. Purchase intention refers to a deliberate decision to acquire a product. Throughout this process, customers engage in various activities, including determining the quantity of product units required within a specific timeframe and assessing their perceptions of the brands and items they currently possess. Previous research has elucidated the factors influencing green purchase intentions and behaviors; however, notable gaps remain in the literature. Wijekoon and Sabri (2021) propose a framework for comprehending the determinants that affect individuals' intentions and behaviors regarding the purchase of green products. Research has examined the efficacy of norm-based messaging in encouraging healthy eating behaviors and intentions. Moreover, purchase intentions are often closely tied to consumer behavior, attitudes, and perceptions. The behavioral intentions of buyers are significantly influenced by their level of engagement in the food industry, particularly regarding healthy beverages. The intention to purchase is substantially affected by personal attitudes, social norms, and perceived behavioral control. The probability of purchasing a product can indicate the intention to obtain it. Purchase intention enhances consumers' propensity to engage in online transactions (Akram et al., 2023). Additionally, a buyer's intention to acquire goods under particular circumstances is referred to as purchase intention. The customer's decision to purchase was complex. Purchase intention was generally associated with consumer behavior, attitudes, and perceptions. The purchasing behavior of customers was essential in evaluating a specific product. The perceived quality and value of price may influence purchase intention. A significant and positive correlation exists between purchase intentions and digital marketing. In their 2023 study, Anas et al. found that social media marketing has a significant and positive effect on consumer purchase intention. Furthermore, a positive correlation has been found between customer engagement and purchase intentions in studies of identity-driven consumer engagement. A multitude of researchers have examined the intent to acquire virtual products on digital platforms (Uhm et al., 2022). Purchase intention is regarded as one of the most dependable indicators of actual buying behavior. An empirical study has demonstrated that information-sharing activities can influence customers' thoughts, emotions, and needs, thereby positively impacting their purchase intentions (Ghahtarani et al., 2020).

3. METHODOLOGY

The PRISMA method was employed in this chapter, following the studies of Siripipatthanakul & Siripipattanakul (a), Siripipatthanakul & Phuangsuwan (2024). There are four steps as follows: identification, screening, eligibility, and inclusion. From more than 500 papers, 50 papers were selected through purposive sampling based on valid sources between 2021 and 2025. The selected papers are only related to theories and variables in this chapter

According to a considerable body of evidence, the practice of consuming healthy beverages has been shown to enhance and develop strategies in the corporate world. To organize the existing knowledge on the practical aspects of curriculum, assessment, student experience, educational leadership, and educational technologies in a manner that is reproducible, valid, and understandable, systematic literature reviews provide a framework that can be utilized. On the other hand, published reviews can often convey a description of the knowledge contained in the sample research as being based on a rigorous methodology. According to the systematic study, the researchers employ Word Cloud and Grammarly as tools to check for instances of plagiarism committed by other individuals. Additionally, writing similarity checking based on artificial intelligence is applied to analyze content from academic papers, specifically between 2021 and 2025, and exclusively in the English language. This content can be located in the databases Scopus, Web of Science (WOS), and Google Scholar.

4. RESULTS

4.1 Grammarly Results

Three experts have proved the chapters' content for its validity. Grammarly results indicate that the similarity is approximately 1%, while the grammar score exceeds 95%. Thus, this chapter is acceptable for publication.

4.2 Word Clouds

Figure 1. Word Clouds

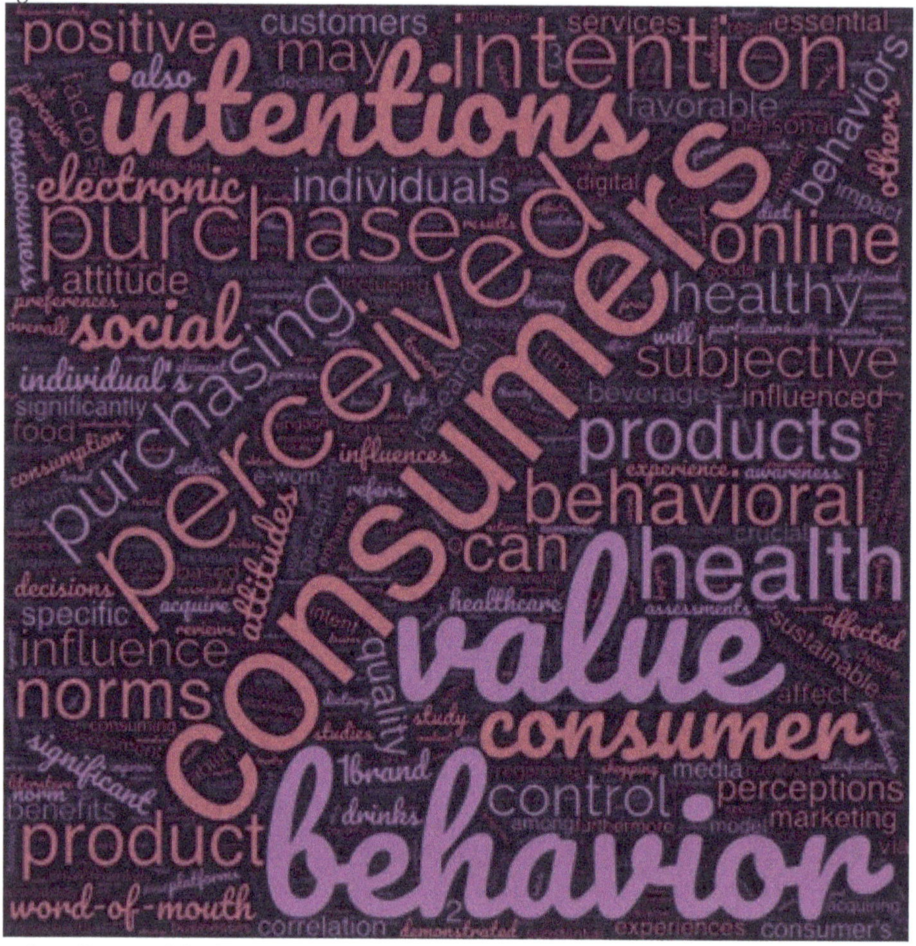

https://www.wordclouds.com/ (July 23, 2025)

4.3 Theoretical Model

Figure 2. Theoretical Model

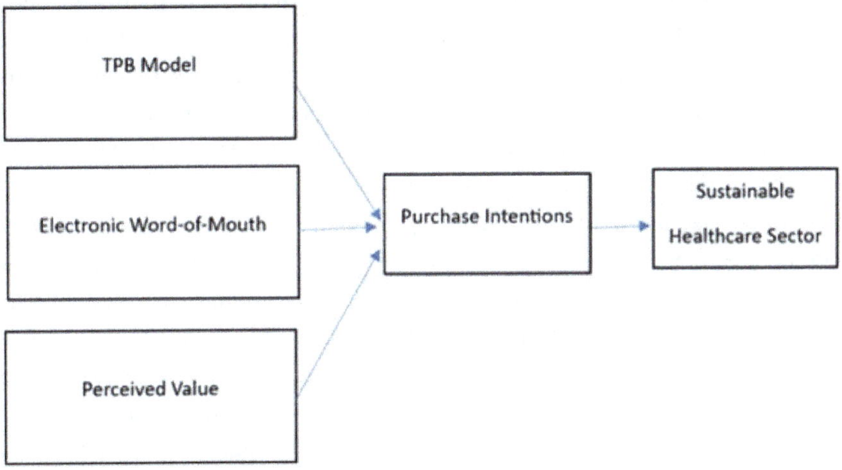

5. DISCUSSIONS

Healthy drinks offer a range of essential nutrients, vitamins, and minerals, making them a desirable choice for individuals seeking to improve their overall well-being. A well-balanced diet is crucial for maintaining good health. A convenient and efficient solution to address this nutritional gap has been the emergence of health drinks. Consuming a nutritious diet and carefully monitoring one's daily caloric intake can enhance immunity. Health consciousness is the ability of an individual to be aware of their health status, enabling them to enhance their well-being and closely monitor their health. In addition, health consciousness refers to the awareness and concern customers have regarding their health. Consumers may be motivated to maintain their quality of life and health by adopting healthy behaviors and cultivating self-awareness about their health.

The demand for health-conscious beverages is increasing as consumers prioritize environmental and health factors in their purchasing decisions. Health consciousness refers to the awareness an individual has about their health and the motivation to maintain it. Health drinks offer a convenient and straightforward way to consume essential nutrients. They are available in various forms, including powders, ready-to-drink bottles, and supplements, which facilitates their integration into daily routines. Health drinks are essential sources of vitamins, minerals, protein, and fiber, whether consumed as a meal replacement or as a dietary supplement. Health consciousness is the driving force behind personal engagement with one's health. Health-conscious customers were motivated to improve or preserve their well-being by engaging in healthy behaviors. Motivation was a significant component that influenced consumer behavior and was crucial to organic consumption. Healthy consumers participated in healthy behaviors to prevent disease and were driven by a desire for a higher quality of life. Intent is a crucial element in marketing literature that companies utilize to predict sales of new products or repeat purchases of existing products. It also demonstrated the propensity of consumers to purchase goods and services from the same retailer and to share their favorable or unfavorable experiences with others. Purchase intentions for healthy products may be affected by several factors, including perceived health benefits, environmental awareness, product availability, perceived quality, distribution channels, and nutritional content, among others. Digital marketing strategies have a significant influence on purchase intentions. The theory of planned behavior posits that customers' purchase intentions are influenced by factors, including attitude, behavioral control, and subjective norms, which ultimately lead to a specific behavior. Consumers' purchasing intentions are positively affected by the behavioral reactions of social media users to social media marketing. Thus, digital marketing and customer relationships will encourage consumers to complete online transactions. All TPB predictors, except for attitude, significantly impacted purchase intention. This study contributes to the existing theoretical framework by applying the Theory of Planned Behavior to the consumption of healthy beverages in a developing economy. Moreover, social norms can promote healthy behaviors. Research has investigated the effectiveness of norm-based messaging in promoting healthy eating behaviors and intentions. The effective integration and application of the Norm Activation Model and the Theory of Planned Behavior. This study endeavors to understand the interplay between these two theories and to investigate the moderating effect of attitude. Padungyos et al. (2020) identified a positive correlation between perceived value and repurchase intention. The majority of consumers employ online product information to assess a product's value before making a purchase. Recent advancements in social networks have enabled consumers to access an infinite quantity of electronic word-of-mouth messages. This study includes subjective norms, perceived behavioral control, and the correlation between personal norms and intended behavior. Moreover, researchers have demonstrated the significant impact of each construct (attitude, subjective norm, and perceived behavioral control) on intended behavior. Data pertinent to product purchase intentions and possible decision-making factors elucidate this finding. The discovery may also be ascribed to the notion that cosmetic products possess social visibility. Consequently, consumers often adhere to the suggestions and perspectives of their family and acquaintances. Guerra-Tamez et al. (2020) and Padungyos et al. (2020) assert that perceived value and repurchase intention exhibit a significant positive correlation. An elevation in the perceived value variable will lead to a substantial and favorable enhancement in repurchase intention. Moreover, consumer behavior, attitudes, and perceptions are often linked to purchase intentions. The degree of involvement in the food sector, particularly regarding healthy beverages, has a profound influence on consumers' behavioral intentions.

5.1. Attitude

The discovery asserts that perceived value relates to the consumer's overall evaluation of the net benefit derived from a particular service or product. Perceptions regarding the acquisition of nutritious food are positive. The intention to acquire sustainable or eco-friendly products is predominantly shaped by attitude. The effectiveness of corporations' macro strategies will be enhanced by the impact of marketing programs on the perceived value derived from brand attitude. Consumers regard the attainment of valuable benefits as a fundamental goal of consumption and purchasing. Consumer attitudes and perceived value are essential elements of consumer behavior concerning products or services. Furthermore, consumers' inclination to purchase products is affected by their perception of uniqueness. Attitude highlights consumer preferences and aversions, fostering their inclination to purchase a product. If customers demonstrate a favorable disposition toward online shopping, their purchasing intentions will be heightened, making it easier for them to make purchasing decisions. The intention of businesses to utilize products was significantly affected by their attitudes and awareness, indicating a strong correlation between attitudes, norms, and purchasing intentions.

5.2. Subjective Norms

Subjective norms influence the development of an individual's self-concept, their belief in self-efficacy, and consequently, the likelihood of establishing particular intentions. Consumer purchasing and recommending behaviors are directly influenced by social media bloggers' recommendations, which also foster trust in products and brands. Social influence is a significant determinant of dietary behaviors and is noteworthy from an academic perspective. It is intriguing to examine the mechanisms and timing of social influence on dietary habits. Social influence possesses the ability to affect individuals' intentions and decisions. Social identity refers to an individual's acknowledgment of their affiliation with a particular social group, along with the emotional and value-related consequences that come with belonging to that group. Consumers' propensity to engage in online shopping will increase if they believe their peers endorse it. The evidence illustrates the subjectivity inherent in consumer perceptions, which are influenced by their cultural backgrounds. A greater intention to purchase arises from the regulation of this decision, leading consumers to perceive the acquisition of green products as an independent choice. Consumers believe that purchasing eco-friendly products has a positive impact on the environment. As a result, their intention to purchase environmentally friendly products will increase as their awareness of these items grows. The acquisition of environmentally sustainable products by consumers, coupled with their belief in the positive environmental impact of such purchases, can affect their purchasing intentions.

5.3. Perceive Behaviour Control

The perceived value of healthier food requires individuals to address the contrast between the often elaborate industrial and convenient food options and the more traditional, yet sometimes unremarkable, selections deemed beneficial. Perceived value is the consumer's overall evaluation of the products or services they have utilized, based on their assessment of the value obtained. In e-commerce, perceived control is a crucial element that must be analyzed to understand the mechanisms affecting consumer behavioral intentions. Consumers' perceptions of control increase when they believe they have additional resources, such as time, money, and skills. As a result, their behavioral intentions are heightened. Perceived behavioral control refers to consumers' ability to overcome obstacles before taking action or engaging in a behavior. Perceived behavioral control has a substantial effect on intention, as widely acknowledged. An individual's behavioral belief is demonstrated by their perceived control over their actions. An individual's normative belief is demonstrated by the societal pressure to conform to specific behaviors. Their control belief demonstrates a person's attitude towards a specific behavior. The more control one has over a perceivable behavior, the stronger the intention to execute a task or desired behavior. Moreover, perceived behavioral control is heightened, and the number of obstacles escalates as the likelihood of an individual's success amplifies.

5.4. E-WOM

The digital sector continued to be infiltrated by social influence. Online ratings, assessments, and endorsements from peers and influencers have a profound influence on purchasing decisions. E-WOM has become essential for information dissemination among social media users. Consumers can enhance their brand perception and purchase intention by sharing and disseminating experiences through various social media platforms, including social networks. These credible messages help consumers evaluate a product's efficacy, quality, value, and perceived value. Perceived quality refers to a consumer's subjective assessment of a product or service's quality, based on their perceptions and experiences. It is a pivotal element in the purchasing decision-making process, influencing consumer attitudes and behaviors—the importance of perceived quality in shaping consumers' online experiences, as shared via electronic word-of-mouth (eWOM). Consumers are more likely to share a favorable experience with a product or service when they perceive it as possessing high quality. A consumer who obtains a product and experiences outstanding quality or performance may be motivated to share this positive experience through online reviews or social media platforms. Favorable electronic word-of-mouth intent yields positive assessments that significantly influence a brand's overall perception. Consumers may reevaluate their brand loyalty due to adverse reviews and electronic word-of-mouth, potentially undermining brand trust. Unfavorable evaluations can significantly impact the brand's overall perception, raising doubts about its quality or reliability. The swift expansion of social media has facilitated real-time communication among consumers. Consumers generally perceive information from online connections, such as peers, as more credible owing to their relevance and trustworthiness.

5.5. Perceived Value

The perceived value of regional products and consumer preferences for these items must be synthesized to elucidate the relationship between consumer attitudes towards a region and their purchasing intentions. Perceived value refers to the customer's assessment of a product or service, and this concept has developed over time. Behavioral intentions have proven to be a crucial predictor of future consumer preferences for a product. Moreover, values serve as the benchmarks that consumers utilize to assess their preferences. The perceived value is more crucial than gratification in elucidating consumers' purchasing intentions. The perceived value was obtained during the pre-purchase stage of the purchasing decision process. Consumers' value perceptions influence their evaluations and preferences. Consumers possess aspirations when acquiring and using brand products, prioritizing the satisfaction of their most paramount desires. Perceived value results from customer preferences and assessments. The consumer's perception of products and services, known as perceived value, fundamentally shapes the exchange transaction. When an online purchasing platform minimizes shopping time, it enhances consumer value perception and cultivates a sustainable relationship. From the consumer's perspective, perceived value enhances the diverse advantages of a product. A positive correlation exists between consumers' purchase intention and their perception of a brand's value, indicating that a specific brand is more likely to be purchased when consumers highly regard both the brand's attitude and values. The perceived value, as a consumer assessment of products or services, is determined by the belief that the benefits received are commensurate with the costs incurred. Furthermore, perceived value is the difference between a prospective client's assessment of all the benefits and all the costs presented. The value of an outcome escalates when it aligns with the client's desires, requirements, and specifications. A higher customer's perceived value of the company's services correlates with increased satisfaction levels.

5.6. Purchase Intention

Customers' purchase intentions accurately predicted their behavior. Purchase intention is one of the best predictors of buying behavior. Purchase intentions are strongly influenced by digital marketing. Virtual experiences influence real-world purchases. Virtual and physical purchasing motivations are linked as people transfer their needs and desires onto virtual things. Purchase intention refers to a consumer's cognitive decision to buy a product or service. By considering product information, consumers can make informed decisions about their selections. The health and environmental implications of food production systems influence food purchasing decisions. The type of green product, its fundamental qualities, and engagement in the food category strongly influence consumers' behavior. Digital consumers' purchasing inclinations are positively influenced by product quality. Marketing literature relied on intent to predict new product sales and repeat purchases. It also showed how consumers buy products and share their positive or negative experiences. Perceived health benefits, environmental awareness, product availability, perceived quality, distribution methods, and nutritional composition can influence the purchase of healthful products. Company or industry performance depends heavily on purchasing intention. The desire to buy creates chances for businesses to build client loyalty. Thus, by fostering consumer purchasing interest, companies can dissuade customers from buying similar items and services from competitors.

6. CONCLUSIONS

Health drinks are popular with those trying to eat better and feel better. Due to their hydration, vitamin contents, and convenience, nutritious beverages can help those with particular diets or busy lifestyles. It is essential to consume healthy drinks in moderation and incorporate them into a balanced diet. Health consciousness significantly influences an individual's ability to adopt and maintain healthy habits independently. Health consciousness—the readiness to do things that could harm your health—was a widespread concept. Wellness-focused consumers were more aware and worried about their health. Associating good behavior with self-consciousness helped people retain their health and quality of life. By incorporating health drinks into a balanced lifestyle, individuals can achieve their wellness goals and boost their vitality. Behavioral intention is the synthesis of subjective norms, volitional behavioral attitudes, and perceived behavioral control. Thus, construction businesses can promote desired behaviors by improving internal organizational processes and managing external forces. Perceived value is crucial to consumers' buying decisions. It is crucial to help consumers evaluate products because their perceived value is based on the assessment of the value they obtain versus the value offered. Many changes must be made to product packaging, communication (both in-store and externally), and pricing to encourage consumers to evaluate quality and value. Manufacturer engagement and in-store samples can boost product value and consumer preference. We also found that perceived value and preference boost customers' purchasing intentions. The desire to buy creates chances for businesses to build client loyalty. Thus, by fostering consumer purchasing interest, companies can dissuade customers from buying similar products or services from competitors. Marketing literature relied on intention to forecast new product sales and repeat purchases. It also showed how consumers buy products and share their positive or negative experiences. Perceived health benefits, environmental awareness, product availability, perceived quality, distribution methods, and nutritional composition can influence the purchase of healthful products.

Due to health consciousness, lifestyle convenience, environmental awareness, and product quality, sustainable healthcare consumers are increasingly buying healthy beverages online. Digital marketing, positive online reviews, transparent labeling, and accessibility of organic, low-sugar, or plant-based beverages influence these intents. Consumer behavior improves healthcare by promoting healthy eating and reducing environmental impact through the use of sustainable packaging and logistics. Internet purchasing lowers store visits, reducing transportation emissions and expanding health-related product selection. This trend inspires organizations to adopt sustainable practices and digitally promote health education. Thus, online healthy beverage consumption promotes preventative care, public health awareness, and environmental stewardship while meeting personal wellness goals.

The growing trend of customers buying healthy drinks online has great promise for sustained growth in the healthcare business. This trend goes beyond consumer wants and signals a shift toward proactive and preventative health management, which is vital to a sustainable healthcare system. First, this movement promotes self-care and disease prevention by making nutritious beverages easily accessible online. Consumers who seek functional drinks, immune system boosters, or natural hydration are investing in their health and may lessen their need for curative medical procedures. This proactive strategy minimizes lifestyle-related chronic diseases, which eases the healthcare infrastructure load on hospitals and clinics. A healthier population requires fewer doctor visits, less medication, and fewer costly medical procedures. These aspects enhance the economic sustainability of healthcare by minimizing alarmingly rising costs. The online marketplace for healthy drinks also promotes transparency and informed customer choices, which are essential for sustainable operations. When provided with thorough nutritional information, ingredient origins, and certifications by online platforms, consumers can make informed, ethical, and health-conscious choices. Transparency drives beverage makers to use organic ingredients, reduce waste, and use eco-friendly packaging. As buyers demand environmentally and socially responsible companies, the internet has spurred businesses to develop sustainable supply chains from component agriculture to product delivery. The environmental pillar of sustainable healthcare is supported by reducing the carbon footprint of health-supporting product manufacturing and delivery.

Further, the fact that online shopping is conducted in a digital format contributes to the sustainability of the industry. Reducing the time spent physically traveling for shopping helps reduce carbon emissions. Although the digital infrastructure (servers, data centers) has its own energy requirements, the impact of this demand is being continuously mitigated by developments in green computing and renewable energy sources for these infrastructures. When compared to traditional retail, the distribution system has the potential to be more resource-efficient due to the efficiency of online logistics and the possibility of optimizing delivery routes. In essence, the confluence of health-conscious consumer behavior and the accessibility of online retail for healthy drinks creates a powerful feedback loop that fosters preventative health, encourages responsible manufacturing, and leverages digital efficiencies, all of which are vital components for building a resilient, equitable, and sustainable healthcare sector for the future.

7. IMPLICATIONS

The relationship between perceived value, subjective norms, perceived behavioral control, social influence, and purchase intention is a good starting point. It can guide consumers to platforms that align with their preferences and offer positive experiences. A more comprehensive examination of consumer behavior during online shopping may help determine the primary reasons for purchasing and repurchasing items. Subjective norms derive from external sources. So that it implements reactive measures involuntarily, rather than employing measured strategies. Perceived value influences purchase intentions by increasing the level of trust and liking for the product. Businesses can develop a marketing strategy that promotes the development of a comprehensive value proposition for consumers.

Social influence influences individuals' likelihood and intention to purchase healthy beverages for both academic and business purposes. Businesses can gain valuable insights and generate more positive E-WOM. The reference groups of consumers and societal pressure have a direct influence on the purchase intentions of healthy drinks. Therefore, these strategies can be deemed effective in enhancing awareness and purchasing intentions for healthy beverages. Businesses can ultimately implement this investigation to assess and personalize their online experiences based on their prior interactions. Lastly, businesses can develop a successful marketing strategy that can add, initiate, or enhance positive outcomes, such as customers' perceived value, subjective norms, perceived behavioral control, and social influence, which ultimately determine purchase intention. The online purchasing intentions of health-conscious beverage consumers pertain to their readiness to acquire healthy drinks online, thus supporting a healthcare system that is economically sustainable, socially just, and environmentally sound. This trend is driven by factors such as convenience, access to diverse product information, and an expanded range of specialized healthy solutions not typically found in physical stores. By deliberately selecting better online options, customers participate in preventative health, thereby alleviating the long-term strain on healthcare resources and endorsing enterprises that adhere to sustainable standards, thereby cultivating a more robust and proactive healthcare ecosystem.

Consumers of healthy beverages substantially contribute to a sustainable healthcare sector through health-oriented purchasing choices shaped by psychological and social influences. The Theory of Planned Behaviour (TPB) posits that buying intentions are influenced by attitudes towards health, perceived social standards, and the accessibility of healthy products. When consumers perceive that nutritious beverages enhance their well-being and conform to societal norms, they are more inclined to purchase them, so fostering preventative health and alleviating long-term healthcare burdens. Electronic Word of Mouth (E-WOM), including online reviews and social media endorsements, bolsters these objectives by shaping perceived norms and trust. Positive electronic word-of-mouth increases awareness and credibility, encouraging others to make comparable healthy decisions. The perceived value of healthy beverages—comprising functional advantages (e.g., nutrition), emotional gratification (e.g., satisfaction from sustainability), and social attractiveness (e.g., wellness identity)—enhances consumer loyalty. These values correspond with overarching environmental and wellness objectives, and purchasing patterns facilitate the advancement of a more sustainable healthcare model. By selecting beverages that are natural, organic, or sustainably produced, consumers inadvertently enhance public health, mitigate risks of chronic illness, and promote environmental and ethical business practices. This establishes a circle in which healthy consumer behavior, influenced by TPB elements, electronic word-of-mouth, and perceived value, enhances both individual well-being and systemic sustainability. The expanding market for healthy beverages is not merely a trend but an essential component of attaining long-term objectives in healthcare sustainability and environmental stewardship.

8. LIMITATIONS AND RECOMMENDATIONS

According to the contemporary studies about sustainable development, such as Siripipatthanakul et al. (2024); Phuangsuwan et al. (2024), Phuangsuwan et al. (2025a, b), Siripipatthanakul & Siripipattanakul (2025b), Yakin et al. (2025), Siripipatthanakul et al. (2025a, b), it is recommended to test the theoretical model using PLS-SEM to confirm the conceptual model regarding the relevant theories and variables related to sustainable development in this sector.

This study focuses on online purchases of healthy drinks. Hence, future research may focus on other healthy products to achieve more comprehensive results. Additionally, this study is limited to assessing the influence of TPB model factors and E-WOM on the prediction of online purchase intention for healthy drink products, with the mediating role of perceived value. So, future research should incorporate and assess additional variables that may influence online purchasing decisions. Online purchase intentions among healthy drink customers in the sustainable healthcare sector refer to customers' desire to buy health-oriented beverages through digital platforms, influenced by characteristics such as health awareness, convenience, trust, and adherence to sustainability principles. These goals support the sustainable healthcare sector by encouraging people to lead healthier lives, reducing carbon footprints through more efficient e-commerce, and promoting the adoption of eco-friendly products that align with public health objectives.

REFERENCES

Ahmad, A., Abuhashesh, M., Obeidat, Z., & AlKhatib, M. (2020). E-WOM and airline e-ticket purchasing intention: Mediating effect of online passenger trust. *Management Science Letters, 10*(12), 2729–2740. DOI: 10.5267/j.msl.2020.4.037

Akram, U., Ansari, A. R., & Yan, C. (2023). Cosmetics makers have always sold 'hope in a jar'! Understanding the cosmetics purchase intention in the Chinese mobile commerce environment. *Journal of Retailing and Consumer Services, 73*, 103337. DOI: 10.1016/j.jretconser.2023.103337

Batjo, F. R., Massie, J., & Saerang, R. T. (2022). The effect of E-WOM, perceived quality, on purchase intention at Shopee online store in Manado. Jurnal EMBA: Jurnal Riset Ekonomi, Manajemen. *Bisnis Dan Akuntansi, 10*(2), 592–599.

Camilleri, M. A., & Kozak, M. (2022). Interactive engagement through travel and tourism social media groups: A social facilitation theory perspective. *Technology in Society, 71*, 102098. DOI: 10.1016/j.techsoc.2022.102098

Casaló, L. V., Flavián, C., & Ibáñez-Sánchez, S. (2020). Influencers on Instagram: Antecedents and consequences of opinion leadership. *Journal of Business Research, 117*, 510–519. DOI: 10.1016/j.jbusres.2018.07.005

Charton-Vachet, F., Lombart, C., & Louis, D. (2020). Impact of attitude towards a region on purchase intention of regional products: The mediating effects of perceived value and preference. *International Journal of Retail & Distribution Management, 48*(7), 707–725. DOI: 10.1108/IJRDM-09-2019-0315

Cotarelo, M., Fayos, T., Calderón, H., & Mollá, A. (2021). Omni-channel intensity and shopping value as key drivers of customer satisfaction and loyalty. *Sustainability (Basel), 13*(11), 5961. DOI: 10.3390/su13115961

Dalziel, R. C., & De Klerk, N. (2021). Media and group influence on Generation Y consumers' attitudes towards beauty products. *Spanish Journal of Marketing - ESIC, 25*(1), 115–136. DOI: 10.1108/SJME-12-2019-0104

Elshaer, I., Sobaih, A. E. E., Alyahya, M., & Abu Elnasr, A. (2021). The impact of religiosity and food consumption culture on food waste intention in Saudi Arabia. *Sustainability (Basel), 13*(11), 6473. DOI: 10.3390/su13116473

Fle eriu, C., Cosma, S. A., & Bocăne , V. (2020). Values and planned behaviour of the Romanian organic food consumer. *Sustainability (Basel), 12*(5), 1722. DOI: 10.3390/su12051722

Gangwar, S., Kumar, S., & Kumari, D. (2023). The Rise of Health Drinks: A Nutritional Boost for a Balanced Lifestyle.

Ghahtarani, A., Sheikhmohammady, M., & Rostami, M. (2020). The impact of social capital and social interaction on customers' purchase intention, considering knowledge sharing in social commerce context. *Journal of Innovation & Knowledge*, *5*(3), 191–199. DOI: 10.1016/j.jik.2019.08.004

Guerra-Tamez, C. R., Dávila-Aguirre, M. C., Barragán Codina, J. N., & Guerra Rodríguez, P. (2021). Analysis of the elements of the theory of flow and perceived value and their influence in craft beer consumer loyalty. *Journal of International Food & Agribusiness Marketing*, *33*(5), 487–517. DOI: 10.1080/08974438.2020.1823929

He, Y., & Tian, W. (2023). Religious participation: Does it shape food consumption? *Religions*, *14*(3), 350. DOI: 10.3390/rel14030350

Husain, F., Shahnawaz, M. G., Khan, N. H., Parveen, H., & Savani, K. (2021). Intention to get COVID-19 vaccines: Exploring the role of attitudes, subjective norms, perceived behavioral control, belief in COVID-19 misinformation, and vaccine confidence in Northern India. *Human Vaccines & Immunotherapeutics*, *17*(11), 3941–3953. DOI: 10.1080/21645515.2021.1967039 PMID: 34546837

Jain, M., Dixit, S., & Shukla, A. (2023). Role of e-service quality, brand commitment and e-WOM trust on e-WOM intentions of millennials. *International Review of Retail, Distribution and Consumer Research*, *33*(1), 23–43. DOI: 10.1080/09593969.2022.2070860

Junaid, M., Fetscherin, M., Hussain, K., & Hou, F. (2022). Brand love and brand addiction and their effects on consumers' negative behaviors. *European Journal of Marketing*, *56*(12), 3227–3248. DOI: 10.1108/EJM-09-2019-0727

Kim, J. M., Park, K. K. C., & Mariani, M. M. (2023). Do online review readers react differently when exposed to credible versus fake online reviews? *Journal of Business Research*, *154*, 113377. DOI: 10.1016/j.jbusres.2022.113377

Liang, L., Abidin, S. B. Z., Shaari, N. B., Yahaya, M. F. B., & Jing, L. (2024). Logo impact on consumer's perception, attitude, brand image and purchase intention: A 5 years systematic review. *International Journal of Academic Research in Business & Social Sciences*, *14*(3), 861–900. DOI: 10.6007/IJARBSS/v14-i3/20084

Madi, J., Al Khasawneh, M., & Dandis, A. O. (2024). Visiting and revisiting destinations: Impact of augmented reality, content quality, perceived ease of use, perceived value and usefulness on E-WOM. *International Journal of Quality & Reliability Management*, *41*(6), 1550–1571. DOI: 10.1108/IJQRM-10-2023-0314

Mimoun, M. S. B., Miltgen, C. L., & Slama, B. (2022). Is the shopper always the king/queen? Study of omnichannel retail technology use and shopping orientations. *Journal of Retailing and Consumer Services, 65*, 102844. DOI: 10.1016/j.jretconser.2021.102844

Molinillo, S., Anaya-Sánchez, R., & Liébana-Cabanillas, F. (2020). Analyzing the effect of social support and community factors on customer engagement and its impact on loyalty behaviors toward social commerce websites. *Computers in Human Behavior, 108*, 105980. DOI: 10.1016/j.chb.2019.04.004

Padungyos, N., Nuangjamnong, C., & Dowpiset, K. (2020). Effects of Service Quality that Leads to Word of Mouth (WOM) A Case Study of Coffee Shop in Bangkok, Thailand.

Panwanitdumrong, K., & Chen, C. L. (2021). Investigating factors influencing tourists' environmentally responsible behavior with extended theory of planned behavior for coastal tourism in Thailand. *Marine Pollution Bulletin, 169*, 112507. DOI: 10.1016/j.marpolbul.2021.112507 PMID: 34029800

Pereira, M. L., de La Martinière Petroll, M., Soares, J. C., Matos, C. A. D., & Hernani-Merino, M. (2023). Impulse buying behaviour in omnichannel retail: An approach through the stimulus-organism-response theory. *International Journal of Retail & Distribution Management, 51*(1), 39–58. DOI: 10.1108/IJRDM-09-2021-0394

Photcharoen, C., Chung, R., & Sann, R. (2020). Modelling theory of planned behavior on health concern and health knowledge towards purchase intention on organic products. *International Business Research, 13*(8), 100–116. DOI: 10.5539/ibr.v13n8p100

Phuangsuwan, P., Siripipatthanakul, S., Chaiprakarn, S., & Rakpathum, W. Muthmainnha, Pariwongkhuntorn, N., & Wattanakul, P. (2024, June). Sustainable Development Adopting Artificial Intelligence (AI) in Marketing and Consumer Behaviour Analysis. In *International Conference on Data Analytics & Management* (pp. 569-587). Singapore: Springer Nature Singapore. https://link.springer.com/chapter/10.1007/978-981-96-3372-2_39

Phuangsuwan, P., Siripipatthanakul, S., Praesri, S., & Rakpathum, W. (2025b). The Relationship between Good Governance and Organizational Performance through the Mediating Role of Employee Satisfaction. *Journal of Governance and Regulation/Volume, 14*(1).

Phuangsuwan, P., Siripipatthanakul, S., Siripipattanakul, S., & Jaipong, P. (2025a). The Impact of Community Participation in Sustainable Learning Resource Development: A Case of Bangkok, Thailand. *Sustainability (Basel), 17*(10), 4620. https://www.mdpi.com/2071-1050/17/10/4620. DOI: 10.3390/su17104620

Roh, T., Seok, J., & Kim, Y. (2022). Unveiling ways to reach organic purchase: Green perceived value, perceived knowledge, attitude, subjective norm, and trust. *Journal of Retailing and Consumer Services, 67*, 102988. DOI: 10.1016/j.jretconser.2022.102988

Setiawan, B., Afiff, A. Z., & Heruwasto, I. (2021). The role of norms in predicting waste sorting behavior. *Journal of Social Marketing, 11*(3), 224–239. DOI: 10.1108/JSOCM-05-2020-0088

Shanbhogue, A. V., & Ranjith, V. K. (2024). Effects of Consumer Dispositional Attitude on Purchase Intention in an Emerging Market. *F1000 Research, 12*, 384. DOI: 10.12688/f1000research.131103.3 PMID: 38434630

Siripipatthanakul, S., Limna, P., Phuangsuwan, P., & Siripipattanakul, S. (2025, b). Enriching Satisfaction With Web-Based Learning (WBL) Among Higher Education Students in Thailand. In *Building Organizational Capacity and Strategic Management in Academia* (pp. 213-236). IGI Global. DOI: 10.4018/979-8-3693-6967-8.ch008

Siripipatthanakul, S., Limna, P., Siripipattanakul, S., & Phuangsuwan, P. (2025, a). Modelling Problem-Based Learning, Student Satisfaction, and Effectiveness Among Higher Education Students in Thailand. In *International Academic Transformations and Cross-Border Collaborations* (pp. 311-332). IGI Global Scientific Publishing. DOI: 10.4018/979-8-3373-0508-0.ch013

Siripipatthanakul, S., & Phuangsuwan, P. (2024). Salutogenic Marketing in Preventive Dentistry. In *Leveraging Digital Technology for Preventive Dentistry* (pp. 255–278). IGI Global., DOI: 10.4018/979-8-3693-3872-8.ch009

Siripipatthanakul, S., Phuangsuwan, P., & Limna, P. Muthmainnha, Siripipattanakul, S., Vui, C. N., & Jaipong, P. (2024, Jun). Artificial Intelligence (AI) Influencing Sustainable Governance: Governance Adopting AI. In *International Conference on Data Analytics & Management* (pp. 551-568). Singapore: Springer Nature Singapore. https://link.springer.com/chapter/10.1007/978-981-96-3372-2_38

Siripipatthanakul, S., & Siripipattanakul, S. (2025a). Rural Dental Health Transformation by Adopting Digital Technologies. *Transforming Dental Health in Rural Communities: Digital Dentistry*, 47-80.

Siripipatthanakul, S., & Siripipattanakul, S. (2025b). Oral Healthcare Knowledge, Attitude, and Practice (KAP) of Primary School Students in Rural Areas Using Digital Technologies. In *Transforming Dental Health in Rural Communities: Digital Dentistry* (pp. 141-172). IGI Global Scientific Publishing. DOI: 10.4018/979-8-3693-7165-7.ch006

Sugajski, M., Buszewska-Forajta, M., & Buszewski, B. (2023). Functional beverages in the 21st century. *Beverages*, *9*(1), 27. https://www.mdpi.com/2306-5710/9/1/27. DOI: 10.3390/beverages9010027

Talwar, S., Jabeen, F., Tandon, A., Sakashita, M., & Dhir, A. (2021). What drives willingness to purchase and stated buying behavior toward organic food? A Stimulus–Organism–Behavior–Consequence (SOBC) perspective. *Journal of Cleaner Production*, *293*, 125882. DOI: 10.1016/j.jclepro.2021.125882

Tuhin, M. K. W., Miraz, M. H., Habib, M. M., & Alam, M. M. (2022). Strengthening consumers' halal buying behaviour: Role of attitude, religiosity and personal norm. *Journal of Islamic Marketing*, *13*(3), 671–687. DOI: 10.1108/JIMA-07-2020-0220

Uhm, J. P., Kim, S., Do, C., & Lee, H. W. (2022). How augmented reality (AR) experience affects purchase intention in sport E-commerce: Roles of perceived diagnosticity, psychological distance, and perceived risks. *Journal of Retailing and Consumer Services*, *67*, 103027. DOI: 10.1016/j.jretconser.2022.103027

Utomo, S. B., Sekaryuni, R., Widarjono, A., Tohirin, A., & Sudarsono, H. (2021). Promoting Islamic financial ecosystem to improve halal industry performance in Indonesia: A demand and supply analysis. *Journal of Islamic Marketing*, *12*(5), 992–1011. DOI: 10.1108/JIMA-12-2019-0259

Watanabe, E. A. D. M., Alfinito, S., Curvelo, I. C. G., & Hamza, K. M. (2020). Perceived value, trust and purchase intention of organic food: A study with Brazilian consumers. *British Food Journal*, *122*(4), 1070–1184. DOI: 10.1108/BFJ-05-2019-0363

Wijekoon, R., & Sabri, M. F. (2021). Determinants that influence green product purchase intention and behavior: A literature review and guiding framework. *Sustainability (Basel)*, *13*(11), 6219. DOI: 10.3390/su13116219

Yakin, A., Khang, A., Muthmainnah, M., Elngar, A. A., Siripipatthanakul, S., & Limna, P. (2025). Unraveling the Quantum Robotics Influence: Transforming Social Interaction for the Future. In *The Quantum Evolution* (pp. 349-372). CRC Press.

Yarmohammadi, S., Mousavi, S., Ajori, L., Mohammadzade, F., & Marashi, T. (2023). Impact of attitude, subjective norms and perceived behavioral control on health behaviors among women with low-risk HPV, and the mediating role of behavioral intention: An interventional study. *International Journal of Health Promotion and Education, 61*(2), 70–82. DOI: 10.1080/14635240.2021.1995776

Chapter 8
Sustainable Development in Hospitals for Elderly Dysphagia In Geriatric Dentistry

Penpim Phuangsuwan
https://orcid.org/0000-0003-2371-7998
University of Phayao, Thailand

Sorasun Rungsiyanont
Srinakharinwirot University, Bangkok, Thailand

Patcharavadee Sriboonruang
https://orcid.org/0000-0002-2171-2387
Kasetsart University, Chatuchak, Thailand

ABSTRACT

Sustainable development in geriatric dental Facilities treating dysphagia in older patients requires a comprehensive approach that encompasses environmental, social, and economic considerations. This chapter uses PRISMA for systematic review meta-analysis. Related keywords determined 2021-2025 scholarly paper selection. We used thematic and content analyses. Adjusted diets reduce waste and make better use of resources, which benefits the environment. Socially, it requires equal access to specialized treatment, patient-centered methods that consider individual needs, and well-supported staff. Financially, cost-effective methods, preventive dental treatment to prevent dysphagia, and long-term value are needed. Geriatric dentistry promotes oral health to prevent and alleviate dysphagia. This improves older patients' quality of life and ensures resource-efficient healthcare.

DOI: 10.4018/979-8-3693-9800-5.ch008

1. INTRODUCTION

Global health concerns, climate change, and chronic disease are making healthcare sustainability more important. Social, economic, and environmental sustainability are crucial for delivering equitable and robust healthcare. It is necessary to bridge the gap between complex health information and people's ability to understand and utilize it by embracing all three elements. Health literacy may be a practical approach to reducing health disparities among demographic groups and enhancing social sustainability by addressing the connection between adverse social and economic conditions and health issues. People can reduce healthcare expenditures by recognizing their health conditions and learning how to manage them effectively. Health literacy and environmental health literacy empower people and communities to understand how environmental factors affect their health and take proactive steps to protect the environment, potentially reducing the environmental impact of healthcare. Health literacy should be incorporated into education and healthcare professional training to promote sustainability. Academia, healthcare institutions, and community organizations can collaborate to enhance health literacy, despite acknowledged obstacles such as low awareness (Zanobini et al., 2024).

Demographic shifts, characterized by a growing percentage of older persons globally and an epidemiological transition leading to increased tooth retention and heightened aspirations, create significant challenges for the oral health of the elderly population (Chávez et al., 2022). Geriatric dentistry must be restructured, shifting from a conventional emphasis to a more comprehensive approach. Specific scenarios that justify the development of a novel conceptual framework for the progression of geriatric dentistry as a clinical specialty.

Based on scientific data and academic expertise, four concepts should guide the discipline in the coming years and serve as its foundational pillars: (a) minimal intervention dentistry, (b) oral functionality, (c) patient-centered care, and (d) interdisciplinary collaboration. Due to the scarcity of data and proof, particular emphasis is placed on impoverished and emerging nations. Modifying clinical recommendations and public health policies based on these principles will enhance access to dental care for the elderly, particularly for individuals facing physical or social barriers, thereby ensuring improved oral health-related quality of life and overall well-being. These notions have a significant impact on the education and training of new dentists and specialists in both public and private sectors (León & Giacaman, 2022).

Swallowing difficulties, or dysphagia, affect patients' quality of life. Dysphagia affects the mortality and hospital stay of older hospitalized patients. Patients with dysphagia may have a lower quality of life. However, its effects are unknown. It is investigated how dysphagia affects home release in elderly rural rehabilitation unit patients. A retrospective cohort study of 65-year-olds discharged from a rural Japanese community hospital rehabilitation unit was used for a secondary analysis. Home discharge was inversely correlated with dysphagia, polypharmacy, and internal medicine hospitalization. Interventional research can enhance the health of rural older persons by identifying effective interventions, such as interprofessional approaches to managing multimorbidity and polypharmacy (Ohta et al., 2022).

Geriatric dentistry experts can contribute to public health campaigns that aim to promote awareness among older persons and their families about the symptoms of dysphagia and the importance of maintaining oral health. Hospitals can create a system that is more efficient, equitable, and environmentally responsible for managing dysphagia in elderly patients within the context of geriatric dentistry by adopting the principles of sustainable development. This will ultimately lead to an improvement in the health and quality of life for a population that is rapidly aging worldwide.

1.1 Research Objective

This chapter explains how dysphagia impacts the elderly and the need for appropriate public health policies.

1.2 Research Question

What are the appropriate public health policies for the elderly with dysphagia in geriatric dentistry?

2. LITERATURE REVIEW

2.1 Dysphagia and the Elderly Prevalence

Dysphagia is relatively common in the general population. However, most studies focus on neurological conditions. Dysphagia is common among older persons, and the population is aging, making it a threat. About 27% of older people in the community have dysphagia. According to clinical settings, 27% to 91% of 70-year-olds are affected, with greater rates in acute hospital wards and nursing homes. Despite its high prevalence, dysphagia is not checked for or handled in clinical settings, and intermediate care (IC) units have not been studied. Transitional care helps older persons, especially those with chronic disease and frailty, recover, improve their abilities, optimize management, and prevent functional decline during care transitions and between settings. Dysphagia is a major Geriatric condition. Dysphagia and other elderly disorders typically overlap and enhance each other, making their relationship significant. Older dysphagia patients, whether chronic or acute, have a significant risk of malnutrition and sarcopenia. Frailty is common in older individuals and a growing public health hazard. Sarcopenia and dysphagia, two age-related disorders in fragile older people, often combine and worsen results. Cognitive impairment raises dysphagia risk in addition to these connections. Dysphagia affects up to 86% of advanced dementia patients, and delirium can cause or worsen dysphagia. Cognitive impairment increases the risk of delirium. Very few acute geriatric and rehabilitation ward studies have examined the relationship between delirium and dysphagia. Finally, a few acute hospital studies indicate conflicting evidence linking dysphagia to polypharmacy and certain drugs (benzodiazepines, antipsychotics, opioids) (Mehraban-Far et al., 2021; Dini et al., 2025).

2.2 Long-Term Sustainable Hospitals by Well-Being Improvement for Elderly Dysphagia

The delivery of individualized health education is a crucial component in managing chronic diseases among the senior population. Disease comprehension, health literacy, the ability to care for oneself, psychological well-being, and physical health are all greatly improved as a result of this initiative. Additionally, it helps reduce the likelihood of experiencing unfavorable health outcomes. it is of the utmost significance to incorporate patient-centered educational initiatives into general practice treatment for elderly patients. By doing so, you can enhance their overall well-being and quality of life, which is why individualized health education is a vital component of the holistic care provided to older patients with chronic diseases. This strategy not only aligns with the fundamentals of contemporary geriatric care but also sets a standard for managing chronic diseases in older populations in the years to come (Zhang et al., 2024).

The performance of healthcare is its ability to restore and preserve health at acceptable societal costs. With the prevalence of chronic diseases, medical care (the majority of healthcare) often underperforms in terms of clinical efficacy, intervention benefit-to-risk ratio, cost-benefit ratio, and population health. Worldwide, most healthcare KPIs focus on process rather than results or depend on activities beyond the control of healthcare decision-makers. The reactive diagnosis-centered organizational approach and biological paradigm, which are inadequate in chronic diseases, limit clinical effectiveness and cost-effectiveness. They delay healthcare intervention, deploy ineffective preventative and treatment tools, and deplete resources. Health promotion and preservation require interdisciplinary and interagency cooperation. Supplementing the present 'reactive' organizational model with a biopsychosocial preventative person-centered model can help the healthcare system fight the chronic illness epidemic. Chronic illness management should prioritize early lifestyle-based interventions, as outlined in the P4 (Participatory, Personalized, Predictive, Preventive) framework. Some even consider adding a fifth P for the term "Precise," suggesting that the degree of customization it enables is increasing. Communication and information technologies should enable the rapid scaling up of optimal person-centered practices (Martyushev-Poklad et al., 2022).

"Sustainable Healthcare" examines the crucial intersection of healthcare and sustainability, providing a comprehensive analysis of strategies that promote both human health and environmental balance. It is crucial to prioritize medical services with environmentally sustainable principles in light of the evolving healthcare landscape. The chapter examines the intricate interconnections among patient care, resource management, technological integration, and environmental stewardship from a multidimensional viewpoint. The innovative projects, case studies, and best practices presented clarify the path to a more sustainable healthcare system. The crucial resource for healthcare practitioners, legislators, and scholars striving to establish a healthier future grounded in care and compassion, highlighting the comprehensive concept of healing that encompasses individuals, communities, and the planet (Singh et al., 2024).

A comprehensive plan that integrates environmental consciousness with patient-centered treatment and economic viability is required for long-term, sustainable institutions that aim to improve the well-being of elderly patients who have dysphagia. Specifically, this entails minimizing waste from modified diets, ensuring equitable access to specialized geriatric dental and dysphagia services, cultivating a supportive environment for healthcare professionals, and implementing cost-effective preventative measures such as promoting optimal oral health to reduce the risk of dysphagia and its complications, which will ultimately lead to an improvement in quality of life and resource efficiency.

2.2.1 Environmental sustainability in Hospitals for the Elderly

Carbon Dioxide (CO2) emissions have a detrimental impact on human health and are a significant contributor to climate change. The probability of reaching the age of 65 diminishes with rising CO2 emissions. Safeguarding the quality of drinking water is essential for maintaining public health. Survival rates will be influenced throughout time by variations in the safety of drinking water. The accessibility of hospitals also affects the probability of surviving to a specific age. Individuals' survival probabilities are elevated in regions with more readily accessible hospitals. Ensuring hospitals operate sustainably and ecologically enhances healthcare provision and accessibility in the context of green hospital management. By enhancing our understanding of the relationship between CO2 emissions, drinking water quality, and hospital accessibility, we can facilitate the transition to a sustainable healthcare system and ensure that patients reach the age of 65 (Supriadi, 2025).

The implementation of sustainability initiatives in hospitals underscores their crucial role in mitigating environmental impacts and promoting public health. The healthcare sector substantially contributes to global greenhouse gas emissions, necessitating immediate improvements in energy use, waste management, building design, transportation, and food systems. Highlight the potential of hospitals to enhance energy efficiency, adopt renewable energy solutions, and reduce waste through the use of innovative technologies and sustainable methodologies. Initiatives such as eco-friendly hospital architecture, environmentally conscious food systems, and sustainable procurement strategies are crucial for minimizing the ecological footprint. Notwithstanding these prospects, obstacles such as manpower shortages, inadequate finance, and technical complexity impede advancement. Confronting these challenges through leadership dedication, effective resource allocation, and staff engagement is crucial for aligning the healthcare industry with national and international sustainability objectives. By emphasizing sustainability, hospitals can achieve enduring economic benefits, improve patient outcomes, and foster a healthier, more resilient society (Schwab et al., 2025).

The "Green Hospital" concept represents a paradigm shift in healthcare, emphasizing resource efficiency and the reduction of environmental effect. This approach includes the integration of renewable energy, natural lighting, sustainable materials, green roofs, and intelligent building management systems. Significant issues persist, including medical waste management, water conservation, chemical utilization, pollution, and plastic consumption in healthcare environments. Furthermore, barriers to green hospital programs must be addressed, including systemic redundancy, regulatory compliance, operational requirements, budgetary limitations, and cultural resistance. In conclusion, an immediate overhaul of healthcare systems is essential to conform to environmentally sustainable practices, emphasizing the need to reduce CO_2 emissions and optimize resource and waste management to address the changing health needs of an expanding and aging global population (Vallée, 2024).

Implementing techniques to limit single-use products in dysphagia management, such as using reusable feeding tools where feasible and safe, and optimizing material use in texture-modified meals, are examples of waste reduction strategies that can be implemented. In the context of food preparation and diagnostic procedures about dysphagia, energy efficiency refers to the utilization of environmentally friendly equipment. To conserve water, it is necessary to implement water-saving methods in the kitchen and when providing oral hygiene treatment to patients who have difficulty swallowing. In the context of patient care and dietary requirements, eco-friendly procurement refers to the selection of products that are of a sustainable and environmentally friendly origin.

2.2.2 Social sustainability in Hospitals for the Elderly

Since 2016, ASEAN—Brunei, Cambodia, Indonesia, Laos, Malaysia, Myanmar, the Philippines, Singapore, Thailand, and Vietnam—has endorsed a "statement on active ageing" to improve the quality of life and well-being of the older population. Long-term care has been established or integrated into the health and social care systems of countries with ageing populations in the region, although it is relatively new. Singapore has the most significant ageing rate in the region, followed by Thailand and Vietnam, according to UN DESA data from 2023. Thailand and Vietnam remain middle-income developing countries with increasing aging populations and inadequate health and social infrastructures. In addition to institutional or nursing home long-term care (LTC), community-integrated care is emerging to help aging adults in their communities. Financial sustainability and personnel stability remain complex issues that require multidisciplinary teamwork (Vo & Fong, 2025).

All elderly patients, regardless of socioeconomic level or location, must get hospital-based dysphagia testing and management. Known as equitable access. Patient-centered treatment tailors treatment to elderly dysphagia patients' cultural background, preferences, and needs. These strategies include involving individuals and their families in decisions related to nutrition and feeding. Provide a supportive and healthful workplace for healthcare personnel treating elderly dysphagia patients. Nurses, nutritionists, speech-language pathologists, and dentists are examples. This may improve care and staff retention. Regularly training hospital staff on the needs of elderly dysphagia patients and sustainable treatment approaches is crucial. Community engagement includes working with local communities and support groups to raise awareness of senior dysphagia and promote care (Office of Disease Prevention and Health Promotion, 2023; Cabañero-Garcia et al., 2025).

2.2.3 Economic Sustainability

The long-term viability of the economy. Cost-effective practices include implementing efficient workflows and effective resource management in the assessment of dysphagia and the preparation of diets, thereby reducing unnecessary costs. Preventive measures include emphasizing the early identification and management of risk factors for dysphagia in order to lessen the likelihood of expensive consequences such as aspiration pneumonia and malnutrition. In this context, geriatric dentistry plays a crucial role in ensuring that patients maintain good dental health. Investing in sustainable solutions that provide long-term benefits for both patients and the hospital, such as durable equipment and efficient service delivery models, is an example of creating long-term value. The process of making informed decisions about resource utilization to provide the most effective and efficient treatment for older patients with dysphagia is referred to as optimizing resource allocation (Hegab et al., 2023; Owolabi et al., 2024).

2.3 Related Studies

Fernández-Ruiz et al. (2020) show oropharyngeal dysphagia (OD) is acknowledged as a geriatric syndrome due to its prevalence among the elderly and the complications that significantly affect quality of life. The primary aim is to analyze the efficacy of telemedicine consultations in re-evaluating nutritional status and quality of life in elderly individuals diagnosed with oropharyngeal dysphagia who actively use thickeners to prevent hospital admissions during the COVID-19 pandemic. An observational, descriptive, longitudinal study with a sample of 33 people aged 65 years or older, diagnosed with OD and possessing intact cognitive function. The nutritional status was assessed using the Mini-Nutritional Assessment (MNA) questionnaire and biochemical markers. At the same time, the quality of life was examined by the Swallowing Quality of Life (SWAL-QOL) questionnaire. Results: Thirty-three elderly patients with OD were recruited (54.5% female), with a mean age of 83.5 ± 7.6 years. The primary etiology of overdose in the study cohort was neurodegenerative illness (51.5%), followed by cerebrovascular disease (33.3%), and other etiologies (15.2%). Sixty-six point six percent of patients were identified as being at risk of malnutrition. The MNA score exhibited a strong correlation with albumin ($r = 0.600$, $p < 0.001$) and total protein ($r = 0.435$, $p = 0.015$), but not with total cholesterol ($r = -0.116$, $p = 0.534$) or lymphocytes ($r = -0.056$, $p = 0.758$). The average overall score of the SWAL-QOL was 75.1 ± 16.4 points. The quality of life for participants associated with the use of a thickening agent is satisfactory. Despite the body mass index (BMI) and average biochemical and nutritional parameters of the subjects falling within normal limits, the MNA has identified a significant proportion of individuals at risk of malnutrition, indicating the necessity for ongoing re-evaluation in these patients and highlighting the efficacy of the telematic approach in this study.

León & Giacaman (2022) demonstrate that demographic shifts, characterized by a growing proportion of older persons globally, combined with an epidemiological transition that leads to increased tooth retention and higher demands and expectations, present new challenges for the oral health of the elderly population. Consequently, geriatric dentistry must be restructured, shifting from a conventional emphasis on prosthetics to a more comprehensive approach that actively integrates geriatric and gerontological elements. Various scenarios that justify the development of a novel conceptual framework for the progression of geriatric dentistry as a clinical specialty. Based on scientific data and our academic expertise, we suggest four concepts that should guide the discipline in the coming years and serve as its foundational pillars:

minimal intervention dentistry, oral functionality, patient-centered care, and interdisciplinary collaboration. Due to the scarcity of data and proof, particular emphasis is placed on impoverished and emerging nations. Modifying clinical recommendations and public health policies based on these principles will enhance access to dental care for the elderly, particularly for individuals facing physical or social barriers, thereby ensuring improved oral health-related quality of life and overall well-being. These concepts have a significant impact on the education and training of emerging dentists and specialists in both public and private sectors.

Arowosola et al. (2022) found Africa's elderly demographic is anticipated to increase by 216%, growing from 74.4 million in 2020 to 235.1 million by 2050. Future forecasts indicate that only Africa will experience a consistent increase of 1% per decade. However, their nutritional needs and food security are not afforded the adequate attention and priority that they deserve compared to other vulnerable populations. Numerous individuals experience health issues resulting from the deterioration of organ functionality. Diverse chronic diseases (e.g., diabetes, hypertension, cancer, Alzheimer's, osteoporosis, arthritis, cardiovascular diseases) are primarily handled through pharmacological interventions; nevertheless, these conditions can also be prevented and managed through proper diets with either broad or particular functionalities. This review aims to outline various meals and their effects on senior health. Furthermore, it examines the impact of proper nutrition on obesity, diabetes, cardiovascular disease, cancer, bone health, oral health, and mental health in the aged population.

Ohta et al. (2022) demonstrate that Dysphagia denotes difficulties in swallowing, which adversely affect patients' quality of life. Dysphagia affects clinical outcomes, such as death rates and duration of hospitalization, in elderly patients. Dysphagia may impact the present and future quality of life of specific patients. Nonetheless, its precise effect remains ambiguous. It was sought to elucidate the influence of dysphagia on home discharge in elderly patients in a rural rehabilitation facility. A secondary analysis was performed utilizing data from a retrospective cohort study involving patients over 65 years old who were discharged from a community hospital rehabilitation unit in rural Japan. Participant data was collected from April 2016 to March 2020. The principal consequence was discharge home. The mean age of participants was 82.1 years (standard deviation, 10.8); 34.5% were male. Brain stroke (44.3%) was the predominant medical diagnosis for admission, whereas femur fracture (42.9%) was the most prevalent orthopedic ailment. Dysphagia (odds ratio [OR] = 0.38, 95% confidence interval [CI]: 0.20–0.73), polypharmacy (OR = 0.5, 95% CI: 0.32–0.90), and hospitalization for internal medicine conditions (OR = 0.44, 95% CI: 0.26–0.77) were inversely correlated with home discharge. The elevated motor domain scores of the Functional Independence Measure were favorably correlated with home discharge (OR = 1.07, 95% CI: 1.05–1.08). Dysphagia, polypharmacy, and hospitalization for internal medicine disorders and conditions were inversely correlated with home discharge. Clarifying successful therapies via interventional studies, particularly strategies for managing multimorbidity and polypharmacy through interprofessional collaboration, may enhance the health conditions of older people in remote locations.

Takeda et al. (2023) show a one-year, multicenter, prospective cohort study aimed to investigate the relationship between observable characteristics of eating and swallowing function and outcomes (mortality/hospitalization, or survival) among senior individuals in long-term care insurance facilities in Japan. Baseline evaluations of parameters, including language, drooling, halitosis, hypersalivation, tongue mobility, perioral muscle function, coughing, respiration post-swallowing, rinsing, and oral residue, among others, were performed. A score of 0 was deemed favorable, while scores of 1 or 2 were considered harmful. Data on patient age, sex, body mass index, Barthel index, and Clinical Dementia Rating were documented. The mortality/hospitalization rates, as well as the survival rates over one year, were documented, and patients were categorized into groups based on their corresponding outcomes (mortality/hospitalization group or survival group) and baseline characteristics. A total of 986 people from 32 facilities participated, comprising 216 in the death/hospitalization cohort and 770 in the survival cohort. Language, salivation, halitosis, perioral musculature, coughing, breathing post-deglutition, washing, and oral residue exhibited significant associations with the outcomes ($p < 0.05$). Consequently, the regular execution of these straightforward evaluations by caregivers may facilitate early identification and intervention to avert mortality, pneumonia, aspiration, and malnutrition in senior individuals.

Roberts et al. (2024) show that dysphagia frequently impacts elderly individuals, rendering them nutritionally susceptible. There is considerable disparity in the documented prevalence of dysphagia in aged care. This systematic review and meta-analysis aimed to ascertain the prevalence of dysphagia among residents of aged care facilities utilizing suitable assessment techniques, focusing on four high-risk subgroups: individuals with neurological disorders, dementia, malnutrition, and inadequate dental health. Scopus, Web of Science, Medline, and CINAHL Plus were queried, and research selection was performed in Covidence. A random effects model was employed in a meta-analysis to determine the pooled prevalence of dysphagia. Seven studies qualified for inclusion. The prevalence of dysphagia varied between 16% and 69.6%. The aggregated prevalence of dysphagia was 56.11% (95% CI, 39.36–72.17, $p < 0.0001$, $I2 = 98.61\%$). The sensitivity analysis assessing the prevalence of dysphagia based solely on the CSE revealed a pooled prevalence of 60.90% (95% CI, 57.55–64.21, $p = 0.9994$, $I2 = 0\%$). Only one study showed dysphagia prevalence in persons with nervous system illnesses (31%), inadequate dentition (92%), and dementia (68.4%), precluding the possibility of a meta-analysis.

No research has documented the prevalence of dysphagia in patients experiencing malnutrition. Dysphagia is highly prevalent among inhabitants of aged care facilities. This evidence needs to inform enhancements in the health outcomes and quality of life for elderly care residents. Future studies should investigate the prevalence among high-risk groupings.

Huang et al. (2025) show that oral disorders have become one of the most widespread non-communicable diseases (NCDs) globally, with an average prevalence of 45%, impacting over 3.5 billion individuals worldwide. As global aging accelerates, oral health concerns among elderly persons have become increasingly significant. The global multi-country epidemiological survey and WHO report indicate a notable rise in the prevalence of oral disorders among individuals aged 65 and older, with a significant burden attributed to dental caries, periodontal disease, and tooth loss. This article consolidates recent epidemiological data on the increasing prevalence of oral health issues in older adults (aged 65 years and above), encompassing both inflammatory and non-inflammatory oral diseases, such as dental caries, periodontal disease, tooth loss, oral cancer, xerostomia, and dysphagia. It elucidates their interconnections with systemic health, identifies risk factors and prevention strategies, and ultimately advocates for the incorporation of oral health into comprehensive geriatric care frameworks.

Kristamuliana et al. (2025) state that dysphagia, or difficulty swallowing, is prevalent among aging populations, particularly those residing in the community, attributable to age-related alterations in sensory and motor capabilities. Efficient preventive interventions are crucial for averting difficulties and enhancing well-being in this demographic. This scoping study aimed to identify and summarize strategies for the prevention of dysphagia in older individuals residing in the community. Nine studies conducted between 2005 and 2023 were identified, comprising seven randomized controlled trials and two quasi-experimental studies. Three forms of dysphagia prevention were identified: exercise, electrical stimulation, and educational programs. Additionally, three trials employed several interventions (combined intervention). Exercise-based therapies represent the most extensively researched techniques for preventing dysphagia in older persons residing in the community, with integrated approaches also demonstrating potential efficacy. Nonetheless, geographic bias, ambiguous sample size determination, and insufficient long-term follow-up undermine the credibility and applicability of all interventions. Subsequent studies must rectify these deficiencies to enhance evidence and bolster dysphagia prevention initiatives.

Cava & Lombardo (2025) conclude that the global rise in elderly populations underscores the need to tackle age-related issues through proper dietary management to improve the well-being of seniors and prevent and treat various diseases. The rising aged population correlates with a surge in conditions including sarcopenia, osteosarcopenia, and frailty, underscoring the necessity for regular malnutrition assessments in older adults and the adoption of tailored nutritional interventions. The significance of diet in managing geriatric disorders, including frailty, sarcopenia, osteosarcopenia, obesity, and metabolic syndrome, is emphasized. Dysphagia, prevalent among the elderly, requires careful management to prevent malnutrition and its associated consequences. Maintaining muscular mass and bone health in advanced age is crucial. Nutrition plays a crucial role in geriatrics, focusing on promoting healthy aging and addressing issues such as malnutrition and overeating. The significance of protein consumption and nutritious dietary frameworks, such as the Mediterranean diet, is then examined. The issues surrounding personalized nutritional treatment, such as the necessity for artificial nutrition or oral supplements, are examined in relation to enhancing quality of life and healthcare in an aging population.

Hegde & Buch (2025) summarized that the aging population is a worldwide phenomena. The size and share of the senior population are increasing globally over time. Chronic diseases impact the oral and systemic health of the elderly population. A comprehensive understanding of the oral health state of the senior population would enhance the ability of healthcare practitioners to provide superior treatment. The information concerning the overall health conditions of the elderly impacting oral health, age-related alterations in dental tissues, oral health status of geriatric patients in India and other nations, the status of the National Oral Health Policy in India, encountered challenges, the state of gerodontology education in India, innovations, and prospective strategies in geriatric oral health care was derived from full-text articles and incorporated into the current review. It shows current state of geriatric oral health care, underscore the obstacles encountered in managing geriatric patients, and showcase technologies that are revolutionizing geriatric oral health care.

Therefore, analyzing current procedures and identifying opportunities for improvement is essential. Establishing defined and verifiable sustainability goals in dysphagia care encourages participation from patients, caregivers, healthcare professionals, and administrators. Sustainable solutions are tested and improved through pilot programs. Monitoring progress and assessing the effects of change, sharing successful ideas, and learning from other healthcare facilities. Hospitals may provide high-quality, patient-centered care for elderly dysphagia patients while improving the globe and society by adopting a sustainable approach. It involves creating innovative solutions that benefit individuals and groups. In conclusion, patient-centered, preventative, and transdisciplinary public health initiatives are needed to address dysphagia in geriatric dentistry. Governments can enhance health outcomes and promote healthy aging by integrating oral health policies with eldercare.

3. METHODOLOGY

The implementation of a comprehensive approach that considers environmental, social, and economic factors is necessary for sustainable development in hospitals addressing dysphagia in older patients within the field of geriatric dentistry. This chapter employs the PRISMA method for meta-analysis in a systematic review. The scholarly papers selected for 2021-2025 were based on related keywords. Thematic and content analyses were employed. The systematic analysis method was applied based on the studies of Siripipatthanakul & Phuangsuwan (2024), Siripipatthanakul et al. (2024), and Phuangsuwan et al. (2024). Purposive sampling was employed, synthesized, and analyzed using content analysis.

Step 1: ***Identifying the Problem*** - Some of the approaches that can be used to identify the early stage of entries include manual searches, literature databases, and other alternatives. The initial stage of this research project involved random sampling, where the subject matter was selected randomly. A total of 266 papers are included in the connected article.

Step 2: ***Screening:*** The remaining records are displayed during this step, which follows the elimination of duplicates. At this point, the titles and abstracts of the records that have been recognized are evaluated to see whether or not they are pertinent to the topic matter or aims of the study. The selection of academic publications from Google Scholar, Scopus, and Web of Science (WOS) was the method that was utilized in the second step of the process, which comprised the execution of purposeful sampling. A total of one hundred seven (107) items were chosen at this stage of the process.

Step 3: ***Eligibility:*** This section provides an overview of the variety of research that may be carried out once the preliminary screening has been completed. Articles that include crucial information are evaluated in this step based on the criteria that have been developed in order to determine eligibility. The third part of the process involved the utilization of a purposive sampling technique, which ultimately led to the selection of thirty papers that were eligible for a systematic review. 30 papers that were chosen were mostly from the years 2021 to 2025 and were based on terms and phrases from AI, Grammarly, Turnitin, and Word Cloud.

Step 4: ***Inclusions:*** This stage is a representation of the overall number of studies that were incorporated into the analysis of the systematic review. It has been determined that the conditions for eligibility have been met, and these studies are suitable for further inquiry. The flow chart contains a visual representation of the quantity of research that was halted at each phase, as well as the reasoning that led to the decision. A lack of relevance to the research issue, an unsuitable study design, an absence of relevant data, or inclusion criteria are some of the most prevalent reasons for exclusion. A lack of relevance to the research subject is another common explanation. In accordance with the PRISMA methodology, the information for the fourth phase was processed by three educational specialists. They demonstrated that the systematic review had valid information by using content analysis as their method of investigation.

4. RESULTS

4.1 Grammarly Results

Grammarly indicates that the accuracy of grammar use is approximately 95% (excluding references) and 1% plagiarism. Thus, the content is acceptable in publication.

4.2 Word Clouds

Figure 1. Word Clouds

https://www.wordclouds.com/ (July 23, 2025)

4.3 Theoretical Model

Figure 2. Sustainable Development for Elderly Dysphagia

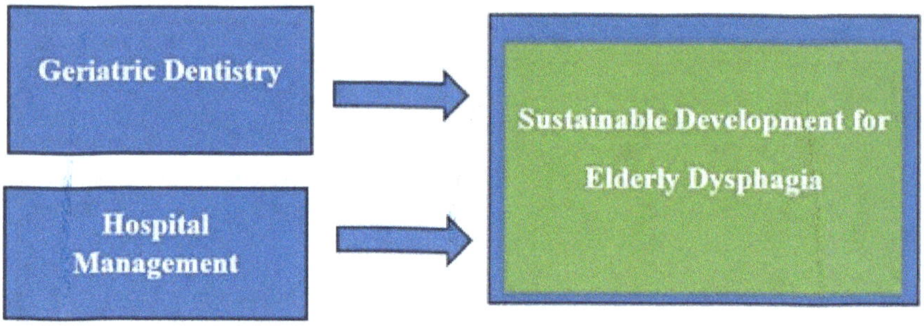

The convergence of clinical care quality, resource efficiency, and long-term patient outcomes in aging populations is where the connection between dysphagia, the elderly, and the sustainability of hospitals may be found. How these three components are connected is as follows:

1. Dysphagia, also known as trouble swallowing, is extremely common in older persons, particularly those who suffer from neurological illnesses such as Parkinson's disease, dementia, or stroke. Its impact on health can result in malnutrition, aspiration pneumonia, dehydration, and increased hospital readmissions, all of which contribute to higher healthcare expenses and increased demands on resources.
2. The goal of sustainable hospitals is to deliver care that is efficient, mindful of resources, and designed for long-term sustainability. The aged population's dysphagia presents many hurdles to this objective:
    - 2.1. To minimize the likelihood of problems and the requirement for emergency medical care, early screening and intervention improve patient outcomes and help shorten the length of stay in cases of elderly dysphagia.
    - 2.2. Preventing malnutrition and hospital-acquired pneumonia can reduce therapy costs and readmissions. Interdisciplinary dysphagia management teams (speech-language pathologists, nutritionists, and nurses) can maximize resources.
    - 2.3. Extended hospital stays and frequent hospitalizations increase the consumption of energy, waste, and resources. Reducing food waste and

packaging can be accomplished through sustainable nutrition techniques such as tailored, texture-modified meals.

3. To enhance the viability of hospitals in the context of dysphagia and populations who are getting older, establish early dysphagia screening techniques for patients who are older inpatients. Staff members should be trained on sustainable methods of geriatric care. Utilize digital health tools to monitor swallowing function. Community-based follow-up should be encouraged to lessen reliance on hospitals. The inability to properly treat dysphagia in older patients can harm the long-term viability of hospitals by increasing the clinical burden, costs, and resource utilization. In contrast, efficient management helps develop resilient, cost-effective, and ecologically conscious healthcare systems for aging societies.

5. DISCUSSIONS

Sustainable hospital development, particularly in the field of geriatric dentistry, emphasizes effective, efficient, and long-term swallowing management systems for older patients. These systems are designed to minimize the negative impact on the environment and maximize the positive effects on society. Not only is it essential to employ environmentally friendly methods, but it is also crucial to have a robust healthcare plan for an aging population. It is common for older persons to suffer from dysphagia, which is characterized by problems in swallowing. Presbyphagia, a physiological change that occurs with aging, chronic disorders such as stroke, Parkinson's disease, and dementia, dry mouth medications, and poor dental health are all associated with this condition. In addition to a decrease in quality of life and an increase in hospitalizations, neglecting one's health can result in malnutrition, dehydration, aspiration pneumonia (which is the leading cause of morbidity and mortality among the elderly), and other adverse health outcomes.

The practice of geriatric dentistry acknowledges that dental health has a profound impact on an individual's overall health and well-being. This insight drives geriatric dentistry, which focuses on the dental needs of older adults. Oral function, which includes chewing, tongue movement, saliva flow, and the presence of healthy teeth or dentures, is evaluated by dentists in older patients who have difficulty swallowing. Every single one of them is essential for generating boluses and for swallowing safely. Caries in the teeth, periodontal disease, and infections that exacerbate dysphagia or cause aspiration pneumonia are all conditions that require treatment to prevent oral problems. To ensure that dentures are functional and well-fitting, dental optimization is performed. This helps to promote healthy chewing and food preparation. Treatment of dysphagia must be approached from a comprehensive perspective, which requires collaboration between speech-language pathologists, physicians, dietitians, nurses, and caretakers. To put sustainable development into action, one must first establish a system that is both economically sustainable and efficient, meaning it is both practical and cost-effective. For early identification and prevention, routine screenings for dysphagia and oral health are performed in older dentistry settings and during hospital admissions among patients. By detecting aspiration pneumonia at an early stage, it is possible to reduce the need for expensive acute care, prolonged hospital stays, and recurrent readmissions owing to secondary aspiration pneumonia.

Oral care and dysphagia management recommendations supported by evidence ensure that patients receive consistent, high-quality care while reducing unnecessary interventions and waste. Bedside swallowing exams are an example of an efficient and cost-effective diagnostic tool that should be used rather than pricey imaging at the beginning of the process. Dental consultations and telemedicine for dental care: Through the provision of follow-up therapy and consultations to homebound or frail elderly patients, technology has the potential to reduce the obligations of both caregivers and patients, as well as the costs associated with transportation. Purchasing oral hygiene products, dental materials, and customized diets from sustainable sources is an example of sustainable procurement for dysphagia patients. This involves taking into consideration the expenditures over the patient's lifespan as well as the impact on the environment. In order to ensure social sustainability, equity, patient-centeredness, and community orientation are essential components. In order to ensure that patients are comfortable and treated with dignity, Person-Centered Care tailors treatment regimens for dysphagia to each patient's needs, preferences, and culture. Dietary preferences are taken into consideration while developing texture-modified diets.

In order to comprehend dysphagia, prevent oral hygiene concerns in vulnerable senior patients, and recognize swallowing problems, education and training are needed for geriatric dentists, dental hygienists, and all other members of the healthcare staff (including nurses and caregivers). Carers are given more agency as a result, and patient outcomes are improved. The expansion of geriatric dental treatment and dysphagia screening beyond hospitals and into community settings, nursing homes, and home-based care is an example of community outreach and integration. In this way, vulnerable groups are able to access and continue receiving care. If we want to eliminate health disparities, we should ensure that all older citizens, regardless of their socioeconomic level or location, have access to specialist dental care. These services include dysphagia and geriatric dentistry programs. Creating a partnership with community centers or mobile dental units is one of the options available. In order to encourage family and caregiver engagement, it is necessary to educate the families and caregivers of elderly dysphagia patients on proper oral hygiene and feeding techniques. On the other hand, this is essential for long-term management and has the potential to lessen the burden on conventional healthcare systems. The preservation of the environment while simultaneously minimizing the ecological footprint. The reduction of waste necessitates the precise segregation of trash and recycling of dental supplies, oral hygiene items, and waste from meals that have been modified and altered in texture. Employ reusable materials whenever it is feasible and safe to do so. In geriatric dentistry clinics and hospitals that treat patients with dysphagia, energy-saving lighting, dental equipment, and water-saving methods, such as low-flow faucets and better sterilization, are implemented. These procedures help save water and energy. Green building concepts are given priority in the construction of hospitals and the rehabilitation of geriatric care units due to the implementation of sustainable infrastructure. In this context, natural light, materials that are not hazardous, and adequate ventilation are all included. These concepts improve the health of both patients and staff members while simultaneously reducing the long-term costs of operations. Public transportation or active commuting techniques should be utilized by both the staff and the patients in order to lessen the influence that transportation has on the environment. Additionally, local food and dental supplies should be purchased. Reducing patient travel is another benefit of telemedicine. Providing dysphagia therapies for older people through the practice of geriatric dentistry. That is. Geriatric dentists, speech-language pathologists, and nutritionists are all medical professionals who work together in hospital-based dysphagia clinics to provide comprehensive treatment for dysphagia. The program known as "Mouth Care Matters" places an emphasis on the significance of maintaining good dental hygiene and preventing aspiration pneumonia. This is accomplished by instituting standardized oral care procedures in nursing homes and hospitals, as well as organizing regular staff training sessions. Food innovations that are innovative, such as 3D food printing for changeable textures and gelling agents for better palatability, have the potential to improve nutritional intake and safety for patients who have dysphagia, which could lead to a reduction in the amount of food that is wasted.

6. CONCLUSIONS

These are fascinating and significant overlaps between dysphagia in the elderly and the sustainability of hospitals. In order to assist the establishment of sustainable hospitals, geriatric dentistry necessitates an approach that is both comprehensive and varied. This is especially true when it comes to the treatment of dysphagia in older patients, which is a review of the most critical variables. The fundamental concerns include the fact that people over the age of 65 are more prone to suffer from dysphagia, which is characterized by difficulties in swallowing. The onset of this syndrome may be brought on by neurological disorders, muscle weakness, adverse drug reactions, or physiological changes that are associated with aging. In addition to having an impact on dietary habits, intake of fluids, adherence to medicine, and overall quality of life, it also raises the probability of developing aspiration pneumonia. Dentistry that focuses on the oral health of elderly patients is known as geriatric dentistry. This field acknowledges the unique difficulties that elderly people encounter, such as dysphagia (which is caused by xerostomia, which affects the generation of boluses) and dentures that do not fit properly, which can create difficulties when chewing. In order to reduce their negative impact on the environment, advance social fairness, and guarantee economic sustainability, hospitals should use sustainable development practices. This should be done without compromising the requirements of future generations. In the context of a hospital, this entails giving priority to the health and safety of both patients and staff, as well as effective use of resources, elimination of waste, and ethical procurement.

The following is an illustration of how the principles of sustainable development might be utilized in the field of geriatric dentistry to address a variety of aspects of hospital care for elderly patients who have trouble swallowing:

6.1 Care Centered On The Patient And Their Well-Being (Sustainable Social Practices)

Person-Centered Assessment and Planning tailors dysphagia treatment to the client's needs, preferences, and culture. This choice should involve the patient and caregivers. Providing accessible and inclusive services means making hospital facilities and services accessible to seniors with mobility and sensory limitations. These include conspicuous signage, proper lighting, and comfortable waiting rooms. Education and empowerment require clear dysphagia, safe swallowing, and dietary information for patients and caregivers. This helps with anxiety and adherence. Interprofessional teamwork helps elderly dentists, speech-language pathologists, dietitians, nurses, and other healthcare practitioners provide holistic care. Recognizing dysphagia's psychological impact and providing methods to treat anxiety, despair, and social isolation promotes mental and emotional well-being.

6.2 The Management of Resources and the Sustainability of the Environment

Implementing techniques to reduce the use of single-use products in managing dysphagia (for example, using reusable feeding aids when suitable and optimizing the use of thickening agents) is an example of efficient resource utilization. Implementing appropriate segregation and recycling systems for medical and food waste produced during dysphagia care is integral to waste reduction and management.

Optimizing the energy consumed in patient rooms and therapeutic spaces is an example of energy and water efficiency, as well as the implementation of water-saving measures in cleaning and preparing food. Sustainable procurement prioritizes the acquisition of products that are both environmentally friendly and ethically sourced. These products include food items, thickening agents, and oral hygiene products. Telehealth and Remote Evaluation will investigate the use of telehealth for follow-up appointments and for evaluating swallowing function remotely, thereby minimizing the need for travel and the associated emissions.

6.3 Long-Term Viability Of The Economy

Cost-effective and evidence-based interventions that improve patient outcomes while reducing wasteful expenditures are referred to as cost-effective interventions. When it comes to older persons, preventive care involves emphasizing oral health promotion and early identification of risk factors for dysphagia to avoid more expensive interventions in the future. By investing in staff training, healthcare personnel are provided with the knowledge and skills necessary to deliver dysphagia care that is both sustainable and of high quality. This results in increased efficiency and reduced errors within the healthcare system.

6.4 Value-Based Treatment Models

Investigating healthcare models that reward the quality of treatment and patient outcomes rather than the quantity of services delivered to provide incentives for developing efficient and successful dysphagia management strategies.

6.5 Real-World Illustrations

For moderate dysphagia, "Food First" stresses naturally textured, safe, and palatable foods over commercially modified ones. Reusable oral hygiene products, such as silicone swabs and specialized toothbrushes, should be taught and provided. Working with local farmers and suppliers to source fresh, seasonal foods for adapted diets saves transportation emissions and promotes the local economy. Online dysphagia management films and documents reduce paper handouts for patient education. Swallowing support groups boost social well-being, increase peer support for dysphagia patients and caregivers, and reduce emotional dependence on formal healthcare. Opportunities and Challenges: The initial investment costs for sustainable infrastructure and equipment, resistance to change, the complexity of coordinating interprofessional teams, the need for ongoing staff training, and ensuring patient safety with reusable products are all significant challenges. Opportunities include improved patient outcomes and quality of life, reduced long-term healthcare costs, increased staff satisfaction, a more positive hospital image, and a more environmentally and socially responsible healthcare system. Moving Forward: Integrating sustainable development into hospital treatment for elderly dysphagia in geriatric dentistry requires a coordinated and collaborative approach.

7. IMPLICATIONS: KEY PUBLIC HEALTH POLICY AREAS FOR ELDERLY HEALTHCARE

Sustainable development in geriatric dentistry institutions that treat dysphagia in older patients entails taking a holistic approach that considers environmental, social, and economic issues to improve care quality and duration. In geriatric dentistry, sustainable development can promote oral health as a key factor in preventing and managing dysphagia, thereby reducing the need for more extensive and expensive therapies and maintaining oral function for safe swallowing using minimally invasive dental treatments. Caregivers and older individuals must learn about oral hygiene practices that affect swallowing and nutrient intake.

7.1 Integrated Screening and Early Detection Policy Objective

Establish routine dysphagia and oral health examinations in dental clinics and establishments that provide care for the elderly. The reason for this is that early diagnosis helps prevent consequences, including malnutrition, aspiration pneumonia, and tooth decay.

7.2 Models of Care That Involve Multiple Disciplines

The goal of this policy is to foster collaboration among dental professionals, speech-language pathologists, dietitians, and geriatric specialists. The reason for this is that dysphagia requires holistic therapy since dental disorders, such as inadequate dentures or missing teeth, can make swallowing difficulties much worse.

7.3 Policy Regarding Access to Dental Services for the Elderly

The goal of this initiative is to ensure that everyone has equal access to specialist dental treatment for the elderly, including home visits and mobile clinics. The reason for this is that many older people who suffer from dysphagia have mobility issues or reside in areas that provide long-term care. The goal of this initiative is to ensure that everyone has equal access to specialist dental treatment for the elderly, including home visits and mobile clinics. The reason for this is that many older people who suffer from dysphagia have mobility issues or reside in areas that provide long-term care.

7.4 Recommendations Related to Nutrition and Oral Health Development

Dissemination of nutritional and oral care guidelines that are specifically designed for older persons who have difficulty swallowing is the objective of this policy. The reason for this is that foods that are soft, non-irritating, and high in nutrients can help. The goal is to educate and raise awareness among caregivers, families, and healthcare staff about the symptoms of dysphagia and its oral implications. Why? Because increasing awareness leads to prompt response, which in turn minimizes health risks that could have been avoided.

7.5 Insurance and Financial Assistance

The objective of this policy is to broaden the scope of coverage for dental and dysphagia-related care for elderly patients under public health insurance. This is because elderly people frequently face financial obstacles that prevent them from receiving therapy on time. To limit the number of expensive hospitalizations, prevention efforts should emphasize early intervention. Supporting effective eating, communication, and dignity in old age is a crucial aspect of maintaining your quality of life. To ensure sustainability, it is essential to promote community-based care options that are long-term and reduce reliance on institutions.

7.6 A Policy Regarding Workforce Training

The goal is to require that dental and public health curricula include training related to dysphagia and geriatric considerations. The reason for this is that it enhances the ability of experts to treat oral-systemic health concerns that are associated with aging. Policy objectives that align with public health principles for the sake of equity should provide comprehensive services to disadvantaged senior groups that are frequently overlooked. Geriatric Dentistry is crucial to promote sustainable development in hospitals for patients with dysphagia in the elderly. The implementation of a comprehensive approach that incorporates health, environmental, and social responsibilities is necessary for the sustainable development of hospitals that provide care for older patients who have dysphagia, particularly within the field of geriatric dentistry.

Dysphagia, or difficulty swallowing, is common in the elderly and can complicate dental, nutritional, and healthcare treatments. Sustainable hospital practices provide interdisciplinary care to manage oral and swallowing processes. Speech therapists, dietitians, and geriatric dentists may help with this treatment. Preventive dental care, digital monitoring, and least-invasive treatment approaches help reduce medical waste and resource utilization. This helps hospitals achieve sustainability. Environmental goals can also be addressed by training staff in geriatric oral care and utilizing eco-friendly dental products. Education and inclusive policies empower caregivers and family members, boosting patients' dignity and engagement. These initiatives support Sustainable Development Goals (SDGs) 3 (Good Health and Well-being) and 12 (Responsible Consumption and Production) by promoting egalitarian, efficient, and environmentally friendly healthcare.

8. LIMITATIONS AND RECOMMENDATIONS

This chapter employs the PRISMA method for a systematic review, focusing on thematic and content analysis. The scholarly papers, mainly from 2021 to 2025, were selected based on keywords and the authors' decisions using purposive sampling. It could be considered a biased evaluation. Further studies are required to enable experts and participants to conduct quantitative and qualitative analyses based on proper sampling and respondent involvement, which could provide general explanations and insightful results.

Participating in collaborative efforts with other healthcare specialists, such as speech therapists and nutritionists, in order to provide comprehensive and long-term care for dysphagia. Hospitals can strive for sustainable development in their approach to senior dysphagia within the field of geriatric dentistry by integrating these environmental, social, and economic factors. This will result in improved patient outcomes, a more resilient healthcare system, and a healthier environment.

REFERENCES

Arowosola, T. A., Makanjuola, O. O., & Olagunju-Yusuf, O. F. (2022). The role of food in the health management of geriatrics. *Food Security and Safety Volume 2: African Perspectives*, 59-81. https://link.springer.com/chapter/10.1007/978-3-031-09614-3_4

Cabañero-Garcia, E., Martinez-Lacoba, R., Pardo-Garcia, I., & Amo-Saus, E. (2025). Barriers to health, social and long-term care access among older adults: A systematic review of reviews. *International Journal for Equity in Health, 24*(1), 1–13. DOI: 10.1186/s12939-025-02429-y PMID: 40075452

Cava, E., & Lombardo, M. (2025). Narrative review: Nutritional strategies for ageing populations-focusing on dysphagia and geriatric nutritional needs. *European Journal of Clinical Nutrition, 79*(4), 285–295. DOI: 10.1038/s41430-024-01513-w PMID: 39414983

Chávez, E. M., Kossioni, A., & Fukai, K. (2022). Policies supporting oral health in ageing populations are needed worldwide. *international dental journal, 72*(4), S27-S38. DOI: 10.1016/j.identj.2022.06.014

Dini, F., Mancini, S., Girelli, A., Ercolini, D. P., Reggiani, A., Alonso, Y. S., Inzitari, M., Bellelli, G., Marengoni, A., Gentile, S., & Morandi, A. (2025). Dysphagia and geriatric syndromes in older patients admitted to an intermediate care unit: Prospective observational study. *Aging Clinical and Experimental Research, 37*(1), 89. DOI: 10.1007/s40520-025-02950-8 PMID: 40095145

Fernández-Ruiz, V. E., Paredes-Ibáñez, R., Armero-Barranco, D., Sánchez-Romera, J. F., & Ferrer, M. (2020). Analysis of quality of life and nutritional status in elderly patients with dysphagia in order to prevent hospital admissions in a COVID-19 pandemic. *Life (Chicago, Ill.), 11*(1), 22. DOI: 10.3390/life11010022 PMID: 33396486

Hegab, H., Shaban, I., Jamil, M., & Khanna, N. (2023). Toward sustainable future: Strategies, indicators, and challenges for implementing sustainable production systems. *Sustainable Materials and Technologies, 36*, e00617. DOI: 10.1016/j.susmat.2023.e00617

Hegde, S., & Buch, S. A. (2025). Geriatric Oral Healthcare Status in India: Challenges, Innovations, and Future Strategies. *Journal of Datta Meghe Institute of Medical Sciences University, 20*(1), 18–23. DOI: 10.4103/jdmimsu.jdmimsu_704_23

Huang, X., Kang, L., & Bi, J. (2025). Epidemiology of oral health in older adults aged 65 or over: Prevalence, risk factors and prevention. *Aging Clinical and Experimental Research, 37*(1), 193. DOI: 10.1007/s40520-025-03110-8 PMID: 40549221

Kristamuliana, K., Sunaryo, E. Y. A. B., Yen, M., & Lee, H. F. (2025). Dysphagia Prevention Strategies for Community-Dwelling Older Adults: A Scoping Review. *Journal of Oral Rehabilitation*, *52*(5), 722–732. DOI: 10.1111/joor.13961 PMID: 40125626

León, S., & Giacaman, R. A. (2022). Proposal for a conceptual framework for the development of geriatric dentistry. *Journal of Dental Research*, *101*(3), 247–252. DOI: 10.1177/00220345211042268 PMID: 34581227

Martyushev-Poklad, A., Yankevich, D., & Petrova, M. (2022). Improving the effectiveness of healthcare: Diagnosis-centered care Vs. Person-centered health promotion, a long forgotten new model. *Frontiers in Public Health*, *10*, 819096. DOI: 10.3389/fpubh.2022.819096 PMID: 35651862

Mehraban-Far, S., Alrassi, J., Patel, R., Ahmad, V., Browne, N., Lam, W., Jiang, Y., Barber, N., & Mortensen, M. (2021). Dysphagia in the elderly population: A videofluoroscopic study. *American Journal of Otolaryngology*, *42*(2), 102854. DOI: 10.1016/j.amjoto.2020.102854 PMID: 33482586

Office of Disease Prevention and Health Promotion. (2023). *Social determinants of health and older adults*. Healthy Aging. [Internet]

Ohta, R., Weiss, E., Mekky, M., & Sano, C. (2022). Relationship between dysphagia and home discharge among older patients receiving hospital rehabilitation in rural Japan: A retrospective cohort study. *International Journal of Environmental Research and Public Health*, *19*(16), 10125. DOI: 10.3390/ijerph191610125 PMID: 36011757

Ohta, R., Weiss, E., Mekky, M., & Sano, C. (2022). Relationship between dysphagia and home discharge among older patients receiving hospital rehabilitation in rural Japan: A retrospective cohort study. *International Journal of Environmental Research and Public Health*, *19*(16), 10125. https://www.mdpi.com/1660-4601/19/16/10125. DOI: 10.3390/ijerph191610125 PMID: 36011757

Owolabi, O. R., Olatoye, F. O., Elufioye, O. A., & Okunade, B. (2024). Reviewing healthcare financial management: Strategies for cost-effective care. *World Journal of Advance Research Reviews*, *21*(2), 958–966. DOI: 10.30574/wjarr.2024.21.2.0523

Phuangsuwan, P., Siripipatthanakul, S., Chaiprakarn, S., & Rakpathum, W. Muthmainnha, Pariwongkhuntorn, N., & Wattanakul, P. (2024, Jun). Sustainable Development Adopting Artificial Intelligence (AI) in Marketing and Consumer Behaviour Analysis. In *International Conference on Data Analytics & Management* (pp. 569-587). Singapore: Springer Nature Singapore. https://link.springer.com/chapter/10.1007/978-981-96-3372-2_39

Roberts, H., Lambert, K., & Walton, K. (2024, Mar). The prevalence of dysphagia in individuals living in residential aged care facilities: A systematic review and meta-analysis. In *Healthcare* (Vol. 12, No. 6, p. 649). MDPI. https://www.mdpi.com/2227-9032/12/6/649

Schwab, R., Schiestl, L. J., & Hasenburg, A. (2025). Greening the future of healthcare: Implementation of sustainability strategies in German hospitals and beyond—a review. *Frontiers in Public Health*, *13*, 1559132. DOI: 10.3389/fpubh.2025.1559132 PMID: 40385621

Singh, K., Srivastava, V. K., & Shukla, A. (2024). Healing with Care: A Roadmap to Sustainable Healthcare. In *Preserving Health, Preserving Earth: The Path to Sustainable Healthcare* (pp. 63-79). Cham: Springer Nature Switzerland._DOI: 10.1007/978-3-031-60545-1_4

Siripipatthanakul, S., & Phuangsuwan, P. (2024). Salutogenic Marketing in Preventive Dentistry. In *Leveraging Digital Technology for Preventive Dentistry* (pp. 255–278). IGI Global., DOI: 10.4018/979-8-3693-3872-8.ch009

Siripipatthanakul, S., Phuangsuwan, P., & Limna, P. Muthmainnha, Siripipattanakul, S., Vui, C. N., & Jaipong, P. (2024, Jun). Artificial Intelligence (AI) Influencing Sustainable Governance: Governance Adopting AI. In *International Conference on Data Analytics & Management* (pp. 551-568). Singapore: Springer Nature Singapore. https://link.springer.com/chapter/10.1007/978-981-96-3372-2_38

Supriadi, B. (2025). Green Hospital Management and Survival to Age 65: Towards Sustainable Health. *Journal of Lifestyle and SDGs Review*, *5*(1), e01771–e01771. DOI: 10.47172/2965-730X.SDGsReview.v5.n01.pe01771

Takeda, M., Watanabe, Y., Taira, K., Miura, K., Ohara, Y., Iwasaki, M., . . . Yamazaki, Y. (2023, June). Association between death or hospitalization and observable variables of eating and swallowing function among elderly residents in Long-Term care facilities: A multicenter prospective cohort study. In *Healthcare* (Vol. 11, No. 13, p. 1827). MDPI._https://www.mdpi.com/2227-9032/11/13/1827

Vallée, A. (2024). Green hospitals face to climate change: Between sobriety and resilience. *Heliyon*, *10*(2), e24769. DOI: 10.1016/j.heliyon.2024.e24769 PMID: 38298726

Vo, M. T. H., & Fong, B. Y. F. (2025). Long-Term Care Initiatives in Southeast Asian Countries with Emerging Ageing Population and the Sustainability of Health and Social Care Systems. In *The Handbook of Public Health in the Asia-Pacific* (pp. 1–32). Springer Nature Singapore., DOI: 10.1007/978-981-97-1788-0_31-1

Zanobini, P., Del Riccio, M., Lorini, C., & Bonaccorsi, G. (2024). Empowering sustainable healthcare: The role of health literacy. *Sustainability (Basel)*, *16*(10), 3964. DOI: 10.3390/su16103964

Zhang, Z., Gu, D., & Li, S. (2024). Effectiveness of Person-Centered Health Education in the General Practice of Geriatric Chronic Disease Care. *Alternative Therapies in Health and Medicine*, *30*(10). PMID: 38330589

Compilation of References

Aamir, A., Iqbal, A., Jawed, F., Ashfaque, F., Hafsa, H., Anas, Z., Oduoye, M. O., Basit, A., Ahmed, S., Abdul Rauf, S., Khan, M., & Mansoor, T. (2024). Exploring the current and prospective role of artificial intelligence in disease diagnosis. *Annals of Medicine and Surgery (London)*, *86*(2), 943–949. DOI: 10.1097/MS9.0000000000001700 PMID: 38333305

Abdeldayem, M. M., Aldulaimi, S. H., & Al-Kaabi, H. (2024). Exploring essential features for developing a human resource management mobile application: Insights from the Middle East. *International Journal of Engineering Business Management*, *16*, 18479790241275306. DOI: 10.1177/18479790241275306

Abdullah, A. R., Cheah, S., Mulia, V. B., & Abdul Fatah, I. A. (2019). *Factors attracting Indonesian medical tourists to Penang. African Journal of Hospitality, Tourism and Leisure* (Special Edition). GCBSS.

Abernethy, A., Adams, L., Barrett, M., Bechtel, C., Brennan, P., Butte, A., Faulkner, J., Fontaine, E., Friedhoff, S., Halamka, J., Howell, M., Johnson, K., Long, P., McGraw, D., Miller, R., Lee, P., Perlin, J., Rucker, D., Sandy, L., & Valdes, K. (2022). The promise of digital health: Then, now, and the future. *NAM Perspectives*, *2022*(22), 10–31478. https://pmc.ncbi.nlm.nih.gov/articles/PMC9499383/. DOI: 10.31478/202206e PMID: 36177208

Ab, F., & Wahyuni, D. U. (2023). Implementation of green human resource management in improving environmental performance at hospital in Makassar. *Innovation Business Management and Accounting Journal*, *2*(3), 157–164. DOI: 10.56070/ibmaj.v2i3.52

Adeniran, I. A., Efunniyi, C. P., Osundare, O. S., & Abhulimen, A. O. (2024). Data-driven decision-making in healthcare: Improving patient outcomes through predictive modeling. Engineering Science & Technology Journal, 5(8).

Aerts, W., & Cormier, D. (2009). Media legitimacy and corporate environmental communication. *Accounting, Organizations and Society*, *34*(1), 1–27. DOI: 10.1016/j.aos.2008.02.005

Agne, I., & Gedrich, K. (2024). Personalized dietary recommendations for obese individuals–A comparison of ChatGPT and the Food4Me algorithm. *Clinical Nutrition Open Science*, *56*, 192–201. DOI: 10.1016/j.nutos.2024.06.001

Ahmad, A., Abuhashesh, M., Obeidat, Z., & AlKhatib, M. (2020). E-WOM and airline e-ticket purchasing intention: Mediating effect of online passenger trust. *Management Science Letters*, *10*(12), 2729–2740. DOI: 10.5267/j.msl.2020.4.037

Ahmad, N., Ullah, Z., Ryu, H. B., Ariza-Montes, A., & Han, H. (2023). From corporate social responsibility to employee well-being: Navigating the pathway to sustainable healthcare. *Psychology Research and Behavior Management*, *16*, 1079–1095. DOI: 10.2147/PRBM.S398586 PMID: 37041962

Ahrens, E., & Elias, M. (2023). Effective communication with linguistically diverse patients: A concept analysis. *Patient Education and Counseling*, *115*, 107868. DOI: 10.1016/j.pec.2023.107868 PMID: 37480794

Akinola, S., & Telukdarie, A. (2023). Sustainable digital transformation in healthcare: Advancing a digital vascular health innovation solution. *Sustainability (Basel)*, *15*(13), 10417. DOI: 10.3390/su151310417

Akinsola, K. (2025). Legal Compliance in Corporate Governance Frameworks: Best Practices for Ensuring Transparency, Accountability, and Risk Mitigation. Accountability, and Risk Mitigation.

Akram, U., Ansari, A. R., & Yan, C. (2023). Cosmetics makers have always sold 'hope in a jar'! Understanding the cosmetics purchase intention in the Chinese mobile commerce environment. *Journal of Retailing and Consumer Services*, *73*, 103337. DOI: 10.1016/j.jretconser.2023.103337

Akther, A., Arobee, A., Adnan, A. A., Auyon, O., Islam, A. S. M., & Akter, F. (2025). Blockchain As a Platform For Artificial Intelligence (AI) Transparency. arXiv preprint arXiv:2503.08699.

Al Shamsi, H., Almutairi, A. G., Al Mashrafi, S., & Al Kalbani, T. (2020). Implications of language barriers for healthcare: A systematic review. *Oman Medical Journal*, *35*(2), e122. https://pmc.ncbi.nlm.nih.gov/articles/PMC7201401/. DOI: 10.5001/omj.2020.40 PMID: 32411417

Alamgir, W., & Shan, H. (2023). Clinical leadership and integration of triple bottom line for planetary health. *Life Sciences*, *4*(3), 180–181. DOI: 10.37185/LnS.1.1.439

Alami, H., Rivard, L., Lehoux, P., Hoffman, S. J., Cadeddu, S. B. M., Savoldelli, M., Samri, M. A., Ag Ahmed, M. A., Fleet, R., & Fortin, J. P. (2020). Artificial intelligence in health care: Laying the foundation for responsible, sustainable, and inclusive innovation in low-and middle-income countries. *Globalization and Health, 16*(1), 52. https://link.springer.com/article/10.1186/s12992-020-00584-1. DOI: 10.1186/s12992-020-00584-1 PMID: 32580741

Alanezi, F. (2024). Examining the role of ChatGPT in promoting health behaviors and lifestyle changes among cancer patients. *Nutrition and Health (Berkhamsted, Hertfordshire)*, 02601060241244563. PMID: 38567408

Al-Emran, M., Abu-Hijleh, B., & Alsewari, A. A. (2025). Examining the impact of Generative AI on social sustainability by integrating the information system success model and technology-environmental, economic, and social sustainability theory. *Education and Information Technologies, 30*(7), 9405–9426. DOI: 10.1007/s10639-024-13201-0

Ali, B. J., Gardi, B., Othman, B. J., Ahmed, S. A., Ismael, N. B., Hamza, P. A., Aziz, H. M., Sabir, B. Y., Sorguli, S., & Anwar, G. (2021a). Hotel service quality: The impact of service quality on customer satisfaction in hospitality. *International Journal of Engineering Business Management, 5*(3), 14–28. DOI: 10.22161/ijebm.5.3.2

Ali, B. J., Saleh, P. F., Akoi, S., Abdulrahman, A. A., Muhamed, A. S., Noori, H. N., & Anwar, G. (2021b). Impact of service quality on the customer satisfaction: Case study at online meeting platforms. *International Journal of Engineering Business Management, 5*(2), 65–77. DOI: 10.22161/ijebm.5.2.6

Alibrandi, A., Gitto, L., Limosani, M., & Mustica, P. F. (2023). Patient satisfaction and quality of hospital care. *Evaluation and Program Planning, 97*, 102251. DOI: 10.1016/j.evalprogplan.2023.102251 PMID: 36806007

Alim, M., & Sulley, S. (2024). Beyond healing: Embracing the triple bottom line approach in post-pandemic healthcare. *Cureus, 16*(2), e54019. DOI: 10.7759/cureus.54019 PMID: 38476781

Ali, S. M., Appolloni, A., Cavallaro, F., D'Adamo, I., Di Vaio, A., Ferella, F., Gastaldi, M., Ikram, M., Kumar, N. M., Martin, M. A., Nizami, A.-S., Ozturk, I., Riccardi, M. P., Rosa, P., Santibanez Gonzalez, E., Sassanelli, C., Settembre-Blundo, D., Singh, R. K., Smol, M., & Zorpas, A. A. (2023). Development goals towards sustainability. *Sustainability (Basel), 15*(12), 9443. DOI: 10.3390/su15129443

Aljunid, S. S., Huda Mohamad Shukri, N. N., Mohd Taib, M. Z., & Samah, Z. A.Shariffah Syafiqah AljunidNurul Nabilah Huda Mohamad ShukriMohd Zafrullah Mohd TaibZanariah Abu Samah. (2020). Determinants of Patient Satisfaction on Interior Design Quality of Public Hospitals in Malaysia. *Malaysian Journal of Public Health Medicine*, *20*(2), 233–241. DOI: 10.37268/mjphm/vol.20/no.2/art.800

AlOmari, F. (2020). Measuring Gaps in Healthcare Quality Using SERVQUAL Model: Challenges and Opportunities in Developing Countries. *Measuring Business Excellence*. DOI: 10.1108/MBE-11-2019-0104

AlOmari, F. (2022). The mediating role of hospital image: The impact of care cost and service quality on patient satisfaction. *Journal of Innovation in Business and Economics*, *6*(01), 1–16. DOI: 10.22219/jibe.v6i01.18475

Al-Worafi, Y. M. (2024, a). Dentistry Education Workforce in Developing Countries. In *Handbook of Medical and Health Sciences in Developing Countries: Education, Practice, and Research* (pp. 1-16). Cham: Springer International Publishing. https://link.springer.com/referenceworkentry/10.1007/978-3-030-74786-2_176-1

Al-Worafi, Y. M. (2024, b). Dentistry Education Challenges in Developing Countries. In *Handbook of Medical and Health Sciences in Developing Countries: Education, Practice, and Research* (pp. 1-15). Cham: Springer International Publishing. https://link.springer.com/referenceworkentry/10.1007/978-3-030-74786-2_200-1

Amit, R., & Schoemaker, P. J. (1993). Strategic assets and organisational rent. *Strategic Management Journal*, *14*(1), 33–46. DOI: 10.1002/smj.4250140105

Andarini, R. (2020). The Influence of Services Quality to Patients Satisfaction at National Brain Center Hospital. *Institutional Repository of* Bakrie University. https://repository.bakrie.ac.id/4383/

An, Q., Kelley, M. M., Hanners, A., & Yen, P. Y. (2023). Sustainable development for mobile health apps using the human-centered design process. *JMIR Formative Research*, *7*, e45694. DOI: 10.2196/45694 PMID: 37624639

Arowosola, T. A., Makanjuola, O. O., & Olagunju-Yusuf, O. F. (2022). The role of food in the health management of geriatrics. *Food Security and Safety Volume 2: African Perspectives*, 59-81. https://link.springer.com/chapter/10.1007/978-3-031-09614-3_4

Asch, D. A. (2023). An interview with ChatGPT about health care. *NEJM Catalyst Innovations in Care Delivery*, *4*(2). https://catalyst.nejm.org/doi/full/10.1056/CAT.23.0043

Asif, R., Hassan, S. R., & Parr, G. (2023). Integrating a blockchain-based governance framework for responsible AI. *Future Internet*, *15*(3), 97. DOI: 10.3390/fi15030097

Asrifan, A., Siripipatthanakul, S., Alaqad, M. H., Saodi, S., & Sadaruddin, S. (2025). Managing Privacy and Security in Research: Effective Practices and Strategies. In *Privacy and Security Management Practices for Organizations* (pp. 151-182). IGI Global Scientific Publishing. DOI: DOI: 10.4018/979-8-3693-9720-6.ch006

Atalla, A. D. G., El-Ashry, A. M., & Khattab, S. M. K. (2025). Fostering eco-friendly excellence: Exploring the relationship between green human resource practices and organizational environmental performance as perceived by nurses: A cross-sectional study. *BMC Nursing*, *24*(1), 495. DOI: 10.1186/s12912-025-03097-7 PMID: 40335971

Aydın, Ö., & Karaarslan, E. (2022). OpenAI ChatGPT generated literature review: Digital Twin in healthcare. *SSRN*, *4308687*, https://papers.ssrn.com/sol3/papers.cfm?abstract_id=4308687. DOI: 10.2139/ssrn.4308687

Ayibuofu-Uwandi, V., & Dyer, T. A. (2024). What are the public health benefits of community-based education in dentistry? A scoping review. *British Dental Journal*, 1–7. https://www.nature.com/articles/s41415-024-7908-4. DOI: 10.1038/s41415-024-7908-4 PMID: 39369154

Azizi, M. R., Atlasi, R., Ziapour, A., Abbas, J., & Naemi, R. (2021). Innovative human resource management strategies during the COVID-19 pandemic: A systematic narrative review approach. *Heliyon*, *7*(6), e07233. DOI: 10.1016/j.heliyon.2021.e07233 PMID: 34124399

Back, D. A., Scherer, J., Osterhoff, G., Rigamonti, L., & Pförringer, D. (2022). Digital implications for human resource management in surgical departments. *European Surgery*, *54*(1), 17–23. DOI: 10.1007/s10353-021-00709-9 PMID: 33936187

Bakker, B. (2025). Reporting Challenges of the Social Dimension ESG in Healthcare (Master's thesis, University of Twente).

Balay-Odao, E. M., Colet, P. C., Almazan, J. U., Kuntuganova, A., Syzdykova, A., Kavashev, Z., Smagulova, M., Dauletkaliyeva, Z., Seidakhmetova, A., & Cruz, J. P. (2024). Environmental sustainability in healthcare: A qualitative study of the perspectives of nursing, medical and public health students in Kazakhstan. *Nurse Education in Practice*, *76*, 103917. DOI: 10.1016/j.nepr.2024.103917 PMID: 38402830

Balkhi, B., Alshahrani, A., & Khan, A. (2022). Just-in-time approach in healthcare inventory management: Does it really work? *Saudi Pharmaceutical Journal : SPJ : the Official Publication of the Saudi Pharmaceutical Society*, *30*(12), 1830–1835. DOI: 10.1016/j.jsps.2022.10.013 PMID: 36601508

Bani-Khaled, S., Azevedo, G., & Oliveira, J. (2025). Environmental, social, and governance (ESG) factors and firm value: A systematic literature review of theories and empirical evidence. *AMS Review*, 1–33. DOI: 10.1007/s13162-025-00303-2

Barney, J. B. (1991). Firm resources and sustained competitive advantage. *Journal of Management*, *17*(1), 99–120. DOI: 10.1177/014920639101700108

Batjo, F. R., Massie, J., & Saerang, R. T. (2022). The effect of E-WOM, perceived quality, on purchase intention at Shopee online store in Manado. Jurnal EMBA: Jurnal Riset Ekonomi, Manajemen. *Bisnis Dan Akuntansi*, *10*(2), 592–599.

Behera, R. K., Gunasekaran, A., Gupta, S., Kamboj, S., & Bala, P. K. (2020). Personalized digital marketing recommender engine. *Journal of Retailing and Consumer Services*, *53*, 101799. https://doi.org/https://doi.org/10.1016/j.jretconser.2019.03.026. DOI: 10.1016/j.jretconser.2019.03.026

BERNAMA. (2020). “MySejahtera application to assist in monitoring COVID-19”. Bernama. https://web.archive.org/web/20210622100036/https://www.bernama.com/en/general/news_covid-19.php?id=1833998. Retrieved 3 July 2025.

BERNAMA. (2025a). Shorter waiting times at government clinics nationwide praised. Bernama. https://www.bernama.com/bm/news.php?id=2389636

BERNAMA. (2025b).Seven Hospitals Identified for Internet Upgrades - Teo. https://www.bernama.com/en/general/news.php?id=2382174

Bhambere, S., Abhishek, B., & Sumit, H. (2021). Rapid digitization of healthcare—A review of COVID-19 impact on our health systems. *Int. J. All Res. Educ. Sci. Methods*, *9*, 1457–1459.

Bhati, D., Deogade, M. S., & Kanyal, D. (2023). Improving patient outcomes through effective hospital administration: A comprehensive review. *Cureus*, *15*(10), e47731. DOI: 10.7759/cureus.47731 PMID: 38021686

Bhutoria, A. (2022). Personalized education and artificial intelligence in the United States, China, and India: A systematic review using a human-in-the-loop model. *Computers and Education: Artificial Intelligence*, *3*, 100068. DOI: 10.1016/j.caeai.2022.100068

Bialas, C., Bechtsis, D., Aivazidou, E., Achillas, C., & Aidonis, D. (2023). Digitalization of the healthcare supply chain through the adoption of enterprise resource planning (ERP) systems in hospitals: An empirical study on influencing factors and cost performance. *Sustainability (Basel)*, *15*(4), 3163. DOI: 10.3390/su15043163

Bornay-Barrachina, M., Guerrero-Villegas, J., López-Fernández, M., & Ruiz-Rodríguez, M. (2023). Pressures for sustainability and strategic responses on employment relationships: The role of the HR manager. *European Research on Management and Business Economics*, *29*(2), 100219. DOI: 10.1016/j.iedeen.2023.100219

Bosco, F., Di Gerio, C., Fiorani, G., & Stola, G. (2024). How to manage sustainability in healthcare organizations? A processing map to include the ESG strategy. *Journal of Public Budgeting, Accounting & Financial Management*, *36*(5), 636–659. DOI: 10.1108/JPBAFM-04-2023-0065

Braganza, A., Chen, W., Canhoto, A., & Sap, S. (2020). Productive employment and decent work: The impact of AI adoption on psychological contracts, job engagement and employee trust. *Journal of Business Research*. Advance online publication. DOI: 10.1016/j.jbusres.2020.08.018 PMID: 32836565

Bratton, J., Gold, J., Bratton, A., & Steele, L. (2021). *Human resource management*. Bloomsbury Publishing.

Buchan, J., & Perfilieva, G. (2015). *Making progress towards health workforce sustainability in the WHO European region*. World Health Organization.

Bvuchete, M., Grobbelaar, S., & Eeden, J. V. (2022). Digitalisation and sustainable supply chain strategy: An instrument for improving efficiencies in the public healthcare sector. *International Journal of Learning and Change*, *14*(5-6), 559–587. DOI: 10.1504/IJLC.2022.126422

Cabañero-Garcia, E., Martinez-Lacoba, R., Pardo-Garcia, I., & Amo-Saus, E. (2025). Barriers to health, social and long-term care access among older adults: A systematic review of reviews. *International Journal for Equity in Health*, *24*(1), 1–13. DOI: 10.1186/s12939-025-02429-y PMID: 40075452

Cahaya, Y. F., Siswanti, I., Putra, Y. M., & Pattiwael, A. C. (2023). Contributions to Customer Satisfaction from Product Quality, Promotion and Price. *Journal of Economics. Finance and Management Studies*, *6*(6), 2434–2440.

Calabrese, M., Suparaku, S., Santovito, S., & Hysa, X. (2023). Preventing and developmental factors of sustainability in healthcare organisations from the perspective of decision makers: An exploratory factor analysis. *BMC Health Services Research*, *23*(1), 797. DOI: 10.1186/s12913-023-09689-w PMID: 37491258

Camilleri, M. A. (2024). Artificial intelligence governance: Ethical considerations and implications for social responsibility. *Expert Systems: International Journal of Knowledge Engineering and Neural Networks*, *41*(7), e13406. DOI: 10.1111/exsy.13406

Camilleri, M. A., & Kozak, M. (2022). Interactive engagement through travel and tourism social media groups: A social facilitation theory perspective. *Technology in Society*, *71*, 102098. DOI: 10.1016/j.techsoc.2022.102098

Campos-García, I., Alonso-Muñoz, S., González-Sánchez, R., & Medina-Salgado, M. S. (2024). Human resource management and sustainability: Bridging the 2030 agenda. *Corporate Social Responsibility and Environmental Management*, *31*(3), 2033–2053. DOI: 10.1002/csr.2680

Canabal, A., & White, G. O.III. (2008). Entry mode research: Past and future. *International Business Review*, *17*(3), 267–284. DOI: 10.1016/j.ibusrev.2008.01.003

Candio, P. (2024). Evolution of ESG and Corporate Performance in Health Care. In *Sustainability and Corporate Performance in Health Care: ESG Implications for the European Industry* (pp. 67–83). Springer Nature Switzerland. DOI: 10.1007/978-3-031-63985-2_4

Candio, P. (2024). *Sustainability and Corporate Performance in Health Care*. Springer., DOI: 10.1007/978-3-031-63985-2

Cao, Z., Zhou, X., Wu, X., Zhu, Z., Liu, T., Neng, J., & Wen, Y. (2023). Data center sustainability: Revisits and outlooks. *IEEE Transactions on Sustainable Computing*.

Casaló, L. V., Flavián, C., & Ibáñez-Sánchez, S. (2020). Influencers on Instagram: Antecedents and consequences of opinion leadership. *Journal of Business Research*, *117*, 510–519. DOI: 10.1016/j.jbusres.2018.07.005

Cava, E., & Lombardo, M. (2025). Narrative review: Nutritional strategies for ageing populations-focusing on dysphagia and geriatric nutritional needs. *European Journal of Clinical Nutrition*, *79*(4), 285–295. DOI: 10.1038/s41430-024-01513-w PMID: 39414983

Caylan, S. (2024). Role of human resource management on strategic management. In Mızrak, F. (Ed.), *Trends, Challenges, and Practices in Contemporary Strategic Management* (pp. 51–69). IGI Global Scientific Publishing., DOI: 10.4018/979-8-3693-1155-4.ch003

Ch, A. S., Pervaiz, F., Nawaz, H., Rafiq, S., Bibi, Y., Almagharbeh, W. T., & Mobeen, M. (2025). Health Equity In Telemedicine: Addressing Disparities In Digital Healthcare Access-A Narrative Review-S. *Insights-Journal Of Life And Social Sciences, 3*(2), 56–62. DOI: 10.71000/rw9xsy20

Chaiprakarn, S. (2022). The Impact of Prices, Services and Facilities on Customer Satisfaction at Drug Stores in Thailand. *PROCEEDING: Volume 1 No. 2 2023*, 304.

Charton-Vachet, F., Lombart, C., & Louis, D. (2020). Impact of attitude towards a region on purchase intention of regional products: The mediating effects of perceived value and preference. *International Journal of Retail & Distribution Management, 48*(7), 707–725. DOI: 10.1108/IJRDM-09-2019-0315

Chávez, E. M., Kossioni, A., & Fukai, K. (2022). Policies supporting oral health in ageing populations are needed worldwide. *international dental journal, 72*(4), S27-S38. DOI: 10.1016/j.identj.2022.06.014

Chiu, W. K., & Fong, B. Y. F. (2023). Environmental, social and governance and sustainable development in healthcare. *Recent trends of research and education in ESG and sustainability*, 99-112. https://doi.org/DOI: 10.1007/978-981-99-1564-4

Chiu, W. K., & Fong, B. Y. F. (2023). Recent trends of research and education in ESG and sustainability. In *Environmental, social and governance and sustainable development in healthcare* (pp. 99–112). Springer Nature Singapore. DOI: 10.1007/978-981-99-1564-4_7

Chiu, W. K., & Fong, B. Y. F. (2023). SDG 3 and ESG—Linkage and the Way Forward. In *Environmental, Social and Governance and Sustainable Development in Healthcare* (pp. 113–116). Springer Nature Singapore. DOI: 10.1007/978-981-99-1564-4_8

Cho, C. H., Michelon, G., Patten, D. M., & Roberts, R. W. (2015). CSR disclosure: The more things change…? *Accounting, Auditing & Accountability Journal, 28*(1), 14–35. DOI: 10.1108/AAAJ-12-2013-1549

Choudhury, A., & Shamszare, H. (2023). Investigating the Impact of User Trust on the Adoption and Use of ChatGPT: Survey Analysis. *Journal of Medical Internet Research, 25*, e47184. https://www.jmir.org/2023/1/e47184. DOI: 10.2196/47184 PMID: 37314848

Chouhan, A. S., Jain, A., Jain, S., & Gupta, P. (2023). Maximizing Efficiency and Minimizing Wait Times: A Case Study on the Use of Technology to Streamline Patient Appointments. *International Journal of Knowledge Based Computer Systems, 11*(1).

Chow, J. C., Sanders, L., & Li, K. (2023). Impact of ChatGPT on medical chatbots as a disruptive technology. *Frontiers in Artificial Intelligence*, *6*, 1166014. DOI: 10.3389/frai.2023.1166014 PMID: 37091303

Consolandi, C., Phadke, H., Hawley, J., & Eccles, R. G. (2020). Material ESG outcomes and SDG externalities: Evaluating the health care sector's contribution to the SDGs. *Organization & Environment*, *33*(4), 511–533. DOI: 10.1177/1086026619899795

Cordoba, L. E. (2021). Well-being and mental health of healthcare workers before, during, and after COVID-19. *Salud Mental*, *44*(5), 211–214. DOI: 10.17711/SM.0185-3325.2021.027

Correia, A. B., Shahzad, M. F., Martins, J. M., & Baheer, R. (2024). Impact of green human resource management towards sustainable performance in the healthcare sector: Role of green innovation and risk management. *Cogent Business & Management*, *11*(1), 1–21. DOI: 10.1080/23311975.2024.2374625

Cotarelo, M., Fayos, T., Calderón, H., & Mollá, A. (2021). Omni-channel intensity and shopping value as key drivers of customer satisfaction and loyalty. *Sustainability (Basel)*, *13*(11), 5961. DOI: 10.3390/su13115961

Crawford, J. (2025). Systematic Literature Reviews: Why I Rejected Your Review. *Journal of University Teaching & Learning Practice*, *22*(2). DOI: 10.53761/10vb5076

da Silva, A. F., Carreira, F., & Cepêda, C. (2025). Does Corporate Governance Impact ESG Performance Reporting in Healthcare? In *Environmental, Social, Governance and Digital Transformation in Organizations* (pp. 51–72). Springer. DOI: 10.1007/978-3-031-86079-9_3

Dalziel, R. C., & De Klerk, N. (2021). Media and group influence on Generation Y consumers' attitudes towards beauty products. *Spanish Journal of Marketing - ESIC*, *25*(1), 115–136. DOI: 10.1108/SJME-12-2019-0104

Daniel-Watanabe, L., Moore, R., England, N. H. S., Tongue, B., & Royston, S. (2024). What is the Carbon Footprint of Digital Healthcare?

Dave, T., Athaluri, S. A., & Singh, S. (2023). ChatGPT in medicine: An overview of its applications, advantages, limitations, prospects, and ethical considerations. *Frontiers in Artificial Intelligence*, *6*, 1169595. DOI: 10.3389/frai.2023.1169595 PMID: 37215063

Dergaa, I., Saad, H. B., El Omri, A., Glenn, J., Clark, C., Washif, J., & Chamari, K. (2024). Using artificial intelligence for exercise prescription in personalised health promotion: A critical evaluation of OpenAI's GPT-4 model. *Biology of Sport*, *41*(2), 221–241. DOI: 10.5114/biolsport.2024.133661 PMID: 38524814

Dhunnoo, P. (2023). ChatGPT In Healthcare: What Science Says. Artificial Intelligence in Medicine. https://medicalfuturist.com/chatgpt-in-healthcare-what-the-science-says/

DiMaggio, P. J., & Powell, W. W. (1983). The iron cage revisited: Institutional isomorphism and collective rationality in organizational fields. *American Sociological Review*, *48*(2), 147–160. DOI: 10.2307/2095101

Dini, F., Mancini, S., Girelli, A., Ercolini, D. P., Reggiani, A., Alonso, Y. S., Inzitari, M., Bellelli, G., Marengoni, A., Gentile, S., & Morandi, A. (2025). Dysphagia and geriatric syndromes in older patients admitted to an intermediate care unit: Prospective observational study. *Aging Clinical and Experimental Research*, *37*(1), 89. DOI: 10.1007/s40520-025-02950-8 PMID: 40095145

Dion, H., & Evans, M. (2024). Strategic frameworks for sustainability and corporate governance in healthcare facilities; Approaches to energy-efficient hospital management. *Benchmarking*, *31*(2), 353–390. DOI: 10.1108/BIJ-04-2022-0219

Dion, H., Evans, M., & Farrell, P. (2023). Hospitals management transformative initiatives; Towards energy efficiency and environmental sustainability in healthcare facilities. *Journal of Engineering. Defence Technology*, *21*(2), 552–584. DOI: 10.1108/JEDT-04-2022-0200

Djakaria, H., Yani, D. A., Wibowo, T. S., & Iswadi, U. (2024). Effect of Price, Location, And Service Quality on onsumer Satisfaction.b 5(1), 548–558. https://journal.yrpipku.com/index.php/msej/article/view/4074/2289

Dobrovolska, O., & Kolomiiets, S. (2024). The Impact of Digitalisation on Social Determinants of Public Health. *Health Economics and Management Review*, *5*(3), 128–142. DOI: 10.61093/hem.2024.3-09

Donaldson, T., & Preston, L. E. (1995). The stakeholder theory of the corporation: Concepts, evidence, and implications. *Academy of Management Review*, *20*(1), 65–91. DOI: 10.2307/258887

Doria, M. (2025). The Application of Blockchain Technology in Securing Electronic Health Records Blockchain for Healthcare Data Security. 324-1.

Dormen, M., & Özkan, P. (2025). Sustainable Dental Approaches for the Environment and Human Health: A Traditional Literature Review. *HRU International Journal of Dentistry and Oral Research*, *5*(1), 51–58. DOI: 10.61139/ijdor.1649869

Duane, B., Stancliffe, R., Miller, F. A., Sherman, J., & Pasdeki-Clewer, E. (2020). Sustainability in dentistry: A multifaceted approach needed. *Journal of Dental Research*, *99*(9), 998–1003. DOI: 10.1177/0022034520919391 PMID: 32392435

Earth911 (2024). Earth911 recycling search https://search.earth911.com..

Easa, N. F., & Orra, H. E. (2021). HRM practices and innovation: An empirical systematic review. *International Journal of Disruptive Innovation in Government*, *1*(1), 15–35. DOI: 10.1108/IJDIG-11-2019-0005

Eliwa, Y., Aboud, A., & Saleh, A. (2021). ESG practices and the cost of debt: Evidence from EU countries. *Critical Perspectives on Accounting*, *79*, 102097. DOI: 10.1016/j.cpa.2019.102097

Elshaer, I., Sobaih, A. E. E., Alyahya, M., & Abu Elnasr, A. (2021). The impact of religiosity and food consumption culture on food waste intention in Saudi Arabia. *Sustainability (Basel)*, *13*(11), 6473. DOI: 10.3390/su13116473

Endeshaw, B. (2021). Healthcare service quality-measurement models: A review. *Warasan Wichai Witthayasat Kanphaet*, *35*(2), 106–117. DOI: 10.1108/JHR-07-2019-0152

Eren, H., Karaduman, Ö., & Gençoğlu, M. T. (2025). Security challenges and performance trade-offs in on-chain and off-chain blockchain storage: A comprehensive review. *Applied Sciences (Basel, Switzerland)*, *15*(6), 3225. DOI: 10.3390/app15063225

Exposto, L. A. S., Mulyati, M. I., Magno, J., & Carvalho, M. (2023). Choosing Service Facilities In The Hospital Interior To Increase Patient Satisfaction. *Asian Journal of Healthy and Science*, *2*(5), 213–224. DOI: 10.58631/ajhs.v2i5.46

Eze, K. C., & Francis, J. (2024). Sustainability in healthcare: An investigation into dynamic employee recruitment, engagement and retention. *British Journal of Management and Marketing Studies*, *7*(3), 31–49. DOI: 10.52589/BJMMS-B7DCYMNV

Faeni, D. P., Oktaviani, R. F., Riyadh, H. A., Faeni, R. P., & Beshr, B. A. H. (2025). Green human resource management and sustainable practices on corporate reputation and employee well-being: A model for Indonesia's F&B industry. *Environmental Challenges*, *18*, 101082. DOI: 10.1016/j.envc.2025.101082

Faggini, M., Cosimato, S., Nota, F. D., & Nota, G. (2018). Pursuing sustainability for healthcare through digital platforms. *Sustainability (Basel)*, *11*(1), 165. DOI: 10.3390/su11010165

Faisal, M., Stanton, P., & Muchiri, M. (2023). Public healthcare in Pakistan: A people management solution? *Asia Pacific Journal of Human Resources*, *61*(2), 462–482. DOI: 10.1111/1744-7941.12360

Fan, Z., Long, R., & Shen, Z. (2024). Regional digitalization, dynamic capabilities and green innovation: Evidence from e-commerce demonstration cities in China. *Economic Modelling*, *139*, 106846. DOI: 10.1016/j.econmod.2024.106846

Fareed, M. A., & Zafar, M. S. (2024). The Path to Sustainable Oral Healthcare to Foster Sustainability in Dentistry. *European Journal of Dentistry*, *18*(03), 701–702. DOI: 10.1055/s-0044-1785187 PMID: 38744325

Fatehi, F., Hassandoust, F., Ko, R. K., & Akhlaghpour, S. (2020). General data protection regulation (GDPR) in healthcare: Hot topics and research fronts. In Digital Personalized Health and Medicine (pp. 1118-1122). IOS Press.

Fernández-Ruiz, V. E., Paredes-Ibáñez, R., Armero-Barranco, D., Sánchez-Romera, J. F., & Ferrer, M. (2020). Analysis of quality of life and nutritional status in elderly patients with dysphagia in order to prevent hospital admissions in a COVID-19 pandemic. *Life (Chicago, Ill.)*, *11*(1), 22. DOI: 10.3390/life11010022 PMID: 33396486

Fle eriu, C., Cosma, S. A., & Bocăne , V. (2020). Values and planned behaviour of the Romanian organic food consumer. *Sustainability (Basel)*, *12*(5), 1722. DOI: 10.3390/su12051722

Freeman, R. E. (1984). *Strategic management: A stakeholder approach.* Pitman.

Furtner, D., Hutas, G., Tan, B. J. W., & Meier, R. (2023). Journey from an enabler to a strategic leader: Integration of the medical affairs function in ESG initiatives and values. *Pharmaceutical Medicine*, *37*(6), 405–416. DOI: 10.1007/s40290-023-00485-9 PMID: 37464231

Gallegos-Rejas, V. M., De Guzman, K. R., Kelly, J. T., Smith, A. C., & Thomas, E. E. (2025). Strategies to improve telehealth access for culturally and linguistically diverse communities: A systematic review. *Journal of Public Health (Oxford, England)*, fdaf030. DOI: 10.1093/pubmed/fdaf030 PMID: 40106706

Gangwar, S., Kumar, S., & Kumari, D. (2023). The Rise of Health Drinks: A Nutritional Boost for a Balanced Lifestyle.

Gao, R. Y. (2024). The diffusion of a US trade-based approach to international personal data transfers and its implications for national data privacy regulations. *International Data Privacy Law*, *14*(4), 352–376.

García-Ramírez, Y., Campoverde, P., Díaz, F., Ortega, J., & Vásquez, J. (2024, Feb). Assessing Ethical Implications of ChatGPT in Higher Education: A Focus on Students. In *International Congress on Information and Communication Technology* (pp. 183–199). Springer Nature Singapore., https://link.springer.com/chapter/10.1007/978-981-97-3302-6_16 DOI: 10.1007/978-981-97-3302-6_16

Garg, V., Kumar, H., Bansal, R., & Bhardwaj, A. (2025). Envisioning Digital Health Technology Innovations for 2025: Enhancing Digital Interventions in the Post-COVID-19 Era. In *Innovations in Healthcare Technologies in India: An Initiative of ICMR-CIBioD (Centre for Innovation and Bio-Design)* (pp. 1-17). Singapore: Springer Nature Singapore. https://link.springer.com/chapter/10.1007/978-981-97-0244-2_1

Gendy, M. E. G., & Yuce, M. R. (2022). Emerging technologies used in health management and efficiency improvement during different contact tracing phases against COVID-19 pandemic. *IEEE Reviews in Biomedical Engineering*, *16*, 38–52. DOI: 10.1109/RBME.2022.3219433 PMID: 36331632

George, A. H., Shahul, A., & George, A. S. (2023). Artificial intelligence in medicine: A New way to diagnose and treat disease. *Partners Universal International Research Journal*, *2*(3), 246–259.

George, A. S., & George, A. H. (2023). A review of ChatGPT AI's impact on several business sectors. *Partners Universal International Innovation Journal*, *1*(1), 9–23. DOI: 10.5281/zenodo.7644359

Ghahtarani, A., Sheikhmohammady, M., & Rostami, M. (2020). The impact of social capital and social interaction on customers' purchase intention, considering knowledge sharing in social commerce context. *Journal of Innovation & Knowledge*, *5*(3), 191–199. DOI: 10.1016/j.jik.2019.08.004

Gherman, A., Andrei, D., Popoiu, C. M., Stoicescu, E. R., Levai, M. C., Stoian, I. I., & Bloancă, V. (2025). Multidisciplinary Telemedicine in Healthcare During and After the COVID-19 Pandemic: A Narrative Review. *Life (Chicago, Ill.)*, *15*(5), 783. DOI: 10.3390/life15050783 PMID: 40430210

Goktas, P., & Grzybowski, A. (2025). Shaping the future of healthcare: Ethical clinical challenges and pathways to trustworthy AI. *Journal of Clinical Medicine*, *14*(5), 1605. DOI: 10.3390/jcm14051605 PMID: 40095575

Golinelli, D., Boetto, E., Carullo, G., Nuzzolese, A. G., Landini, M. P., & Fantini, M. P. (2020). Adoption of digital technologies in health care during the COVID-19 pandemic: Systematic review of early scientific literature. *Journal of Medical Internet Research*, *22*(11), e22280. DOI: 10.2196/22280 PMID: 33079693

Gomes, D. R., Ribeiro, N., Gomes, G., Ortega, E., & Semedo, A. (2024). Green HRM's effect on employees' eco-friendly behavior and green performance: A study in the Portuguese tourism sector. *Sustainability (Basel)*, *16*(22), 10005. DOI: 10.3390/su162210005

Gray, B. J., Bright, D., Bolton, S., & Davies, A. R. (2020). Towards a healthy and sustainable workforce for the future. Public Health Wales. www. nati o nalar chives. gov. uk/doc/open-gover nment-licen ce/versi on/3.

Greenwood, R., Raynard, M., Kodeih, F., Micelotta, E. R., & Lounsbury, M. (2011). Institutional complexity and organizational responses. *The Academy of Management Annals*, *5*(1), 317–371. DOI: 10.5465/19416520.2011.590299

Grieco-Page, H., Black, C. J., Berent, J. M., Gautam, B., & Betancourt, T. S. (2021). Beyond the pandemic: Leveraging rapid expansions in US telemental health and digital platforms to address disparities and resolve the digital divide. *Frontiers in Psychiatry*, *12*, 671502. DOI: 10.3389/fpsyt.2021.671502 PMID: 34421669

Guerra-Tamez, C. R., Dávila-Aguirre, M. C., Barragán Codina, J. N., & Guerra Rodríguez, P. (2021). Analysis of the elements of the theory of flow and perceived value and their influence in craft beer consumer loyalty. *Journal of International Food & Agribusiness Marketing*, *33*(5), 487–517. DOI: 10.1080/08974438.2020.1823929

Gusti, O. I., Ardana, N., & Gede, A. A. (2014). Interior Lobi Rumah Sakit yang Didesain Berdasarkan Kebijakan Sistem Pelayanan. *Jurnal Seni Dan Pendidikan Seni*, 1–10.

Habibie, W. L., Hardjosoekarto, S., & Kasim, A. (2017). Health reform in Indonesia towards sustainable development growth (Case study on BPJS Kesehatan, health insurance in Indonesia). *Review of Integrative Business and Economics Research*, *6*(3), 375–383. http://buscompress.com/journal-home.html

Hackley, D. M., & Luca, J. (2024). Sustainability in Dentistry: An Overview for Oral Healthcare Team Members. *Journal of the California Dental Association*, *52*(1), 2422150. DOI: 10.1080/19424396.2024.2422150

Hadi, S., Purnasari, E., Hidayat, R., Lukitaningsih, A., Kirana, K. C., & Siripipatthanakul, S. (2025). Challenges and Management Practices in Protecting Employee Personal Data in the Digital Era. In Privacy and Security Management Practices for Organizations (pp. 89-116). IGI Global Scientific Publishing. DOI: DOI: 10.4018/979-8-3693-9720-6.ch004

Hadian, M., Jelodar, Z. K., Khanbebin, M. J., Atafimanesh, P., Asiabar, A. S., & Dehagani, S. M. H. (2024). Challenges of implementing telemedicine technology: A systematized review. *International Journal of Preventive Medicine*, *15*, 8. DOI: 10.4103/ijpvm.ijpvm_48_23 PMID: 38563036

Haimi, M., Goren, U., & Grossman, Z. (2024). Barriers and challenges to telemedicine usage among the elderly population in Israel in light of the COVID-19 era: A qualitative study. *Digital Health*, *10*, 20552076241240235. DOI: 10.1177/20552076241240235 PMID: 38550265

Hameed, K., Naha, R., & Hameed, F. (2024). Digital transformation for sustainable health and well-being: A review and future research directions. *Discover Sustainability*, *5*(1), 104. DOI: 10.1007/s43621-024-00273-8

Harrington, L. M. B. (2016). Sustainability theory and conceptual considerations: A review of key ideas for sustainability, and the rural context. *Papers in Applied Geography*, *2*(4), 365–382. DOI: 10.1080/23754931.2016.1239222

Hart, S. L. (1995). A natural-resource-based view of the firm. *Academy of Management Review*, *20*(4), 986–1014. DOI: 10.2307/258963

Heaslip, V., & Holley, D. (2023). Ensuring digital inclusion. *Clinics in Integrated Care*, *17*, 100141. DOI: 10.1016/j.intcar.2023.100141

Hegab, H., Shaban, I., Jamil, M., & Khanna, N. (2023). Toward sustainable future: Strategies, indicators, and challenges for implementing sustainable production systems. *Sustainable Materials and Technologies*, *36*, e00617. DOI: 10.1016/j.susmat.2023.e00617

Hegde, S., & Buch, S. A. (2025). Geriatric Oral Healthcare Status in India: Challenges, Innovations, and Future Strategies. *Journal of Datta Meghe Institute of Medical Sciences University*, *20*(1), 18–23. DOI: 10.4103/jdmimsu.jdmimsu_704_23

He, Y., & Tian, W. (2023). Religious participation: Does it shape food consumption? *Religions*, *14*(3), 350. DOI: 10.3390/rel14030350

Hosseini, M., Gao, C. A., Liebovitz, D. M., Carvalho, A. M., Ahmad, F. S., Luo, Y., . . . Kho, A. (2023). An exploratory survey about using ChatGPT in education, healthcare, and research. medRxiv, 2023-03.DOI: 10.1101/2023.03.31.23287979

Hou, M. (2023). Digital economy, enterprise digital transformation, and digital business model: Evidence from China. DOI: 10.1080/13602381.2023.2241762

Hsu, M. S., Yeh, C. L., Cheng, S. J., & Lin, C. P. (2025). Integrating digital technologies in dental technician education: A comparative study of national examination in Asian countries. *Journal of Dental Sciences*, *20*(1), 28–35. DOI: 10.1016/j.jds.2024.10.017 PMID: 39873091

Huang, X., Kang, L., & Bi, J. (2025). Epidemiology of oral health in older adults aged 65 or over: Prevalence, risk factors and prevention. *Aging Clinical and Experimental Research, 37*(1), 193. DOI: 10.1007/s40520-025-03110-8 PMID: 40549221

Huang, Y. K., & Chang, Y. C. (2022). Oral health: The first step to sustainable development goal 3. *Journal of the Formosan Medical Association, 121*(7), 1348–1350. DOI: 10.1016/j.jfma.2021.10.018 PMID: 34732302

Hua, S., Jin, S., & Jiang, S. (2024). The limitations and ethical considerations of ChatGPT. *Data Intelligence, 6*(1), 201–239. DOI: 10.1162/dint_a_00243

Husain, F., Shahnawaz, M. G., Khan, N. H., Parveen, H., & Savani, K. (2021). Intention to get COVID-19 vaccines: Exploring the role of attitudes, subjective norms, perceived behavioral control, belief in COVID-19 misinformation, and vaccine confidence in Northern India. *Human Vaccines & Immunotherapeutics, 17*(11), 3941–3953. DOI: 10.1080/21645515.2021.1967039 PMID: 34546837

Hussain, A., Umair, M., Khan, S., Alonazi, W. B., Almutairi, S. S., & Malik, A. (2024). Exploring sustainable healthcare: Innovations in health economics, social policy, and management. *Heliyon, 10*(13), e33186. DOI: 10.1016/j.heliyon.2024.e33186 PMID: 39027491

Hussey, P. S., Wertheimer, S., & Mehrotra, A. (2013). The association between health care quality and cost: A systematic review. *Annals of Internal Medicine, 158*(1), 27–34. DOI: 10.7326/0003-4819-158-1-201301010-00006 PMID: 23277898

Iakovets, A. (2022). BalogMand ˇZidekK. The use of mobile application for sustainable development of SMEs in the context of industry 4.0. *Applied Sciences (Basel, Switzerland), 13*(1), 429. DOI: 10.3390/app13010429

Iftikhar, L. (2023). Docgpt: Impact of ChatGpt-3 on health services as a virtual doctor. *EC Paediatrics : Open Access, 12*(1), 45–55.

Ige-Olaobaju, A. Y., Ganiyu, I. O., Atiku, S. O., & Olarewaju, O. M. (Eds.). (2025). *Advances in ethical work climate and employee well-being*. IGI Global Scientific Publishing., DOI: 10.4018/979-8-3693-8819-8

Ilori, O., Lawal, C. I., Friday, S. C., Isibor, N. J., & Chukwuma-Eke, E. C. (2023). A framework for Environmental, Social, and Governance (ESG) auditing: Bridging gaps in global reporting standards. *International Journal of Social Science Exceptional Research, 2*(1), 231–248. DOI: 10.54660/IJSSER.2023.2.1.231-248

Ilyas, G. B., & Mustafa, H. (2022). Price, Promotion, and Supporting Facilities on Customer Satisfaction. *Golden Ratio of Marketing and Applied Psychology of Business, 2*(1), 01-11.

Ishaq, S., Hoang, T. G., Tanveer, U., Hoang, T. H., & Truong, H. Q. (2024). Transformative capabilities of MedTech organizations in driving circularity in the healthcare industry: Insights from multiple cases. *Journal of Cleaner Production*, *446*, 141370. DOI: 10.1016/j.jclepro.2024.141370

Jain, M., Dixit, S., & Shukla, A. (2023). Role of e-service quality, brand commitment and e-WOM trust on e-WOM intentions of millennials. *International Review of Retail, Distribution and Consumer Research*, *33*(1), 23–43. DOI: 10.1080/09593969.2022.2070860

Jaipong, P. (2023). Business Model and Strategy: A Case Study Analysis of TikTok. *Advance Knowledge for Executives, 2*(1), 1-18. https://papers.ssrn.com/sol3/papers.cfm?abstract_id=4335962

Jamalabadi, S., Winter, V., & Schreyögg, J. (2020). A systematic review of the association between hospital cost/price and the quality of care. *Applied Health Economics and Health Policy*, *18*(5), 625–639. DOI: 10.1007/s40258-020-00577-6 PMID: 32291700

Javaid, M., Haleem, A., & Singh, R. P. (2023). ChatGPT for healthcare services: An emerging stage for an innovative perspective. *BenchCouncil Transactions on Benchmarks. Standards and Evaluations*, *3*(1), 100105. DOI: 10.1016/j.tbench.2023.100105

Javaid, M., Haleem, A., Singh, R. P., & Suman, R. (2023). Towards insighting cybersecurity for healthcare domains: A comprehensive review of recent practices and trends. *Cyber Security and Applications*, *1*, 100016. DOI: 10.1016/j.csa.2023.100016

Jawad, L. A. (2024). Security and privacy in digital healthcare systems: Challenges and mitigation strategies. *Abhigyan*, *42*(1), 23–31.

Jensen, M. C. (2002). Value maximization, stakeholder theory, and the corporate objective function. *Business Ethics Quarterly*, *12*(2), 235–256. DOI: 10.2307/3857812

Jerjes, W., & Harding, D. (2024). Telemedicine in the post-COVID era: Balancing accessibility, equity, and sustainability in primary healthcare. *Frontiers in Digital Health*, *6*, 1432871. DOI: 10.3389/fdgth.2024.1432871 PMID: 39233772

Jeyaraman, M., Ramasubramanian, S., Balaji, S., Jeyaraman, N., Nallakumarasamy, A., & Sharma, S. (2023). ChatGPT in action: Harnessing artificial intelligence potential and addressing ethical challenges in medicine, education, and scientific research. *World Journal of Methodology*, *13*(4), 170–178. DOI: 10.5662/wjm.v13.i4.170 PMID: 37771867

John, J., Durward, C., Kruger, E., Mani, S. A., & Tennant, M. (2025). Dental Education Without Borders. In *Handbook of Dental Education Technology* (pp. 1–28). Springer., DOI: 10.1007/978-981-97-0275-6_3-1

Junaid, M., Fetscherin, M., Hussain, K., & Hou, F. (2022). Brand love and brand addiction and their effects on consumers' negative behaviors. *European Journal of Marketing*, *56*(12), 3227–3248. DOI: 10.1108/EJM-09-2019-0727

Kailay, M., Paposa, K. K., & Chhibber, P. (2024). Employee well-being as a mediating variable in sustainable human resource management, organizational commitment, and job satisfaction of healthcare professionals: A structural equation modeling approach. *International Journal of Healthcare Management*, •••, 1–14. DOI: 10.1080/20479700.2024.2405327

Kalia, D., & Aggarwal, D. (2023). Examining impact of ESG score on financial performance of healthcare companies. *Journal of Global Responsibility*, *14*(1), 155–176. DOI: 10.1108/JGR-05-2022-0045

Kalla, D., & Smith, N. (2023). Study and Analysis of Chat GPT and its Impact on Different Fields of Study. *International Journal of Innovative Science and Research Technology*, *8*(3), 827–833. https://papers.ssrn.com/sol3/papers.cfm?abstract_id=4402499

Kalogirou, M. R., & Baumbusch, J. (2025). Examining Canadian hospitals' support for planetary health through the implementation of green teams and sustainability offices. *Journal of Healthcare Leadership*, *17*, 269–284. DOI: 10.2147/JHL.S517669 PMID: 40525086

Kamar, K., Lewaherilla, N. C., Ausat, A. M. A., Ukar, K., & Gadzali, S. S. (2022). The influence of information technology and human resource management capabilities on SMEs performance. *International Journal of Artificial Intelligence Research*, *6*(1.2), 1.

Kanyama, J., Nurittamont, W., & Siripipatthanakul, S. (2022). Hotel service quality and its effect on customer loyalty: The case of Ubon Ratchathani, Thailand during COVID-19 Pandemic. *Journal of Management in Business. Health Care Education*, *1*(2), 1–20. https://papers.ssrn.com/sol3/papers.cfm?abstract_id=4004388

Kaur, D., & Kaur, R. (2022). Elucidating the role of gender differences via TAM in e-recruitment adoption in India: A multi-group analysis using MICOM. *The Bottom Line (New York, N.Y.)*, *35*(2/3), 115–136. DOI: 10.1108/BL-11-2021-0104

Kelvin-Agwu, M. C., Adelodun, M. O., Igwama, G. T., & Anyanwu, E. C. (2024). Strategies for optimizing the management of medical equipment in large healthcare institutions. *Strategies (La Jolla, Calif.)*, *20*(9), 162–170.

Khurshid, Z. (2023). Digital dentistry: Transformation of oral health and dental education with technology. *European Journal of Dentistry*, *17*(04), 943–944. https://www.thieme-connect.com/products/ejournals/abstract/10.1055/s-0043-1772674. DOI: 10.1055/s-0043-1772674 PMID: 37729928

Kim, J. M., Park, K. K. C., & Mariani, M. M. (2023). Do online review readers react differently when exposed to credible versus fake online reviews? *Journal of Business Research*, *154*, 113377. DOI: 10.1016/j.jbusres.2022.113377

Knevel, R., & Liao, K. P. (2023). From real-world electronic health record data to real-world results using artificial intelligence. *Annals of the Rheumatic Diseases*, *82*(3), 306–311. DOI: 10.1136/ard-2022-222626 PMID: 36150748

Kok, S. L. (2023). A Strategic Cooperative Model: The Case of Islamic Financing Hub. *Advance Knowledge for Executives, 2*(1), 1-15. https://papers.ssrn.com/sol3/papers.cfm?abstract_id=4393073

Koman, G., Boršoš, P., & Kubina, M. (2024). Sustainable human resource management with a focus on corporate employee recruitment. *Sustainability (Basel)*, *16*(14), 6059. DOI: 10.3390/su16146059

Kong, D., Qi, J., & Fu, X. (2023). Would You Accept Doctor ChatGPT: An Empirical Study

Konttila, J., Siira, H., Kyngäs, H., Lahtinen, M., Elo, S., Kääriäinen, M., Kaakinen, P., Oikarinen, A., Yamakawa, M., Fukui, S., Utsumi, M., Higami, Y., Higuchi, A., & Mikkonen, K. (2019). Healthcare professionals' competence in digitalisation: A systematic review. *Journal of Clinical Nursing*, *28*(5-6), 745–761. DOI: 10.1111/jocn.14710 PMID: 30376199

Kotcher J, Maibach E, Miller J, et al. Views of health professionals on climate change and health: a multinational survey study. Lancet Planet Health 2021; 5: e316e23

Kristamuliana, K., Sunaryo, E. Y. A. B., Yen, M., & Lee, H. F. (2025). Dysphagia Prevention Strategies for Community-Dwelling Older Adults: A Scoping Review. *Journal of Oral Rehabilitation*, *52*(5), 722–732. DOI: 10.1111/joor.13961 PMID: 40125626

Kruk, M. E., Gage, A. D., Arsenault, C., Jordan, K., Leslie, H. H., Roder-DeWan, S., Adeyi, O., Barker, P., Daelmans, B., Doubova, S. V., English, M., García-Elorrio, E., Guanais, F., Gureje, O., Hirschhorn, L. R., Jiang, L., Kelley, E., Lemango, E. T., Liljestrand, J., & Pate, M. (2018). High-quality health systems in the Sustainable Development Goals era: Time for a revolution. *The Lancet. Global Health*, *6*(11), e1196–e1252. DOI: 10.1016/S2214-109X(18)30386-3 PMID: 30196093

Kumi, E., Amoako, G. K., Appiah, T., & Dartey-Baah, K. (2025). The impact of digital transformation on organisational dynamics, HR practices, and wellbeing in Ghana's healthcare sector: A social exchange perspective. *Future Business Journal*, *11*(1), 64. DOI: 10.1186/s43093-025-00449-2

Kuo, C. L. (2023). *Revolutionizing healthcare paradigms: The integral role of artificial intelligence in advancing diagnostic and treatment modalities. International Microsurgery Journal.* IMJ.

Kwiatkowska, E. M., & Skórzewska-Amberg, M. (2019). Digitalisation of healthcare and the problem of digital exclusion. *Central European Management Journal*, *27*, 48–63.

Leal Filho, W., Lisovska, T., Fedoruk, M., & Taser, D. (2023). Medical waste management and the UN Sustainable Development Goals in Ukraine: An assessment of solutions to support post-war recovery efforts. *Environmental Challenges*, *13*, 100763. DOI: 10.1016/j.envc.2023.100763

Lee, J. Y., & Divaris, K. (2014). The ethical imperative of addressing oral health disparities: A unifying framework. *Journal of Dental Research*, *93*(3), 224–230. DOI: 10.1177/0022034513511821 PMID: 24189268

Lee, S. M., & Lee, D. (2021). Opportunities and challenges for contactless healthcare services in the post-COVID-19 Era. *Technological Forecasting and Social Change*, *167*, 120712. DOI: 10.1016/j.techfore.2021.120712 PMID: 33654330

Leiva, V., & Castro, C. (2025). Artificial intelligence and blockchain in clinical trials: Enhancing data governance efficiency, integrity, and transparency. *Bioanalysis*, *17*(3), 161–176. DOI: 10.1080/17576180.2025.2452774 PMID: 39844748

Leogrande, A. (2024). Integrating ESG Principles into Smart Logistics: Toward Sustainable Supply Chains.

León, S., & Giacaman, R. A. (2022). Proposal for a conceptual framework for the development of geriatric dentistry. *Journal of Dental Research*, *101*(3), 247–252. DOI: 10.1177/00220345211042268 PMID: 34581227

Lescher, M., & Sirven, N. (2019). Healthcare quality, patients' satisfaction, and hospital incentives in France. Revue d′ ′economie politique. *Dalloz, 129*, 525–551.

Leung, T. C. H., & You, S. X. (2023). Environmental, Social and Governance (ESG) of Listed Companies in the Healthcare Industry of Hong Kong. In *Gaps and Actions in Health Improvement from Hong Kong and Beyond: All for Health* (pp. 421–436). Springer Nature Singapore. DOI: 10.1007/978-981-99-4491-0_28

Liang, L., Abidin, S. B. Z., Shaari, N. B., Yahaya, M. F. B., & Jing, L. (2024). Logo impact on consumer's perception, attitude, brand image and purchase intention: A 5 years systematic review. *International Journal of Academic Research in Business & Social Sciences, 14*(3), 861–900. DOI: 10.6007/IJARBSS/v14-i3/20084

Liang, X., & Li, J. (2024). Sustainable human resource management and employee performance: A conceptual framework and research agenda. *Human Resource Management Review, 35*(2), 101060. DOI: 10.1016/j.hrmr.2024.101060

Liebrenz, M., Schleifer, R., Buadze, A., Bhugra, D., & Smith, A. (2023). Generating Scholarly content with ChatGPT: Ethical challenges for medical publishing. *The Lancet. Digital Health, 5*(3), e105–e106. DOI: 10.1016/S2589-7500(23)00019-5 PMID: 36754725

Lim, L. (2023). Digital Marketing Strategies: A Case of Charles & Keith. *Advance Knowledge for Executives, 2*(2), 1-11. https://papers.ssrn.com/sol3/papers.cfm?abstract_id=4426397

Limna, P., Jakwatanatham, S., Siripipattanakul, S., Kaewpuang, P., & Sriboonruang, P. (2022). A review of artificial intelligence (AI) in education during the digital era. *Advance Knowledge for Executives, 1*(1), 1-9. https://papers.ssrn.com/sol3/papers.cfm?abstract_id=4160798

Limna, P., Kraiwanit, T., Jangjarat, K., Klayklung, P., & Chocksathaporn, P. (2023). The use Of ChatGPT in the digital era: Perspectives on chatbot implementation. *Journal of Applied Learning and Teaching, 6*(1), 1–11. DOI: 10.37074/jalt.2023.6.1.32

Limna, P., Siripipatthanakul, S., Siripipattanakul, S., & Auttawechasakoon, P. (2023). The UTAUT model explaining intentions to use telemedicine among Thai people during the COVID-19 pandemic: A qualitative study in Krabi, Thailand. *International Journal of Computing Sciences Research, 7*, 1468–1486. DOI: 10.25147/ijcsr.2017.001.1.111

Liu, J., Wang, C., & Liu, S. (2023). Utility of ChatGPT in Clinical Practice. *Journal of Medical Internet Research, 25*, e48568. https://www.jmir.org/2023/1/e48568/. DOI: 10.2196/48568 PMID: 37379067

Lu, M. K., Moslehpour, M., Lin, P. K., & Chen, T. W. (2025). Impact of sustainable HRM practices on employee well-being in health organizations: The mediating role of perceived organizational support. *American Journal of Health Behavior*, *49*(2), 78–92. DOI: 10.5993/AJHB.49.2.8

Luo, J. (2024, Nov). Validating the impact of gamified technology-enhanced learning environments on motivation and academic performance: enhancing TELEs with digital badges. In *Frontiers in Education* (Vol. 9, p. 1429452). Frontiers Media SA. https://www.frontiersin.org/journals/education/articles/10.3389/feduc.2024.1429452/full

Luu, T. T. (2020). Linking authentic leadership to salespeople's service performance: The roles of job crafting and human resource flexibility. *Industrial Marketing Management*, *84*, 89–104. https://doi.org/https://doi.org/10.1016/j.indmarman.2019.06.002. DOI: 10.1016/j.indmarman.2019.06.002

Lv, B., Deng, Y., Meng, W., Wang, Z., & Tang, T. (2024). Research on digital intelligence business model based on artificial intelligence in post-epidemic era. *Management Decision*, *62*(9), 2937–2957. https://www.emerald.com/insight/content/doi/10.1108/md-11-2022-1548/full/html. DOI: 10.1108/MD-11-2022-1548

Madi, J., Al Khasawneh, M., & Dandis, A. O. (2024). Visiting and revisiting destinations: Impact of augmented reality, content quality, perceived ease of use, perceived value and usefulness on E-WOM. *International Journal of Quality & Reliability Management*, *41*(6), 1550–1571. DOI: 10.1108/IJQRM-10-2023-0314

Mainardes, E. W., Alves, H., & Raposo, M. (2011). Stakeholder theory: Issues to resolve. *Management Decision*, *49*(2), 226–252. DOI: 10.1108/00251741111109133

Makda, F. (2025). Digital education: Mapping the landscape of virtual teaching in higher education–a bibliometric review. *Education and Information Technologies*, *30*(2), 2547–2575. https://link.springer.com/article/10.1007/s10639-024-12899-2. DOI: 10.1007/s10639-024-12899-2

MalayMail. (2025). Health Ministry says RM18.9m allocated for digital transformation of 100 public health clinics nationwide. MalayMail. 8 February 2025. Retrieved 3 July 2025 from https://www.malaymail.com/news/malaysia/2025/02/08/health-ministry-says-rm189m-allocated-for-digital-transformation-of-100-public-health-clinics-nationwide/166001

Malik, A., Nguyen, M., Budhwar, P., Chowdhury, S., & Gugnani, R. (2024). Leveraging high-performance HRM practices and knowledge sharing for managing technological and social change in emerging market healthcare providers. *Technological Forecasting and Social Change*, *205*, 123463. DOI: 10.1016/j.techfore.2024.123463

Malik, S. Y., Hayat Mughal, Y., Azam, T., Cao, Y., Wan, Z., Zhu, H., & Thurasamy, R. (2021). Corporate social responsibility, green human resources management, and sustainable performance: Is organizational citizenship behavior towards environment the missing link? *Sustainability (Basel)*, *13*(3), 1044. DOI: 10.3390/su13031044

Man, L. C., Lin, Y., Pang, G., Sanderson, J., & Duan, K. (2024). Digitalization to achieve greener healthcare supply chain. *Journal of Cleaner Production*, *463*, 142802. DOI: 10.1016/j.jclepro.2024.142802

Marnovita. 2020. Hubungan kualitas pelayanan dengan kepuasan pelanggan. *Jurnal Ilmiah Psikologi* 8(1):100-106.

Martyushev-Poklad, A., Yankevich, D., & Petrova, M. (2022). Improving the effectiveness of healthcare: Diagnosis-centered care Vs. Person-centered health promotion, a long forgotten new model. *Frontiers in Public Health*, *10*, 819096. DOI: 10.3389/fpubh.2022.819096 PMID: 35651862

Mataruka, L., Zishiri, C., Muzurura, J., Mkumbuzi, W. P., & Garatsa, C. (2024). Enhancing Performance of Zimbabwean Service-based Firms through Digital Transformation and Sustainable Competitive Advantage: A Structural Equation Analysis. *African Journal of Commercial Studies*, *5*(1), 7–20. DOI: 10.59413/ajocs/v5.i1.2

Mehraban-Far, S., Alrassi, J., Patel, R., Ahmad, V., Browne, N., Lam, W., Jiang, Y., Barber, N., & Mortensen, M. (2021). Dysphagia in the elderly population: A videofluoroscopic study. *American Journal of Otolaryngology*, *42*(2), 102854. DOI: 10.1016/j.amjoto.2020.102854 PMID: 33482586

Mensah, L. E., Shukla, S., & Iqbal, H. F. (2023). Green human resource management practices and employee innovative behaviour: Reflection from Ghana. *IIMBG Journal of Sustainable Business and Innovation*, *1*(1), 58–74. DOI: 10.1108/IJSBI-02-2023-0002

Menvielle, L., Audrain-Pontevia, A. F., & Menvielle, W. (Eds.). (2017). *The digitization of healthcare: new challenges and opportunities*. DOI: 10.1057/978-1-349-95173-4

Meskó, B., Kristóf, T., Dhunnoo, P., Árvai, N., & Katonai, G. (2024). Exploring the Need for Medical Futures Studies: Insights From a Scoping Review of Health Care Foresight. *Journal of Medical Internet Research*, *26*, e57148. https://www.jmir.org/2024/1/e57148/. DOI: 10.2196/57148 PMID: 39383528

Methnani, J., Latiri, I., Dergaa, I., Chamari, K., & Saad, H. B. (2023). ChatGPT for sample-size calculation in sports medicine and exercise sciences: A cautionary note. *International Journal of Sports Physiology and Performance, 1(aop), 1-5.* https://journals.humankinetics.com/view/journals/ijspp/18/10/article-p1219.xml

Mgaya, T. W., & Gwahula, R. (2024). The Effect of Service Quality on Customer Satisfaction at St. Joseph Referral Hospital-Peramiho, Tanzania. *European Journal of Theoretical and Applied Sciences*, *2*(2), 223–233. DOI: 10.59324/ejtas.2024.2(2).19

Mhaskey, S. V. (2025). Optimizing healthcare distribution: The role of enterprise resource planning systems.

Mijwil, M. M., Aljanabi, M., Abotaleb, M., Shukur, B. S., Al Sailawi, A. S. A., Bala, I., Hiran, K. K., Doshi, R., & Dhoska, K. (2025). Exploring the Impact of Blockchain Revolution on the Healthcare Ecosystem: A Critical Review. *Mesopotamian Journal of CyberSecurity*, *5*(1), 78–89. DOI: 10.58496/MJCS/2025/006

Mimoun, M. S. B., Miltgen, C. L., & Slama, B. (2022). Is the shopper always the king/queen? Study of omnichannel retail technology use and shopping orientations. *Journal of Retailing and Consumer Services*, *65*, 102844. DOI: 10.1016/j.jretconser.2021.102844

Mirbabaie, M., Langer, M., Hofeditz, L., & Frowerk, J. (2025). AI'll Be There: Challenges and Opportunities in the AI-Supported Doctor-Patient Relationship.

Mitchell, R. K., Agle, B. R., & Wood, D. J. (1997). Toward a theory of stakeholder identification and salience: Defining the principle of who and what really counts. *Academy of Management Review*, *22*(4), 853–886. DOI: 10.2307/259247

Moch, E. (2023). The Industrial Revolution of Artificial Intelligence: A New Era of Automation and Innovation. *International Journal of Public Administration Management and Economic Development*, *8*(2), 1–12. DOI: 10.60026/ijpamed.v8i2.104

Moglia, V., Johnson, O., Cook, G., de Kamps, M., & Smith, L. (2025). Artificial intelligence methods applied to longitudinal data from electronic health records for prediction of cancer: A scoping review. *BMC Medical Research Methodology*, *25*(1), 24. DOI: 10.1186/s12874-025-02473-w PMID: 39875808

Molero, A., Calabrò, M., Vignes, M., Gouget, B., & Gruson, D. (2021). Sustainability in healthcare: Perspectives and reflections regarding laboratory medicine. *Annals of Laboratory Medicine*, *41*(2), 139–144. DOI: 10.3343/alm.2021.41.2.139 PMID: 33063675

Molinillo, S., Anaya-Sánchez, R., & Liébana-Cabanillas, F. (2020). Analyzing the effect of social support and community factors on customer engagement and its impact on loyalty behaviors toward social commerce websites. *Computers in Human Behavior*, *108*, 105980. DOI: 10.1016/j.chb.2019.04.004

Moons, K., Waeyenbergh, G., & Pintelon, L. (2019). Measuring the logistics performance of internal hospital supply chains – A literature study. *Omega*, *82*, 205–217. DOI: 10.1016/j.omega.2018.01.007

Moreno Serrano, R., & Ocampo-Corrales, D. B. (2022). The ability of European regions to diversify in renewable energies: The role of technological relatedness. *Research Policy*, *51*(5), 104508. DOI: 10.1016/j.respol.2022.104508

Mostepaniuk, A., Akalin, T., & Parish, M. R. (2023). Practices pursuing the sustainability of a healthcare organization: A systematic review. *Sustainability (Basel)*, *15*(3), 2353. DOI: 10.3390/su15032353

Mourya, A., Jobanputra, B., & Pai, R. (2024). AI-powered clinical trials and the imperative for regulatory transparency and accountability. *Health and Technology*, *14*(6), 1071–1081. DOI: 10.1007/s12553-024-00904-0

Mousa, S. K., & Othman, M. (2020). The impact of green human resource management practices on sustainable performance in healthcare organisations: A conceptual framework. *Journal of Cleaner Production*, *243*, 118595. DOI: 10.1016/j.jclepro.2019.118595

Muftić, F., Kadunić, M., Mušinbegović, A., & Abd Almisreb, A. (2023). Exploring Medical Breakthroughs: A Systematic Review of ChatGPT Applications in Healthcare. *Southeast Europe Journal of Soft Computing, 12*(1), 13-41. https://scjournal.ius.edu.ba/index.php/scjournal/article/view/252

Mursyid, P., Maidin, A., & Syamsuddin, S. (2022). The influence of price, service quality and relationship marketing on patient satisfaction in the outpatient installation of the haji hospital, South Sulawesi province. *Journal of Asian Multicultural Research for Medical and Health Science Study*, *3*(2), 59–68. DOI: 10.47616/jamrmhss.v3i2.292

Nabivi, E. (2025). The Role of Social Media in Green Marketing: How Eco-Friendly Content Influences Brand Attitude and Consumer Engagement. [measurements.]. *Sustainability (Basel)*, *2025*(17), 1965. DOI: 10.3390/su17051965

Nadarzynski, T., Miles, O., Cowie, A., & Ridge, D. (2019). Acceptability of artificial intelligence (AI)-led chatbot services in healthcare: A mixed-methods study. *Digital Health, 5*, 2055207619871808. https://pubmed.ncbi.nlm.nih.gov/31467682/. DOI: 10.1177/2055207619871808 PMID: 31467682

Namahoot, K. S. (2024). Adoption and Impact of Chat-Gpt in Thailand: Analyzing Service Quality and Technology Acceptance Through a Structural Equation Modeling Approach. *SSRN, 4898056*, https://papers.ssrn.com/sol3/papers.cfm?abstract_id=4898056

Nassiri, S., Adida, E., & Mamani, H. (2022). Reference pricing for healthcare services. *Manufacturing & Service Operations Management, 24*(2), 921–937. DOI: 10.1287/msom.2021.0986

Nazem, G., & Mohamed, B. (2015). Understanding medical tourists' perception of private hospital service quality in Penang Island. *Asian Culture and History, 8*(1), 100–111. DOI: 10.5539/ach.v8n1p100

Ng'andu, D., & Haabazoka, L. (2024). A Study of the Effect of Health Records Digitalization on Healthcare Facility Operational Efficiency. *Open Journal of Business and Management, 12*(2), 1135–1157. DOI: 10.4236/ojbm.2024.122060

Niranjana, J., Daniel, E., Durga, S., & Kathiresan, V. (2024) Enhancing Storage Efficiency for Health Data Records through Block chain-Based Storj Mechanism. In Proceedings of the 2024 3rd International Conference on Intelligent Technologies, Control, Optimization, and Signal Processing, Krishnankoil, 14–16; pp. 1–7. DOI: 10.1109/INCOS59338.2024.10527538

Njah, J., Hansoti, B., Adeyami, A., Bruce, K., O'malley, G., Gugerty, M. K., Chi, B. H., Lubimbi, N., Steen, E., Stampfly, S., Berman, E., & Kimball, A. M. (2021). Measuring for success: Evaluating leadership training programs for sustainable impact. *Annals of Global Health, 87*(1), 63. DOI: 10.5334/aogh.3221 PMID: 34307066

O'Donnell, S., Quigley, E., Hayden, J., Adamis, D., Gavin, B., & McNicholas, F. (2023). Psychological distress among healthcare workers post COVID-19 pandemic: From the resilience of individuals to healthcare systems. *Irish Journal of Psychological Medicine, 40*(3), 508–512. DOI: 10.1017/ipm.2022.35 PMID: 35938227

Obeng, H. A., & Atan, T. (2024). Understanding turnover intentions: The interplay of organizational politics, employee resilience, and person-job fit in Ghana's healthcare sector. *Sustainability (Basel), 16*(22), 9980. DOI: 10.3390/su16229980

Oberai, H., & Anand, I. (2025). Unifying green HRM with sustainable development goals: Ways to develop capabilities and skills. In Tripathi, V., Rastogi, S., & Singh, N. (Eds.), *Implementing ESG Frameworks Through Capacity Building and Skill Development* (pp. 237–260). IGI Global Scientific Publishing., DOI: 10.4018/979-8-3693-6617-2.ch011

Office of Disease Prevention and Health Promotion. (2023). *Social determinants of health and older adults*. Healthy Aging. [Internet]

Ohta, R., Weiss, E., Mekky, M., & Sano, C. (2022). Relationship between dysphagia and home discharge among older patients receiving hospital rehabilitation in rural Japan: A retrospective cohort study. *International Journal of Environmental Research and Public Health, 19*(16), 10125. DOI: 10.3390/ijerph191610125 PMID: 36011757

Oke, G. I., & Sibomana, O. (2025). Adoption of Digital Health Technology in Nigeria: A Scoping Review of Current Trends and Future Directions. *Advances in Public Health, 2025*(1), 4246285. DOI: 10.1155/adph/4246285

Olawade, D. B., Popoola, T. T., Egbon, E., & David-Olawade, A. C. (2025). Sustainable healthcare practices: Pathways to a carbon-neutral future for the medical industry. *Sustainable Futures : An Applied Journal of Technology, Environment and Society, 9*, 100783. DOI: 10.1016/j.sftr.2025.100783

One health global. (n.d.) https://www.who.int/health-topics/one-health#tab=ta

Ong, R. (2025). How Are AI and ERP Systems Reshaping Healthcare in Penang, Malaysia? Multiable. https://multiable.com.my/2025/06/25/how-are-ai-and-erp-systems-reshaping-healthcare-in-penang-malaysia/

Ong, H., Ong, J., Cheng, R., Wang, C., Lin, M., & Ong, D. (2023). GPT technology to help address longstanding barriers to care in free medical clinics. *Annals of Biomedical Engineering, 51*(9), 1906–1909. DOI: 10.1007/s10439-023-03256-4 PMID: 37355478

Onn, Y. (2022). MySejahtera services to include booking for hospital, clinic appointments. NST Online. https://www.nst.com.my/news/nation/2022/12/865062/mysejahtera-services-include-booking-hospital-clinic-appointments Retrieved 3 July 2025.

Oră tean, R., Sava, R., & Mărginean, S. (2022). Measuring Healthcare Digitalisation In The European Union: Trends And Challenges. *Revista Economica (Sibiu), 74*(4), 64–74. DOI: 10.56043/reveco-2022-0038

Othman, N., & Babulal, V. (2020). MySejahtera app disseminates COVID-19 information. NST Online. https://www.nst.com.my/news/nation/2020/04/583117/mysejahtera-app-disseminates-COVID-19-information

Oviedo-Trespalacios, O., Peden, A. E., Cole-Hunter, T., Costantini, A., Haghani, M., Kelly, S., & Reniers, G. (2023). The risks of using ChatGPT to obtain common safety-related information and advice. *SSRN*, *4346827*, https://papers.ssrn.com/sol3/papers.cfm?abstract_id=4346827

Owolabi, O. R., Olatoye, F. O., Elufioye, O. A., & Okunade, B. (2024). Reviewing healthcare financial management: Strategies for cost-effective care. *World Journal of Advance Research Reviews*, *21*(2), 958–966. DOI: 10.30574/wjarr.2024.21.2.0523

Padungyos, N., Nuangjamnong, C., & Dowpiset, K. (2020). Effects of Service Quality that Leads to Word of Mouth (WOM) A Case Study of Coffee Shop in Bangkok, Thailand.

Panwanitdumrong, K., & Chen, C. L. (2021). Investigating factors influencing tourists' environmentally responsible behavior with extended theory of planned behavior for coastal tourism in Thailand. *Marine Pollution Bulletin*, *169*, 112507. DOI: 10.1016/j.marpolbul.2021.112507 PMID: 34029800

Papademetriou, C., Anastasiadou, S., Belias, D., & Ragazou, K. (2025). Integrating sustainability into human resource management: Building a greener workforce for the future. *Sustainability (Basel)*, *17*(3), 1113. DOI: 10.3390/su17031113

Parashakti, R. D., Febrian, W. D., Tarmizi, A., Satria, E., Hikmah Perkasa, D., & Yuliana, L. (2024). The role of green human resource management: Analysis of organizational culture, innovation and leadership. *Dinasti International Journal of Education Management and Social Science*, *6*(1), 475–485. DOI: 10.38035/dijemss.v6i1.3436

Parija, S. C., & Poddar, A. (2024). Artificial intelligence in parasitic disease control: A paradigm shift in health care. *Tropical Parasitology*, *14*(1), 2–7. DOI: 10.4103/tp.tp_66_23 PMID: 38444798

Parzhanova, A. (2025). Human resource management – Sustainable practices. *Edelweiss Applied Science and Technology*, *9*(1), 1100–1110. DOI: 10.55214/25768484.v9i1.4325

Pathak, A. (2023). Exploring Chatgpt: An Extensive Examination of its Background, Applications, Key Challenges, Bias, Ethics, Limitations, and Future Prospects. Applications, Key Challenges, Bias, Ethics, Limitations, and Future Prospects. https://papers.ssrn.com/sol3/papers.cfm?abstract_id=4499278

Pennucci, F., De Rosis, S., Murante, A., & Nuti, S. (2022). Behavioural and social sciences to enhance the efficacy of health promotion interventions: Redesigning the role of professionals and people. *Behavioural Public Policy*, *6*(1), 13–33. DOI: 10.1017/bpp.2019.19

Perceka, A. L. (2020). Quality of Nursing Services with Patient Satisfaction in the Emergency Room at RSUD Dr. Slamet Garut. *Scientific Journal of Public Administration*, *6*(2). DOI: 10.21776/ub.jiap.2020.006.02.14

Pereira, M. L., de La Martinière Petroll, M., Soares, J. C., Matos, C. A. D., & Hernani-Merino, M. (2023). Impulse buying behaviour in omnichannel retail: An approach through the stimulus-organism-response theory. *International Journal of Retail & Distribution Management*, *51*(1), 39–58. DOI: 10.1108/IJRDM-09-2021-0394

Pesqueira, A., Fitzgerald, J., Kurman, P. A., Jaimes, S. D. G., Curado, J., & Gianico, S. (2025). Balancing Ethical, Data Privacy, and Security Dimensions in Blockchain-Based Healthcare Governance: Aligning With ESG Principles. Navigating Privacy, Innovation, and Patient Empowerment Through Ethical Healthcare Technology, 1-38.

Photcharoen, C., Chung, R., & Sann, R. (2020). Modelling theory of planned behavior on health concern and health knowledge towards purchase intention on organic products. *International Business Research*, *13*(8), 100–116. DOI: 10.5539/ibr.v13n8p100

Phuangsuwan, P. & Rakpathum, W. (2024). Social Media and Its Effect on Higher Education: A Review Article. Advance Knowledge for Executives. 3(2), No. 43, 1-11.

Phuangsuwan, P., Siripipatthanakul, S., Chaiprakarn, S., & Rakpathum, W. Muthmainnha, Pariwongkhuntorn, N., & Wattanakul, P. (2024, Jun). Sustainable Development Adopting Artificial Intelligence (AI) in Marketing and Consumer Behaviour Analysis. In *International Conference on Data Analytics & Management* (pp. 569-587). Singapore: Springer Nature Singapore. https://link.springer.com/chapter/10.1007/978-981-96-3372-2_39

Phuangsuwan, P., Siripipatthanakul, S., Chaiprakarn, S., & Rakpathum, W. Muthmainnha, Pariwongkhuntorn, N., & Wattanakul, P. (2024, June). Sustainable Development Adopting Artificial Intelligence (AI) in Marketing and Consumer Behaviour Analysis. In *International Conference on Data Analytics & Management* (pp. 569-587). Singapore: Springer Nature Singapore. https://link.springer.com/chapter/10.1007/978-981-96-3372-2_39

Phuangsuwan, P., Siripipatthanakul, S., Limna, P., & Pariwongkhuntorn, N. (2024). The Impact of Google Maps Application on the Digital Economy. Corporate and Business Strategy Review, 5(1), 192-203. https://papers.ssrn.com/sol3/papers.cfm?abstract_id=4785205

Phuangsuwan, P., Siripipatthanakul, S., Praesri, S., & Rakpathum, W. (2025). The Relationship between Good Governance and Organizational Performance through Mediating Role of Employee Satisfaction. *Journal of Governance and Regulation/ Volume, 14*(1).

Phuangsuwan, P., Siripipatthanakul, S., Praesri, S., & Rakpathum, W. (2025b). The Relationship between Good Governance and Organizational Performance through the Mediating Role of Employee Satisfaction. *Journal of Governance and Regulation/Volume, 14*(1).

Phuangsuwan, P., Siripipatthanakul, S., Hadi, S., Suttipong, R., & Wattanakul, P. (2023). A Review of Sustainable Development Guidelines for Green Universities in Thailand. *Advance Knowledge for Executives, 2*(4), 1–11.

Phuangsuwan, P., Siripipatthanakul, S., Limna, P., & Pariwongkhuntorn, N. (2024). c). The impact of Google Maps application on the digital economy. *Corporate & Business Strategy Review, 5*(1), 192–203. DOI: 10.22495/cbsrv5i1art18

Phuangsuwan, P., Siripipatthanakul, S., Praesri, S., & Rakpathum, W. (2025). The Relationship Between Good Governance and Organizational Performance Through the Mediating Role of Employee Satisfaction. *Journal of Governance and Regulation, 14*(1), 100–108. DOI: 10.22495/jgrv14i1art9

Phuangsuwan, P., Siripipatthanakul, S., Siripipattanakul, S., & Jaipong, P. (2025). The Impact of Community Participation in Sustainable Learning Resource Development: A Case of Bangkok, Thailand. *Sustainability (Basel), 17*(10), 4620. DOI: 10.3390/su17104620

Pichler, P. P., Jaccard, I. S., Weisz, U., & Weisz, H. (2019). International comparison of health care carbon footprints. *Environmental Research Letters, 14*(6), 064004. DOI: 10.1088/1748-9326/ab19e1

Pisarenco, C., & Pisarenco, S. (2024). Digitalisation of Health Data: Impact on Patient-Centredness and Safety. Buletinul Academiei de Ştiinţe a Moldovei. Ştiinţe Medicale, 80(3), 139-143.

Plugmann, P. (2021). Digitalization in dentistry. *Digitalization in Healthcare:* https://link.springer.com/chapter/10.1007/978-3-030-65896-0_6

Popescu, C. R., Martínez-Falcó, J., Marco-Lajara, B., Sánchez-García, E., & Millán-Tudela, L. (Eds.). (2024). *Building sustainable human resources management practices for businesses*. IGI Global Scientific Publishing., DOI: 10.4018/979-8-3693-1994-9

Prastyanti, R. A., & Sharma, R. (2024). Establishing Consumer Trust Through Data Protection Law as a Competitive Advantage in Indonesia and India. Journal of Human Rights. *Culture and Legal System*, *4*(2), 354–390. DOI: 10.53955/jhcls.v4i2.200

Pratici, L., Salvatore, F. P., Fanelli, S., Zangrandi, A., & Milone, M. (2025). Using ESG paradigm as a basis for social reporting in nonprofit organizations: Evidence from cases in healthcare. *Management Decision*, *63*(2), 586–609. DOI: 10.1108/MD-10-2023-2012

Pulka, B. M., & Tijjani, T. S. (2023). Revisiting resource-based view of a firm: A conceptual framework. Sustainable Governance, Citizenship and National Development, 707.

Purohit, A., Smith, J., & Hibble, A. (2021). Does telemedicine reduce the carbon footprint of healthcare? A systematic review. *Future Healthcare Journal*, *8*(1), e85–e91. DOI: 10.7861/fhj.2020-0080 PMID: 33791483

Purwadi, P., Widjaja, Y. R., Junius, J., & Mahmudah, N. (2024). Strategic human resource management in healthcare: Elevating patient care and organizational excellence through effective HRM practices. *Golden Ratio of Data in Summary*, *4*(2), 236–241. DOI: 10.52970/grdis.v4i2.540

Puspitasari, D. A., Anggraeni, A. W., & Rachmaniyah, N. (2017). 140321-ID-desain-interior-ruang-inap-dan-fasilitas. *Jurnal Sains Dan Seni ITS, 6*(1).

Putri, I. Ivana. (2021). The Relationship between Nurse Performance and Patient Satisfaction in an Inpatient Room. *Faculty of Health Repository Sari Mulia University*.http://repository.unism.ac.id/id/eprint/2010

Raja, J., Ashish, A., Boianapalli, S., & Rashid, S. Z. (2025). Blockchain Technology in Supply Chain Management Enhancing Transparency and Efficiency. In ITM Web of Conferences (Vol. 76, p. 02011). EDP Sciences. DOI: 10.1051/itmconf/20257602011

Rajagopalan, S., Pronovost, P., & Al-Kindi, S. (2023, Jun). Implementing a sustainability framework in healthcare: a three-lens framework. In *Healthcare* (Vol. 11, No. 13, p. 1867). MDPI. https://www.mdpi.com/2227-9032/11/13/1867

Raj, R., Singh, A., Kumar, V., & Verma, P. (2023). Analyzing the potential benefits and use cases of ChatGPT as a tool for improving the efficiency and effectiveness of business operations. *Bench Council Transactions on Benchmarks. Standards and Evaluations*, *3*(3), 100140. DOI: 10.1016/j.tbench.2023.100140

Rakpathum, W., Siripipatthanakul, S., Phuangsuwan, P., & Charoenporn, C. (2025). Enhancing Sustainable Development Goals (SDGs) for Rural Tourism Communities: The Case of Mae Kampong Village, Chiang Mai, Thailand. *Journal of Lifestyle and SDGs Review*, *5*(1), e04755–e04755. https://www.sdgsreview.org/LifestyleJournal/article/view/4755. DOI: 10.47172/2965-730X.SDGsReview.v5.n01.pe04755

Rakshit, S., Islam, N., Mondal, S., & Paul, T. (2021). Mobile apps for SME business sustainability during COVID-19 and onwards. *Journal of Business Research*, *135*, 28–39. DOI: 10.1016/j.jbusres.2021.06.005 PMID: 34751197

Ramgolam, G., Ramphul, N., & Chittoo, H. (2024). Sustainable human resource management—A systematic literature review and directions for future research. *Journal of the Knowledge Economy*, •••, 1–38. DOI: 10.1007/s13132-024-02273-5

Rashah, R. A. S. A., Al Rashah, K. A. H., Al Rashah, S. M. R., Saleh, I. A., Al Shaiban, M. A., Alrashah, M. A., & Al Musharraf, N. H. N. (2024). Comprehensive review of sustainability practices, innovation, and resource management in healthcare. *Journal of Ecohumanism*, *3*(8), 5457–5466. DOI: 10.62754/joe.v3i8.5245

Rasul, T., Nair, S., Kalendra, D., Robin, M., de Oliveira Santini, F., Ladeira, W. J., & Heathcote, L. (2023). The role of ChatGPT in higher education: Benefits, challenges, and future research directions. *Journal of Applied Learning and Teaching*, *6*(1), 41–56. DOI: 10.37074/jalt.2023.6.1.29

Rathore, N., Kumari, A., Patel, M., Chudasama, A., Bhalani, D., Tanwar, S., & Al-abdulatif, A. (2025). Synergy of AI and Blockchain to Secure Electronic Healthcare Records. *Security and Privacy*, *8*(1), e463. DOI: 10.1002/spy2.463

Ray, P. P. (2023). ChatGPT: A comprehensive review on background, applications, key challenges, bias, ethics, limitations and future scope. *Internet of Things and Cyber-Physical Systems*, *3*, 121–154. DOI: 10.1016/j.iotcps.2023.04.003

Read, J., & Meath, C. (2025). A conceptual framework for sustainable evidence-based design for aligning therapeutic and sustainability outcomes in healthcare facilities: A systematic literature review. *HERD*, *18*(1), 86–107. DOI: 10.1177/19375867241302793 PMID: 39655601

Renger, F., Patzke, K., & Alrayes, M. (2025). Dental Care Models and their Contribution to Reducing Health Inequalities: A Public. *Health Perspectives*. DOI: 10.71123/jrnhc.v2.i1.25002

Ren, S., Cooke, F. L., Stahl, G. K., Fan, D., & Timming, A. R. (2023). Advancing the sustainability agenda through strategic human resource management: Insights and suggestions for future research. *Human Resource Management*, *62*(3), 251–265. DOI: 10.1002/hrm.22169

Reyazat, F. (2023). The New Path for Humanity. *Artificial Intelligence*.

Rice, S., Crouse, S. R., Winter, S. R., & Rice, C. (2024). The advantages and limitations of using ChatGPT to enhance technological research. *Technology in Society*, *76*, 102426. DOI: 10.1016/j.techsoc.2023.102426

Rivas, P., & Zhao, L. (2023). Marketing with ChatGPT: Navigating the ethical terrain of GPT-based chatbot technology. *AI*, *4*(2), 375–384. DOI: 10.3390/ai4020019

Roberts, H., Lambert, K., & Walton, K. (2024, Mar). The prevalence of dysphagia in individuals living in residential aged care facilities: A systematic review and meta-analysis. In *Healthcare* (Vol. 12, No. 6, p. 649). MDPI. https://www.mdpi.com/2227-9032/12/6/649

Roh, T., Seok, J., & Kim, Y. (2022). Unveiling ways to reach organic purchase: Green perceived value, perceived knowledge, attitude, subjective norm, and trust. *Journal of Retailing and Consumer Services*, *67*, 102988. DOI: 10.1016/j.jretconser.2022.102988

Rowland, S. P., Fitzgerald, J. E., Holme, T., Powell, J., & McGregor, A. (2020). What is the clinical value of mHealth for patients? *NPJ Digital Medicine*, *3*(1), 4. https://www.nature.com/articles/s41746-019-0206-x. DOI: 10.1038/s41746-019-0206-x PMID: 31970289

Sadeghi, T. S., Ourang, S. A., Sohrabniya, F., Sadr, S., Shobeiri, P., & Motamedian, S. R. (2025). Performance of artificial intelligence on cervical vertebral maturation assessment: A systematic review and meta-analysis. *BMC Oral Health*, *25*(1), 187. DOI: 10.1186/s12903-025-05482-9 PMID: 39910512

Sadr, H., Nazari, M., Khodaverdian, Z., Farzan, R., Yousefzadeh-Chabok, S., Ashoobi, M. T., Hemmati, H., Hendi, A., Ashraf, A., Pedram, M. M., Hasannejad-Bibalan, M., & Yamaghani, M. R. (2025). Unveiling the potential of artificial intelligence in revolutionizing disease diagnosis and prediction: A comprehensive review of machine learning and deep learning approaches. *European Journal of Medical Research*, *30*(1), 1–36. DOI: 10.1186/s40001-025-02680-7 PMID: 40414894

Saharkhiz, M., Rao, T., Parker-Lue, S., Borelli, S., Johnson, K., & Cataife, G. (2024). Telehealth expansion and Medicare beneficiaries' care quality and access. *JAMA Network Open*, *7*(5), e2411006–e2411006. DOI: 10.1001/jamanetworkopen.2024.11006 PMID: 38739388

Sajwani, R. A. (2024). Sustainability in healthcare practice. In Al Marri, K., Mir, F.A., David, S.A., Al-Emran, M. (eds), *BUiD Doctoral Research Conference 2023. Lecture Notes in Civil Engineering* (vol. 473). Springer. DOI: 10.1007/978-3-031-56121-4_25

Sallam, M. (2023, Mar). ChatGPT utility in healthcare education, research, and practice: Systematic review on the promising perspectives and valid concerns. *Health Care*, *11*(6), 887. DOI: 10.3390/healthcare11060887 PMID: 36981544

Saruchera, F. (2025). Sustainability: A concept in flux? The role of multidisciplinary insights in shaping sustainable futures. *Sustainability (Basel)*, *17*(1), 326. DOI: 10.3390/su17010326

Sarwar, A., & Shahzad, S. (2024). Fostering sustainability in the healthcare organization through green HRM practices: The mediation analysis of perceived organizational support. *Employee Relations*, *46*(8), 1666–1688. DOI: 10.1108/ER-07-2023-0368

Schellenberg, M., Harker, M. J., & Jafari, A. (2018). International market entry mode–a systematic literature review. *Journal of Strategic Marketing*, *26*(7), 601–627. DOI: 10.1080/0965254X.2017.1339114

Schwab, R., Schiestl, L. J., & Hasenburg, A. (2025). Greening the future of healthcare: Implementation of sustainability strategies in German hospitals and beyond—a review. *Frontiers in Public Health*, *13*, 1559132. DOI: 10.3389/fpubh.2025.1559132 PMID: 40385621

Selvakumar, P., Muralidharan, V., Kumar, G. S., Kumar, D. S., Anand, T., & Manjunath, T. C. (2025). Reducing the Carbon Footprint in Healthcare. *Journal of Environmental Nanotechnology*, *14*(1), 453–463. DOI: 10.13074/jent.2025.03.2511154

Sepetis, A., Rizos, F., Pierrakos, G., Karanikas, H., & Schallmo, D. (2024). A sustainable model for healthcare systems: The innovative approach of ESG and digital transformation. In Healthcare (Vol. 12, No. 2, p. 156). mdpi.

Sepetis, A., & Parlavantzas, I. (2025). Circular economy behavior and sustainable healthcare. *Circular Economy and Sustainability*, 1–23. DOI: 10.1007/s43615-025-00601-8

Seraj, Z. (2025). Klang Valley takes medical tourism crown from Penang. Malay-Mail. https://www.malaymail.com/news/malaysia/2025/02/17/klang-valley-takes-medical-tourism-crown-from-penang/165936.

Setiawan, B., Afiff, A. Z., & Heruwasto, I. (2021). The role of norms in predicting waste sorting behavior. *Journal of Social Marketing*, *11*(3), 224–239. DOI: 10.1108/JSOCM-05-2020-0088

Setyaningrum, R. P., & Muafi, M. (2022). The role of digital HRM: contribution to the improvement of business sustainability. In: *International Conference on Business and Technology*. Cham: Springer International Publishing, pp. 840–848. DOI: 10.1007/978-3-031-26953-0_78

Shahsavar, Y., & Choudhury, A. (2023). User Intentions to Use ChatGPT for Self-Diagnosis and Health-Related Purposes: Cross-sectional Survey Study. *JMIR Human Factors*, *10*(1), e47564. https://humanfactors.jmir.org/2023/1/e47564. DOI: 10.2196/47564 PMID: 37195756

Shanbhogue, A. V., & Ranjith, V. K. (2024). Effects of Consumer Dispositional Attitude on Purchase Intention in an Emerging Market. *F1000 Research*, *12*, 384. DOI: 10.12688/f1000research.131103.3 PMID: 38434630

Shankar, D. S., Li, Z. I., Hoberman, A. R., Blaeser, A. M., Gonzalez-Lomas, G., & Youm, T. (2024). Patient Satisfaction with Postoperative Telemedicine Versus In-Office Visits Following Primary Hip Arthroscopy: A Prospective Observational Study Before and During the COVID-19 Pandemic. *Telemedicine Journal and e-Health*, *30*(2), 464–471. DOI: 10.1089/tmj.2023.0157 PMID: 37585554

Shan, S., Luo, Y., Zhou, Y., & Wei, Y. (2019). Big data analysis adaptation and enterprises' competitive advantages: The perspective of dynamic capability and resource-based theories. *Technology Analysis and Strategic Management*, *31*(4), 406–420. DOI: 10.1080/09537325.2018.1516866

Sharma, P., & Dash, B. (2023). The digital carbon footprint: Threat to an environmentally sustainable future. *SSRN*.

Sharma, R., Soni, G., & Sethia, S. (2025). Bias and Ethical Concerns in Generative AI-driven Medical NLP Models. Available at *SSRN* 5255346. DOI: 10.2139/ssrn.5255346

Shrivastava, U., & Song, J. (2022). Digitization and public trust in health system during COVID pandemic. In *Trust and Digital Business* (pp. 177–187). Routledge. DOI: 10.4324/9781003266525-16

Shukla, K., & Attar, A. M. (2025). Integration of dental patient-reported outcomes (dPROs) in tele dentistry to enhance patient-centered care: A scoping review. *The Journal of Evidence-Based Dental Practice*, *25*(1), 102084. DOI: 10.1016/j.jebdp.2024.102084 PMID: 39947782

Sidiropoulos, D., & Anagnostopoulos, C. N. (2024). Applications, challenges and ethical issues of AI and ChatGPT in education. *arXiv preprint arXiv:2402.07907*. https://arxiv.org/abs/2402.07907

Siemens-Healthineers. (2025). Gleneagles Hospital Penang Introduces Southeast Asia's First SOMATOM Pro.Pulse Dual Source CT Scanner. https://www.siemens-healthineers.com/en-my/press-room/press-features/first-somatom-pro-pulse-gleneagles-penang

Singh, K., Srivastava, V. K., & Shukla, A. (2024). Healing with Care: A Roadmap to Sustainable Healthcare. In *Preserving Health, Preserving Earth: The Path to Sustainable Healthcare* (pp. 63-79). Cham: Springer Nature Switzerland._DOI: 10.1007/978-3-031-60545-1_4

Singh, V., Sharma, M. P., Jayapriya, K., Kumar, B. K., Chander, M. A. R. N., & Kumar, B. R. (2023). Service quality, customer satisfaction and customer loyalty: A comprehensive literature review. *Journal of Survey in Fisheries Sciences*, *10*(4S), 3457–3464.

Sinsky, C. A., Biddison, L. D., Mallick, A., Dopp, A. L., Perlo, J., Lynn, L., & Smith, C. D. (2020). Organizational evidence-based and promising practices for improving clinician well-being. *NAM Perspectives*, 1–15. DOI: 10.31478/202011a PMID: 35291739

Sipos, D., Goyal, R., & Zapata, T. (2024). Addressing burnout in the healthcare workforce: Current realities and mitigation strategies. *The Lancet Regional Health. Europe*, *42*, 42. DOI: 10.1016/j.lanepe.2024.100961 PMID: 39070752

Siripipattanakul, S., Siripipatthanakul, S., Limna, P., & Auttawechasakoon, P. (2022). Determinants of hotels' customer loyalty during the COVID-19 pandemic in Thailand. *Journal of Management Information and Decision Sciences*, *25*(4), 1–14. https://papers.ssrn.com/sol3/papers.cfm?abstract_id=4118267

Siripipatthanakul, S. (2020). Service Quality, Patient Satisfaction and Patient Loyalty in the Private Dental Care Sector: A Case of Smile Family Dental Clinic. *Graduate School of Advanced Technology Management* (Doctoral dissertation, ASSUMPTION UNIVERSITY OF THAILAND).

Siripipatthanakul, S. (2022). *Determinant Factors Influencing Patient Satisfaction and Patient Loyalty at Dental Clinics in Laem Chabang, Thailand* (Doctoral dissertation, Doctoral Dissertation (DBA), Manipal GlobalNxt University, Malaysia).

Siripipatthanakul, S., & Siripipattanakul, S. (2025a). Oral Healthcare Knowledge, Attitude, and Practice (KAP) of Primary School Students in Rural Areas Using Digital Technologies. In *Transforming Dental Health in Rural Communities: Digital Dentistry* (pp. 141-172). IGI Global Scientific Publishing. DOI: 10.4018/979-8-3693-7165-7.ch006

Siripipatthanakul, S., & Siripipattanakul, S. (2025a). Rural Dental Health Transformation by Adopting Digital Technologies. *Transforming Dental Health in Rural Communities: Digital Dentistry*, 47-80.

Siripipatthanakul, S., & Siripipattanakul, S. (2025a). Rural Dental Health Transformation by Adopting Digital Technologies. *Transforming Dental Health in Rural Communities: Digital Dentistry*, 47-80. DOI: DOI: 10.4018/979-8-3693-7165-7.ch003

Siripipatthanakul, S., & Siripipattanakul, S. (2025b). Oral Healthcare Knowledge, Attitude, and Practice (KAP) of Primary School Students in Rural Areas Using Digital Technologies. In *Transforming Dental Health in Rural Communities: Digital Dentistry* (pp. 141-172). IGI Global Scientific Publishing.

Siripipatthanakul, S., & Siripipattanakul, S. (2025b). Talent Management Ensuring the Safety and Cybersecurity in Schools. *Cultivating Creativity and Navigating Talent Management in Academia*, 383-402. DOI: DOI: 10.4018/979-8-3693-6880-0.ch018

Siripipatthanakul, S., Limna, P., Phuangsuwan, P., & Siripipattanakul, S. (2025, b). Enriching Satisfaction With Web-Based Learning (WBL) Among Higher Education Students in Thailand. In *Building Organizational Capacity and Strategic Management in Academia* (pp. 213-236). IGI Global. DOI: 10.4018/979-8-3693-6967-8.ch008

Siripipatthanakul, S., Limna, P., Siripipattanakul, S., & Auttawechasakoon, P. (2022). The Impact of TPB Model on customers' intentions to buy organic foods: A qualitative study in Angsila-Chonburi, Thailand. *Psychology and Education Journal, 59*(2), 419-434. https://papers.ssrn.com/sol3/papers.cfm?abstract_id=4109868

Siripipatthanakul, S., Limna, P., Siripipattanakul, S., & Phuangsuwan, P. (2025, a). Modelling Problem-Based Learning, Student Satisfaction, and Effectiveness Among Higher Education Students in Thailand. In *International Academic Transformations and Cross-Border Collaborations* (pp. 311-332). IGI Global Scientific Publishing. DOI: 10.4018/979-8-3373-0508-0.ch013

Siripipatthanakul, S., Nyen Vui, C., & Phuangsuwan, P. (2024a). Strategic Management Adopting Digital Intelligence (Business Intelligence) for Dentistry and Dental Clinics. *Open Access Journal of Dental Sciences, 9*(1), 000388. https://papers.ssrn.com/sol3/papers.cfm?abstract_id=4739624

Siripipatthanakul, S., Phuangsuwan, P., & Limna, P. Muthmainnha, Siripipattanakul, S., Vui, C. N., & Jaipong, P. (2024, Jun). Artificial Intelligence (AI) Influencing Sustainable Governance: Governance Adopting AI. In *International Conference on Data Analytics & Management* (pp. 551-568). Singapore: Springer Nature Singapore. https://link.springer.com/chapter/10.1007/978-981-96-3372-2_38

Siripipatthanakul, S., Phuangsuwan, P., & Limna, P., Muthmainnha, Siripipattanakul, S., Vui, C. N., & Jaipong, P. (2024, Jun). Artificial Intelligence (AI) Influencing Sustainable Governance: Governance Adopting AI. In *International Conference on Data Analytics & Management* (pp. 551-568). Singapore: Springer Nature Singapore.

Siripipatthanakul, S. (2011). Development of a Model for Administration of Student Dental Health Promotion Work for Basic Education Schools in Thailand. *International Journal of Learning, 17*(12), 137–150. DOI: 10.18848/1447-9494/CGP/v17i12/47373

Siripipatthanakul, S. (2021). Service quality, patient satisfaction, word-of-mouth, and revisit intention in a dental clinic, Thailand. [IJTSRD]. *International Journal of Trend in Scientific Research and Development, 5*(5), 832–841. https://papers.ssrn.com/sol3/papers.cfm?abstract_id=3910239

Siripipatthanakul, S. (2025) *Privacy and Security Management Practices for Organizations, 2025*, 1–306.

Siripipatthanakul, S., & Chana, P. (2021). Service marketing mix (7Ps) and patient satisfaction in clinics: A review article. [IJTSRD]. *International Journal of Trend in Scientific Research and Development, 5*(5), 842–850.

Siripipatthanakul, S., & Phuangsuwan, P. (2024). *Salutogenic Marketing in Preventive Dentistry: Leveraging Digital Technology for Preventive Dentistry*. IGI Global Publishing. DOI: 10.4018/979-8-3693-3872-8.ch009

Siripipatthanakul, S., Phuangsuwan, P., Jaipong, P., & Pholphong, L. (2024). b). A Management Model for Leadership in Diversity and Equality Affecting Human Resource Satisfaction and Performance in Dentistry. *Journal of Dental Sciences, 9*(3), 000401. https://papers.ssrn.com/sol3/papers.cfm?abstract_id=4919825

Siripipatthanakul, S., & Puttharak, S. (2021). Marketing mix analysis in private dental healthcare service sector. [IJTSRD]. *International Journal of Trend in Scientific Research and Development*, *5*(5), 827–831. https://papers.ssrn.com/sol3/papers.cfm?abstract_id=3910242

Siripipatthanakul, S., & Siripipattanakul, S. (2025c). Online Gambling of Higher Education Learners. In *International Academic Transformations and Cross-Border Collaborations* (pp. 377–400). IGI Global Scientific Publishing.

Siripipatthanakul, S., & Vui, C. N. (2021). A conceptual review on the mediating effect of patient satisfaction towards patient loyalty in the dental practice in Thailand. *International Journal of Behavioral Analytics*, *1*(2), 1–16.

Snoswell, C. L., Chelberg, G., De Guzman, K. R., Haydon, H. M., Thomas, E. E., Caffery, L. J., & Smith, A. C. (2023). The clinical effectiveness of telehealth: A systematic review of meta-analyses from 2010 to 2019. *Journal of Telemedicine and Telecare*, *29*(9), 669–684. DOI: 10.1177/1357633X211022907 PMID: 34184580

Snowden, B., Lahiri, S., Dutton, R., & Morton, L. (2023). Achieving and sustaining change through capacity building train-the-trainer health initiatives in low-and middle-income countries: A systematic review. *The Journal of Continuing Education in the Health Professions*, *43*(2), 96–103. DOI: 10.1097/CEH.0000000000000458 PMID: 36215155

Soekotjo, S., Sosidah, , Kuswanto, H., Setyadi, A., & Pawirosumarto, S. (2025). A conceptual framework for sustainable human resource management: Integrating ecological and inclusive perspectives. *Sustainability (Basel)*, *17*(3), 1241. DOI: 10.3390/su17031241

Sok, S., & Heng, K. (2023). ChatGPT for education and research: A review of benefits and risks. *Cambodian Journal of Educational Research*, *3*(1), 110–121. DOI: 10.62037/cjer.2023.03.01.06

Solomou, T., Mappouras, S., Kyriacou, E., Constantinou, I., Antoniou, Z., Canciu, I. C., Neophytou, M., Lantos, Z., Schizas, C. N., & Pattichis, C. S. (2025). Bridging language barriers in healthcare: A patient-centric mobile app for multilingual health record access and sharing. *Frontiers in Digital Health*, *7*, 1542485. DOI: 10.3389/fdgth.2025.1542485 PMID: 40041125

Sophia, E. (2025). Adoption of Teleradiology during the COVID-19 Pandemic: Opportunities and Challenges in the UAE Healthcare System.

Squires, A. (2018). Strategies for overcoming language barriers in healthcare. *Nursing Management, 49*(4), 20–27. DOI: 10.1097/01.NUMA.0000531166.24481.15 PMID: 29528894

Sribanasarn, W., Kaewplang, S., Khotdee, M., Phumiphan, A., Sivanpheng, O., & Kangrang, A. (2025). Sustainable Development Goals for Education and Research in the Ranking of Green Universities of Mahasarakham University Advancing Sustainability: An Analysis of Education, Research, and University Operations In 2024. *Journal of Lifestyle and SDGs Review, 5*(3), e04627–e04627. DOI: 10.47172/2965-730X.SDGsReview.v5.n03.pe04627

Stahl, B. C., & Eke, D. (2024). The ethics of ChatGPT–Exploring the ethical issues of an emerging technology. *International Journal of Information Management, 74*, 102700. DOI: 10.1016/j.ijinfomgt.2023.102700

Stolarchuk, C., Kumar, P., Lionis, C., Anastasaki, M., Conde, M. G., Chowdhury, M., & Awankem, B. (2025). Optimizing healthcare delivery: Strategies for workforce retention and resource allocation. *Journal of Surgical Specialties and Rural Practice, 6*(1), 3–8. DOI: 10.4103/jssrp.jssrp_7_25

Strielkowski, W., Grebennikova, V., Lisovskiy, A., Rakhimova, G., & Vasileva, T. (2025). AI-driven adaptive learning for sustainable educational transformation. *Sustainable Development (Bradford), 33*(2), 1921–1947. DOI: 10.1002/sd.3221

Suchman, M. C. (1995). Managing legitimacy: Strategic and institutional approaches. *Academy of Management Review, 20*(3), 571–610. DOI: 10.2307/258788

Sudirjo, F., Violin, V., Abdullah, A., & Iswahyudi, M. S. (2023). The Effect of Promotion, E-Service Quality and Price on Customer Satisfaction and Its Implication on Loyalty of Tokopedia Customers. *JEMSI (Jurnal Ekonomi, Manajemen, dan Akuntansi), 9*(5), 1724-1728.

Sugajski, M., Buszewska-Forajta, M., & Buszewski, B. (2023). Functional beverages in the 21st century. *Beverages, 9*(1), 27. https://www.mdpi.com/2306-5710/9/1/27. DOI: 10.3390/beverages9010027

Supartiningsih, S. (2017). Kualitas Pelayanan an Kepuasan Pasien Rumah Sakit: Kasus Pada Pasien Rawat Jalan. *Jurnal Medicoeticolegal Dan Manajemen Rumah Sakit, 6*(1), 9–15. DOI: 10.18196/jmmr.6122

Supriadi, B. (2025). Green Hospital Management and Survival to Age 65: Towards Sustainable Health. *Journal of Lifestyle and SDGs Review, 5*(1), e01771–e01771. DOI: 10.47172/2965-730X.SDGsReview.v5.n01.pe01771

Szabo, A. (2023). ChatGPT is a breakthrough in science and education but fails a test in sports and exercise psychology.

Takeda, M., Watanabe, Y., Taira, K., Miura, K., Ohara, Y., Iwasaki, M., . . . Yamazaki, Y. (2023, June). Association between death or hospitalization and observable variables of eating and swallowing function among elderly residents in Long-Term care facilities: A multicenter prospective cohort study. In *Healthcare* (Vol. 11, No. 13, p. 1827). MDPI. https://www.mdpi.com/2227-9032/11/13/1827

Talwar, S., Jabeen, F., Tandon, A., Sakashita, M., & Dhir, A. (2021). What drives willingness to purchase and stated buying behavior toward organic food? A Stimulus–Organism–Behavior–Consequence (SOBC) perspective. *Journal of Cleaner Production*, *293*, 125882. DOI: 10.1016/j.jclepro.2021.125882

Tan-McGrory, A., Schwamm, L. H., Kirwan, C., Betancourt, J. R., & Barreto, E. A. (2022). Addressing virtual care disparities for patients with limited English proficiency. *The American Journal of Managed Care*, *28*(1). PMID: 35049259

Tebeje, T. H., & Klein, J. (2021). Applications of e-health to support person-centered health care at the time of COVID-19 pandemic. *Telemedicine Journal and e-Health*, *27*(2), 150–158. DOI: 10.1089/tmj.2020.0201 PMID: 32746750

Teece, D., Pisano, G., & Shuen, A. (1997). Dynamic Capabilities and Strategic Management. *Strategic Management Journal*, *18*(7), 509–533. DOI: 10.1002/(SICI)1097-0266(199708)18:7<509::AID-SMJ882>3.0.CO;2-Z

Temsah, O., Khan, S. A., Chaiah, Y., Senjab, A., Alhasan, K., Jamal, A., & Senjab, A. M. (2023). Overview of early ChatGPT's presence in medical literature: Insights from a hybrid literature review by ChatGPT and human experts. *Cureus*, *15*(4), 1–7. https://pubmed.ncbi.nlm.nih.gov/37038381/. DOI: 10.7759/cureus.37281 PMID: 37038381

Thapa, P. P. (2024). Digital Education and Awareness for Oral Health: Exploration of Digital Tools and Educational Platforms to Promote Awareness About the Importance of Oral Health. In *Leveraging Digital Technology for Preventive Dentistry* (pp. 225–254). IGI Global. DOI: DOI: 10.4018/979-8-3693-3872-8.ch008

The Malaysian Reserve. (2024). Malaysia's advanced healthcare attracts international patients. The Malaysian https://themalaysianreserve.com/2024/06/04/malaysias-advanced-healthcare-attracts-international-patients/

Thomas, T. S. P., & Leon, L. (2025). Artificial Intelligence in Health and Well-Being: Advancing Diagnostics, Personalized Medicine, and Global Health Initiatives. In Smart Healthcare, Clinical Diagnostics, and Bioprinting Solutions for Modern Medicine (pp. 39-62). IGI Global Scientific Publishing.

Thomas, A. (2024). Challenges in dental education. *Indonesian Journal of Prosthodontics*, *5*(1), 86–88. DOI: 10.46934/ijp.v5i1.268

Tran, V. A., Tran, Q. N., Doan, H. M., La, G. L., Vu, T. D., & Pham, T. H. (2025). How sensory marketing affects perceived service quality and customer satisfaction: Study in Vietnam public hospitals. *Journal of Health Organization and Management*, *39*(4), 568–583. DOI: 10.1108/JHOM-03-2024-0125 PMID: 39657827

Tuhin, M. K. W., Miraz, M. H., Habib, M. M., & Alam, M. M. (2022). Strengthening consumers' halal buying behaviour: Role of attitude, religiosity and personal norm. *Journal of Islamic Marketing*, *13*(3), 671–687. DOI: 10.1108/JIMA-07-2020-0220

Tully, J., Selzer, J., Phillips, J. P., O'Connor, P., & Dameff, C. (2020). Healthcare challenges in the era of cybersecurity. *Health Security*, *18*(3), 228–231. DOI: 10.1089/hs.2019.0123 PMID: 32559153

Tunio, R. (Ed.). (2024). *Intersecting human resource management and organizational culture for environmental sustainability*. IGI Global Scientific Publishing., DOI: 10.4018/979-8-3693-2699-2

Tushar, S. R., Moktadir, M. A., Kusi-Sarpong, S., & Ren, J. (2023). Driving sustainable healthcare service management in the hospital sector. *Journal of Cleaner Production*, *420*, 138310. DOI: 10.1016/j.jclepro.2023.138310

Ugwu, C. N., Ugwu, O. P. C., Alum, E. U., Eze, V. H. U., Basajja, M., Ugwu, J. N., Ogenyi, F. C., Ejemot-Nwadiaro, R. I., Okon, M. B., Egba, S. I., & Uti, D. E. (2025). Sustainable development goals (SDGs) and resilient healthcare systems: Addressing medicine and public health challenges in conflict zones. *Medicine*, *104*(7), e41535. DOI: 10.1097/MD.0000000000041535 PMID: 39960902

Uhm, J. P., Kim, S., Do, C., & Lee, H. W. (2022). How augmented reality (AR) experience affects purchase intention in sport E-commerce: Roles of perceived diagnosticity, psychological distance, and perceived risks. *Journal of Retailing and Consumer Services*, *67*, 103027. DOI: 10.1016/j.jretconser.2022.103027

Ullah, Z., Nasir, A. R., Alqahtani, F. K., Ullah, F., Thaheem, M. J., & Maqsoom, A. (2023). Life cycle sustainability assessment of healthcare buildings: A policy framework. *Buildings (Basel, Switzerland)*, *13*(9), 2143. DOI: 10.3390/buildings13092143

Upadhyai, R., Jain, A. K., Roy, H., & Pant, V. (2019). A review of healthcare service quality dimensions and their measurement. *Journal of Health Management, 21*(1), 102–127. DOI: 10.1177/0972063418822583

US Environmental Protection Agency. (2024, 16 Jul) Criteria for the definition of solid waste and solid and hazardous waste exclusions.. https://www.epa.gov/hw/criteria-definition-solid-waste-and-solid-and-hazardouswaste-exclusions.

Utomo, S. B., Sekaryuni, R., Widarjono, A., Tohirin, A., & Sudarsono, H. (2021). Promoting Islamic financial ecosystem to improve halal industry performance in Indonesia: A demand and supply analysis. *Journal of Islamic Marketing, 12*(5), 992–1011. DOI: 10.1108/JIMA-12-2019-0259

Uzkurt C, Ekmekcioglu EB, Ceyhan S, et al. Digital technology use of SMEs during the COVID-19 pandemic in Turkey: mobile applications' role on motivation and job performance.

Vaishya, R., Misra, A., & Vaish, A. (2023). ChatGPT: Is this version good for healthcare and research? *Diabetes & Metabolic Syndrome, 17*(4), 102744. DOI: 10.1016/j.dsx.2023.102744 PMID: 36989584

Vallée, A. (2024). Green hospitals face to climate change: Between sobriety and resilience. *Heliyon, 10*(2), e24769. DOI: 10.1016/j.heliyon.2024.e24769 PMID: 38298726

Van Wynsberghe, A., & Sustainable, A. I. (2021). AI for sustainability and the sustainability of AI. [CrossRef]. *AI and Ethics, 1*(3), 213–218. DOI: 10.1007/s43681-021-00043-6

Vashu, D., Masri, R., Huei, C. T., & Lee, K. C. S. (2021). Destination image as a healing destination among medical tourists: An exploratory case study of Penang, Malaysia. *ABAC Journal, 41*(2), 156–176.

Vasileiou, A., Sfakianaki, E., & Tsekouropoulos, G. (2024). Exploring sustainability and efficiency improvements in healthcare: A qualitative study. *Sustainability (Basel), 16*(19), 8306. DOI: 10.3390/su16198306

Verdonck, P., & Verniers, I. (2024). Environmental sustainability in healthcare: Managerial concerns and solutions. *Baillière's Best Practice and Research in Clinical Anaesthesiology, 38*(4), 379–385. DOI: 10.1016/j.bpa.2025.03.006

Victor, O., Ugochukwu, S., Macdonald, N., & Ebuka, M. (2025). Public Perception of Artificial Intelligence and Its Role in Achieving the Sustainable Development Goals.

Vo, M. T. H., & Fong, B. Y. F. (2025). Long-Term Care Initiatives in Southeast Asian Countries with Emerging Ageing Population and the Sustainability of Health and Social Care Systems. In *The Handbook of Public Health in the Asia-Pacific* (pp. 1–32). Springer Nature Singapore., DOI: 10.1007/978-981-97-1788-0_31-1

Vrontis, D., Christofi, M., Pereira, V., Tarba, S., Makrides, A., & Trichina, E. (2022). Artificial intelligence, robotics, advanced technologies and human resource management: A systematic review. *International Journal of Human Resource Management, 33*(6), 1237–1266. DOI: 10.1080/09585192.2020.1871398

Wang, Q., Su, M., Zhang, M., & Li, R. (2021). Integrating digital technologies and public health to fight Covid-19 pandemic: Key technologies, applications, challenges and outlook of digital healthcare. *International Journal of Environmental Research and Public Health, 18*(11), 6053. DOI: 10.3390/ijerph18116053 PMID: 34199831

Wang, W., Chen, L., Xiong, M., & Wang, Y. (2023). Accelerating AI adoption with responsible AI signals and employee engagement mechanisms in health care. *Information Systems Frontiers, 25*(6), 2239–2256. DOI: 10.1007/s10796-021-10154-4

Wang, X., Wang, R. S., Qin, X., Huang, Y. N., Chiu, H. C., & Wang, B. L. (2024). Exploring human resource management in the top five global hospitals: A comparative study. *Frontiers in Public Health, 11*, 1–10. DOI: 10.3389/fpubh.2023.1307823 PMID: 38249385

Washif, J., Pagaduan, J., James, C., Dergaa, I., & Beaven, C. (2024). Artificial intelligence in sport: Exploring the potential of using ChatGPT in resistance training prescription. *Biology of Sport, 41*(2), 209–220. DOI: 10.5114/biolsport.2024.132987 PMID: 38524820

Watanabe, E. A. D. M., Alfinito, S., Curvelo, I. C. G., & Hamza, K. M. (2020). Perceived value, trust and purchase intention of organic food: A study with Brazilian consumers. *British Food Journal, 122*(4), 1070–1184. DOI: 10.1108/BFJ-05-2019-0363

White SM, Shelton CL, Gelb AW, (2022) Principles of environmentally-sustainable anaesthesia: a global consensus statement from the World Federation of Societies of Anaesthesiologists. Anaesthesia; 77: 201e12

Whitehead, L., Talevski, J., Fatehi, F., & Beauchamp, A. (2023). Barriers to and facilitators of digital health among culturally and linguistically diverse populations: Qualitative systematic review. *Journal of Medical Internet Research, 25*, e42719. DOI: 10.2196/42719 PMID: 36853742

Wijekoon, R., & Sabri, M. F. (2021). Determinants that influence green product purchase intention and behavior: A literature review and guiding framework. *Sustainability (Basel), 13*(11), 6219. DOI: 10.3390/su13116219

Willie, M. M. (2025). Strategies for enhancing training and development in healthcare management. *Advances in Human Resource Management Research, 3*(1), 44–59. DOI: 10.60079/ahrmr.v3i1.408

Willms, A., & Liu, S. (2024). Exploring the feasibility of using ChatGPT to create just-in-time adaptive physical activity mHealth intervention content: Case study. *JMIR Medical Education, 10*, e51426. https://mededu.jmir.org/2024/1/e51426. DOI: 10.2196/51426 PMID: 38421689

Wolf, R. M., Abramoff, M. D., Channa, R., Tava, C., Clarida, W., & Lehmann, H. P. (2022). Potential reduction in healthcare carbon footprint by autonomous artificial intelligence. *NPJ Digital Medicine, 5*(1), 62. DOI: 10.1038/s41746-022-00605-w PMID: 35551275

Wu, A., Roemer, E. C., Kent, K. B., Ballard, D. W., & Goetzel, R. Z. (2021). Organizational best practices supporting mental health in the workplace. *Journal of Occupational and Environmental Medicine, 63*(12), e925–e931. DOI: 10.1097/JOM.0000000000002407 PMID: 34840320

Wulansari, R., & Pratama, M. S. R. (2022). The Influence of Services Quality and Facilities on Patient Satisfaction at Wijaya Kusuma Hospital Lumajang, East Java. *Adpebi International Journal of Multidisciplinary Sciences, 1*(1), 166–174. DOI: 10.54099/aijms.v1i1.254

Wu, X., Duan, R., & Ni, J. (2024). Unveiling security, privacy, and ethical concerns of ChatGPT. *Journal of Information and Intelligence, 2*(2), 102–115. DOI: 10.1016/j.jiixd.2023.10.007

Xi, M., Liu, Y., Fang, W., & Feng, T. (2024). Intelligent manufacturing for strengthening operational resilience during the COVID-19 pandemic: A dynamic capability theory perspective. *International Journal of Production Economics, 267*, 109078. DOI: 10.1016/j.ijpe.2023.109078

Xinxin, C., Umair, M., Rahman, S., & Alraey, Y. (2024). RETRACTED: The potential impact of digital economy on energy poverty in the context of Chinese provinces. *Heliyon, 10*(9), e30140. Advance online publication. DOI: 10.1016/j.heliyon.2024.e30140 PMID: 38707298

Xu, G., Wu, Y., Minshall, T., & Zhou, Y. (2017). Exploring the Innovation Ecosystems Across Science, Technology and Business: A Case of 3D Printing in China. *Technological Forecasting and Social Change*. DOI: 10.1016/j.techfore.2017.06.030

Yadav, S. (2024). Transformative frontiers: A comprehensive review of emerging technologies in modern healthcare. *Cureus*, *16*(3), e56538. DOI: 10.7759/cureus.56538 PMID: 38646390

Yakin, A., Khang, A., Muthmainnah, M., Elngar, A. A., Siripipatthanakul, S., & Limna, P. (2025). Unraveling the Quantum Robotics Influence: Transforming Social Interaction for the Future. In The Quantum Evolution (pp. 349-372). CRC Press.

Yaraghi, N. (2023). *ChatGPT And Health Care: Implications For Interoperability And Fairness*. Health Affairs Forefront., DOI: 10.1377/forefront.20230605.938282

Yarmohammadi, S., Mousavi, S., Ajori, L., Mohammadzade, F., & Marashi, T. (2023). Impact of attitude, subjective norms and perceived behavioral control on health behaviors among women with low-risk HPV, and the mediating role of behavioral intention: An interventional study. *International Journal of Health Promotion and Education*, *61*(2), 70–82. DOI: 10.1080/14635240.2021.1995776

Yong, S. P., Goh, Y. N., Ting, M. S., & Lunyai, J. (2021). Revisit intention for medical services: An investigation on Penang as a medical tourism hub. *Malays J Consum Fam Econ*, *26*, 127–157.

Yoo, D. Y. (2024). Eco-leadership in action: Integrating green HRM and the new ecological paradigm to foster organizational commitment and environmental citizenship in the hospitality industry. *Sustainability (Basel)*, *16*(20), 9044. DOI: 10.3390/su16209044

Yu, M., Wang, Y., & Umair, M. (2024). Minor mining, major influence: Economic implications and policy challenges of artisanal gold mining. *Resources Policy*, *91*, 104886. DOI: 10.1016/j.resourpol.2024.104886

Yun, Y. M., Kirby, C., Bob, N., Calabria, C., Hernandez, A., Cook, B., Krolczyk, J., & Jee, S. H. (2023). Promoting sustainability practices in the outpatient pediatric setting. *The Yale Journal of Biology and Medicine*, *96*(2), 261–265. DOI: 10.59249/VCAH6394 PMID: 37396977

Zahari, A. I., Said, J., Muhamad, N., & Ramly, S. M. (2024). Ethical culture and leadership for sustainability and governance in public sector organisations within the ESG framework. *Journal of Open Innovation*, *10*(1), 100219. DOI: 10.1016/j.joitmc.2024.100219

Zaman, M. (2023). ChatGPT for Healthcare Sector: SWOT Analysis. *International Journal of Research in Industrial Engineering*. DOI: 10.22105/riej.2023.391536.1373

Zanobini, P., Del Riccio, M., Lorini, C., & Bonaccorsi, G. (2024). Empowering sustainable healthcare: The role of health literacy. *Sustainability (Basel)*, *16*(10), 3964. DOI: 10.3390/su16103964

Zeb, A., Ullah, R., & Karim, R. (2024). Exploring the role of ChatGPT in higher education: Opportunities, challenges, and ethical considerations. *The International Journal of Information and Learning Technology*, *41*(1), 99–111. DOI: 10.1108/IJILT-04-2023-0046

Zeithaml, V. A., Berry, L. L., & Parasuraman, A. (1996). The behavioral consequences of service quality. *Journal of Marketing*, *60*(2), 31–46. DOI: 10.1177/002224299606000203

Zhang, Z., Gu, D., & Li, S. (2024). Effectiveness of Person-Centered Health Education in the General Practice of Geriatric Chronic Disease Care. *Alternative Therapies in Health and Medicine*, *30*(10). PMID: 38330589

Zheng, R., Wu, G., Cheng, Y., Liu, H., Wang, Y., & Wang, X. (2023). How does digitalization drive carbon emissions? The inverted U-shaped effect in China. *Environmental Impact Assessment Review*, *102*, 107203. DOI: 10.1016/j.eiar.2023.107203

Zhou, J., Müller, H., Holzinger, A., & Chen, F. (2023). Ethical ChatGPT: Concerns, Challenges, and commandments. *arXiv preprint arXiv:2305.10646*. https://doi.org//arXiv.2305.10646DOI: 10.48550

Zournatzidou, G., Ragazou, K., Sklavos, G., & Sariannidis, N. (2025). Linking HRM with sustainability: Achieving the goals of the 2030 agenda. In K. Ragazou, A. Garefalakis, C. Papademetriou, & A. Samara (Eds.), *Sustainability Through Green HRM and Performance Integration* (pp. 281-304). IGI Global Scientific Publishing. DOI: 10.4018/979-8-3693-5981-5.ch012

About the Contributors

Supaprawat Siripipatthanakul got his Doctor of Dental Surgery from Chiang Mai University in 1998. He also has degrees from Sukhothai Thammathirat Open University, including B.Ed. (Educational Measurement & Evaluation), B.PH. (Public Health Administration), B.Art. (Information & Technology), B.Art. (Production & Management), B.Art. (Thai Studies), and an English Certificate for Healthcare Providers. He held two master's degrees in science, one in oral medicine from Mahidol University (3.67/4) and another in management from Assumption University (3.73/4), Thailand. In 2010, Sukhothai Thammathirat Open University awarded him a PhD in educational administration with a scholarship based on his excellent score (4/4). His PhD research was presented at an international conference in HK, and his PhD paper is included in a Q4 Scopus-USA journal. He has been a lecturer in education at Bangkokthonburi University, Thailand, since 2011. He received another doctorate in DBA in 2022 from Manipal GlobalNxt University (MGNU), MY, with a distinguished score (3.95/4). He became an Adjunct and Visiting Professor. He has published more than 90 papers and books on Google Scholar. He has a CEFR Level 5 (C1), an English Teacher certificate from AAARYA Business College in Singapore, a Teaching English as a Foreign Language (TEFL) certificate, and a Teaching English to Speakers of Other Languages (TESOL) certificate. He lectures on research methodology (business/ education/ healthcare) for international universities. He has been invited to review the manuscripts of Q1 and Q2-Scopus, WOS journals/Scopus, and Springer books (118 verified reviews by WOS/ 146 verified reviews by ORCID) since 2022. Research Interests: Healthcare; Business; Education, IT-Computer Sciences, Management, Behavioural Analytics, Asian Studies; and English Language

***

|Seng Loong (Stanley) Kok - Contributing Author|Doctor of Business Administration, CA(M) FCCA (UK), Researcher (DBA Holder)

Pongsakorn Limna, also known as Palm, is currently a postdoctoral researcher in the Digital Business program at the International College, Pathumthani University, Thailand. He is an active scholar with numerous publications in leading academic journals, including those indexed in Scopus and the Thai Citation Index (TCI). He also serves as a reviewer for several national and international journals and academic conferences, demonstrating his strong commitment to academic excellence and scholarly contribution. His research interests span a wide range of interdisciplinary fields, including the digital economy, digital business, business administration, management, communication, technology, artificial intelligence (AI), and consumer behavior. In 2012, Dr. Limna was awarded a prestigious scholarship jointly provided by the Office of the Basic Education Commission of Thailand and the Wisconsin Department of Public Instruction, USA, to participate in the Thailand–Wisconsin International Sunrise Program in Wausau, Wisconsin. He holds a Bachelor of Arts (B.A.) degree from the Faculty of Humanities and Social Sciences at Burapha University, Thailand, with a major in English and a minor in tourism management. He later earned an Executive Master of Business Administration (Executive MBA) from the Faculty of Business and Technology at UNITAR International University in Malaysia. He completed his Doctor of Philosophy (Ph.D.) in Digital Economy at Rangsit University, Thailand, with the support of the esteemed Prasit – Khunying Pattana Ourairat Scholarship.

Sorasun Rungsiyanont is an associate professor in the Department of Oral surgery and Oral medicine, Faculty of Dentistry, Srinakharinwirot University, Thailand. He received his bachelor degree in Doctor of Dental Surgery from Chiangmai University, Thailand in 1995, MSC in Oral Biology from Chulalongkorn University, Bangkok, Thailand in 2002. He obtained Thai Board in Oral Diagnostic Sciences from Royal council of Thailand in 2007 and PhD. in Tissue Engineering and regenerative Medicine from Tokyo Medical and Dental University, Tokyo, Japan in 2012. He is also a Senior Fellowship (SFHEA) from UK Professional Standard Framework for teaching and learning support in higher education in 2020. His research focuses on hard tissue engineering, biomaterials and probiotics. He is ex-president of Thai Society of Oral Diagnostic Sciences and The Oral diseases group of Thailand and now he is the advisory board of both societies.

Chok Nyen Vui serves as the Dean of the School of Business at Manipal GlobalNxt University (MGNU). His skill set encompasses the areas of instruction, scholarly inquiry, oversight, and administration within the Graduate School of various esteemed institutions of higher education. The individual's primary responsibility involves the development of new programmes aimed at enhancing the university's offerings to align with market demand. In addition to his involvement in the development of new programmes, he also possesses expertise in the evaluation of the existing curriculum to ensure its alignment with industry standards, while simultaneously maintaining a high level of quality. As a member of the Globalnxy University Board of Governors, he actively participates in the development of strategic plans aimed at enhancing the university's global visibility and marketability, while also emphasising its value and reputation. Dr. Chok holds a Doctor of Philosophy (Ph.D.) in management, Master of Business Administration (MBA) and Bachelor of Business Administration (BBA), from University Putra Malaysia. He is passionate about teaching as he has more than 15 years of teaching experience at the undergraduate and postgraduate levels. He is also an Associate Member of The Chartered Institute of Marketing (CIM), United Kingdom and a certified HRDF Trainer registered under the Ministry of Human Resources. He is appointed as one of the Research Grant Management Committee members to identify potential partners from other universities or industry players for project collaboration. Apart from developing new postgraduate programs and handling administrative matters, he actively involves in academic and research activities, focusing on conference collaboration between the universities. He was awarded the best paper in conferences at the World Marketing Conference and International Conference of Innovation and Entrepreneurship, International Conference of Innovation and Entrepreneurship indexed in SCOPUS. Besides handling the accreditation of postgraduate programs, he chairs departmental meetings and monitors students' academic performance to ensure graduation on time. He always believes that being a leader by example will inspire his fellow team members to achieve a greater height. He has been lecturing Research Methodology at the postgraduate level and encouraging his fellow students to publish their thesis/dissertation into articles actively. As a postgraduate research methodology examiner, ethical issues arise at various business and management research stages that consist of lesson delivery. As a researcher and research methodology module leader, professionalism and ethics within social sciences have keen to spell out through part of our paper review.

Index

U

www.ingramcontent.com/pod-product-compliance
Lightning Source LLC
LaVergne TN
LVHW081526300926
849161LV00006B/1315